SHAKESPEARE SURVEY

ADVISORY BOARD

1 Shakespeare and his Stage
2 Shakespearian Production
3 The Man and the Writer
4 Interpretation
5 Textual Criticism
6 The Histories
7 Style and Language
8 The Comedies
9 *Hamlet*
10 The Roman Plays
11 The Last Plays (with an index to *Surveys 1–10*)
12 The Elizabethan Theatre
13 *King Lear*
14 Shakespeare and his Contemporaries
15 The Poems and Music
16 Shakespeare in the Modern World
17 Shakespeare in his Own Age
18 Shakespeare Then Till Now
19 *Macbeth*
20 Shakespearian and Other Tragedy
21 *Othello* (with an index to *Surveys 11–20*)
22 Aspects of Shakespearian Comedy
23 Shakespeare's Language
24 Shakespeare: Theatre Poet
25 Shakespeare's Problem Plays
26 Shakespeare's Jacobean Tragedies
27 Shakespeare's Early Tragedies
28 Shakespeare and the Ideas of his Time
29 Shakespeare's Last Plays
30 *Henry IV* to *Hamlet*
31 Shakespeare and the Classical World (with an index to *Surveys 21–30*)
32 The Middle Comedies
33 *King Lear*
34 Characterization in Shakespeare
35 Shakespeare in the Nineteenth Century
36 Shakespeare in the Twentieth Century
37 Shakespeare's Earlier Comedies
38 Shakespeare and History
39 Shakespeare on Film and Television
40 Current Approaches to Shakespeare through Language, Text and Theatre
41 Shakespearian Stages and Staging (with an index to *Surveys 31–40*)
42 Shakespeare and the Elizabethans
43 *The Tempest* and After
44 Shakespeare and Politics
45 *Hamlet* and its Afterlife
46 Shakespeare and Sexuality
47 Playing Places for Shakespeare

Aspects of *Macbeth*
Aspects of *Othello*
Aspects of *Hamlet*
Aspects of *King Lear*
Aspects of Shakespeare's 'Problem Plays'

SHAKESPEARE SURVEY

AN ANNUAL SURVEY OF SHAKESPEARE STUDIES AND PRODUCTION

47

EDITED BY

STANLEY WELLS

CAMBRIDGE UNIVERSITY PRESS

Published by the Press Syndicate of the University of Cambridge
The Pitt Building, Trumpington Street, Cambridge CB2 1RP
40 West 20th Street, New York, NY 10011–4211, USA
10 Stamford Road, Oakleigh, Melbourne 3166, Australia

First published 1994

Printed in Great Britain at the University Press, Cambridge

A cataloguing in publication record for this book is available from the British Library

ISBN 0 521 47084 6 hardback

Shakespeare Survey was first published in 1948. Its first eighteen volumes were edited by Allardyce Nicoll. Kenneth Muir edited volumes 19 to 33.

CE

EDITOR'S NOTE

Volume 48 of *Shakespeare Survey*, which will be at press by the time this volume appears, will have as its theme 'Shakespeare and Cultural Exchange' and will include papers from the 1994 International Shakespeare Conference. The theme of Volume 49 will be '*Romeo and Juliet* and its Afterlife'.

Submissions should be addressed to the Editor at The Shakespeare Institute, Church Street, Stratford-upon-Avon, Warwickshire CV37 6HP, to arrive at the latest by 1 September 1995 for Volume 49. Pressures on space are heavy; priority is given to articles related to the theme of a particular volume. Please either enclose postage (overseas, in International Reply coupons) or send a copy you do not wish to be returned. All articles submitted are read by the Editor and at least one member of the Editorial Board, whose indispensable assistance the Editor gratefully acknowledges.

Unless otherwise indicated, Shakespeare quotations and references are keyed to the modern-spelling Complete Oxford Shakespeare (1986).

Review copies of books should be addressed to the Editor, as above. In attempting to survey the ever-increasing bulk of Shakespeare publications our reviewers inevitably have to exercise some selection. We are pleased to receive offprints of articles which help to draw our reviewers' attention to relevant material.

S. W. W.

CONTRIBUTORS

S. P. Cerasano, *Colgate University*
Richard Foulkes, *University of Leicester*
Mark Gauntlett, *University of Newcastle, Australia*
Andrew Gurr, *University of Reading*
Franklin J. Hildy, *University of Georgia*
Peter Holland, *Trinity Hall, Cambridge*
Dennis Kennedy, *University of Pittsburgh*
Werner Von Koppenfels, *University of Munich*
David Lindley, *University of Leeds*
Jane Moody, *Girton College, Cambridge*
J. R. Mulryne, *University of Warwick*
John Orrell, *University of Alberta*
Niky Rathbone, *Birmingham Shakespeare Library*
Naseeb Shaheen, *Memphis State University*
Alan Somerset, *University of Western Ontario*
Martin Wiggins, *The Shakespeare Institute, University of Birmingham*
George Walton Williams, *Duke University*
H. R. Woudhuysen, *University College, London*

CONTENTS

CONTENTS

ILLUSTRATIONS

FIGURES

PLATES

SHAKESPEARE PLAYED SMALL: THREE SPECULATIONS ABOUT THE BODY

DENNIS KENNEDY

Any space we occupy deeply affects how we perceive events inside it. We are bodies which occupy space and, metaphorically speaking, are occupied by it; especially when we are present in a space marked off from the mundane, like a holy temple or a chamber for the exercise of power, we are likely to alter not only our behaviour but our frame of mental reference. Theatres, which are spaces separate from ordinary life by definition, affect us not only by their architecture and decor but also by the spatial relationship established between actor and spectator. From the hillside amphitheatres of Athens in the fifth century BC to the concrete cinema bunkers of late twentieth-century suburban shopping malls, a theatre space is inscribed with ideas about the position of drama within the culture that built it.

For Shakespeare the issue of space has assumed particular importance, and in the modern era has been highly contested, partly because the status of Shakespeare's plays has focused attention on where they can be seen to best advantage. While most of us imagine Burbage's the Theatre or the Globe when we think of the original productions, the plays were performed in their own time in a variety of public, private and royal spaces, a fact that should make us question the common notion that they were 'written for' the public theatre or were somehow contained by it. Yet the Elizabethanist movement of the end of the nineteenth century, associated with William Poel in London and Jocza Savits in Munich, made that proposition the basis for much subsequent worry over the right space for Shakespeare. Taking the radical inference that the performance space was inscribed in the text itself, Poel and Savits, and their more successful heirs like Granville Barker and Tyrone Guthrie, have vastly affected how Shakespeare relates to the spectator in the physical environment of the stage.[1]

Though Poel and Savits sought spatial authenticity, the spaces they established were conscious compromises with practicality and unconscious compromises with their ingrained theatrical biases. The right space for Shakespeare, regardless of any claims its architect might make about fidelity to a lost epitome, is always going to be the right space for a specific culture. The reified proscenium productions of Charles Kean at the Princess's Theatre were as right for mid-nineteenth-century London as Guthrie's open-stage productions at the Ontario

[1] In preparing this essay I was fortunate to have the research assistance of Melissa Gibson, who made a number of important contributions to the work. For a discussion of royal and other non-public performances by Shakespeare's company, see Peter Thomson, *Shakespeare's Professional Career* (Cambridge, 1992), pp. 150–65. I treat the issue of the right space for Shakespeare in more detail in *Looking at Shakespeare: A Visual History of Twentieth-Century Performance* (Cambridge, 1993), pp. 34–42 and 152–64. On the cultural implications of theatre buildings, see Marvin Carlson, *Places of Performance: The Semiotics of Theatre Architecture* (Ithaca, 1989).

Festival Theatre were for mid-twentieth-century North America. Yet the intensity of the search for space in the twentieth century, causing enormous expense in building and in remodelling, has been motivated by two ambitions specific to modernity: to get Shakespeare out of the boxed-in stages of proscenium theatres, and (thereby) to create a rejuvenated or urgent sense of intimacy between the actor and spectator. Especially since the Second World War, producers of Shakespeare have repeatedly appealed to the need for connection, hoping for a revitalized mode of performance that would affect audiences directly and (re)-capture the intensity presumed to be present in the texts.

For my purposes the crucial aspect of this story is that most theatres playing Shakespeare in the modern era, whether pre-existing or purpose-built, have been large. Of course, 'large' is a relative term: the Theatre of Dionysos sat at least 13,000 bodies, the first Globe upwards of 3,000, and the second Shakespeare Memorial Theatre in Stratford about 1,500; all of them seem large by our contemporary standards, with substantial distance between the ludic space and farthest spectator. (In some cases even to the closest spectator: at the SMT, for example, rebuilt in 1932 after a fire, the scenic system in operation for many years discouraged the use of the forestage, so that the action was often at least 30 feet (over 9 metres) away from the front row.)[2] Guthrie's Festival Stage in Ontario, designed for Shakespearian 'intimacy', seats an extraordinary 2,258 people, 858 of them in a balcony; though no spectator is more than 65 feet (20 metres) from the stage, that is nonetheless an enormous audience.

All proscenium theatres coercively discipline the gaze, but large auditoria amplify the separation between audience and performer by sheer force of distance. As Guthrie himself put it, spectator and actor in a proscenium arrangement are separated by two barriers, 'a barrier of fire, which is the footlights, then a barrier of space called the orchestra'.[3] The bodies of actors on stage are therefore made to look smaller than the body of the viewer, more like puppets or imagined creatures in an autonomous and visually consistent world, and the farther away from the stage a spectator sits the more dream-like the actors will appear. This phenomenon is well-suited to the affection of power the audience can assume over the players by virtue of the ocular relationship between silent watcher and speaking doer. (On the issue of power, it's useful to recall that the proscenium stage was developed to display the expensive and scenographically complex court musical entertainments that eventually led to seventeenth-century opera, a form historically associated with royal authority.) In a standard proscenium theatre the best seats for viewing, which are not necessarily the closest seats, are by custom the most expensive, and a clear downward grading is established for those with progressively inferior sightlines. Thus inscribed in the seating plan of large theatres – even those with open stages – is a scopic hierarchy that unconsciously replicates an antiquated social hierarchy. Especially in a turn-of-the-century theatre, with stalls, boxes, circle, pits, and galleries built to distinguish the classes by space and to rank their regard of the stage, audiences today still form an ordered opticon of reception.

At about the time that Poel and Savits were reacting against Shakespeare in the wrong spaces, a similar reaction occurred in Europe against the general habits of performance in large spaces. The historical avant-garde, working against the grain of the established or commercial theatre, began to experiment with small and unconventional venues as part of its oppositional project. Unable to secure a regular theatre for the first production of the Théâtre Libre in 1887, André Antoine was forced to use a hastily arranged performance space that sat

[2] Richard and Helen Leacroft, *Theatre and Playhouse* (London, 1984), p. 159.

[3] Tyrone Guthrie, 'Theatre at Minneapolis', in *Actor and Architect*, ed. Stephen Joseph (Toronto, 1964), p. 37.

only 349.[4] What was a necessity for Antoine soon became a mark of avant-garde distinction, and small spaces and small audiences were taken to signal a seriousness of artistic purpose and disdain for bourgeois values. The Studio Theatre of the Moscow Art Theatre, which Stanislavsky created for Meyerhold's experiments with Symbolism in 1905, became the model (even though it never performed for the public): the MAT opened a series of Studios later, the Intimate Theatre in Stockholm was formed for Strindberg's chamber plays, Max Reinhardt started both Schall und Rauch and the Kammerspiele in Berlin, Georg Fuchs made the Künstlertheater in Munich a centre of analysis and reform. A studio, of course, is a place for study, a laboratory; the names of the other small theatres implied a similar emphasis on marginality or artist–audience process.

Most of these institutions did not survive the Great War. Though their aesthetic customs were sometimes kept alive by amateur players, it was the self-conscious revival of avant-garde attitudes in the 1960s and early 1970s that found renewed profit from the tradition. In the Off-Off-Broadway movement in New York, in the fringe movement in London, in left-bank theatres in Paris, in basement theatres in Rome, and in university and alternative theatres from Moscow to Tokyo, theatrical marginality was exemplified and cherished. Indeed it was in this environment, usually associated with leftist political inclinations, that some of the most exciting theatre work of our time was hatched in small or unconventional spaces: the Théâtre du Soleil, the Schaubühne, the Living Theatre and the Open Theatre, the Taganka, and directors like Konrad Swinarski, Jerzy Grotowski, Richard Foreman, Robert Wilson, JoAnne Akalaitis, Tadashi Suzuki, and Yukio Ninagawa, to name but a few, investigated the relationship between actor and spectator, trying to break down or lessen the separation between them, literally and metaphorically.

Prior to the 1970s Shakespeare was infrequently connected to the studio movement. The size of the casts, the length of the plays, the expense of production, and the continued appropriation of Shakespeare as genteel high art, all colluded to discourage the radical experimentation and small purses associated with the fringe. (There were exceptions, most notably the collage Shakespeare of Charles Marowitz at the Open Space Theatre in London.) In 1974, however, the British branch of the socially committed, marginalized theatre suddenly appeared in the centre of Shakespeare-land, when under the leadership of Buzz Goodbody a corrugated metal storage shed up the street from the Royal Shakespeare Theatre in Stratford was converted to a playing space. Seating about 140 people in a rough environment with a temporary feel, it was consciously constructed as an alternative to the mainstream traditions of the large theatre. Even its name, The Other Place, suggested its eccentricity.[5] Since then small-scale or chamber performance has become an important part of the RSC's work, and some of its most gripping and innovative productions have been staged for the intimate surroundings of The Other Place or its London variants, the Donmar Warehouse (opened in 1977) and its replacement, a small flexible theatre in the Barbican called the Pit (1982). Meanwhile the chamber movement for Shakespeare had spread around the world.

Chamber performances place a burden on the finances of theatrical organizations because it is normally impossible for audiences of 150 or less to cover enough of the costs to make

---

[4] See Jean Chothia, *André Antoine* (Cambridge, 1991), p. 7. I discuss the issue of the audience for the avant-garde in a paper called 'The New Drama and the New Audience', in *Edwardian Theatre*, ed. Michael Booth and Joel Kaplan (Cambridge, forthcoming 1995).

[5] See Colin Chambers, *Other Spaces: New Theatre and the RSC* (London, 1980). On the visual implications of chamber performance see *Looking at Shakespeare*, pp. 250–7. It is interesting that the building had originally been put up in 1962 as a studio for the RSC acting work conducted by Michel Saint-Denis. Only later was it used for storage.

professional production feasible, even when expenses have been drastically reduced; some form of subsidy is necessary, whether external or internal, which means the producers must be firmly committed to the project to maintain it. Yet it's clear that many performers as well as many spectators are attracted to Shakespeare in reduced environments, preferring the intimacy achieved to the grander gestures and more detailed images in larger spaces. As Peter Holland wrote in 1982 about Stratford, 'the myth has grown up – however hard the company may try to rebut it – that the productions at the Royal Shakespeare Theatre itself are for tourists and school parties, while the productions at The Other Place are the justification for a long and miserable drive or an impossible confrontation with British Rail'.[6] Myth or no, the importance of chamber Shakespeare is undeniable. Though postmodern performance often seeks the coolness and spectacle of proscenium staging, at the same time there has been a general movement in western culture away from representation displayed on a large scale and toward psychological intimacies familar from film and television. I now propose to investigate the reasons for the success of small Shakespeare through three speculations based on performance theory, using as examples the work of Trevor Nunn.

Speculation 1. The impact of performance in small spaces results from the parity between the performer's body and the spectator's body.

As Erika Fischer-Lichte succinctly points out, the theatre event occurs when an actor (A) represents a character (X) while a spectator (S) looks on. The triadic relationship A–X–S is irreducible. But because the actor is a three-dimensional body and always needs room, 'the stage space also represents an irreducible element of the theatrical code'; it is '(1) the space in which A acts, and (2) the space in which X is found'.[7] I add to the formula the requirement of space for spectation, since S is also a three-dimensional body, and usually a number of three-dimensional bodies, taking up room. So there are two necessary spaces: the ludic space for A, and the watching space for S. The boundary of where X can be found is at the line where the two spaces meet. In these terms the distance between X and S in large theatres reduces the apparent size of A, making it difficult and often impossible for much of the audience to read facial and gestural details and encouraging, as I noted above, a sense of S's superiority over A. This tendency is so much a part of the experience of the theatre in history that little attention has been paid to its psychological and physiological effects, though a number of theatrical moments have been forced to deal with it. There seems little doubt, for example, that the outsized masks of Greek actors were designed at least in part to make symbolic facial postures visible to spectators far up the hillside; opera glasses, introduced as early as the 1730s but gaining significantly in popularity as playhouses expanded in size in the nineteenth century, were optical compensations with a similar purpose, adding an element of spying to the theatrical experience. Of course the spatial distance between A and S has traditionally been offset by make-up, large gestures, and loud voices; for Shakespeare that has meant a routine of acting variously called 'big' or 'inflated' or 'classical'. To compensate for a reduced physical impression, the actor in a large space performs in a larger-than-life manner.

Thus when a performance occurs in a small theatre, especially one where the ludic space is not architecturally divided from the watching space, the proximity of A's body is the dominant physical impression made upon S. While distant views of a proscenium performance normally affect only the eyes and ears, keeping the danger of A's body at bay, the corporeal

[6] Peter Holland, 'The RSC and Studio Shakespeare', *Essays in Criticism* 32 (1982), 205–18; p. 206.

[7] Erika Fischer-Lichte, *The Semiotics of Theatre*, trans. Jeremy Grimes and Doris L. Jones (Bloomington, 1992), p. 101.

contiguity of small space performance can affect the range of senses. The results are not necessarily pleasant – especially when touch and smell are involved – but they provoke the audience to recognize that the actor is not merely a representation. As an undeniable presence, as a space-occupying creature distinctly like the watcher in size, vitality, and desire, the actor in a studio becomes both more human and more threatening. For Shakespeare the proximity of A to S, and the less rigorous distinctions between ludic and watching spaces, can be more powerful than in other types of presentation. The transgressive opportunities of performance, particularly those violating common notions of where Shakespeare belongs and how he should be represented, can dominate normal fictive issues like story and character and theme. The space in which *Hamlet* is played, in other words, can be more important than *Hamlet* itself.

At the same time the spoken text becomes more emphatic. Most of the renovations in Shakespeare stage space since Poel have attempted to recentre the word, recognizing that the actor on a bare stage, especially when partly surrounded by spectators and untrammelled by decorations, is chiefly perceived as a body speaking text. In a small theatre the spoken word becomes as intimate as the environment, insidious, urgent and intrusive. Because the vocal qualities are close to those of everyday life, the stage events seem domestic in scale, a condition that cuts both ways: the performance can show violent or hilarious upheavals of that domesticity, or show mere banalities. By the simple fact of their proximity A and S become familiar. Sighs, whispers, ironic inflections, the electricity of sudden outbursts, these appear direct and genuine to the late twentieth-century spectator, whereas large-scale Shakespearian acting may appear stagey or artificial. Why contemporary spectators seem to prefer one over the other is a complicated question, and I'll defer my attempt at an answer until later. First I hope to establish through an example some of the ways that audiences are affected by chamber Shakespeare.

There have been many notable successes on small stages, and some failures as well, but the performance that gets discussed the most in English is Trevor Nunn's *Macbeth* at The Other Place in 1976. The production is doubly interesting to us because Nunn had staged the play in the main house in 1974, then restaged it for the Aldwych Theatre in London the following year; dissatisfied both times by a lack of intensity, he mounted a chamber version using two of the company's stars, Ian McKellen and Judi Dench, to experiment with a 'big' play in a small space. Nunn, who was at the time the Artistic Director of the RSC, had been a strong supporter of Buzz Goodbody's work at The Other Place. He had supervised the final dress rehearsals of her 'village hall' production of *Hamlet* in 1975 after her suicide in April, and the experience convinced him of the distinctive opportunities of studio performance. His *Macbeth* has particular weight as an historical example because it was one of the earliest of the RSC chamber productions; the comments of reviewers may be accorded more consequence than usual because they were not habituated to the rewards and dangers of such a Shakespearian enterprise.

Nunn and the designer John Napier notably set out to limit size and spectacle. The ludic space was a circle of about 20 feet in diameter, outlined by a black line painted on bare floorboards. The watching space consisted of a few rows of seats on the floor on three sides of the circle and a few more rows on raised scaffolding, all with a quality of impermanence. The spatial relationship created the sense that spectators were staring at an intimate ritual of evil, helpless to act, even though it was close enough to touch. A circle of wooden beer crates was set at the boundary of the ludic space, just outside the magic circle; seated on them, actors not involved in a scene could watch the action, mediating between the positions of A–X and S. The crates were also used as props inside the circle, along with an extremely limited number of other items: a richly decorated coronation robe, a bell, a thunder sheet.

In such a minimized visual field, the smallest movements and the smallest voices were severely focused. Almost all commentators recorded some reaction to how the cramped space heightened their discomfort over witnessing a dark intimacy, and many spoke of their sense of voyeurism at perverse acts. 'Everything is cribbed, cabined and confined', said the *Birmingham Post*, 'lit by sulphurous gleams.' Maurice Daniels, a long-time staff director and lighting designer at Stratford (though not connected with this production), reported that he felt 'like a voyeur watching with horror and fascination as Lady Macbeth and Macbeth became aroused, really unable to keep their hands off each other, as they planned Duncan's murder'. The theatre is voyeuristic by nature, of course, and the proscenium theatre lends itself especially well to the spirit of peering through a keyhole. The voyeurism of this *Macbeth*, however, struck many viewers as distinctly disturbing. Gareth Lloyd Evans related his 'sense of almost unbearable proximity to, and identification with, the world of the play: terror, apprehension, pity counterpointing with revulsion'. And Robert Cushman said that 'we are brought so close to Macbeth, and to evil itself (we are practically locked up with them), that we cannot disown them'.[8]

I suggest that the source of spectators' disturbance lay in the condition of studio playing adopted at The Other Place: the actors publicly performed actions that should be hidden, as they do whenever *Macbeth* is staged, but in this case they did so almost unframed, tangibly close, *and as if the spectators were not present*. They performed inside the conventions of psychological realism, overtly ignoring the presence of the audience, maintaining fourth-wall illusion though the fourth wall of a proscenium did not divide ludic space from watching space and was most plainly not implied. The performance created a disjunction between two attitudes to corporeality: spectators acknowledged the actors' bodies, indeed could not resist their carnal closeness, while actors (at least officially) denied the spectators' bodies and concentrated on their own.

The spectators' inescapable awareness of the actors' bodies in a closed space can be demonstrated by the frequency with which commentators reported physical details and movements, often noting unusually small matters. I could make a very long list, but some samples will serve:

> Jaggedness of movement and gesture ... characterised the whole production. [On first seeing the witches, Macbeth and Banquo] twirled rapidly around, with daggers drawn, to face them. This 'twirl' became a feature of the playing and was sometimes continued until the actor's body had passed through 360 degrees in a complete pirouette.[9]

> The meeting between them was orgasmic in movement, and we later remembered the pushing movement of her hips and thighs when she gently but insidiously pulled Duncan into her castle.[10]

> [In the scene with the murderers] Macbeth was at his most briskly administrative, busy with papers ... [until he sent them away with a] dismissive jerk of the head.[11]

> At Macbeth's return to court there is an instant outburst of cheers and embraces, abruptly cut off as soon as the point has been made. For the coronation, Macbeth performs a stately walk round the perimeter of the acting area clad in Duncan's robe ... If [the Macbeths] are sure of one thing it is that nothing can drive them apart, a process that begins with the murder and is ruthlessly articulated up to the

8 *Birmingham Post*, 13 September 1976. Daniels cited in Michael Mullin, 'Stage and Screen: The Trevor Nunn *Macbeth*', *Shakespeare Quarterly*, 38 (1987), 350–9; p. 355. Lloyd Evans in a review in *Shakespeare Quarterly*, 28 (1977), 190–5; pp. 193–4. Cushman's report of the London run, *New York Times*, 5 February 1978.

9 Richard David, *Shakespeare in the Theatre* (Cambridge, 1978), p. 87.

10 Gareth Lloyd Evans, *Shakespeare Quarterly*, p. 194.

11 Roger Warren, *Shakespeare Survey 30* (1977), p. 178.

moment of Ian McKellen lugging Judi Dench off like a carcass.[12]

This kind of characterized movement and gesture, which reveals inner state as well as conveys emotional attitudes about the story, is familiar to us from the cinema, where a raised eyebrow or an impassive face in close-up can be used to enunciate enterprises of great pith and moment. 'There's no art / To find the mind's construction in the face', Duncan holds, but in filmed performances audiences find it automatically. All audiences, including theatre audiences, are now habituated to the psychological–realist acting associated with films and television, what one television critic has called 'micro-acting'.[13] I suspect that familiarity made the production more accessible. Certainly the acting used techniques of gesture and voice to create emotional closeness, as Holland noted:

> All the incisive detail of McKellen's performance was aimed to make Macbeth recognisable, to encourage us to empathise in the most complex way possible. His presentation of the part had nothing to do with sympathy – indeed this was the least sympathetic Macbeth I have ever seen – but the evil was explicable rather than terrifying, closer to malice than an abstracted principle of negativity.[14]

Reading the face became the central interpretative task and, when a spectator's line of sight was obscured, the production was in danger of losing its hold. Roger Warren felt he missed a number of important moments because of his seat location: 'I should dearly have liked to see Judi Dench's face, for instance, as she greeted Duncan', he wrote.[15]

Other features of the production also replicated filmic patterns. Though it's already the shortest of the tragedies, Nunn cut *Macbeth* down to two and a quarter hours and played it without interval, like a film; and some of its visuals were clearly cinematic, like the line of red blood on Lady Macduff's neck when a murderer cut her throat as the lights faded. Yet the moment remained highly theatrical, since Macduff himself, impassive and helpless, was watching the murder of his wife and children from a crate outside the circle. And the general feel of the production was theatrical as well, its best instances deriving from simple images of actors' bodies in space, like the magnificent moment after Lady Macbeth's death when McKellen stood frozen under a bare lightbulb which hung from a cord. He set it swinging in a long arc, his face alternately in shadow and light, precisely indicating the rhythm of elation and despair he had traced in the play:

> I 'gin to be aweary of the sun,
> And wish th'estate o'th'world were now
> undone. (5.5.47–8)

But overt theatricality only worked to a point. It was not able to include Ian McDiarmid's Porter, for example, which was almost universally condemned; McDiarmid played the role as a music-hall turn, addressing the audience directly and forcing the obscenities and jokes. Not only did his performance seem too big for the small space, it violated the basic assumption of the production by admitting the spectators' presence. Even more telling, prior to its run at the Warehouse Nunn briefly mounted the production in the main theatre at Stratford in 1977, where its cinematic details and theatrical intimacy were hopelessly lost in the large space.

Speculation 2. The absence of the performer's body in film and video is offset by magnified body-gesture.

Actors in film and video, emerging only as simulacra of light and shadow or as pixels of cathode rays, obviously cannot acknowledge a

---

12 Irving Wardle, *The Times*, 14 September 1977.

13 An unsigned review of Derek Jacobi's performance in the BBC production of *Hamlet*, *New York Times*, 16 November 1980, as quoted in *Shakespeare on Television: An Anthology of Essays and Reviews*, ed. J. C. Bulman and H. R. Coursen (Hanover, NH, 1988), p. 264.

14 Holland, 'The RSC and Studio Shakespeare', p. 214.

15 Roger Warren, *Shakespeare Survey 30* (1977), p. 179.

spectator's presence or be acknowledged in turn. If our starting point is that Shakespeare's work was intended to be seen in the theatre, then the absence of the performer's body is the most significant phenomenological difference in Shakespeare on film and television, a circumstance frequently acknowledged by commentators. 'Film occurs in a kind of virtual space', William Flesch notes. 'Lacking a dimension it lacks a basic *presence* in the world we live in. Nothing in film can touch or be touched.'[16] It's not the actual touching of or by actors in live performance that is notable, but the possibility that it can occur, especially in a studio space; with the possibility gone, film and video spectation belongs to a different category of experience. The 'loss of the actor', as W. B. Worthen calls it, which characterizes all mechanically reproduced performance, is usually assumed to be a severe detriment. 'Although the camera simulates intimacy with the characters, it also keeps us safe from them', Worthen says, so that we are permitted 'to watch without risk'; denied the public dimension of Shakespeare's work, we are prevented 'from playing our part'.[17]

Yet the simulation of intimacy in film and television is very powerful. What causes it, and why do spectators feel it? I'm not at all sure that I have the answer, but it's important to stress first that watching films and videos has significantly altered the perception of any kind of drama. Prior to the invention of motion pictures, when the term 'live performance' was a tautology, dramatic representation was an uncommon experience, whereas film, radio, and especially television have made drama in the late twentieth century all-pervasive and practically universal. In much of the world it is difficult to get through an ordinary day without some exposure to electronic enactments, and many people spend an inordinate amount of time engaged by the various dramatic, pseudo-dramatic, and speciously dramatic representations on television. Despite their recent arrival, film and video are now deeply part of us, and our cultural habituation to them has deeply affected the way we perceive the world.

Further, film and television have thoroughly altered the social construction of audiences. Though the body of the actor is absent in mechanical drama, quite obviously the spectator of film and video remains corporeal and has (or can have) an affiliation to other spectators. But film-going, despite its similarity to theatre-going, does not encourage the same sense of community among spectators because of the impersonality of enacted event. Occasionally an audience in a cinema will clap at the end of a film, for example, but since the actors are not present to receive approbation, any more than they have been present to receive the gaze, the applause seems forced and awkward: it is applause for the machine. (Though in some cases applause in a cinema may signify the sense of community that has developed among the spectators.) And television, where the gathered audience may be a few persons or a single person only, suggests a private, one-to-one relationship of each spectator to the talking head on the screen. As Sheldon Zitner writes, 'from stage to film to television, the audience changes from active collective to passive collective to passive individual'.[18]

---

16 William Flesch, 'Proximity and Power: Shakespearean and Cinematic Space', *Theatre Journal*, 39 (October 1987), 277–93; p. 277. The issue of the fixity of film's performance text is raised in Patricia Ferrara, 'Towards a Theory of Shakespearean Film', *Literature/Film Quarterly*, 16 (1988), 167–73; p. 172. Catherine Belsey addresses the question of cinematic and Shakespearian illusion in 'Shakespeare and Film: A Question of Perspective', *Literature/Film Quarterly*, 11 (1983), 152–8.

17 W. B. Worthen, 'The Player's Eye: Shakespeare on Television', *Comparative Drama*, 18 (Fall 1984), 193–202; pp. 197, 200, 201.

18 Sheldon, P. Zitner, 'Wooden O's in Plastic Boxes: Shakespeare and Television', *University of Toronto Quarterly*, 51 (Fall 1981), 1–12; p. 2. See also Neil Taylor, 'Two Types of Television Shakespeare', *Shakespeare Survey 39* (1987), pp. 103–11; p. 104. Two essays by Graham Holderness are important for the institutional

These McLuhanesque commonplaces become important for my subject because both film and television, whether delivering news or drama, tend to present themselves as realist texts, as transparent windows on the world. We watch images of people engaged in ordinary or tenable actions, often dressed and speaking like us, inviting us to figure them out. If intimacy in live performance comes from the actors' presence, the simulation of intimacy in film and video, emphasized by close ups and by amplified but unstressed voices, comes from their absence. Paradoxically, it is metaphoric distance which appears to make the actors closer, since the human images can be much larger than life without becoming a physical threat, the voices sinuous and alluring or enhanced and coercive without becoming abusive. The intrusive intervention of the actor's face, glowing from a screen that is a metonym of the spectator's desire, invites psychological speculation and infinite fantasias of meaning. The actors' magnified absence encourages individualized readings of their images, creating an illusory but intense sensation of veracity. We look at the screen and we fill it with ourselves.

The Trevor Nunn *Macbeth* on stage was already in psychological close up. When it was shot for Thames Television in 1978, using the same sixteen actors and the same cut-down version of the text, it fitted quite naturally into the new medium. The video director, Philip Casson, had simply to accent its imbedded mode of performance and bring the camera in close. This he did with great and almost tedious regularity, so that the dominant impression is of faces in turmoil. Television, of course, normally compensates for the small screen by replacing the panoramas of film with full-screen images of faces. (Though the video monitors currently available in many countries are much larger than the standard in 1978, so that faces filling the screen can now be larger than life.) Television is thus – by convention, if not inherently – suited to a drama of psychologizing, a characteristic that works well in the domestic environment where we normally see it. Since we are in a space resonant with the ordinary, we are less likely to accept representations of the extraordinary on the screen.

'Your face, my thane, is as a book where men / May read strange matters' (1.5.61–2) became the theme of the Thames production, and the camera provided ample opportunity to read faces. Filmed in a studio, there were no long shots and few shots of groups. Actors appeared as if from a misty darkness and were immediately subjected to the camera's scrutiny. Even the prologue, replayed from the stage version, in which all the actors entered and sat on the crates at the circle's edge, focused on individual faces as the camera panned from one to the next. For 'Is this a dagger which I see before me', only McKellen's face and hands were lit, his black costume invisible; at the end of the soliloquy he rolled back his sleeve in preparation for stabbing Duncan, and the length of his white arm in all that darkness was terrifying. After the regicide his arm was streaked with bright blood. Similarly, on discovering the King's murder Macduff revealed horror in his face rather than in his words. The acoustic effects were directly parallel to the visuals; like the camera, the microphone amplifies extreme intimacies while maintaining the illusion of the typical. Sighs, intakes of breath, whispers, and softly uttered cries were as much a part of the television version as the enlarged faces.

Reviewing the original broadcast, Sean Day-Lewis noted how strikingly effective this method is for television: 'The chamber-music style, allowing nothing except some dubiously muddled costumes to detract from the words and the talking heads, was as far as could be travelled from the expensive naturalism

issues of the BBC Shakespeare project: 'Radical Potentiality and Institutional Closure' in *Political Shakespeare*, ed. Jonathan Dollimore and Alan Sinfield (Manchester, 1985), pp. 182–201; and 'Boxing the Bard' in *The Shakespeare Myth*, ed. Holderness (Manchester, 1988), pp. 172–89.

adopted by Cedric Messina for his complete Shakespeare on BBC-2.'[19] *Macbeth* was successful on television because on stage the production had domesticated the supernatural. Witchcraft and murder were arranged to fit inside the homey environment of the theatre-within-the-box by relying on faces to convey inner states rather than on external effects, and by making those faces indisputable. Speaking of Shakespeare video acting in a slightly different context, Robert Lindsay (who played Benedick in the BBC series' *Much Ado About Nothing*) said that 'the subtleties, the subtext, which are difficult to project on stage, you can do on television. Just the fact that you can stand next to someone and say one thing, while your eyes are saying something else, is wonderful.'[20]

In *Macbeth* subtext was also conveyed by non-facial gestures and actions in the same close-up manner. Holding two daggers after Duncan's murder, Macbeth's hands were shaking: the blades lightly but insistently clicked against each other. At the end Macbeth's head on a pole would have been out of keeping with the extreme psychological realism, on stage and on television; instead an actor brought the crown to Macduff's hands, which were holding two similar daggers still smeared with the tyrant's blood. For the video version the camera tightly focused on this final image, searing it in the spectator's mind in a still frame that made the final moment darker and considerably more pessimistic than on stage.

Speculation 3. Film and video have altered the reception of the performer's body in the theatre.

Recent scholarship has emphasized that the way the body is represented and perceived is historically determined, and our most 'natural' corporeal attributes are conditioned, shaped, and controlled by culture. The actor's body is probably more subject to historical forces than the bodies of non-performers; regardless of its size, shape, or beauty, the actor's body is almost inevitably read as exemplary because it is the object of the most intense and profound gaze in a culture. Indeed it seems fair to say that accepting the culture's gaze is a condition of acting. As Joseph Roach notes, 'the complex values of a culture' become concentrated in the performing body as observed by the spectator. Fischer-Lichte goes even farther, holding that the performer's body is representative of the whole of culture.[21] When notions of the body undergo change, the actor's body becomes a site where that cultural crisis is represented.

In the past fifteen or twenty years we have undergone a major transformation in the way Shakespeare is perceived on stage. As I have been suggesting, this change has been informed by the prevalence of film and television in the culture at large, and their increasing bias to psychic revelation through close-ups and through small but precise signifiers of meaning. The actor's animate body on stage is now seen with eyes thoroughly accustomed to the actor's inanimate body on film, eyes that in many cases may prefer the distance of the screen. Further, there are substantially more films and videos of Shakespeare's plays available now than twenty years ago, and because video recorders are so common it is at least possible for the general public to see performances of the plays on demand. The success of the recent films by Kenneth Branagh and Franco Zeffirelli, relying on the old Hollywood formula for Shakespeare of spectacle and stars, demonstrates that the

---

19 Sean Day-Lewis, *The Daily Telegraph*, 5 January 1979.

20 Quoted in Susan Willis, *The BBC Shakespeare Plays* (Chapel Hill, 1991), pp. 220–1.

21 Joseph R. Roach, *The Player's Passion: Studies in the Science of Acting* (Ann Arbor, 1993), p. 11. Erika Fischer-Lichte, 'Theatre and the Civilizing Process: An Approach to the History of Acting', *Interpreting the Theatrical Past: Essays in the Historiography of Performance*, ed. Thomas Postlewait and Bruce A. McConachie (Iowa City, 1989), pp. 19–36. On historicizing the human body, see Thomas W. Laqueur, *The Making of the Modern Body: Sexuality and Society in the Nineteenth Century* (Berkeley, 1987); and Laqueur, 'Bodies, Details, and Humanitarian Narrative', *The New Cultural History*, ed. Lynn Hunt (Berkeley, 1989), pp. 176–204.

market is reasonably large. In their video versions those films join a burgeoning cinematic industry, dominated by the BBC complete Shakespeare project: for the first time in history, you can walk down the street and hire a Shakespeare production, and at very little expense.

A very large number of people have now been introduced to Shakespeare performance through video in the classroom. This form of Shakespearian spectation, because it fits with culturally accustomed habits of viewing, strikes many students as less foreign or intimidating than watching Shakespeare in the theatre, but it comes with a cost: it tends to suggest that the plays are essentially about psychological states. (Not all television productions have restricted themselves to naturalistic techniques; in the BBC series Jane Howell has been successful in directing performances that retain something of Shakespeare's overt theatricality. Yet even her versions have focused on intimate character portrayal in the traditional televisual manner.)[22] Further, students have been spontaneously advocated to deconstruct video performances, and to investigate very small details in them, by means of the pause and rewind buttons. The technology of video encourages us to treat performances as if they were printed scripts, searching back and forth in them as we do in a text, replaying moments, taking them out of their performative context, realigning them according to our own choices. With a VCR remote control in hand, any viewer is a textual editor and perhaps a playwright, and able to control (the simulacra of) the actor's body and voice.

I don't mean to suggest that spectators who have grown up with video Shakespeare are inclined to stop live performances and ask for an instant replay. But it is likely that the electronic reification of the actor's body has affected the way those spectators watch in the theatre. They are more likely to look for psychological explanations of action, more likely to heed small intense moments that clarify inner states, unlikely to listen for rhetorical structure or be patient with self-conscious theatricality. These spectators are more likely attracted to the underplaying characteristic of studio theatres and to imperial themes treated as intimate occasions. It's intriguing to notice that from the start the most successful productions at The Other Place have been tragedies or dark comedies rooted in family matters. Goodbody's *King Lear* (1974) and *Hamlet*, Nunn's *Macbeth*, John Barton's *The Merchant of Venice* (1978), John Caird's *Romeo and Juliet* (1984), and on up to Sam Mendes's *Richard III* (1992) – all worked by using micro-acting and homespun theatrical virtues to underline the domestic situations of the plays. The lighter comedies or the more public histories have rarely been tried there, probably because they rely on broader styles which are difficult to play up close.

The domesticating effect of film and television on chamber work can be seen through Nunn's *Othello* of 1989 at The Other Place, some thirteen years after *Macbeth*. The cast was assembled specially for the occasion, and played for limited runs in Stratford and at the Young Vic in London. Unlike *Macbeth*, cut to the length of a film, this *Othello* used a nearly complete text and lasted over four hours. While magnificently theatrical, the performance nonetheless refined the micro-characteristics of its predecessors, especially in the acting of Ian McKellen. As Iago, McKellen was a military iceman, obsessive about orderliness and under notable control: he was often brushing his uniform, straightening a carpet, or pedagogically explaining to Roderigo exactly how to accomplish his aims. His face could show dedication to his general and perfidy to the audience at the same moment, yet be psychologically in tune with a nineteenth-century martial code assumed by the setting. 'The stiff military back, the fastidiously groomed moustache and the clipped northern accent persuades them all',

22 See Hardy M. Cook, 'Jane Howell's BBC First Tetralogy', *Literature/Film Quarterly*, 20 (1992), 326–37.

wrote Christopher Edwards; 'only we seem to see how cold are his blue eyes.' The 'microscopic scrutiny' of Iago's character 'repeatedly puts you in mind of Strindberg. The locations may ostensibly be Venice and Cyprus, but spiritually we are inside the four walls of bourgeois naturalist drama.'[23] Othello, on the other hand, was played by Willard White, a Jamaican opera singer acting Shakespeare for the first time – and acting in a large, unrestrained, indulgent style, allowing his voice to range in pitch and volume and his gestures to become grand and contrived. His passion was readily apparent, but it cast doubt on his mental state. McKellen was on television, as it were, and White at Covent Garden: so we, strangely, trusted Iago and were suspicious of Othello.

The visuals of the production, designed by Bob Crowley, specifically elicited a cinematic reference. The Senate scene in Act 1, for example, sat Othello at a small table to recount the story of his love: the council took place, according to Robert Smallwood, 'in a haze of cigar smoke around a table on which the maps jostled with the brandy decanter and glasses under a green-shaded lamp – a gentlemen's-club atmosphere'.[24] It was a powerful image of a familiar world where decisions about women are made by men with the same brusque presumption that drives them to occupy and defend a distant island. That world was evoked in part by the numerous small hand props that allowed actors characterized tasks. McKellen rolled his own cigarettes, for example, as quickly and neatly as he misled Othello; Imogen Stubbs as Desdemona dropped her handkerchief after trying to cool her husband's troubled brow with it. McKellen mixed wine punch in a white enamel basin in the barracks scene, and later the drunken Cassio vomited into it. Stanley Wells noted that the physical details and psychological acting lent an 'almost Ibsenite social realism'; indeed, he said, 'a fully written account of this production would read like a Victorian novel'.[25]

In Cyprus it gradually became apparent that the costumes and props were derived from the American Civil War: blue Union tunics with brass and leather accessories, folding camp cots, wooden washstands. Because Willard White is black, this raised intriguing questions about slavery, but Crowley told me that he was not after a political statement: 'I tried rather to elicit key objects from the period that would have a huge resonance in a small space. This was Shakespeare under the microscope.'[26] With a few deft strokes the designer had evoked a major cultural quotation, not to the Civil War but to movies about the Civil War. Collective images of the past have always come from popular sources; they are now defined by Hollywood films more than by ballads or books or plays. Crowley explained he wanted to give spectators swift access to the situation of men travelling to a remote outpost for war, a few women tagging along, out of place in a male world. 'It's hard to do that with doublets and hose', he said, but military uniforms from more recent and visually accessible periods can quickly establish ranks, emotional dispositions, and character displacements.

Cinema and video were important to Nunn's *Othello* in two ways, then: through the range of visual references that drew on period movies, and through a psychological acting (especially McKellen's) that stressed intimate facial gesture and quiet vocal practice. The production's power derived not from its imitation of film and video, but rather from the selective reconditioning of their methods, including the naturalistic habit of defining character through environment and objects. At the end of the

[23] Christopher Edwards, 'Tragedy in Close-Up', *The Spectator*, 2 September 1989, pp. 37, 36.

[24] Robert Smallwood, 'Shakespeare on Stage', *Shakespeare Quarterly*, 41 (1990), 101–14; p. 111.

[25] Stanley Wells, 'Shakespeare Production in England in 1989', *Shakespeare Survey 43* (1991), pp. 183–203; pp. 191, 192.

[26] Bob Crowley, in an interview in London, October 1989. See *Looking at Shakespeare*, pp. 255–6.

piece McKellen stood unrepentant and unbowed in a fading spotlight, coldly staring at spectators only a few feet away, his face revealing nothing – 'Demand me nothing' fixed in a physical gesture – which meant we were free to read his face with impunity. It was intimate Shakespeare at its best: chillingly intense, psychologically convincing, and thoroughly alien.

Actors' bodies, existent and incontestable before spectators' bodies in a studio theatre, will never be mistaken for the electronic and luminant phantasms of television and films. But by drawing on the kind of acting and scenography familiar from the mass media, Nunn's productions, and chamber Shakespeare in general, have profited from contemporary cultural habituations while aggressively reapplying them to live art. Caught between a premodern and a postmodern mode of representation, we are surprised by the antique pleasure of corporeal presence. Confronting the Shakespearian other in a claustrophobic space, we sense the familiar performative modes of film and television, and at the same time the inescapable danger of other bodies occupying a shared present.

THE ARCHITECTURE OF THE FORTUNE PLAYHOUSE

JOHN ORRELL

Edward Alleyn embarked on his Fortune playhouse project late in 1599, soon after the Globe had opened on Bankside. On 22 December he leased a site near Cripplegate, and within three weeks had signed up Peter Street, the Globe's carpenter.[1] Only two years earlier he had quitted the stage to concentrate on business affairs, but short retirement urges sweet return, and already he was planning his comeback, for which the new playhouse was to be the elegant setting. He paid for it himself, and looked for another sort of return from the income generated by its galleries. The Fortune was the player's investment in his own confident talent.

The contract drawn up between Alleyn, his partner Philip Henslowe, and their builder is a tantalizing document, holding back as much information as it offers. To save going into a mass of particulars it cites another building – the Globe – as a defining prototype, a shortcut often found in such agreements,[2] and made especially effective in this case by the carpenter's intimate knowledge of the model. The Fortune was, in untold ways though certainly not in everything, a replication of the 'round' Bankside playhouse.

Yet its plan, the contract tells us, was to be 'sett square', a radical if not altogether surprising departure from the Globe's example. To Alleyn, contemplating the building of a new playhouse during the closing months of 1599, London offered a variety of models. The old public theatre type, perhaps initiated as long ago as 1567 at the Red Lion in Whitechapel, was still the main standard. The Theatre, with its high turret rising from the central yard, had gone, though it was now substantially resurrected as the Globe. The Shoreditch Curtain remained, a 'round' or polygonal house in which the yard stood open to the weather, ringed by storeys of covered galleries. The Swan was of a similar pattern, though possibly built in a more sophisticated idiom and more elegantly decorated. The Rose, originally 'round', had been radically reconstructed in 1592 into a D-shaped house, no longer a regular polygon in plan but still with roofed galleries and an open yard. At the Boar's Head in Whitechapel a stage had been fitted up in the middle of the rectangular innyard, forward of each of its ranges, rather like a boxing ring totally surrounded by its audience. That arrangement proving unsatisfactory, the stage was later – in 1599 – removed towards the

1 See the contract, dated 8 January 1600, printed in *Henslowe's Diary*, edited by R. A. Foakes and R. T. Rickert (Cambridge, 1961), pp. 306–15. Only circumstantial evidence exists to show that Street had built the Globe, but it is persuasive.

2 The Hope, built by Gilbert Katherens for Henslowe and Jacob Meade in 1613, was contracted to be 'of suche large compasse, fforme, widenes, and height as the Plaie house Called the Swan' (*Henslowe Papers*, edited by Walter W. Greg (London, 1907), p. 20); in 1732, John Rich sent his builder Edward Shepherd off to survey the third Lincoln's Inn Fields theatre as a model for Covent Garden, the survey becoming part of the Articles of Agreement between them (PRO C11/2662/1).

south-western side of the court, where a tiring house (or houses: the records sometimes use the plural form) was constructed and a roof extended over the stage.[3] And of course the Globe, though it almost certainly repeated the shape and size of the original Theatre, must have introduced some new elements of stage design, including the sort of integrated roof over the stage that had been found earlier at the Rose.

But the most striking innovation was not among the public arenas at all. The Blackfriars, unfortunately dark during the latter part of 1599, had been designed by James Burbage two years earlier as a new type of enterprise for the Lord Chamberlain's Men. Unlike the public playhouses it was an enclosed auditorium, intended for the commercial presentation of plays to comparatively small audiences by candlelight. The U-shape of its galleries appears to have been influenced by the plan of a theatre published in Sebastiano Serlio's *Architettura*.[4] Already in 1584–5 the Elizabethan Banqueting House at Whitehall had been equipped with a semi-permanent U-shaped auditorium[5] perhaps derived from the same source, which is clearly invoked in the earliest surviving English theatre plan, that for the hall at Christ Church, Oxford, when it was fitted up for plays in 1605.[6]

Theatrical innovation was in the air. Blackfriars, barred from opening by the protests of important neighbours, was not yet in use, and its enforced idleness was enough to discourage Alleyn from proposing to build a similar enclosed playhouse, at least for the present.[7] But Henslowe's transformation of the Rose into a D-shaped structure, possibly in imitation of ancient Roman theatres as they were known from Serlio's archaeological chapters,[8] together with the experiments at the Boar's Head, showed that even the central tradition of the public amphitheatre was open to question and modification. Alleyn's decision to build the Fortune square was one such experiment, devised no doubt with the help of Peter Street.

STREET, ALLEYN AND ARCHITECTURE

Unfortunately too little is known of Street and his work as a whole to allow us to assess his habits of design,[9] but to judge by the company he kept he was probably up-to-date in fashion and technique. He was the official carpenter at Bridewell, once Henry VIII's palace and now run by the City of London as 'a workehouse for the poore'.[10] Here Street had his own wharf to handle the timber and pre-built frames which he brought to his yard by river.[11] He became Second Warden of the Carpenters' Company in 1598, and Mary Edmond has observed that he must have been acquainted with the Master Carpenter of the Royal Works, William Portington, whom the Company often entertained (they still have his portrait on the wall).[12] Portington had overseen the reconstruction of the Banqueting House auditorium of 1584–5, and was later to fit the place out again for Jonson's *Masque of Blackness* (1605), with its great mobile stage, 40 feet square, four feet high and made 'wth wheles to go on'.[13] He was

3 Herbert Berry, *The Boar's Head Playhouse* (Washington, 1986), pp. 106–19.

4 John Orrell, 'The Private Theatre Auditorium', *Theatre Research International*, 9 (1984), 79–91

5 PRO E351/3219, discussed in John Orrell, *The Human Stage: English Theatre Design 1567–1640* (Cambridge, 1988), pp. 111–12.

6 Orrell, *The Human Stage*, pp. 119–29.

7 In 1617–18 Alleyn seems to have attempted to rescue the nearby Puddle Wharf private theatre, which closed because of the neighbours' objections: Gerald Eades Bentley, *The Jacobean and Caroline Stage*, vol. 6 (Oxford, 1968), pp. 77–86.

8 Sebastiano Serlio, *Tutte l'opere d'architettura* (Venice, 1566), III. fols. 70^{r}, 72^{r}, 74^{r}.

9 The best recent work on Street is by Mary Edmond, 'Peter Street, 1553–1609: Builder of Playhouses', *Shakespeare Survey 45* (Cambridge, 1992), pp. 101–14.

10 John Stow, *A Survay of London* (London, 1603), p. 398.

11 PRO Req. 2/91/57.

12 'Peter Street, 1553–1609', p. 111.

13 PRO E351/3240, Whitehall. The masque was designed by Inigo Jones.

thoroughly used to theatre work: for forty years, from 1579 until his death in 1620, he supervised the carpentry needed for the staging of plays at court, including many performed by the Admiral's Men, for whom Edward Alleyn was often a payee.

Two important projects early in the new reign give some idea of how the Works thought about theatre design. Though he is not specifically named in contemporary accounts, Portington was almost certainly one of 'two of his Ma$^{ts.}$ M$^{r.}$ Carpenters' who accompanied Simon Basil to Oxford in 1605 to fit up a decidedly Serlian scenic stage and auditorium in the hall at Christ Church.[14] The plan survives, and shows that the structure was carefully set out along Serlian lines: the whole work was contained within a double square (proportioned 2:1), the radial depth of the auditorium was twice the width of the orchestra, and so on.[15] The second undertaking was the new Banqueting House at Whitehall, for which Portington provided the massive carpentry as well as the stage for the opening production, Jonson's *Masque of Beauty* (1608), complete with its elaborate rotating machinery and self-conscious presentation of the Ionic and Corinthian orders.[16]

One of the few records of Street's professional work links him with the Banqueting House carpentry, whose style may well have resembled his own. The building was the most impressive piece of Court architecture that Street's generation had seen. Most of the Works' leading craftsmen and designers were involved, including Portington and the new Surveyor, Simon Basil. It was an aisled hall, 120 feet long, with brick walls and a flat leaded timber roof. According to a survey plan by Robert Smythson, the clear span of the nave was 37 feet, too wide for ordinary joisting.[17] Someone called Acheson was offered the large sum of £54 to make a 'Module of a Geometricall roof for the banqueting house'; no doubt this was framed, as Colvin and Summerson have suggested, to a pattern published in Serlio's First Book, for a floor made of timbers none of which is as long as the span.[18] The same scheme had interested Robert Stickells when he designed a roof at Lyveden New Build; his drawing, which neatly adapts Serlio to the specific requirements of the job, is extant.[19] Stickells, who was Clerk of the Royal Works at Richmond, drew the elevations for the Banqueting House,[20] with its great wooden columns, Ionic superimposed on Doric, made of select timbers felled in the forest at Pamber. Special equipment was needed to hollow them out to prevent splitting, and it was Street to whom the Works turned 'for the lone of y^{e} greate pumpaugurs for boringe the greate Collumbes in the Banquettinge house'.[21]

One cannot, on the basis of such evidence,

---

14 'Ffor the better contrivinge and finishinge of their stages, seates, and scaffoldes in S$^{t.}$ Maries and Christchurch, they intertayned two of his Ma$^{ts.}$ M$^{r.}$ Carpenters, and they had the advise of the Comptroler of his workes.' Cambridge University Library, Add. MS 34, fol. 44^{v}. Basil was the Comptroller; he became Surveyor in 1606.

15 See the analysis in *The Human Stage*, pp. 127–8.

16 The mobile throne of beauty, with eight Ionic pilasters below and a Corinthian order above, was 'put in act (for the *Motions*) by the *Kings* Master Carpenter'. C. H. Herford and Percy and Evelyn Simpson, eds., *Ben Jonson*, vol. 7 (Oxford, 1941), p. 190.

17 Reproduced in Stephen Orgel and Roy Strong, *Inigo Jones: the Theatre of the Stuart Court*, 2 vols. (London, 1973), vol. 1, p. 81.

18 B. L. Lansdowne MS 165, fol. 103^{v}; H. M. Colvin and John Summerson, *The History of the King's Works, Volume IV 1485–1660 (part II)* (London, 1982), p. 322; Serlio, *Tutte l'opere d'architettura*, I, fol. 15^{v}.

19 In the British Library, Add. MS 39831, fol. 3^{r}. It is reproduced in *The Human Stage*, p. 54. Robert Smythson had used the Serlian scheme in the great hall at Wollaton in the 1580s: Mark Girouard, *Robert Smythson and the Architecture of the Elizabethan Era* (London, 1966), p. 82.

20 PRO E351/3240, Rewards (1604–5).

21 PRO E351/3243, Rewards (1606–7). Edmond, 'Peter Street 1553–1609', p. 113, speculates that Street may have assisted in the carpentry for the earlier Jacobean court masques and in the preparation of Blackfriars for the adult company in 1608–9.

prove that Street talked about architectural theory with men like Portington and Stickells, but it is clear that he had contact with them and may have shared their idiom. Alleyn too had an interest in architecture. Later in life he became a friend of Inigo Jones, with whom he sometimes worked. John Chamberlain noted one such occasion during the preparations for the aborted visit of the Infanta in 1623. The Duke of Richmond and other noblemen went down to Southampton to make arrangements

> for mending the high ways, and for Shews and Pageants, to which purpose Inigo Jones and Allen the old Player went along with them, who alone with two or three Harbengers, or such officers, might have performed all this as well as so many Privy-counsellors . . .[22]

Among the superfluous councillors was the earl of Arundel, Jones's aristocratic patron and mentor, in whose circle Alleyn now customarily moved.[23] Both Arundel and Jones had been present at the inauguration of Alleyn's Dulwich College on 13 September 1619, and a few months earlier Alleyn had visited the earl at Arundel House, 'wher my Lord showed me all his statues and pictures that came from Italy',[24] a collection which already formed the very heart of Jonesian classicism. When, therefore, his Fortune playhouse burned in 1622, and the workmen were busy putting up a new brick theatre in its place, Alleyn sought the earl's approval of the new design.[25] On 12 June he entered in his diary: 'I went to ye Lord off Arundle showed ye fortune plott . . .'.[26] The second Fortune drawings were evidently fit to be exposed to the great arbiter's criticism; it would hardly be surprising to discover that the first Fortune had also been a piece of deliberate 'architecture'.

In their time both Alleyn and Street came to know a thing or two about current architectural styles. What the state of their knowledge was in 1600 is less clear, and the Fortune contract, with its technical and legal language, is hardly the place we should choose to look for enlightenment. Yet even here among the unexpressive clauses there are signs of three related matters, all tending to show that the playhouse was designed according to the precepts of Renaissance architectural classicism. First, although Alleyn named the Globe as his prototype, and retained a good many of its features including some of its dimensions, he rejected its old-fashioned polygonal plan in favour of the simpler square. Second, the contract gives evidence of rational, commensurate proportioning in the Fortune's design. And third, it shows that Street was instructed to use a modified architectural 'order' for the internal elevations.

THE FORTUNE AND THE GLOBE

The new theatre was to be 'sett square', 80 feet each way outside, with a 55 foot courtyard

---

22 Chamberlain to Carleton, 14 June 1623, in John Nichols, *The Progresses . . . of King James the First . . .* 4 vols. (London, 1828), vol. 4, p. 873. The journey was also noted in a letter from Dr Meddus to the Revd Joseph Meade, dated 5 June 1623, again linking 'Allein, some time a player, now squire of the bears' and 'Inigo Jones, surveyor of the king's works': Thomas Birch, *The Court and Times of James I*, 2 vols. (London, 1849), vol. 2, pp. 402–3.

23 David Howarth, *Lord Arundel and his Circle* (New Haven, 1985), p. 104.

24 Alleyn's diary, 17 April 1618, in William Young, *The History of Dulwich College*, 2 vols. (London, 1889), vol. 2, p. 80.

25 The second Fortune was constructed jointly by the carpenter Anthony Jarman and the bricklayer Thomas Wigpitt, 'according to a plottforme by them allready drawne' by 20 May 1622: *Henslowe Papers*, p. 29. Both men were among the sharers of the new enterprise. Jarman was Master of the Carpenters' Company in 1633; in the following year he submitted designs for the Goldsmiths' Hall; and in 1638 he was paid for making a 'modell' of St Michael le Querne, which was 'then about to be rebuilt with advice from Inigo Jones': Howard Colvin, *A Biographical Dictionary of British Architects 1600–1840* (London, 1978), p. 459, citing Guildhall Library MS 2895/2. Jarman's elder son Edward, a more famous architect than his father, made a survey of the second Fortune in 1656, working with the City Bricklayer John Tanner: *Henslowe Papers*, pp. 95–7.

26 Young, *History of Dulwich College*, vol. 2, p. 238.

centrally placed within.[27] The contract had to give dimensions because some of them could hardly have come unaltered from the polygonal Globe. It tells us – as it told Street – to compare the two houses and to allow for certain specified modifications. But what was clear for Street has become obscure for us, because until recently no one knew for certain what the plan of the Globe was like. Now, however, the archaeological investigation of its site has turned up enough of the foundations to give some idea of the underlying geometry of its polygonal plan. Parts of two bays have come to light, together with the footings of an attached lobby or possibly stair turret. The overall depth of the bays, from the gallery fronts to the external surface of the outer wall, is 12 feet 6 inches, the same measure that Street worked with at the Fortune. The width of the one bay that can be measured with any confidence is about 11 feet 6 inches at the front, and 15 feet 6 inches at the rear. A careful study of the site drawings leads to the conclusion that the overall diameter of the house, excluding the lobby or staircase, was 99 feet, and the building probably consisted of a polygon of twenty sides.[28]

Alleyn's Fortune was certainly smaller than that, though not so small as Henslowe's original Rose of 1587, which archaeology has shown to have been a regular polygon of fourteen bays, about 74 feet across.[29] The Rose was reconstructed in 1592 only a little larger, and Alleyn was used to its comparative intimacy. He must have been dismayed by the broad expanse of the Globe's yard, as wide at ground level as the whole of the original Rose. If some of this yard area were to be sacrificed in the new theatre a seated audience as big as the Globe's could be brought closer to the stage without itself being reduced. Alleyn had a particular interest in the income generated by the Fortune's galleries, which would be the major source of his profit. It was probably to maintain the gallery revenue, therefore, that he decided on a fundamental principle of his new theatre's design: despite its smaller area overall, its galleries would be just the same size as the Globe's. To achieve this end in a traditional centrally designed house of the Globe type he had to reduce the number of sides to four, the area of a square being smaller than that of a many-sided polygon of equal perimeter.[30]

The area of the 99-foot twenty-sided Globe apparently discovered by archaeology was 7571.69 square feet overall, excluding any attached stair turrets. Its yard was 4194.89 square feet gross, and the area covered by the gallery structure amounted to 3376.8 square feet. Similarly measured, the 80-foot Fortune covered 6400 square feet; 3025 square feet of that was taken up by the 55-foot yard, leaving 3375 square feet as the area of the main frame at ground level. In this respect the Globe was larger than the Fortune by a mere 1.8 square feet, or 0.05 per cent. A contemporary calculation, dealing in fractions rather than decimals, might not have recognized any difference at all. Street's measurement of the Globe's bays would have shown him that they were 15½ feet wide externally and 11½ feet at the front (for a diameter of 99 feet overall, a pocket calculator expresses these figures as 15.49 and 11.52 respectively). The average width of a bay would therefore have been 13 feet 6 inches. The Globe, made up of twenty such bays, each 12 feet 6 inches deep and joined together as a

[27] *Henslowe's Diary*, p. 307.

[28] The figures are of course provisional, derived as they are from limited evidence. Only the completion of the dig can confirm them; see the discussion and reports reprinted in Andrew Gurr, Ronnie Mulryne and Margaret Shewring, eds., *The Design of the Globe* (London, 1993), pp. 5–14 and 20–52.

[29] See C. Walter Hodges, 'Reconstructing the Rose', and John Orrell, 'Beyond the Rose: Design Problems for the Globe Reconstruction', in *New Issues in the Reconstruction of Shakespeare's Theatre*, ed. Franklin J. Hildy (New York, 1990), pp. 79–94 and 100–7.

[30] Although the result at the Fortune was generally a more intimate theatre, the building contained places in its corners that were 7 feet further from the stage than any at the Globe.

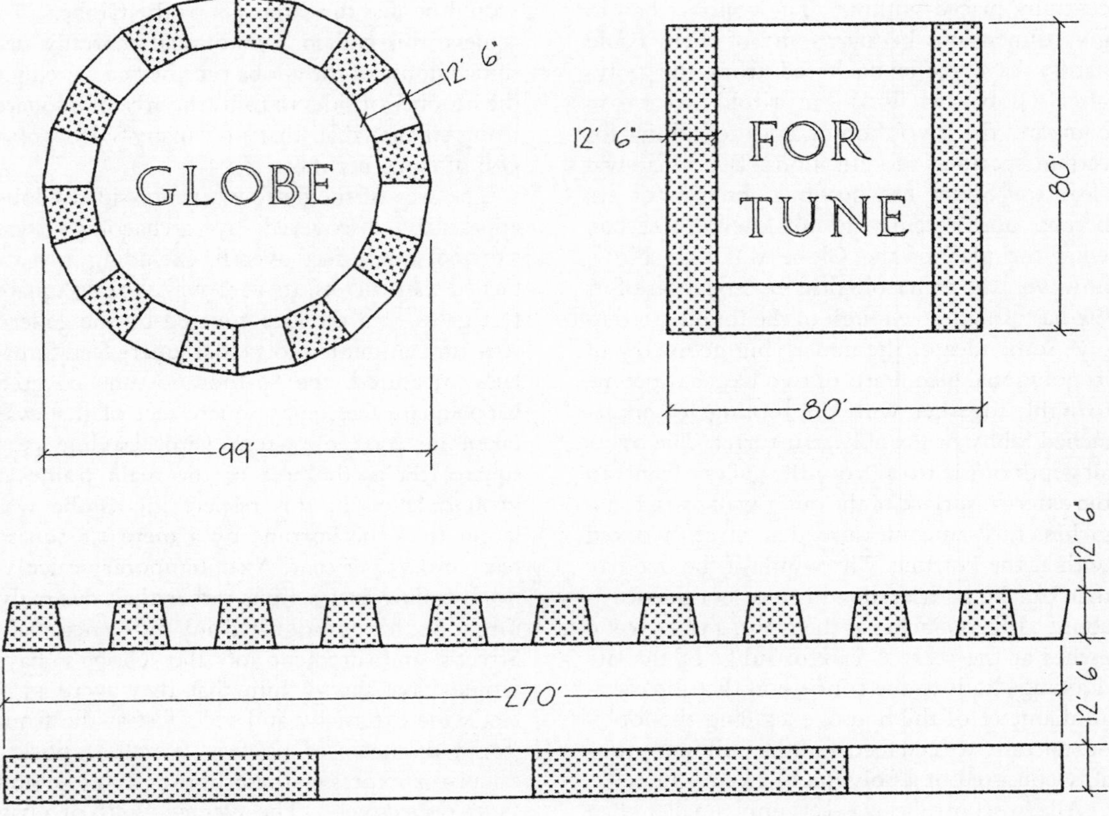

Fig. 1 The area of the Fortune's galleries equals that of the Globe's

polygon, consisted of 270 running feet of work. At the Fortune, where the galleries were also 12 feet 6 inches deep, Street constructed what we might for this purpose consider as two ranges each 80 feet long, linked by flanking ranges of 55 feet, for a total – as at the Globe – of 270 running feet. In Figure 1 I have shaded alternate bays and ranges to make this matter clear; for both theatres the bars at the foot of the diagram represent the baywork rearranged as a straight run. They are equal in area.[31]

PROPORTION AT THE FORTUNE

Renaissance architectural theory, derived from Vitruvius but developed by more recent commentators such as Cesariano or Daniele Barbaro, was a vast subject. Two parts of it concern us here: the conviction that a fine building should be proportioned according to simple commensurate ratios, and the insistence on the use of an architectural 'order' in the development of the structure. The first was

[31] In both theatres some of the bays were devoted to the use of the actors, probably in connection with a separate tiring house built independently between the frame and the stage. The logic of the framing of the Fortune, where the corners must have been built with diagonal 'dragon beams' to accommodate the displacements of the jettied corner posts from storey to storey, suggests that one entire range of the theatre was devoted to backstage uses. It may be that a quarter of the bays were similarly occupied at the Globe; the new Bankside reconstruction has adopted the scheme.

discussed by Robert Stickells in two theoretical memoranda of 1595 and 1597; the second is the theme of John Shute's *First and Chief Groundes of Architecture*, published in 1563. Neither was new, therefore, in the London of 1600, and although the Fortune contract has no reason to raise such matters explicitly, it nevertheless implies some version of them both.

The preference of Renaissance architects for simple mathematical ratios is well known. Serlio, following Vitruvius, looked with much favour on the square: 'Among the quadrangular forms I find the rectangle the most perfect. And the more the rectangle moves away from the perfect square the more it loses its perfection . . .'[32] In the first book of the *Architettura* he illustrates the most useful proportions for rooms as rectangles derived from the square: a square-and-a-quarter, a square-and-a-third, and so on.[33] The forms may be expressed as ratios: 1:1, 5:4, 4:3, 3:2, 2:1. Into this elementary series he also inserts 5:3 and √2:1. All except the last are composed of rational numbers, making possible the sort of design that is called 'commensurate' because both elements – say the width and length of a chamber – may be expressed as integers. Such thinking had become the common currency of Renaissance architectural theory, and in the 1590s was beginning to emerge in London building practice. Robert Stickells' theoretical notes contrasted medieval geometric design practices – what he called 'the moddarn' – with the architecture of antiquity ('the antikes'), which used rational proportions.[34] By 1635, when John Webb designed an auditorium in the hall at Whitehall, proportion was everywhere: he made the 'orchestra' or dancing floor 15 feet 4 inches wide by 23 feet long, a proportion of 2:3; the height of the frontispiece was 30 feet 8 inches, or in a proportion of 2:1 to the width of the orchestra (and 4:3 to the orchestra's length); just about every part of the structure was related to the rest through the system of integral ratios.

The Fortune contract gives the plan dimensions at ground level, but above that they change because of a 10-inch jetty forwards in each floor. The most important storey was unlikely to have been the one next to the yard, with its crowd of stinkards jostling for a view. In fact this floor was barricaded from contact with the yard, 'paled in belowe', as the contract puts it, like the stage itself 'wth good stronge and sufficyent newe oken bourdes'. It was also to be 'laide over and fenced wth stronge yron pykes',[35] forerunners of the fearsome rows of spikes that fortified the interiors of Georgian playhouses. English social custom had for some time favoured the upper floor of buildings, the ground-level Great Hall having been largely abandoned to the servants while the gentry moved upstairs to the Great Chamber, the withdrawing room and the gallery. In town houses the notable rooms were increasingly to be found at the upper level, the *piano nobile*, where they remain to this day.[36] In the Elizabethan public theatres the lords' rooms were located in a balcony over the stage, decorously above the action.

The best gallery – the dress circle, as it were – was the middle one, with its modest elevation above the stage, its greater distance from the groundlings and its propinquity to the lords' rooms. At the Fortune it appears that the middle gallery was the normative one for the proportionate design of the house. Down below, at ground level, the yard was 55 feet

---

32 *Tutte l'opere d'architettura*, I, fol. 9^v^, translated by George Hersey, *Pythagorean Palaces* (Ithaca, 1976), p. 53.

33 *Tutte l'opere d'architettura*, I, fol. 15^r^.

34 British Library Lansdowne MS 84, no. 10, ii, printed by John Summerson, 'Three Elizabethan Architects', *Bulletin of the John Rylands Library*, 40 (1957), 227–8.

35 *Henslowe's Diary*, p. 308.

36 See, for example, Simon Basil's designs for a town house of *c.*1600 reproduced in A. P. Baggs, 'Two Designs by Simon Basil', *Architectural History*, 27 (1984), 104–10; Mark Girouard, *Life in the English Country House: a Social and Architectural History* (New Haven and London, 1978), pp. 88–100; and the same author's *The English Town* (New Haven and London, 1990), p. 121.

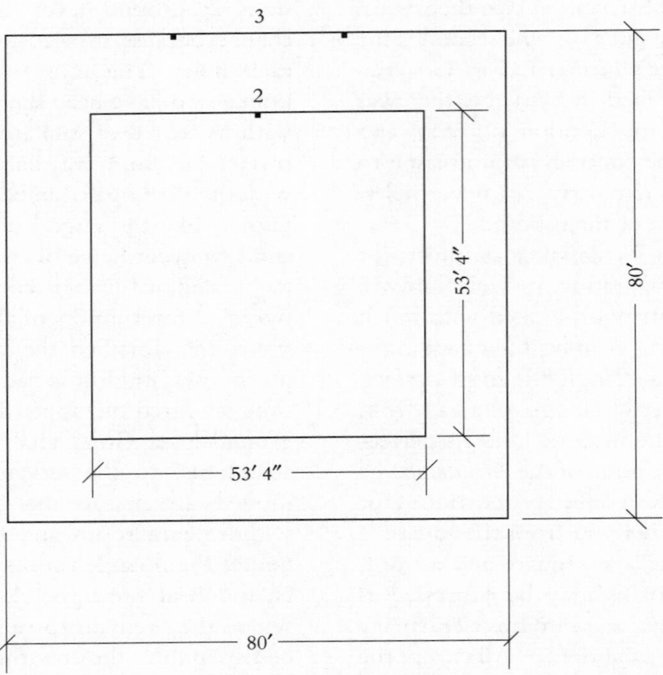

Fig. 2 The proportion of the Fortune's plan at the middle-storey level

wide, related to the overall width of the building as 11:16, not at all the kind of ratio to be found in Vitruvius or Serlio. At the top, where the yard was diminished by two jetties to either side, or 40 inches altogether, the space between opposite sides was 51 feet 8 inches, for a proportion of 31:48, a ratio even less arresting than that of the ground floor. But at the middle level, where a single jetty to either side produced a yard width of 53 feet 4 inches, the case was altogether different. Here the yard width stood in relation to that of the whole theatre as 2:3 (53 feet 4 inches × 3/2 = 80 feet; see Figure 2).

Of course the principal ratio here entailed others: the middle gallery depth of 13 feet 4 inches was one-sixth of the whole building's width, and a quarter that of the yard. The area of the yard, measured at this level, related to that of the gallery as 4:5. Experienced at the first floor, the building fairly sang a proportionate harmony: even the elevation, at 32 feet from the plinth to the plates, stood in relation to the yard width as 3:5. Furthermore, if we consider the ground floor as a podium on which a *piano nobile* of 11 feet and an attic of 9 feet were superimposed, the upper part of the frame was a structure 20 feet high, one quarter of the width of the whole house and related to the gallery depth at the middle floor as 3:2 (13 feet 4 inches × 3/2 = 20 feet). Like the 1605 theatre at Christ Church, Alleyn's new playhouse was designed to a rationally proportionate scheme.

THE ORDER OF TERMS

The Fortune also used something resembling an architectural order, though not a canonical one. The contract required that '. . . all the princypall and maine postes of the saide fframe and Stadge forwarde shalbe square and wroughte palasterwise wth carved proporc*i*ons Called

Satiers to be placed & sett on the Topp of every of the same postes'.[37] The principal posts were load-bearing members at the bay divisions, a total of some forty-eight if all three storeys of three ranges were to be similarly decorated. How many stood around the stage it is impossible to say. There were, it would seem, satyrs everywhere, their function and their pilaster shape giving them the character of an order, not of columns but of terms.

The provision of the satyrs is one of those clauses in the contract that distinguishes the Fortune from the Globe, which presumably had some other treatment of the posts, perhaps round to suit its 'round' plan. At the polygonal Hope arena in 1613 there were 'Turned Cullumes vppon and over the stage', and de Witt shows what look like round columns at the Swan. Square posts for the square Fortune, then. But there is something else resonating in the language of the contract. The standard definition of the ancient Greek Herm insisted on the square section of its shaft: 'Hermes of stone', wrote North, in his translation of Plutarch, '(which are foure square pillers) vpon the toppes of the which they set vp heades of *Mercurye* . . .'[38] By Street's time the Athenian Herm had long been confused with the Roman Term, originally an effigy of the god Terminus, used to mark all manner of boundaries.[39] But the Term, as strictly understood, had itself generated yet another architectural form, as it became confused with the caryatids and atlantes of ancient buildings. At the beginning of his *Ten Books* Vitruvius tells the story of the women of Caryae, enslaved for their state's treachery, who were forced to go on wearing what they were dressed in at the moment of their capture as a permanent sign of their shame. Architects placed statues of them where they would bear a structural load, their immobile servitude a lesson to posterity (Vitruvius I.1.5).[40] Similarly Persians were shown supporting entablatures and the like, as a Lacedaemonian triumph after the battle of Plataea (Vitruvius I.1.6). Such anecdotes match the idea that the architectural orders stem from various types of human figure, the Doric stolid and masculine, the Ionic feminine and matronly, the Corinthian 'an imitation of the slenderness of a maiden' (Vitruvius IV.1.8). To a modern sensibility, used to thinking of architecture as artistic engineering, this location of human forms within the load-bearing members may seem quaint; the only human figure we might expect to find holding up a motorway would be a dead gangster encased in the concrete. Designers trained in the classical tradition have always thought otherwise; John Shute, for example, illustrated the orders with appropriate human figures, and repeated the stories of the Caryatides and the Persians.

Terms, as generally understood in the sixteenth century, marked boundaries; but they also contained imprisoned figures put to work. In 1611 Randle Cotgrave could define the French word 'Terme' as, amongst other things, 'a Pillar fashioned, at the vpper end, like an armeless man or woman; and (more generally) any arme-lesse Image: . . . also, a stone, bound, limit, mere, diuiding land from land'.[41] The armlessness of many terms (I adopt the lower-case to distinguish the feature from that strictly devoted to Terminus) was a sign of their conquest, for it recalled the antique ritual of the dismemberment of slain enemies.[42] A term

---

37 *Henslowe's Diary*, p. 308.

38 Thomas North, *The Lives of the Noble Grecians and Romanes, Compared . . . by Plutarke of Chaeronea* (London, 1579), p. 533.

39 The Term was adopted by Erasmus as his device, signifying either a refusal to yield or a recognition of the inevitability of death (perhaps both): Edgar Wind, 'Aenigma Termini', *Journal of the Warburg and Courtauld Institutes*, 1 (1937–8), 66–8; compare Henry Peacham, *Minerva Brittana* (London, 1612), part 2, p. 193.

40 *Vitruvius: the Ten Books on Architecture*, trans. Morris Hickey Morgan (New York, 1960).

41 *A Dictionarie of the French and English Tongues* (London, 1611), 'Terme'.

42 George Hersey, *The Lost Meaning of Classical Architecture* (Cambridge, Mass, 1988), p. 132.

represented energy vanquished, disabled and put to architectural use.

The Fortune's terms were not mere flummery. The study and enjoyment of such figures flourished in Alleyn's time, a matter for scholars as well as artisans. The two founding texts were Cesariano's edition of Vitruvius, published in 1521, and the *Vitruvius Teutsch* (1548).[43] Many kinds of term appeared in Jan Vredeman de Vries's *Caryatidum (vulgus termas vocat) sive Athlantidum multiformum* ... (Antwerp, 1565?), which was in the library of Sir Thomas Tresham where it was available to Tresham's architectural adviser Robert Stickells (along with volumes of Vitruvius, Serlio, Palladio and others, including Shute).[44] Hughes Sambin's *Oeuvre de la diversite des termes* (Lyon, 1572) contained a systematic arrangement, on hierarchical principles, of eighteen pairs of terms, increasingly complex as their forms ascended from the subhuman to the divine, but even the highest supporting a heavy entablature.[45] There were further elaborations in Joseph Boillot, *Nouveaux pourtraitz et figures de terms* (Langres, 1592). Eventually terms lost much of their remarkable energy, smothered by decorum. By the eighteenth century a much-reprinted account defined them as

> a Sort of Statue or Column, adorn'd at the Top with the Figure of the Head of a Man, a Woman, or Satyr, as the Capital, and the lower Part ending in a kind of Sheath or Scabbard ... you may give them what Degree of Delicacy you please, by lengthening out their Sheath, and raising the Figures to any Height that you would have ... To give them a Figure proper to represent a delicate Column, their Arms are lop'd off, and their Body does not appear below the Girdle; these *Terms* are very proper in the Decorations of a Theatre ...[46]

That terms were commonly shaped as satyrs, whether armed or not, is especially evident from the title-pages of printed books, where their presence at the gateway into the work recalls the classic role of Terminus. I reproduce a border used by the London printer T. Marshe and his successor from 1567 to 1592 (Plate 1); many similar ones are illustrated by McKerrow and Ferguson.[47] In buildings satyr-terms appeared most often at gateways, doorways and beside the grate, at the meeting place of room and chimney. They usually supported the upper part of the structure, sometimes cheerfully, as if displaying the area they bounded, but more often with blank indifference. In 1606 Peter Street built a decorative window over the entrance to Alleyn's Beargarden which illustrates the theme: it was constructed, complete with its classical pediment and obelisks, 'standinge upone twoe carved Satyres', which flanked the threshold.[48] Two years earlier, at the Londinium arch erected in Fenchurch Street for the ceremonial entry of James I into the city, the king passed through a gateway whose liminality was similarly distinguished: 'On either side of the Gate, stood a great French Terme, of stone, aduanced vpon wodden Pedestalls; two half Pilasters of Rustick, stand ouer their heads.'[49]

---

43 Cesare Cesariano, *Di Lucio Vitruvio Pollione de architectura* ... (Como, 1521); *Vitruvius Teutsch* (Nuremberg, 1548), fols. 14ʳ–19ʳ includes numerous illustrations of terms and satyrs among the cuts of Caryatides and Persians.

44 'Caryatid vulgus term vocat' in Tresham's catalogue of *c.*1605, BL Add. MS 39830.. See Lucy Gent, *Picture and Poetry 1560–1620: Relations between Literature and the Visual Arts in the English Renaissance* (Leamington Spa, 1981), pp. 71–2 and 86.

45 See Hersey, *Lost Meaning*, pp. 135–47.

46 *The Builder's Dictionary: or, Gentleman and Architect's Companion*, 2 vols. (London, 1734), vol. 2, T5ᵛ.

47 R. B. McKerrow and F.S. Ferguson, *Title-Page Borders Used in England & Scotland 1485–1640* (London, 1932), *passim*.

48 W. J. Lawrence and Walter H. Godfrey, 'The Bear Garden Contract of 1606 and what it Implies', *Architectural Review* 47 (1920), p. 153. Compare William Portington's garden seat for the queen at Greenwich in 1598–9, 'standing upon terms arched and carved'. The decorative scheme also included 'pyramides' and 'Perymentes', as did Street's: PRO E351/3234.

49 Thomas Dekker, *The Magnificent Entertainment ... (London, 1604)*, B4ʳ⁻ᵛ. There were similar terms at the *Hortus Euporiae* arch in Cheapside, where at the bottom of the stairs '(on two pillers) were fixed two Satiers carued out in wood' (G1ʳ).

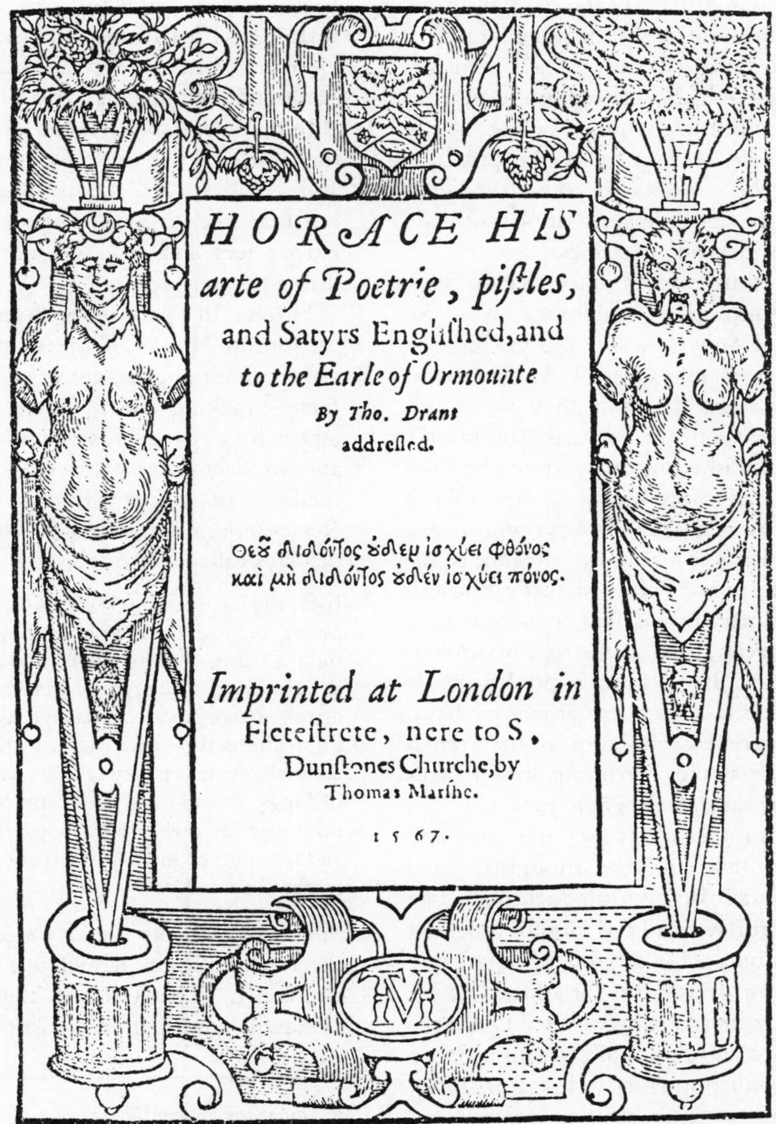

HORACE HIS
arte of Poetrie, pistles,
and Satyrs Englished, and
to the Earle of Ormounte
By Tho. Drant
addressed.

Θεοῦ διδόντος οὐδὲν ἰσχύει φθόνος
καὶ μὴ διδόντος οὐδὲν ἰσχύει πόνος.

Imprinted at London in
Fletestrete, nere to S.
Dunstones Churche, by
Thomas Marshe.

1567.

1 *Horace his arte of Poetrie* . . . (London, 1567), frontispiece. A border used by the London printer T. Marshe and his successor from 1567 to 1592

Six feet to the left, dangerously perched in a niche at the same level as the pilasters, teetered Edward Alleyn as the 'Genius of the City', ready with a speech.[50]

The satyr-terms at the Fortune marked the boundaries of the bays and – at the middle level – the fulcrum of its proportionate design, the colon, so to speak, in the ratio 2:3. To their

50 See Andrew Gurr, *The Shakespearean Stage 1574–1642*, 3rd edn (Cambridge, 1992), p. 10.

sense of limit, as guardians of the bays, we must add their condition of servitude: they were free spirits tamed into labour. Their square-sectioned pilaster-shafts, carved no doubt to seem to taper almost to a point below, in the manner of a *stele*, were actually the principal posts of the gallery fronts and the satyr-heads took the weight of the beams along with the live load of a thousand spectators.

The values thus pressed into service were notoriously equivocal. Ambiguity was the satyrs' style: '*A Satyre*', wrote Cotgrave, is '*a monster halfe man halfe Goat.*'[51] As woodland creatures they were shy, but they were also aggressively lascivious. In Edward Wilkinson's *Thameseidos*, published in the year of the Fortune, 1600, the nymph Medway, one of the attendants of Isis, is raped by a satyr whose idea of foreplay consists of a reasoned defence of his appearance. He points 'vnto his little hornes', justifies the redness of his face, confesses to a rough, hairy breast, and claims that his cloven feet are no worse than Vulcan's 'pool-foote'.[52] And then he sets to. Such sexual energy has a name, and Cotgrave's translation of the French word 'Satyriase' makes a rousing list: '*Pricke-pride, lust-pride; the standing of the yard . . .*'[53]

The satyrs in *Oberon* (1611) use unchaste language and think unchaste thoughts; these and other attributes Ben Jonson documents in a series of notes for which he is largely indebted to Isaac Casaubon's *De satyrica Graecorum & Romanorum satira* (1605). But for all the learned commentary, with its allusions to Diodorus Siculus, Nonnos and Synesius, as well as Plato and Virgil, the salient quality of his satyrs is not their Bacchic provenance but their athleticism. It is their nature to leap and run. Jonson insists on the leaping, using the verb four times to describe their ordinary stage movement. Their balletic performance, when it comes, is '*an antique dance, full of gesture, and swift motion . . .*',[54] contrasting with the more measured pieces of the masque proper. The same athletic prowess bounds across Shakespeare's stage in *The Winter's Tale* (4.4.340), during '*a dance of twelve satyrs*', originally perhaps the very performers who had distinguished themselves in *Oberon*.[55] They are punningly introduced as 'saultiers' (or leapers); a trio of them, Polixenes is told, 'hath danced before the King: and not the worst of the three but jumps twelve foot and a half by th' square' (4.4.335–7). At the Fortune the satyrs jumped nowhere; their cloven feet and crooked legs were crammed into a pilaster.

Horace, in a part of the *Ars poetica* duly noted by Jonson, speaks of the satyrs' unchaste language, while the ancient poet Nonnos refers to their 'mocking throat'.[56] An early confusion, especially in the scholarly understanding of the ancient satyr-play, attributed to them the biting qualities of satire. Thomas Godwin, in his *Romanae historiae anthologia*, described the sort of plays called '*Satyrae*',

> from the lascivious and wanton country-Gods called *Satyri*, because the Actors in these *Satyricall* playes, did vse many obscene poems, and vnchast gestures to delight their spectators. Afterwarde these kind of actors as wee may coniect, did assume such liberty vnto themselves, that they did freely and without controlement, sharpely taxe & censure the vices even of kings, as wel as of the commons, insomuch that now wee call every witty poeme, wherein the liues and manners of men are sharpely taxed, *A satyre*, or *satyricall* poeme.[57]

Spite might make the satyrs dangerous, but at the Fortune their ill-will was imprisoned and controlled. The Oxford theologian George Hakewill recorded an ancient belief that their

51 *Dictionarie*, 'Satyre'.

52 (London, 1600), C2v.

53 *Dictionarie*, 'Satyriase'.

54 *Ben Jonson*, vol. 7, p. 351.

55 The theory that the satyr-dancers in *The Winter's Tale* had already appeared in *Oberon* was first put forward by Ashley H. Thorndike, 'Influence of the Court-masques on the Drama, 1608–15', *PMLA*, 15 (1900), 116–19.

56 Horace, *Ars poetica*, 225; Nonnos, *Dionysiaca*, trans. W. H. D. Rouse, 3 vols. (London, 1940), vol. 3, p. 65.

57 *Romanae historiae anthologia: an English exposition of the Romane antiquities* . . . (Oxford, 1614), p. 69.

presence attached to buildings was at once magical and prophylactic:

> . . . *Plinie* giues the reason of placing *Satyres*, and *Antikes* to be looked on, in the entries & portales of great mens houses, to haue beene the possessing by that meanes, of the thoughts of that malitious kinde of people, by which their strength in hurting might either bee diverted, or abated.[58]

We need hardly go so far as this to understand why satyrs should be posted around a playhouse; their chief ambiguity was that they were both anarchic and critical, an ideal state of mind for a serious theatre audience.

Such qualities as these were tamed into the carved supporters of the Fortune's galleries. Analysis of the acquittances found on the verso of the contract shows that the timbers were extensively worked on before they were sent down the Thames on barges, carted to the site and promptly erected during May 1600.[59] The principal posts must have been given their 'palasterwise' shape at the framing place which Street had established in the woods; if, as seems most likely, the 'carved proporc*i*ons Called Satiers' were integral with the posts they will have been carved there too, in the forest where their type belonged. The vigorous spirit of the woodlands was captive in the Fortune's auditorium. And with it came the satyrs' sardonic gaze.

Alleyn's new theatre was a replica of the Globe, its revenue-packed galleries precisely the same size but set square to diminish the overall area and incorporate the architectural virtues of fit proportion. Its carved timbers expressed the classical theme of contained energy. In the event the scheme was only partly successful, for the square shape proved to be a theatrical dead end. But the terms and satyrs became the familiars of the English theatre: they often appeared in masques and entertainments, and showed up repeatedly in the playhouses. Inigo Jones's drawings, probably for the Cockpit in Drury Lane,[60] offer terms with arms, their lower portions wrapped in spiral sheaths. They flank the central opening over the stage, where they support urns. There were urns too at Christopher Rich's Lincoln's Inn Fields playhouse, held by satyrs crouching on bombé plinths. One of them appears stage right in Hogarth's caricature of *The Beggar's Opera*, made in 1728; another stage left in the same artist's composite portrait of the company.[61] At Covent Garden in 1732 John Rich had what he called 'Thermes' specially carved. They were removed from the bombé plinths, on which there now stood figures of Melpomene and Thalia, and instead flanked the upper stage boxes, supporting the 'pigeon holes' or slips above. Here they were again imprisoned in tapering shafts, but retained their arms, with which they held up the entablature overhead.[62] They seem to have presided over Covent Garden's stage until Inigo Richards swept them away in 1782.

---

58 *The Vanitie of the Eie*, 2nd edn (Oxford, 1608), p. 32.

59 See the discussion in John Orrell, 'Building the Fortune', *Shakespeare Quarterly*, 44 (1993), p. 137.

60 Reproduced in *The Human Stage*, p. 175.

61 David Thomas and Arnold Hare, *Restoration and Georgian England, 1660–1788*, Theatre in Europe: a Documentary History (Cambridge, 1989), nos. 69 and 98. The most detailed record, including the bombé plinths, is in an anonymous stage design for *The Necromancer* (1723), Thomas and Hare no. 93. The figure without the plinth is given in the frontispiece, entitled 'The Masque at the Old House', to George Bickham, *The Musical Entertainer* (London, 1737).

62 The terms are illustrated in James Miller, *Harlequin Horace: or the Art of Modern Poetry*, 3rd edn (London, 1735), frontispiece (Thomas and Hare no. 94); and by Gabriel Dumont in his section of the theatre in *Parallèle de plans des plus belles salles de spectacles d'Italie et de France* (Paris, 1774) (Thomas and Hare no. 71).

THE BARE ISLAND

ANDREW GURR

When Prospero begs the audience not to spellbind him 'in this bare island' it is not unreasonable to wonder where we are supposed to think we are. From the unique and startling shipwreck scene that set us on shore to that unique and peculiar octosyllabic Epilogue,[1] we have been on an island full of noises and magic that hurt not. At the end, after the '*Exeunt all*', the courtiers still in their clothes for Claribel's wedding, the seamen dry again, and Prospero's robe, book and staff all gone, Prospero speaks his last speech bare of his trappings. Is his adjective a transferred epithet? I think not, even in the wake of all the colourful apparel that has just walked offstage. Prospero stands alone on the stage island in the middle of a sea of faces, asking for human breath to blow his sail to Naples, if he is not to be imprisoned on the island. Like Hamlet's ground, that other 'stale promontory', Prospero's stage island has lost its fresh decorations. What, in the original performances, was it bared of, though? A lot of people, certainly, some of them colourfully dressed. Prospero's own props, his magic gown and staff, must have gone too. Was the stage shorn of fabric and colour? Was it all bare boards? Were there no hangings left across the front of the tiring house and Prospero's cell? Was there no painting on the stage posts to make them look like marble as De Witt described them? It would be nice to know. For all the riches of the recent archaeological findings, the Shakespearian *mise en scène*, the geography of the stage island, is not so much bare as undiscovered.

We can be sure that it was an island, a three-dimensional entity. Thanks largely to the flatness of paper, until very recently the only durable form for recording performance details on, the essential three-dimensional character of the Shakespearian theatre is given too little account in modern thinking. We rely on the invention of perspective to facilitate the use of paper as a representation of the Globe's three-dimensional stage and as a result still use misleading terms like front stage and back stage. Van Eyck's invention of perspective and its ultimate exploitation on the cinema screen condition us to think, if not in two dimensions, then from the position that a two-dimensional picture of a three-dimensional scene invites. Henry Peacham drew the figures he saw on stage in 1595 in *Titus Andronicus* in a linear spread from 'in front'. De Witt drew his Swan in 1596 from the perspective of a cinema's projection booth. The inescapably two-dimensional form that recording on paper invites seduces us into a two-dimensional mode of thinking. De Witt's actor figures are posed not at the stage 'front' but in the centre of a circle of audience, as near as they can get to 'the middle of the yard', the central point where the Fortune contract ordered its stage to extend. The only audience De Witt's drawing depicts is

[1] Stephen Orgel in his Oxford edition of *The Tempest* notes that this Epilogue is unique in being spoken by a character in the fiction, not an actor in the play.

sitting where we now think is 'behind' the actors. Paper pictures are not only two-dimensional but static. They encourage us to think of humans as capable of facing only forwards, in one direction. It would help to think of Prospero's epilogue as spoken by a rotating figure, not a still.

There is a limited but highly specific value in trying to learn more about the original staging of Shakespeare's plays. Theatre is always invented for an occasion. A performance is an event, not a text. Like buildings or stage scenes in pictures, it does not belong naturally on paper.[2] Each new performance of a play that has established itself in a repertory and achieved fixity through print is a new event. The history of theatre is full of plays that died on their first performance and were resurrected successfully a generation or more later. Printed texts of playscripts work against that feature of the play in performance as a transient event or occasion. Each event, and especially each theatrical or performance event, is unique to its moment. It cannot be 'recuperated'. So the exploration of Shakespeare's original staging has to be not a story of texts, even of lost texts, but of their frames, the contexts. Since they are Shakespearian contexts, they are useful when they offer insights that other ways of recuperating the Shakespeare text cannot. So such fragments of evidence about the bare stage island that can be retrieved are worth fitting into the Shakespearian mosaic.

In this exercise what calls for the greatest care is an evaluation of the different kinds of evidence, fragmentary as it all is, and the relative weight that might be attached to one item against the often contradictory indications of the others. What follows is an attempt to give a sense of relative values to the different kinds of evidence about a number of the features that might have stood on Prospero's bare island.

The first consideration is the radically different testimonies from the different amphitheatre playhouses about their shapes. De Witt's drawing of the Swan shows a square stage and a flat *frons* with two entry doors, whereas the Rose had a stage in the form of an elongated hexagon, with its *frons* on three angles. The Rose's outside diameter was about 74 feet, while the Globe's seems to have been 99 feet. The closest similarity among all the amphitheatres appears to have been not the stage area but the gallery bays. The Rose, the Globe and the Fortune all seem to have had galleries with bays of about the same size, despite the radical variation in their shapes (square at the Fortune, twenty-sided at the Globe, fourteen-sided at the Rose) and the difference in their overall dimensions. This radical variation in auditorium and stage at the playhouses of the 1590s is at odds with the demonstrable fact that until at least 1594 all the playhouses were treated by the playing companies as interchangeable. The Queen's Men in the late 1580s are recorded at one time or another as playing at every amphitheatre and every inn available to them in London. Not until the Privy Council started designating playhouses for the two approved companies after 1594 could a company expect to have a settled tenure at any playhouse.[3] The Globe and the Fortune were the first playhouses built for particular tenant companies. From this it might be expected that the amphitheatre stages all had similar configurations until 1599. That expecta-

[2] It is hardly necessary here to go into the long debate between printed text and performance text, Shakespeare on page and stage, Formalist 'text' against New Historicist 'context'. Harry Berger Jr has put the former case brilliantly in *Imaginary Audition: Shakespeare on Stage and Page* (University of California Press, Berkeley, 1989). The 'performance' case, which I think has more substance, has not yet been thoroughly set out. It lies somewhere between the position Louis Montrose sets out in 'New Historicisms', in *Redrawing the Boundaries: The Transformation of English and American Literary Studies*, eds. Stephen Greenblatt and Giles Gunn (University of Chicago Press, Chicago, 1988), and the position and illuminations that Bernard Beckerman offered long ago in his ur-theoretical *Shakespeare at the Globe 1599–1609* (Macmillan, New York, 1962).

[3] See Gurr, 'Three Reluctant Patrons and Early Shakespeare', *Shakespeare Quarterly*, 44 (1993), 159–74.

tion is rubbished by the radical differences of the Rose from its near neighbour the Swan.

The evident difference of one amphitheatre from another complicates the tendency to generalize about the original staging on the basis of internal evidence in the plays. It puts a premium on the value in evidence from stage directions of reconciling the demands in specific plays with the playhouses they were written for. This gives priority most notably to the Rose plays of the 1590s and the Globe plays of the following decade. Such a premium marginalizes the Swan, and that one piece of paper evidence from Utrecht which has ruled thinking about the stages for the last century. It also makes the question of a play's date more important. Plays written before the late 1590s were designed to be staged anywhere. Only the post-1594 plays staged at the Rose, the plays written subsequently for the Globe and the Fortune, and probably in the seventeenth century some plays written for companies settled at the Red Bull and the Cockpit and Salisbury Court hall theatres can be said with any confidence to be designed for a specific venue and its peculiar stage features.

The evidence from the Rose excavation of 1989 has the advantage over other evidence of being what you might loosely call concrete. The paper evidence of De Witt's oddly irregular dimensions in his Swan drawing, and his 'ingressus' from the yard to the galleries, marked in a theatre which we know had at least one stair turret, gives ample ground for us to doubt what we can make of the papers surviving from the time, quite apart from their two-dimensionality. The square stage on the Swan's paper has to be set against the elongated hexagon of the Rose's brick foundations. The large, round, marbled stage posts set so firmly on a line across the middle of the Swan's platform have to be compared with the Rose's small and square pile base abutting the stage 'front'. The three thousand said to cram into the Swan contrast with the two thousand now known to be able to get into the original Rose. Should the Rose's concrete displace De Witt's paper, or should we acknowledge the likelihood of radically different designs and dimensions for the first two Southwark theatres? In their different ways, whether De Witt's paper or the Rose's brick foundations, both of them offer evidence that is two-dimensional. All the fragments, the Rose dig, the papers of De Witt, Norden, and Hollar, and the play-texts themselves, need to be reassessed in concert. It is no small task. A beginning might be made with a few of the stage features that the uncovering of the Rose foundations throws into question.

THE DISCOVERY SPACE

Two-dimensional pictures of the Shakespearian stage create more problems than they solve, not least that current version of the inner stage, the discovery space. The stage foundations for the Rose, the only recent piece of fresh evidence, give no indication about what Henslowe built for the players to use in 1587 and rebuilt in 1592. The floor plan shows that the Rose probably had a tiring-house front or *frons* with three faces, but there is little to suggest what openings stood in those faces. And a *frons* with three angled walls counters the only other tangible evidence for the Rose's neighbour the Swan of 1595, with its flat-faced two-door wall. Neither piece of evidence helps answer the most vexed question, what occupied the central part of the *frons*. Despite the absence of any central opening at all in De Witt's Swan drawing, the assumption that there was a wide central recess or discovery space has dominated all reconstructions of the *frons*, infecting calculations not only about the entry doors but about the balcony or 'above' and the stage hangings. The long life of the inner stage theory reflects the two-dimensional thinking of earlier theatre historians. Its continuing life, transformed into a long and deep curtained alcove in the centre of the *frons*, dominates thinking about staging. The need to have it has called in doubt the strong evidence that there were lords' rooms over the stage, the location of which in a flat-walled *frons* would prevent the highest-paying customers from seeing any of the set-pieces uncovered in the central alcove. It has also, rather paradoxically, prevented the central opening in the *frons* from being used as an ordinary entry door and has consigned even royal and processional entrances to the flanking doors. It has been invoked as the only access big enough to be used for carrying large stage properties on and off the stage, an assumption that has allowed the two great double doors on each side of the Swan's stage to be replaced with single doors. It now operates as the fall-back position into which are pitched most of the unresolvable puzzles about routine Renaissance staging practices.

De Witt's Swan drawing shows audience sitting in all six of its balcony rooms. The familiar references about Jonson talking to lords who sat over the stage and other casual namings of 'the lords' room over the stage', wherever we put the apostrophe, suggest that De Witt was right to place spectators where they could not see the openings in the *frons*. That is the position for the gallants noted in Everard Guilpin's *Skialetheia* (1598), and at the Globe in Jonson's *Every Man Out*. Dekker mocked Jonson in *Satiromastix* for exchanging courtesies with the gallants in the lords' rooms. Later references to playgoers sitting 'over the stage' come from Dekker in 1607 and E. S. in *c.*1608.[4] Such casual references may be more reliable than stage directions. Privileged access to those rooms by means of the tiring-house back door instead of the common entry doors to the auditorium would offer an amphitheatre equivalence to the means of entry with a stool to sit on the stage that the hall playhouses offered their gallants. I think that this reading of the evidence, consistent as it is, makes a strong case for finding the lords' rooms adjacent to Juliet's central balcony room which later became the music room,[5] and so in a position that prevented the payers of the highest prices from seeing any 'discoveries'. We can speculate endlessly about the implications of that for the price the lords paid in order to be seen better than they could see, or for the minimization of discovery scenes by the playwrights in order to prevent the lords from feeling deprived.

Some kind of space behind the stage hangings there was for 'discoveries' such as Volpone's gold at the Globe or Faustus in his study at the Rose ('This the man that in his study sits', as the prologue draws back the curtain).[6] Hangings across the *frons* concealed the king and Polonius in *Hamlet*, and later hid the body of Polonius until Hamlet uncovered it. The problems for the over-the-stage watchers in the lords' rooms of viewing what was 'discovered' would have been markedly worse at the Swan than at the Rose, where the angled *frons* might have allowed the viewers in the flanking boxes to see something of what was displayed behind the hangings. The flat plane of the Swan's tiring house front not only makes the watchers above the stage incapable of viewing any 'discovery', but omits any indication of a discovery space between the two large doors of the *frons*. What kind of *frons* the Globe had is a question that can only be answered by excavating under Anchor Terrace, which would require a radical change of policy by English Heritage and is unlikely to happen quickly.

The shape of the alcove (if that is the right word for the part of the tiring-house *frons* from which the players emerged onto the stage: the

---

4 *Jests to Make You Merry, Non-Dramatic Works*, II.292; E. K. Chambers, *The Elizabethan Stage* II.535.

5 For the introduction of a music room after 1608 at the Globe in order to accommodate the newly acquired Blackfriars musicians, see Richard Hosley, 'Was there a Music-Room in Shakespeare's Globe?', *Shakespeare Survey 13* (1960), p. 113.

6 The relation between the 'discovery space' and the stage hangings does no good to the theory that the space may have been a fit-up booth or tent-like structure forward of the *frons*. In any case there would be little room for such a structure on the Rose's broad but shallow stage. This problem also damages Evert Sprinchorn's theory of a raised platform at the rear (see below, note 14).

word presupposes a frontal position for the audience, which inhibits thinking of the stage as the centre of a complete circle of spectators), is unclear. The hangings were variously a traverse to be drawn back (*Volpone*) or an arras to hide behind (*Hamlet*). And the space to be 'discovered'? If it was a deep walled-off room, the minimal 390 square feet of free space given the players in the Rose's tiring house would be reduced even further. Comedies required a set of hangings in front of the tiring-house wall, so that the clowns could enter by first sticking their heads through. The evidence for them doing this stretches from 1592 (Nashe) to 1639 (Glapthorne). Such entries needed nothing more than a doorway behind the hangings. Polonius needed little more. The only hint I know of that suggests a size for the discovery space is in the 1647 Folio text of *The Maid in the Mill*, written by Fletcher and Rowley for the Globe in about 1623. It has an anticipatory stage direction at the end of Act 1 which says '*Six Chaires placed at the Arras*'. They have no direct role in the following Act. Were they placed in line? If so, the space for the alcove or discovery behind the arras must have been close to twelve feet, much wider than even the double doorways of De Witt's Swan.

The evidence of Heywood's 1 *If You Know Not Me, You Know Nobody* and its royal 'state', written for the Fortune, supports Fletcher and Rowley's evidence about the Globe with its chair scene. A throne was needed at beginning and end of the play, and for Scene 12 in the middle. Was it permanently positioned on the stage platform? The 'discovery space' is needed for other scenes in the play, notably the bed in Scene 3 and the seven chairs of Scene 5. That raises the whole question of localities on stage and the realism of designated space. In use, a throne obviously designated a throne room or 'presence', and sometimes a lawcourt. If it remained as a passive presence through other scenes, we have to rein in our assumptions about realistic localities and assume that when the dialogue called for a specific locality the audience shut out of its consciousness the obtrusive properties that did not fit the designated place. The trouble is that just as Shakespeare and other playwrights, and even the stage managers who compiled the seven extant 'plots' of players' comings and goings, often failed to mark exits for their characters they invariably failed to mark exits for their props.

There are a few indicators. One certain thing about the discovery space is that it must have been big enough not just to provide an entryway for ceremonial entrances, but also to carry on and off the largest properties. There was no other form of access to the stage platform. We might also wonder just how many properties of each kind the players had. In that there may be a hint to confirm the belief that properties were not generally left on stage throughout the play. Dekker and Middleton's 1 *The Honest Whore*, written in 1603–4 for the Fortune, like Heywood's 1 *If You Know Not Me, You Know Nobody*, calls for a table in two successive scenes, 3.3 and 4.1. The stage direction for the first runs '*Enter Bellafronte with a Lute, pen, inke and paper being placde before her*'. A table is not specified, but it is hardly likely that the stage hand would have left the writing instruments on the floor. Bellafronte sings to the lute and then starts writing. There is no opportunity for anyone to carry the table off before the next scene. But that, 4.1, opens with a stage direction '*Enter a servant setting out a table, on which he places a scull, a picture, a booke, and a Taper*', traditional devices for a malcontent scene. The writer of this stage direction clearly expected the servant to carry the table in, and for it to be a different table. The first speech in the scene is the servant's address to the table he has just set. Conceivably the writer expected an act break to intervene between one table going out and the other being brought in, but there are no other indications of act breaks in the play, and the Fortune did not use act breaks with any frequency for another decade.

SQUARE OR TAPERED STAGES

Even the tangible foundations of the Rose's stage offer a new uncertainty. The row of its foundation bricks, strong enough to support a five-foot high wall though not much more, presumably set the wall high enough to serve as lodging for the joists that supported the stage's planking. Such a solid brick wall would have made unnecessary the Fortune's 'Stadge to be paled in belowe with good, strong and suffi-cyent newe oken bourdes', and also the hangings that Heywood said the Roman theatres had around the fore-front of the stage. It was a radically different design from De Witt's Swan, where the dark objects under the stage might be seen as openings in the hangings for devils to run into the yard through the crowd. There is no sign that the Rose's stage foundations had any doorways in them to give the devils access to the yard, and no provision in the Fortune contract of any access from under the stage to the yard.

Besides the conflict of evidence between the Swan's square stage as De Witt presented it and the Rose's irregular hexagon as the archaeologists found it lies the even larger question of where at the Rose the tiring-house *frons* was set. This has large implications not only for what size of stage each playhouse had but for the capacity of the tiring house behind it. De Witt's Swan gives central place to the stage platform, a huge nearly square space with behind it six (or five) bays of the scaffolding for the tiring house, augmented by the planar surface of the tiring-house front which makes a chord across the polygon of the inner gallery walls. Following Glynne Wickham's reconstruction based on De Witt, Richard Hosley has measured the likely space for the players inside the Swan's tiring house behind the stage front (in a 24-sided structure) at roughly 1045 square feet.[7] Even if the stage was foreshortened by a tiring-house front cutting a chord across the stage-front bays, the Rose evidently had far less space than that. The bays of its polygon were trapezoids measuring roughly ten feet between the outer and inner walls, with the outer wall measuring sixteen feet and the inner eleven feet.[8] If its tiring-house front was angled, each of its three bays would be more or less eleven feet in length on the inner side with a door in each of the three, angled around the rear of a stage with a total width of thirty-seven feet. The tiring-house space in the three bays behind that would give a floor space of about 390 square feet. If the front ran straight, on a chord across the thirty-seven-foot width of the stage's central line, the backstage space would increase to nearly 630 square feet. This is not a great deal more than the space available for the original stage platform if its tiring-house front was angled to follow the three bays. Such a minute tiring-house space, not enlarged noticeably in the 1592 rebuilding, must have suffered further encroachments too. Space would have been taken up by the stairway up to the balcony or 'above', another stair up to the third-level 'heavens' and its machinery over the stage, and most obtrusively by the 'discovery space', the walls around the enclosure that made Faustus' study. Walls would be vital if the hangings across the centre of the tiring-house *frons* were not when opened to reveal the entire company in the process of re-costuming itself for the next scenes. Even a 'study' for Faustus as little as six feet wide would cut the tiring house's floor space by another forty or so square feet.

If it followed the larger hexagonal plan, at 475 square feet the Rose's stage area was also markedly smaller than others for which we have measurements – 1200 at the Red Lion, and only slightly less for the stage at the Fortune that replaced the Rose. Such a small stage with its even smaller tiring-house area made the Rose a peculiarly little playhouse by com-

---

7 See 'A Postscript on the Swan', in 'The Shape of the Globe and the Interior of the Globe', *Renaissance Drama Newsletter*, 8 (Coventry, 1987), 61–78.

8 Orrell and Gurr, 'What the Rose can tell us', *Antiquity*, 63 (1989), 421–9.

parison with its contemporaries. That being so, it is the more remarkable that the 1592 enlargement, increasing the auditorium space by over twenty per cent and demolishing and rebuilding the whole stage area, only negligibly increased the size of the stage platform, giving one extra foot or so from the stage's front edge to the tiring-house *frons*, and nothing to the tiring house area itself. This smallness puts a premium on the question whether the tiring-house front took a straight chord across the thirty-seven feet at the centre of the hexagon or followed the lines of the three bay walls. If it ran straight, the stage area would be reduced by half, and the tiring-house would be enlarged by the same amount. It is difficult to believe that even the thought-to-be-tall Alleyn, whose arrival at the Rose seems to have prompted Henslowe to make his enlargements, would have preferred more backstage space at the expense of a reduced scaffoldage under his stretched footing. There is no sign of any foundation for a straight tiring-house *frons*. It is almost impossible to believe that both the original and the later tiring-houses would not have to compensate for the tapers at each side by having a recessed stage *frons* that followed the walls of the bays at the rear: a stage in the shape of an elongated hexagon, with behind it a small tiring house occupying three gallery bays.

The only points of comparison for this small dimension come from the hall playhouses, which had smaller dimensions all round than the amphitheatres. R. A. Foakes[9] measures the stage of the royal Cockpit-in-Court as a space about 34 feet wide and 16 feet deep at the centre, with the curve of its *frons* cutting the space at the sides to about five feet. The central door space is about four feet, which Foakes notes is hardly enough for the properties that the plays staged there require – *Volpone* and *The Maid's Tragedy*, which call for beds, and the discovery-scenes of *The Duchess of Malfi*. Its curvature and its five doors might be thought to correspond roughly to the Rose *frons* if it followed the three inner walls of the tiring-house bays. There is little basis for any valid generalizations here. Radical variety in the design of stage areas is the only possible conclusion.

STAGE POSTS

Judging from the archaeological evidence turned up so far, the early Rose may not have had stage posts, though what little evidence there is about plays staged there before the 1592 alterations indicates that it did.[10] The one pile base uncovered in 1989 was added after the new foundation wall for the pushed-back stage was built for the reconstruction of 1592. It must have been meant for a post to uphold the new stage cover. Unless this base covers an earlier cap for the original stage posts, so far undiscovered, there is no sign of any base for a stage post at the first Rose. I think it is conceivable that the new post base was positioned over the old one, which would mean that the original stage posts were positioned seven feet back from the stage front. But that still leaves the 1592 Rose with stage posts right forward by the new stage's edge. These posts were positioned so close to the 'front' line of the stage platform that they would have left little if any room for players to walk round them or hide behind them. It is possible that just enough of the stage's floor timbers protruded forward of the foundation wall to allow the posts to be used for concealment, but the evidence is against it. The erosion line in the original mortar surface of the yard that runs in front of the first stage is too close to the foundation to

---

[9] R. A. Foakes, *Illustrations of the English Stage 1580–1642* (London, 1985), p. 68.

[10] Gurr, 'The Rose Repertory: What the Plays might tell us about the Stage', in *New Issues in the Reconstruction of Shakespeare's Theatre* (New York, 1990), pp. 119–34. There is also the erosion line across the 'front' of the original stage, matching the depth of the erosion line in the yard that runs round the front of the galleries. These lines were all made by dripping from the thatched roof.

allow much room for any substantial protrusion forward of the stage flooring's timbers. That throws doubt on the possibility that the second stage protruded much either. And since they built a new post base for the second Rose the builders could have felt no need to economize by incorporating the old structure. They were free to position the new post wherever the users wanted it.

Stage posts are certainly called for in some of the post-1592 Rose plays. In *Englishmen for my Money*, written by William Haughton for the Rose early in 1598, the clown guides a group of comic foreigners, complaining that they are lost in London, around the stage. One asks 'but watt be dis Post?', and is told it is 'the May-pole on Ivie-bridge going to Westminster'. Their guide then says 'Soft, heere's an other: Oh now I know in deede where I am; wee are now at the fardest end of Shoredich, for this is the May-pole' (lines 1654–61). Two posts identified as maypoles do imply that they were set in enough open space to allow dancing round them. But there might also be a joke built into the visuals in this play, if the characters blundering blindly through the London streets are seen coming dangerously close to the edge of the stage when they encounter the posts. It is necessary to be careful about deducing too much from stage directions. Posts are explicitly invoked for the staging in some plays, and they might have been used for concealment in eavesdropping scenes. But whether they were the mighty structures that De Witt drew is doubtful.

A play written for the Red Bull and acted by the company which once used the Rose provides a test for the evidence from stage directions and text. *Swetnam the Woman Hater*, staged at the Red Bull in about 1619, has two courtroom scenes. To judge from the woodcut on the titlepage of the 1620 quarto, the stage court was set up with a seat for the judge that resembled, and probably was, the same chair of state or throne used for scenes at royal courts. In the woodcut, however, in front of the judge's chair there is a 'bar', behind which the prisoner stands facing the judge and flanked by jury and spectators. Whatever one's qualms about how faithful to the staging the makers of titlepage woodcuts felt it necessary to be, this woodcut does depict the disposition we might expect to see on stage for such scenes of judgement as *Swetnam* 3.1. In that scene, the first of the two judgement scenes, the judge is royal, and the throne would have been placed centrally. An order is given at line 13 to 'Bring to the Barre the Prisoners'. A marginal note at line 31 in the 1620 edition calls for 'A Barre', and 14 lines later a stage direction reads '*The Prisoners brought to the Barre by a Gard*'. It seems reasonable to conclude that this courtroom scene would probably have been staged more or less as in the woodcut, with throne and bar placed centrally. The main difference is that the woodcut depicts the second courtroom scene.

The play's first courtroom scene, in 3.1, is the trial of the lovers. The subsequent populist and feminist call in 5.2 for the trial of Joseph Swetnam is a parodic imitation of the 3.1 formal trial. The woodcut on the *Swetnam* titlepage was clearly intended to depict this scene, with the Queen sitting as judge and the women jurors surrounding the court. In the woodcut Swetnam himself stands at a bar made of a short wooden pillar and two large foils, one stuck in the floor, the other suspended across from its handle to a short pillar. For this burlesque scene the women have taken the men's places, and the courtroom 'bar' is set up explicitly as a home-made affair. Atlanta says

> We want a Barre. O, these two foyles shall serve:
> One stucke i'the Earth, and crosse it from this Tree.
> Now take your places, bring him to the Barre.

This is clearly the scene that should have been depicted in the woodcut, which has swords positioned to make a bar as Atlanta specifies, but no tree.[11] Acts 4 and 5 are full of swords and swordplay, which make the properties the author calls for to set up the improvised courtroom bar apt enough, even in a scene dominated by the women of the play.

The trouble here is the confused and contradictory nature of the evidence. The Swetnam woodcutter might have merged his idea of the 3.1 courtroom with the 5.2 makeshift courtroom, or may have merely used the familiar set for every Jacobean courtroom. Possibly he was not thinking of the stage set at all (which given the windows at the rear seems likely), and just did as he thought fit to show Swetnam at his trial/arraignment. But even the text and stage directions do not make clear how it was staged.

THE 'HEAVENS'

Hamlet's heaven fretted with golden fire is almost certainly a Global phenomenon. The stage traditionally represented the earth, with the heavens above and hell beneath. Faustus and Barabbas went down to a hell under the stage. The stage trapdoor opened Hamlet's grave, which is also the suicided Ophelia's and had been the entry-point for the ghost of his father. It also gives access to Malvolio's hellishly dark cell.[12] William Cartwright's *The Ordinary* (1634–5), a play which may have been written for performance at Oxford but which is soaked in the London plays of the time, has a statement by Moth (3.1.)

> . . . with it my Carcasse entire I bequeathen
> Under my foot to Hell, above my head to
> heaven.

Nashe had registered a similar three-level cosmos as early as 1591, when the Theatre, the Curtain and the Rose were the only purpose-built amphitheatres in town. In the introduction to the 1591 printing of *Astrophil and Stella*, he wrote

> here you shal find a paper stage streud with pearle, an artificial heav'n to overshadow the fair frame, & christal wals to encounter your curious eyes, whiles the tragicommedy of love is performed by starlight.[13]

This may or may not mean that the Rose had the same kind of stage cover as the Theatre and Curtain, and therefore had stage posts to support it. John Norden's depiction of the Rose, although he simplified what we now know was a fourteen-sided structure into a hexagon, does show a stage cover in the right position, to the north, where the 1989 excavation confirmed that the stage was. Unfortunately Norden also makes it gable-fronted. This is unlikely. A broad erosion line runs through the mortar flooring across the front of the first stage at the Rose. It appears to have been made by water dripping from the thatch cover over the stage, like the line around the rim of the yard from the gallery roofing. If so, the first stage's cover must have had a penthouse roof sloping down towards the front, like the one De Witt shows at the Swan. A gable front requires a roof that would drain its water sideways, down the flanks of the stage, not across the front. The stage front's erosion line is similar in depth to the lines in the yard's mortar fronting the galleries, though it is much more scuffed. Either Norden was wrong in showing a gable-fronted stage cover, or else the first Rose of 1587 had a stage cover like a penthouse, with its roof ridge running across a chord of the polygon, while the second was altered to give it a ridge at right angles to the northern gallery wall and a gable front, as depicted by Norden. This is a substantial contradiction between different kinds of evidence, more substantial than others because both relate to the same structure. The archaeological evidence seems the more tangible, especially since Norden simplified the

---

11 See George Fulmer Reynolds, *The Staging of Elizabethan Plays at the Red Bull Theatre 1605–1625* (New York, 1940), pp. 46–7; R. A. Foakes, *Illustrations of the English Stage 1580–1642*, pp. 116–17.

12 See John Astington, 'Malvolio and the Dark House', *Shakespeare Survey 41* (1989), pp. 55–62.

13 *Works*, ed. McKerrow, III.329.

original fourteen sides of the polygon into six.

'CHRISTAL WALS' AND THE LORDS' ROOMS OVER THE STAGE

Did the richest spectators complete the circuit of audience in the round by sitting on the stage balcony at all the amphitheatres? Nashe knew the Rose and its brave Talbot, and may have had it in mind in the contrasting picture he drew of a stage strewn with pearls and surrounded with see-through walls. A see-through crystal may indicate that he was thinking that some of the crystal-wall gazers were looking from over the stage. An angled tiring-house front would provide a better structure for lords' rooms over the stage if the central space was for the players and the gentry were positioned in the flanking rooms, the angle of which gave at least some view of the stage entrances and the discovery space.

What was on the upper level in the tiring house at the Rose? The post-1592 Rose has a plethora of plays written specifically for it, and we might expect an ample supply of stage directions indicating the furniture that its bare island was equipped with. But stage directions rarely give straight evidence. One in *A Woman Killed with Kindness*, written for Worcester's at the Rose in early 1603, suggests that there may have been a playing space over the stage. It reads '*Enter over the stage* Frankford, Anne and Nicholas' (Scene 5). Wendoll, already on stage, sees them ('There goest thou'), but they do not see him. This is one of the pieces of evidence cited by Allardyce Nicoll for his concept of steps from the yard on each side up to the stage so that players could be seen 'passing over the stage' from one side to the other.[14] The lack of any evidence for steps, or any place for them on a platform with tapered sides, makes it more likely that 'over the stage' meant the same place as the gentlemen's places, the eight-foot-wide central balcony. Using such testimony falls easily into the swirl of circular arguments.

Other stage directions in plays written specifically for the Rose are, mercifully, less ambiguous. In *Englishmen for my Money* a burlesque Romeo and Juliet balcony scene has the Falstaffian lover hoisted up to his love in a buckbasket ('How heavie the Asse is', says his reluctant Juliet) and left suspended in midair while he is mocked and pelted with a cushion (lines 1746–94). The poet assumed the availability of a playing-space 'above' and possibly some form of hoist machinery as well.

The 'lords' rooms' were evidently distinct from the 'twopenny galleries' and even from the 'gentlemen's rooms' noted in the Fortune and Hope contracts. Access to them, unlike the galleries, was through the tiring house. Their position was on the stage balcony, where they are shown in De Witt's Swan drawing. Gentlemen's rooms, probably the ones that Platter notes as costing an extra penny for a cushion and the best view, were the bays closest to the stage at the lowest level of the galleries, to judge from the Hope contract's 'boxes'. The twopenny galleries or rooms were presumably the remaining bays of the polygonal frame stretching around the rest of the gallery circuit. The Fortune contract calls for the gentlemen's rooms and the twopenny rooms to be lined with plaster. At the Rose and probably other amphitheatres both the lords' and the gentlemen's rooms had plastered ceilings, while the lesser gallery bays had no formal ceiling other than the timbers forming the degrees for the level above.

THE *FRONS SCENAE*

Windows in the tiring-house frons

In Foakes's *Illustrations*, four of the scenes shown on the titlepages of play quartos have

[14] Evert Sprinchorn, 'An Intermediate Stage Level in the Elizabethan Theatre', *Theatre Notebook*, 46 (1992), 73–94, offers a thoughtful reconsideration of the old case about players 'passing' literally up to and 'over' some structure on the stage, or the stage itself.

windows in the rear wall. *Faustus* in 1616 has one, *Swetnam* in 1620 has two, *Bacon and Bungay* in 1630 has one, and *Arden of Faversham* (1633) and *A Maidenhead Well Lost* (1634) both have two. Three of them (*Faustus*, *Swetnam* and *Bacon and Bungay*) have squared floors, like the stage floor in Fludd's Theatrum Orbis. All have flat rear walls, and no tapering sides like the Rose's stage. Against this indication that the illustrators thought of stage rooms as possessing windows, few stage directions for any playhouse offer any function for such windows. Neither De Witt's Swan drawing nor either of Inigo Jones's stage designs for the Cockpit and the Cockpit-in-Court shows windows either. The unison of stage plans and stage directions weighs heavily against the illustrators.

Positioning the stage furniture

Where was the stage furniture positioned on stage in the different playhouses? Where were the royal stage, the row of chairs, the bed and even features such as trees or arbours placed, and where did they stand in relation to the stage posts? There is no evidence that can provide any confident answer to these questions apart from De Witt. His players are at 'stage front', or rather in the centre of the Swan's circuit of audience. The bench the lady sits on is a long way from the tiring house, far enough to give some justification to the arguments that claim the two-line gap between entries and speech that occur in some texts is a measure of how long it took to get from an entry door to the centre-stage or centre-auditorium speaking position.[15] There is a case, too, for thinking that the royal throne or judicial chair of state might have been positioned not facing the 'front' but towards the tiring house where the watching grandees sat. Everyone concerned directly in the royal presence would stand in front of the throne, but lesser beings stood behind. If the throne was placed in the centre of the playhouse it might have faced either way, depending on what players and audience thought their status was. The only evidence for the positioning of a judicial throne is *Swetnam*'s titlepage, which unequivocally places it facing away from the tiring-house wall. But the reliability of the titlepage illustrators has been called in question once already. There is just not enough evidence to answer this potent question.

Stage hangings

A *frons* with two angles in it, and doors in each of the flanking angles, might suggest that any hangings would front the discovery space in the central section of the wall. Such a positioning would have allowed the hangings to be used not only for discoveries but for entries, especially the clown sticking his head through, a trick recorded of Tarlton before 1588 and of Timothy Reade in the 1630s. One problem with that is Heywood's seemingly unequivocal if anachronistic description, in the *Apology*, of the Roman theatres with curtains of arras tapestry hanging around what he calls the 'fore-front' of the stage. His Melpomene laments the loss of the golden age when 'Then did I tread on Arras, cloth of Tissue, / Hung round the fore-front of my stage: the pillars / That did support the Roofe of my large frame / Double appareld in pure Ophir gold: / Whilst the round Circle of my spacious orbe / Was throng'd with Princes, Dukes and Senators' (B2v). She notes elsewhere (F2r) that Rome's stages were 'hung with rich Arras'. Such a general framing for the stage would be appropriate for Dekker's suggestion that the stage could be 'hung with black' for tragedies, but it counters the need for a traverse and a cloth of arras for the Globe in *Hamlet* and *Volpone*. In this case I think the balance of probability lies

15 Mariko Ichikawa and others have noted the frequent incidence in some texts of a two-line interim between characters arriving on stage and starting to speak. See Ichikawa, 'Exits in Shakespeare's Plays: Time Allowed to Exiters', *Studies in English Literature*, 68 (Tokyo, 1992), 189–206.

with the stage directions rather than the vaguer mentions by Heywood and Dekker.

AUDITORIUM ENTRANCES

The size of the auditorium, only 74 feet in outside diameter at the Rose, probably 99 feet at the Globe and the Swan, is as large a factor in calculations about the bare island as the actual stage design. The semiotic potential of a theatre where half the audience is visible to the other half behind Hamlet as he speaks his ostensibly solitary soliloquies has too potent a bearing on the use of the stage island to be set down as a minor consideration. The same is true of the social divisions within the audience. How consistently the workingmen kept themselves to the yard, citizens to the galleries and lords to the rooms over the stage, and what social cachet there was in a gentleman's seat in the gallery near the stage compared with a twopenny gallery bench, are all questions with a bearing on the ways performances were received and responded to. Consideration of the bare island cannot afford to ignore such heavy details as the disposition, geographical and social, of the surrounding sea of theatre audience.

Many assumptions need challenging besides the shape of the stage island. One in particular puts to the test what has been more a conditioning concept or metaphor than an assumption about the design of the amphitheatres. That their development was evolutionary, and that in the forty-seven years between the building of the Red Lion and the Hope the design improved step by step and theatre by theatre is a Darwinian concept that is not very readily supported by the evidence. Building the nine theatres of Elizabethan and Jacobean London was a novel, demanding and infrequent activity, and it is reasonable to expect that each new design would incorporate the best features of its predecessors. That assumption can be tested most thoroughly by a look at the evidence for the means of audience access to the auditorium. Access to the galleries through the yard or by stair turrets is not a new question, but testing the evidence about it shows up as many contradictions as the geography of the bare island.

Control of access for the spectators, and a means of securing the right payment from them, must always have been a high priority in commercial playhouses. So there is an inherent plausibility in the idea of a consistent development in design from the early buildings which were simple erections of scaffolding around the stage and its yard, and which gave access first through the scaffolding into the yard and then from the yard up into the galleries, into a better system which advantaged the firstcomers. By this theory, in the early system latecomers into the yard would have had to stand at the back, furthest from the stage. If they wanted a seat and a roof they would have to push into the galleries through the firstcomers who, on crowded days, would have used the steps or degrees of the 'ingressus' to sit on. That there would be a consequent jostling for position on the ingressus stairways is not out of keeping with what we know about audience behaviour even in modern theatres where the seating is numbered, and everyone expects a guaranteed place. So the stair turret system, making latecomers enter the galleries from the rear, had the inherent advantage of reducing the occasion for audience aggression. At the same time it reduced the number of gatherers spread through the auditorium and concentrated them in the stair turret lobbies, where they could take money from yard and gallery patrons alike. It is plausible, but the available evidence does not support it.

The Globe's remains exposed in 1989 seem to show the foundations for a stair turret butting onto the outer gallery wall. Lines of bricks are subtended from the centre of two adjacent outer panels of the polygon for eight feet, each of them turning at right angles to run parallel to the main walls and stopping about six feet from each other, well short of the angle that they would form if they met each other. From one side of the two more or less square bays thus enclosed, a pair of walls make a corridor through to the yard. One of these corridor walls runs from outer wall angle to inner wall angle, while the other runs parallel to it at a distance of four feet. If the outer foundations were for a stair turret, the second of the two square bays must have been occupied by a narrow set of stairs less than four feet wide at ground level zigzagging up to each of the three levels of gallery above the ground. At the upper levels these stairs would have given access to lobbies into each gallery on either side of the main wall angle. Such a design is speculative, and it does not fit well with the much narrower flat-fronted lobbies shown in Hollar's drawing of the second Globe. But it is all the concrete evidence we have.

From written accounts it seems that a stair turret system of access to the galleries became current in or before 1600. It is on and after that date that references to the occupants of the 'twopenny galleries' start appearing. This used to bother me a little, because specifying seats in the galleries that cost twopence implied that other seats cost more, and for all William Lambarde's and Thomas Platter's claims that threepence got you a better place and a cushion there are no references to threepenny galleries. The 'twopenny gallery' term must, it seems, have entered with the stair turrets, where the single gatherer at the foot of the stair in the entrance lobby would collect both pennies at the same time. The concept of a 'twopenny' place would not have existed under the old system where patrons entered door by door and gatherer by gatherer, paying one penny at each, unless the 'twopenny gallery' was the place for Platter's cushion, a twopenny access from the one-penny yard separate from the one-penny access to the bare-benched galleries. That would require another single entry-point for such a privileged gallery, where the gatherer collected twopence, which is extremely unlikely and almost impossible in terms of ready access from the yard. We might conjecture that Lambarde's and Platter's third penny went for a place in a lord's room, or more likely for a cushion in one of the twopenny galleries closest to the stage which qualified as a gentleman's room. The sixpence identified as the price of the lords' rooms is an inference from the prices paid on visits to the Globe by people like Mildmay in the 1620s. That may have been a price peculiar to the lords' rooms at the Globe only after the company's extended use of the Blackfriars had pushed up the social status of their clientele and their prices.

On the face of it, a change in the method for audience access between the early and the later amphitheatres is proclaimed by contemporary testimony. Lambarde, writing before 1596, and Platter writing in 1599, are quite specific. Lambarde wrote that at the Theatre, 'they first pay one pennie at the gate, another at the entrie of the Scaffolde, and the third for a quiet standing'. Platter said

> whoever cares to stand below only pays one English penny, but if he wishes to sit he enters by another door, and pays another penny, while if he desires to sit in the most comfortable seats which are cushioned, where he not only sees everything well, but can also be seen, then he pays another English penny at another door.[16]

Such a system of entry does not need stair turrets. The more tangible evidence, both from archaeology and from contemporary pictures, seems to support this. The absence of any turret in the sixty per cent of the Rose's groundplan so far excavated, and the 'ingressus' from the yard to the gallery scaffolding shown in De Witt's Swan drawing both support Lambarde's and Platter's accounts. The Theatre, the Rose and the Swan thus seem to have belonged to the older design of playhouse, without stair turrets. That suggests an evolution in playhouse design, with the more sophisticated form of audience access to the

[16] *Thomas Platter's Travels in England,* trans. Clare Williams (London, 1951), p. 167.

gallery seats developing later than the system Lambarde and Platter describe.

But it is, of course, not so simple. Against this evidence there are two substantial pieces of evidence that need to be reconciled very carefully against the statements made by Lambarde and Platter. The first is the Utrecht view of the Theatre, which appears to show it with a pair of stair turrets on opposite flanks.[17] The other is the pair of testimonies that the Swan had at least one and probably two examples of the newer form of access. In the 1627 map of Paris Garden Manor[18] the single stair turret on the northeast flank of its polygonal 'Swan' would have made De Witt's 'ingressus' from the yard unnecessary. That is one conflict of evidence. And there is another. However unreliable we think De Witt was the 1627 map might also be questioned, not for its marking of a stair turret but for marking only one. The Hope contract, with all the precision of a building specification, notes that the Swan has plural 'stearcasses . . . without and adjoyninge' its frame. This testimony that the Swan had two stair turrets is at odds with De Witt, with the Paris Garden Manor map and with the Lambarde and Platter evidence.

The Paris Garden Manor map is a problem in another way. Francis Langley when he built his Swan in 1595 close to the Rose was the first impresario to follow Henslowe onto the south bank. His design was evidently larger than Henslowe's since the Swan was claimed to have a capacity of three thousand. Besides its evident differences, the square stage, the planar *frons* and De Witt's testimony to its having walls of flint and timbers painted to look like marble, it may have copied the Rose in the kind of audience access that Henslowe's first playhouse could have had: a single stair turret on its northeastern flank. Until the eastern segment of the Rose's polygon can be excavated, we cannot know for sure that the Rose did not have a stair turret where the Paris Garden map suggests the Swan had one. If so, then Lambarde's and Platter's evidence from 1596 and 1599 about the penny-by-penny access to the galleries through the yard in the early amphitheatres is quite wrong for the Rose and the Swan. Even De Witt's 'ingressi' could then only be correct if they were built for the few spectators who might be expected to change their minds after first deciding to stand in the yard. A secondary means of access from the yard to the galleries would be useful for when it rained and the penny-payers decided to pay extra to get a roof over their heads, but the opportunity for such second thoughts would intensify the problem of crowding and conflict with the spectators already in position on the access steps. Lambarde, Platter and De Witt all tell a consistent but unconvincing story about audience access.

Worse is to come. James P. Lusardi[19] has argued strongly that Abram Booth's 'The View of the Cittye of London from the North towards the South' (Foakes, *Illustrations*, p. 8), made in the late 1590s, shows that the Theatre had stair turrets. If that is true, and stair turrets were in use as early as 1576, Lambarde and Platter are again contradicted. Neither the Rose, Swan nor the Theatre had the penny-by-penny form of audience entry. Moreover, this means that the stair-turreted Globe, with its framing timbers taken from the Theatre, was built even more like its predecessor than conventional expectation admits.

The obvious advantage of a stair turret for gallery access is twofold: it removes the need to provide stairway space inside the auditorium, where seating space is more profitable, and it admits latecomers to the back of the gallery instead of the front, which is the confrontational access that seems to be required by the step-by-step admission system through the Swan's and the Rose's 'ingressus'. If the

17 See James P. Lusardi, 'The Pictured Playhouse: Reading the Utrecht Engraving of Shakespeare's London', *Shakespeare Quarterly*, 44 (1993), 202–27.

18 Foakes, *Illustrations of the English Stage 1580–1642*, p. 24.

19 Lusardi's well-illustrated article considers the stair turrets on page 215.

Theatre, the Swan and possibly the Rose all had stair turrets, what playhouses did Lambarde and Platter attend that might have justified their generalizations? Lambarde cited the Bel Savage inn and the baiting house in Paris Garden in his original account of the playhouses, adding the Theatre's name to the list for his 1596 revision. But citing the baiting house raises another question about the Lambarde and Platter testimonies. The baiting-house yards were inaccessible to audiences because they were occupied by the animals. Neither of the Bankside scaffolds shown in the Agas map of 1572 shows any sign of stair turrets, but it seems inherently improbable that their owners would have expected customers to enter through the yard, even if the audience was all required to be in place before the baitings started. Access must have been from the outside, by stairs. The baiting houses must therefore have provided some kind of early model for the stair-turret design of audience access to the playhouse galleries.

Platter must have been even looser than Lambarde in his generalizing, because he certainly went to some amphitheatres which had stair turrets, although he makes no mention of them. Besides at least one visit to a bear-baiting house, where stair turrets were essential, he specified a visit to the Globe ('the house with the thatched roof'), where on 21 September 1599 he saw *Julius Caesar*. We can be fairly sure from the 1989 excavation that the Globe had at least one stair turret. So what led Platter to record a generalization that certainly did not apply to at least two of the amphitheatres he visited? Like the references that appeared in sermons about the decadence of the Theatre long after it was pulled down, Platter may have been repeating out-of-date information the locals had given him, and overlooking his own direct experience. Such a possibility strengthens the case for relying on archaeological concrete rather than written testimonies from the time.

'HOW CHANCES IT THEY TRAVEL?' PROVINCIAL TOURING, PLAYING PLACES, AND THE KING'S MEN

ALAN SOMERSET

I

Hamlet's question provides our earliest surviving evidence of curiosity about actors' provincial touring – his interest is aroused because, as he realizes, 'their [the actors'] residence both in reputation and profit was better both ways' (2.2.331–2). Rosencrantz replies, puzzlingly, with two explanations, alluding to 'the late innovation' and the 'eyrie of children' as the reasons why the tragedians of the city have taken to the road.[1] The moment in the play passes, but curiosity about provincial touring does not; attempts to answer Hamlet's query have recurred throughout the three hundred and ninety-odd years since he asked it. This essay tackles an old question, then, in the hope that some new light may be shed on it. As well as asking why players toured, we will try to discover when tours took place (a question closely related to the first) and how they were organized. I am curious, as well, about the physical conditions and economics of touring along with the related issue of the type of reception the touring players might expect. Finally, we will enquire into where players toured – their touring routes – and most importantly, about the playing places in which they acted during their sojourns in provincial cities and towns through the length and breadth of England, Scotland and Ireland.[2]

Records of Early English Drama has been engaged for sixteen years on an intense examination of provincial dramatic activities, and this paper grows out of my collaboration in that project.[3] I must begin with a note of caution, well sounded by Giles Dawson in 1965 and as true today:

> The accounts for no town in Kent are complete for the years between 1450 and 1642: there are always lost and fragmentary years. But even if they were all preserved complete and flawless, they would fall short of providing a full record of performances by travelling players. If a company of players came to a town, performed, and departed without cost to the corporation, their presence would not be shown in

---

[1] In the 1603 (bad) Quarto, the only reason offered is the competition of the children's companies, where in the 1604 (good) Quarto the reason given is simply the late innovation. In the 1623 Folio the two reasons appear, for the first time, side by side.

[2] That English troupes of players visited Edinburgh is well-attested; it is less widely known that at least one troupe, the Queen's Men, journeyed across the Irish Sea to perform in Dublin in 1588–9, where they were rewarded with £3, as is found by examination of the Irish documents for Records of Early English Drama (currently being undertaken by Alan Fletcher).

[3] I gratefully acknowledge Sally-Beth MacLean's research into tour organization and routes, in her recently published 'Tour Routes: "Provincial Wanderings" or Traditional Circuits?' *Medieval and Renaissance Drama in England*, 6 (1993), 1–14, and her paper, 'Tracking Leicester's Men: Patterns and Incentives', delivered at the Shakespeare Association of America meeting in 1991. Dr MacLean has also kindly read and commented on this paper, with many helpful suggestions. As well, I have been able to make use of collections of as yet unpublished documents in her care at the REED editorial offices; these are acknowledged individually.

the accounts and we should have no knowledge of it.[4]

From Chester, for example, there survive only sporadic accounting records, in which occur only six payments to touring entertainers, but much more activity than that took place. Edward Alleyn wrote to his wife in August, 1593, and stated that 'west Chester' was on the itinerary of the Lord Strange's men,[5] but their visit is otherwise unknown. On 8 October 1596 the city prohibited plays and bear-baitings upon the city's charges because, in the words of the order, 'by daylie experience it has fallen out what great inconvenences there haue Arrysen by playes and bearebeat*es*', clearly implying that such activities occurred frequently. Plays apparently continued to be performed, because on 20 October 1615 a further order alluded to the number of plays performed and banned plays from the common hall, and in any other place after 6 pm (not a single visit appears in the records from 1600–15, but such must have taken place). Interestingly, the order names 'Innehowses' as possible alternative playing places.[6] The other aspect of incompleteness arises from the nature of the records, which are mostly accounting payments with a scattering of legal records, prohibitions and the like. Only very rarely does one uncover any evidence of the dynamics of a visit, the physical conditions of performance or the reactions of audiences. Similarly difficult to determine are the realities of touring, because of Elizabethan (and later) attitudes and misconceptions about it.

The ever-accelerating growth of England's capital city in the sixteenth century, spurred by the importance of the royal court, the law courts, and trade caused country gentry and aristocracy to flock to the capital, particularly after 1590, as Lawrence Stone has pointed out; London became by 1650 the 'inn-general of the gentry and nobility', despite sporadic government attempts to force persons with country estates to return to them.[7] An aversion to the country (or a preference for London) becomes a matter of frequent comment, as does the cliché of the boorish and stupid country dweller – Kastril, in Ben Jonson's *The Alchemist*, provides an example. Significantly, the word 'urbane' in the sense of 'having the manners, refinement or polish regarded as characteristic of a town' (*OED*) is first recorded in 1624. There survive many literary expressions of this anti-provincial bias, which surely were aimed to make London dwellers think well of themselves – a favourite is Robert Herrick's 'His Return to London':

> From the dull confines of the drooping west,
> To see the day spring from the pregnant east,
> Ravished in spirit, I come, nay more, I fly
> To thee, blest place of my nativity!
> Thus, thus, with hallowed foot I touch the
> ground
> With thousand blessings by thy fortune
> crowned . . .

One has difficulty squaring these sentiments with the playful and idealizing poems of country life and festivals which also came from Herrick's pen. What chance had, or have, the provinces against the force of this view of London?

London playwrights fed London's self-esteem in a number of ways, one of which was to celebrate the wit and sophistication of the city in the numerous plays set within its boundaries. They also presented audiences with scenes and characters from rural life, the attitudes to which vary from sardonic enjoyment to sarcastic ridicule. Shakespeare's Justice Shallow and Master William Silence, or Audrey and William are memorable good-natured examples. The point is, the players were reinforcing audiences'

---

[4] Giles Dawson, ed. *Records of Plays and Players in Kent 1450–1642*, Malone Society Collections, 8 (Oxford, 1965), p. xxvi.

[5] Alleyn's letter is preserved at Dulwich College, MS 1. See R. A. Foakes and R. T. Rickert, eds. *Henslowe's Diary* (Cambridge, 1968), pp. 276–7.

[6] Lawrence M. Clopper, ed. *Chester*, Records of Early English Drama (Toronto, 1979), pp. 184, 292–3.

[7] Lawrence Stone, *Crisis of the Aristocracy, 1558–1641* (Oxford, 1965), pp. 387–8.

stereotypes, as they were when presenting their attitudes to provincial touring. Nobody would argue that the London companies of actors preferred touring – Hamlet's point is a good one; it was no doubt a second choice[8] – but the question remains, did actors embark on a provincial season with feelings of utter loathing, or with a sense of adventure? One might in passing compare the provincial tours, or royal progresses, of Queen Elizabeth and King James. What did they think about the provinces, preferring as they doubtless did to be at the centre of things in London? They certainly toured with vigour, and the public reaction to the boroughs and households they visited was invariably one of pleasure and delight.

Any metatheatrical commentary must be used with care because it may not accurately reflect realities. For example, Ben Jonson's habit of attacking other plays, other theatres or other theatre techniques in his prologues is not evidence, but raillery. 'Where neither Chorus wafts you o'er the seas / Nor creaking throne comes down, the boys to please' (*Every Man In His Humour*) doesn't mean that public-theatre windlasses always squeaked, any more than 'Nor quaking custards with fierce teeth affrighted / Wherewith your rout are so delighted' (*Volpone*) is evidence that this particular comic turn was invariably included in other productions. Jonson's aim is to compliment his auditory (and himself!), reminding them that they are not 'boys' or members of a 'rout' and that what they are about to see and hear will be something special.

The same caution must be used when considering actors' public commentaries upon touring. During what Andrew Gurr aptly terms 'the war of railing',[9] the period during which London's audience became divided between different theatres with contrasting repertoires, the most remarkable attacks on provincial touring are contained within two plays written for the private boys' theatres, Marston's *Histriomastix, or the Player Whipped* (Paul's, 1599) and Jonson's *Poetaster, or the Arraignment of the Humorous Poet* (Chapel, 1601). We must be doubly cautious here, because these plays hold other theatres, players and playwrights up to ridicule; since London boys' companies did not tour but rather emphasized the eliteness of their refined urban audiences, an attack on provincial playing was likely inevitable.[10] In Marston's *Histriomastix* a troupe of irregular local players call themselves Sir Oliver Owlet's men although they are, really, unlicensed vagabonds. These local mechanicals provide a vehicle whereby Marston can attack their company poet, Posthaste (Anthony Munday); some of their 'base brown-paper stuff', their opening song, is relevant here:

> Besides that we travel, with pumps full of
> gravel,
> Made all of such running leather:
> That once in a week, new masters we seek
> And never can hold together.

This gaggle of incompetents can fool or please nobody; their artless and precarious brief existence ends when they are pressed into the army. Jonson alludes to a line from this song in *Poetaster*, 3.4, where Captain Tucca recommends Chrisogonus, the Poetaster, to a troupe of players whose touring activities are ridiculed:

> thou has fortie, fortie shillings, I meane, stinkard, giue it him in earnest, doe, he shall write thee, slaue. If hee pen for thee once, thou shalt not need to trauell, with thy pumps full of grauell, any more, after a blinde iade and a hamper: and stalke vpon boords, and barrell heads, to an olde cract trumpet.

---

[8] Professor David Bevington has emphasized this point in a careful and helpful critique of an earlier version of part of this paper.

[9] Andrew Gurr, *Playgoing in Shakespeare's London* (Cambridge, 1987), pp. 153–9.

[10] James P. Bednarz, 'Marston's Subversion of Shakespeare and Jonson: *Histriomastix* and the War of the Theaters', *Medieval and Renaissance Drama in England*, 6 (1993), 103–28, suggests that Marston's attack on the public theatre implies that all professional players (in London or without) are little more than vagabonds, and that select audiences should abandon them altogether (p. 104).

Chrisogonus (Marston) in the last scene is compelled to vomit forth words like 'oblatrant', 'furibund', 'fatuate' and 'strenuous'. Jonson's aim is to attack Marston's ineptitude as a writer, not to present an objective picture of players on tour. A third provincial touring troupe in Middleton's *Hengist, King of Kent, or The Mayor of Queenborough* (1618), serves as vehicle for an attack on provincial audiences. The foolish mayor eagerly receives the visiting troupe, which is really a gang of thieves masquerading as players, and he is easily gulled – the point is, the mayor is so enamoured of clowns that he cannot tell real players from counterfeits, and the playwright's intent is to ridicule him. What about, on the other hand, depictions of tourers where the writer's intention is not satirical?

Three touring professional companies make visits whose outcomes are sympathetically portrayed, in *The Booke of Sir Thomas More*, *The Taming of the Shrew* and *Hamlet*; perhaps significantly, each troupe visits a household (household accounts have received less thorough attention than borough records, but assuredly deserve more complete investigation). All three troupes are politely or even eagerly received and a play is arranged. Two of the companies acquit themselves wholly admirably (surely we cannot blame the players for the disorder that interrupts *The Murder of Gonzago*!'). Hamlet, in particular, is fulsome in his praise of the actors, the 'abstracts and brief chronicles of the time' (2.2.527–8). In *The Book of Sir Thomas More* a missed cue gives More the opportunity to step up amongst the players and take a part, a talent made memorable by Roper's *Life*, and a matter of legend. A final piece of evidence about players on tour is Simon Jewell's will, in which he alludes to himself and five partners having pooled £37 for horses, a wagon and new apparel – a considerable outlay, assuredly invested in hopes of welcomes on the road and profits from playing.[11]

The negative attacks on provincial touring are balanced, then, by more sympathetic portrayals and some objective evidence. But the negative portrayals have largely come to be accepted as factual depictions of the touring life, to the point where many assume that *Poetaster* gives us Jonson's description of a typical provincial stage. Why? One answer is that the records that indicate trouble are inherently more colourful, and often are more detailed – take for example the following, from Newcastle-under-Lyme in 1610:

It is agreed by the assemblie aforesaid, y*a*t Thomas Dale Alder*man* for ent*er*tayninge into his howse Certaine Wandringe fellows by the title of players or rath*er* rouges & sufferinge theim to play in his howse after hee had warninge by m*aste*r Maior to ye Contrarie ys fyned in xl *s*./[12]

In contrast, payments are usually run-of-the-mill accounting entries, and lack emotion or drama, such as this Shrewsbury payment from 1603:

It*em* geven to the kinges his ma*ies*ties players xx *s*.

A second reason, of course, is that the anti-provincial bias of the Elizabethan period has persisted and has become a rooted attitude among Londoners – 'Watford, then wilderness' – reflecting the concentrated centralization of British cultural, political and economic institutions in the capital. In general it reflects the growing urbanization of our century across the developed world, which has resulted in ever-increasing proportions of the population living in large cities. The anti-provincial attitude has also persisted in the theatre; for example Lord Olivier once reportedly contrasted himself to Sir Donald Wolfit with the quip, 'some of us are a *tour de force*; others are forced to tour'. And the anti-provincial bias has affected theatre historians, leading to a number of little-examined presuppositions that have long affected scholar-

11 Mary Edmond, 'Pembroke's Men', *RES*, n.s. 25 (1974), 129–36.

12 Newcastle-under-Lyme Public Library, 'Red Book', fol. 29v.

ship; among these we might examine the idea that the players only travelled when they absolutely had to, especially when the plague was raging, or the notion that little theatrical activity occurred outside London. I will return to these, but first let us consider some assumptions about the conditions of touring and the reception of troupes.

For every investigator who suggests that Hamlet's warm welcome to the travelling tragedians is typical of the treatment afforded to touring professional entertainers, scores have emphasized the examples in the records where players received the cold shoulder, or worse. For example, a recent authority, G. E. Bentley, in *The Profession of Player* (1984), states as follows: 'there is no evidence that touring was ever very profitable, and it was certainly uncomfortable in the mire and the rain'; touring was 'an unpleasant and comparatively unprofitable expedient to compensate for London misfortunes'; 'permission to play was sometimes granted . . . often they were not allowed to perform at all . . . there is little evidence that the local authorities received the travellers with enthusiasm.'[13] Bentley goes on to outline the procedures followed by companies on town visits, and in his account he presents two examples of permission to play being granted as opposed to thirteen records of control, refusal or trouble, including the 1580 affray at Norwich and the 1627 wounding at a performance in Ludlow.[14] Are these proportions defensible? We may grant the discomfort of the mire and the rain (while remembering that London auditorium playhouses were open to the sky), but later we will suggest that there were even some counterbalancing advantages offered by provincial touring. However, we must first ask, does Bentley present an accurate picture of the reception expected when a company of actors visited a town?

To answer I have read through a large body of stable and reliable evidence, choosing Shakespeare's lifetime (1563–4–1616–17) as chronological limits: Malone Society and REED collections of provincial records that cover the period.[15] They can be used with confidence because they have been carefully collected according to the same scholarly criteria. As outlined above, they must be used with caution because no collection of records can be thought to be 'complete', and as well methods of record-keeping varied from place to place. The following list of cities and counties shows that the collections come from all parts of the country, and include many major provincial cities. A county collection includes all boroughs within its boundaries. The list comprises city and county collections in published REED volumes, as well as REED collections in the course of publication (indicated by an asterisk) and Malone Society collections, marked (M).

Bristol*	Cumberland
Cambridge	Devon
Chester	Gloucestershire
Coventry	Herefordshire
Leicester*[16]	Kent*[17]

[13] G. E. Bentley, *The Profession of Player in Shakespeare's Time, 1590–1642* (Princeton, 1984), pp. 177–84.

[14] Bentley's view of the difficulties faced by provincial companies is a long-held one. Writing about a case at Norwich in 1623 (see below, note 35), Bentley states that the 'affair in which Wambus figured at Norwich must be fairly characteristic of the adventures of the provincial companies . . .' (*The Jacobean and Caroline Stage*, vol. 2 (London, 1941), p. 614).

[15] With regret, I have excluded Stanley J. Kahrl, ed. *Records of Plays and Players in Lincolnshire 1300–1585*, Malone Society Collections, 8 (Oxford, 1969 (1974)), because it does not survey the whole period chosen here. James Stokes is currently working on the Lincolnshire records to 1642 for REED, but his survey is not yet completed.

[16] The Leicester collection was researched by the late Alice Hamilton as part of a projected REED volume on Leicestershire; the city records have been checked by Dr Abigail Young.

[17] Here I have used the records collected from east Kent by James Gibson for his forthcoming edition in the REED series, and for other parts of the country I have used Giles Dawson's collection for the Malone Society (see note 4). Gibson's collection includes 140 records not in Dawson.

Newcastle upon Tyne	Norfolk (M – including separately edited Ipswich and Aldeburgh)
Norwich	Shropshire*
York	Somerset (including Bath)*[18]
	Suffolk (M)
	Westmorland
	Worcestershire

I noted every reference to touring professional entertainers (players, minstrels, bearwards, jugglers, and other public performers) as being either 'positive' (that is, performing was allowed, rewarded or otherwise welcomed) or 'negative' (performing was prohibited, players were paid to go away without playing, playing was controlled, forged licences were detected, and so on). The results are startling. Where Bentley implied that performers were welcomed only twice in fifteen attempts (a 13.3 per cent success rate), the recorded proportions are more than the reverse: 3,119 successful visits out of a total of 3,279 records, giving an actual success rate of 95.12 per cent. These numbers provide, as well, evidence of an astonishing amount of entertainment activity. It is time to revise our stereotypes, and perhaps to look a little more closely at these records of provincial touring.

A second generalization to re-examine is the idea that provincial tours were undertaken 'to compensate for London misfortunes', particularly visitations of the plague. While escape from the plague may have been the case with a few London companies on occasion (for example, in 1592–4), one notes from reading the provincial records that there was not an observable rise in the numbers of visits during plague outbreaks. Rather the reverse. Plague epidemics were national in their effect and often led provincial boroughs to take preventive action, by preventing troupes from acting for fear of infection,[19] or by taking stronger measures. In Shrewsbury, for example, the borough assembly ordered that no visitor or wares be allowed within four miles of the town gates, if the journey taken originated in any place infected with plague, until the traveller or goods had been absent from the place of origin and remained free of infection for at least two months.[20] Travellers were also wary of infected places; when King James went on his annual progress, he required each borough he was to enter to certify in writing that it was free from infection. I think it is probably truer to say that the lives of entertainers (and people in general) everywhere became much harder during plague epidemics. I wonder, further, if evidence of troupes on tour during times of national plague outbreaks is typical at all of usual experiences while on tour.

From the evidence examined, provincial prohibitions to players became more frequent (just as they did in London) as time went on and the influence of Puritanism became more prevalent. However, provincial touring continued vigorously to the end of the period surveyed – it is mistaken to suppose that it died out early, soon after the establishment of the permanent playhouses in London. Negative reactions to visiting troupes do not become prevalent until the 1620s, except in a few places, and even as late as the 1630s about a quarter of the localities that had rewarded touring companies since 1550 were continuing to do so.[21] Hostility to players' visits appears to have been concentrated in particular regions, such as East Anglia – eighty-six of the negative responses to entertainment, or 66 per cent of the total, come from Norwich (45), Cambridge (26) and Norfolk/Suffolk (15), while this area provides

[18] The Somerset records, excluding Bath, are edited by James Stokes; they will appear with the separately edited Bath records, edited by Robert Alexander.

[19] For examples, at Norwich in 1583–4, at Worcester in 1626 or across Lancashire in 1631. For the national spread of plague epidemics see Paul Slack, *The Impact of Plague in Tudor and Stuart England* (Cambridge, 1985).

[20] Shrewsbury Assembly minute books, Shrewsbury and Atcham Corporation Borough Council Offices, Book 76, fol. 62v. The Shropshire records have been edited by the present writer.

[21] MacLean, 'Tour Routes', pp. 10–11.

596 positive responses, or 19.9 per cent of that total. From Norwich and Cambridge, it is clear that a corporation could prevent touring performances if it was determined to do so. The Vice-Chancellor of Cambridge University actively, and successfully, prevented performances within five miles of the town to protect the students from distraction.[22] Norwich began in 1584–5 to reward troupes but prevent performances, and in 1588–9 it banned attendance at performances by the townspeople, although visits continue to be rewarded after the latter date. The city began to issue limited licences to play, for short seasons of only two or three days, and to punish troupes that disobeyed.[23] The cumulative effect of these actions was impressive; although Norwich was the second largest city in the realm, and within easy access from London and other centres, it recorded only a total of 156 visits through the period (in passing, we note that a company's chance of a welcome at Norwich, which recorded the highest number of negative responses of any locality in the country, was still better than 76 per cent). Norwich welcomed far fewer troupes than smaller Ipswich, which welcomed professional entertainers on 202 occasions (and prevented them playing only once). If a city or borough did not hold out the promise of profit it would be avoided in favour of greener pastures; the greenest pasture was the city of Coventry, which welcomed 418 individuals or troupes and recorded only two minor misdemeanours through the period under consideration. Obviously, word got around about where to go and where to avoid.

II

It is only reasonable to suppose that companies of players usually found a welcome, and sought out localities where this was more likely, because touring with a company cost money. Sizes of troupes varied from the four men and a boy of tradition to as high as twenty members of Lady Elizabeth's players in 1618–19.[24] As William Ingram has argued, if we posit a company size of six people (the number of investers in additional equipment for a provincial tour mentioned in Simon Jewell's will), what we know about prices for accommodation, feed for horses and meals for the company leads us to conclude that a company of six persons on the road needed something in the order of ten shillings to fourteen shillings per day simply to survive.[25] Some companies were, as noted, much larger and would require proportionately greater sums for subsistence. Careful organization would be necessary to avoid running into deficit, and this care is amply in evidence when we look at tour routes and organization.

Inspecting, on a map, the 126 boroughs, parishes and households visited throughout England shows that the companies favoured well-travelled routes between major market towns, with smaller but considerable numbers of visits to large households.[26] Difficult terrain

---

[22] Alan H. Nelson, ed. *Cambridge*, Records of Early English Drama (Toronto, 1989), vol. 1, pp. 395–7, prints a 1603 letter from James I to the university that continues the authority of the Vice-Chancellor to intervene against 'commo*n* Plaies, Publique shewes, Enterlud*es*, C<o>modies & tragedies, in the English Tongue' (p. 395).

[23] David Galloway, ed. *Norwich, 1540–1642*, Records of Early English Drama (Toronto, 1984), pp. 81, 91, 117.

[24] R. W. Ingram, ed. *Coventry*, Records of Early English Drama (Toronto, 1981), p. 394. Bentley, *Profession of Player*, pp. 184–6, notes that up to twenty players were licensed by the Master of the Revels to tour as a company in 1624, and fifteen in 1635. Lord Derby's players numbered fourteen at Chatsworth in 1611 and at Londesborough in 1612. Lady Elizabeth's men numbered sixteen at the latter household in 1612, and the Queen's men visited there in 1619 with fifteen players. In the same year, Lady Elizabeth's men included twenty players when they visited Plymouth.

[25] William Ingram, 'The Cost of Touring', *Medieval and Renaissance Drama in England*, 6 (1993), 57–62, p. 59. Ingram uses comparative wage and price analyses to suggest that 10s would translate now to approximately £750 (p. 60).

[26] MacLean, 'Tour Routes', Maps 1–8, locates the known localities of provincial performances. The following discussion is greatly indebted to Dr MacLean's researches.

was usually avoided to ensure ease (and hence speed) of travel. Tour itineraries were developed by different companies. Some companies favoured those parts of the country where their patrons were influential – an example is the company under the patronage of the Lord President of the Council of the Marches of Wales, who are frequently traceable in those counties where that body held sway. Where the records are sufficiently plentiful the direction of various itineraries is traceable. A south-eastern circuit taken by both the Queen's men (in 1584) and Worcester's men (in 1591) followed the Roman road through Maidstone and Canterbury to the Kent coast, and then traversed the coast road between towns such as Dover, Folkestone, Hythe, Lydd and Rye; here were towns close together and easy of access. Access to Bristol and the west was either by the southerly Roman road to Exeter, or to the north via the Marlborough road, and after a stop at Bath and Bristol a company could either proceed along the Severn river via Gloucester, Tewkesbury, Worcester and Bridgnorth to Shrewsbury and north into Cheshire, or they could follow a more westerly route, crossing the Bristol Channel by ferry and proceeding north through Hereford, Leominster and Ludlow to Shrewsbury. In 1593 Edward Alleyn, writing to his wife from Bristol, announced his plan to travel northwards to York via Shrewsbury and Chester before returning south.[27]

To focus upon a particular company through a long career gives insight into touring practices. Robert Dudley, created Earl of Leicester in 1564, was patron of a company over a thirty-year period, 1559–88. A continuing investigation of the activities of the company has resulted in a paper that is in the nature of a 'progress report', but some of the conclusions reached so far are surprising.[28] Leicester was a powerful courtier, appointed Master of the Horse in the opening months of Elizabeth's reign and enjoying a special status as a royal favourite until his death. His was an eminent company that profited from frequent appearances at court (annually or more frequently from 1572–81), and they are known to have toured in twenty-six of the thirty years of their existence, often extensively – ninety-two records unknown to Murray or Chambers have been discovered to help complete the picture of their tours.[29] Their routes, in order of frequency, took them through East Anglia (in eighteen years), the south east (in fifteen years), the Midlands (in seventeen years) and via the Great North Road extending to the north-east (in combination with a Midlands tour, in ten of those seventeen years). These were areas with strong associations with Dudley, where rewards were higher and, one supposes, welcomes were more easily assured. Other areas were visited far less frequently (the south-west) or virtually ignored (the Welsh marshes). Touring could occur in any season, with the summer preferred (twenty-one years), although the company can be found in seven seasonal tours during December and January. The company's touring activities were pursued with no less energy during the years of their special favour at court, although they planned and timed their tours to ensure their availability to the queen at court, where rewards were highest. Their tours seem to have been similarly unaffected by the building of the Theatre in 1576, their permanent playhouse in London which gave them a secure base. In summary, Leicester's men were a highly organized and successful company, whose tours were a carefully planned major part of their life as a company. Their letter to the Earl in 1572 asking for a licence clearly implies that a yearly tour was to be expected and was customary. The licence would 'certifye that we are your houshold Servaunts when we shall have occasion to travayle amongst our frendes as we do usuallye

[27] See note 5.

[28] MacLean, 'Tracking Leicester's Men'.

[29] John Tucker Murray, *English Dramatic Companies 1558–1642* (2 vols., London, 1910) and E. K. Chambers, *The Elizabethan Stage*, vol. 3 (London, 1923), pp. 85–91.

once a yere, and as other noble-mens Players do and have done in tyme past'.[30] The wording suggests that 'our frendes' may include the Earl's associates and allies, and that the annual tour was planned with his preferences in mind.

Turning to the King's Men after 1603, it is of interest to contrast their touring with the tours of the company when under the patronage of the Lord Chamberlain during 1594–1603. As the Lord Chamberlain's Men the company toured in four of these nine years, including tours outside periods of inhibition in London; their most extensive tours were in 1597. They favoured the south-east and south-west, as far west as Bristol. Once under royal patronage, however, the company expanded the duration and extent of its tours, and are found in the provinces in every season from 1603–15; E. K. Chambers notes, but does not comment upon, this annual touring, to the evidence for which fourteen additional records have now come to light and a few have been found to be incorrect.[31] Should we not ask why the King's Men, the premier acting company of the realm, in control of the Globe (and after autumn, 1609 the Blackfriars) should have taken to the road in this way, both during and outside periods of London inhibition? The King's Men were by no means the most active touring company during this period, but it is nonetheless remarkable that their provincial activities increased just as they achieved pre-eminence in London. They continued to tour mainly in East Anglia, the south and the south west, but they are recorded as far north as Congleton, Cheshire, in 1615.[32] How chances it they travelled?

As an admittedly speculative answer, I think we might examine anew the patent issued to the company by King James, which announces that the king had 'licenced and aucthorized' the company 'freely to vse and exercise the Arte and faculty of playinge . . . aswell within theire nowe vsual howse called the Globe . . . as alsoe within anie towne halls or Moute halls or other conveniente places within the liberties and freedome of anie other Cittie, vniversitie, towne, or Boroughe whatsoever . . .'[33] Does this 'licence' imply simple permission (as does, say, a fishing licence)? Or does it imply authoritative permission, amounting to an expectation that the licensed activity will occur, or almost to a command that it take place (as does a licence to preach, or to practise medicine)? In 1612, the city authorities at York interpreted the Lady Elizabeth's Men's royal licence as conveying authority:

> And whereas the Ladie Elizabeth Players . . . haue brought with them his maiesties Commission for to be licensed to playe . . . in all moote halls skoolhowses towne halls within any other Citties or townes . . . Wherupon it is thought good to permitt them to play within this Cittie in such places as they shall procure or gett so as they do not play on the sabaoth daies or in the night tyme.[34]

---

30 Quoted in Chambers, *Elizabethan Stage*, vol. 3, p. 86.

31 The fullness and variety of the surviving Shrewsbury accounts have allowed us to arrive at a more accurate picture of the activities of the King's Men in that town. In many years original payment claims, bailiffs' day-to-day notes of expenses, bailiffs' rough accounts and the final audited versions all survive. The payment claims or day-to-day expenses specifically note each company rewarded, whereas the final audited accounts will record only a single 'grouped' payment, in summary form, such as (from 1608–9): 'Item to the king*es* ma*ies*ties players and the queene & princes players and other noblemens players.' Examples survive of these audited summary accounts with no sums entered, indicating that the scribe created them in advance of the audit, presumably on a day when he was not busy with other duties. In cases where the sum of the payment claims or day-to-day expenses equals that given in the summary account but the identity of companies differs (as here, in 1608–9) we know that the summary account was formulaic and we can identify companies that did not put in an appearance although they are mentioned. This is the case for the King's Men in 1608–9, 1609–10 and 1612–13. It is significant, however, that the scribe who wrote the formula expected the company to visit and provided for the possibility.

32 MacLean, 'Tour Routes', p. 10 and Map 7.

33 Chambers, *Elizabethan Stage*, vol. 3, p. 209.

34 Alexandra F. Johnston, ed. *York*, Records of Early English Drama (Toronto, 1979), p. 538.

At Norwich in 1623–4 Francis Wambus of the same company similarly attempted to claim that the company's licence conveyed authority to play '& accused mr Maior to his face that he contemned the kynges authority'.[35] When he set up a bill announcing a play at the sign of the White Horse near Tombland in defiance of the city's prohibition, however, Wambus was jailed for two months. The claim of authority, similarly made on these different occasions about another royal company, may suggest why the King's Men travelled. Provincial touring under the King's name was probably part of their expected duties, as was entertaining the monarch at court or the London populace at the company's permanent theatres.

III

The inclusive language used in both licences about actual playing places within provincial boroughs ('towne halls or Moute halls or other conveniente places'; 'moote halls skoolhowses towne halls') is both indicative and maddeningly elusive, as is the task of attempting to describe actual playing places and performance conditions. Because the vast majority of our records are accounts they usually specify only the amount of payment, and perhaps mention the playing place. We lack the eyewitness descriptions, diary accounts, letters, views, drawings and so on that we depend upon so heavily for our knowledge of the permanent London theatres, not to mention recent and exciting archaeological findings. However, we are not completely bereft of evidence; I wish first of all to survey what we know about performance conditions, and then turn to the actual playing places themselves. In surveying, we must be ready to extrapolate from the known to the unknown, and at the same time be cautious about doing so. For example, there is ample evidence from Norwich and elsewhere that companies' visits were not one-night stands. At Norwich the city authorities again and again chose to limit the number of days that a company might act before leaving, clearly implying that the companies would have stayed longer if they were allowed. What was the normal duration of a troupe's 'season'? It must have varied from locality to locality, depending upon expectations of audience size; but what might the average have been? Again, there are numbers of prohibitions from different localities against performing at night (Norwich and Chester provide examples). How prevalent were evening performances? Were they condoned elsewhere, or were they furtive? At Hythe, in Kent, the borough authorities decided in 1615–16 that 'conveient tymes' to play would be no later than 8 pm in the winter or 9 pm in the summer – later than our usual expectations of playing.[36] Evidence from Shropshire further fills in the picture here, because in both Shrewsbury (in 1613) and Ludlow (in 1627) evening performances were connected to disorders – the robbery of the Exchequer at Shrewsbury, and a wounding in Ludlow. Despite these misfortunes there is no trace of an attempt in either borough to limit performances in the evening. Being limited to playing during the working day would drastically reduce the potential audience, and hence late-afternoon or evening performances were preferable, just as they are today.

We may look a little more closely at the two Shropshire events just mentioned, and consider them along with the affray at Norwich in 1582, because all three were occasions for taking eyewitness evidence which affords insights into the conditions of provincial playing (lest we might think that such disorders only took place in the provinces, we should remember the affray at the Fortune Theatre in 1626, as a parallel). The events in Norwich, Shrewsbury and Ludlow are widely separated in time and all

35 Norwich Mayors' Court Books XV, fol. 525. See Galloway, ed. *Norwich, 1540–1642*, p. 181.

36 Hythe Mayors' Books and Chamberlains' Account, HBA MS 1209; to be published in REED: *Kent*, ed. James Gibson (forthcoming).

involved important companies: the Queen's Men, the Lady Elizabeth's Men, and the King's Men. One undoubtedly occurred at an outdoor inn-yard afternoon performance (Norwich), one undoubtedly was an indoor evening performance (Shrewsbury), and the third probably occurred at an inn, beginning at a door which issued directly into the streets at about 10 or 11 pm. The testimony in each case is not directed at reviewing the plays being put on but some details about the production conditions are preserved. At Norwich, the yard of the Red Lion Inn had a stage constructed within it, and admission was being taken at the gate. The stage was not too high to jump from, because two of the players pursued the malefactor into the street with their stage (real) swords, where unfortunately for us most of the testimony concentrates. The audience at the play included a worsted weaver, a yeoman, a servant, a draper, the brother of a grocer and two others whose occupations are not given.[37] In Shrewsbury, the robbery of the Exchequer had nothing to do with the Lady Elizabeth's company or the performance, except that the Exchequer was next to the Booth Hall where the play took place and the bailiffs suspected and examined some of the audience members. The respondents were being asked to provide alibis for the whole of Saturday evening and night, so if they are truthful they provide a fascinating picture of the pastimes of a provincial borough. The evening performance was attended by a troupe of local musicians, Ludnam's Men, who presumably had been hired to provide additional entertainment. One respondent claimed that he had left early because the crowd was unruly; others do not corroborate this testimony, so perhaps this was just an excuse. This was not the initial performance of the company's visit; their reward from the bailiffs was dated Friday 26 November (presumably claimed after payment was made at a performance a day or two before), and the robbery took place on the Saturday, with the examinations on the following Thursday.[38] Finally in Ludlow, at an evening performance, a wounding took place that is very reminiscent of the affray at Norwich both in the way it began at the door and spilled out into the street. Again, most of the testimony centres upon the affray outside and adds little to what we know about playing conditions. Beyond this, there are a number of questions I should like to ask about 'Old*es*treete et Galford*es*' where the incident happened. Can the house be located? Was it an inn, an alehouse or private house – and who were its owners? Was it the usual playing place for visiting troupes, or was this an unusual performance? Most important, can anything be determined about its size or location? One might think that answers to such matters are lost in the sands of time (as, until recently, were the Rose and the Globe); however details can sometimes be turned up, often in unsuspected places, and the aggregation of such details from across the country will prove fruitful. To give only one example, a Shrewsbury antiquarian, Thomas Phillips, described the Booth Hall as it appeared about 1770 (when the building was somewhat over 300 years old):

> [the Booth Hall is] . . . an old low timber building consisting of a large room 63 feet in length and 25 1/2 in breadth, in which the assizes, sessions and other courts are held; it is commodious but in no respect elegant; adjoining to it is a large room, commonly called the Green Room, but more properly the agreeing room, or Chamber of Concord . . . [where] the assemblies were generally held . . . At one end of the Green Room is the Exchequer, where the Magistrates attend . . .[39]

Phillips might have added that the hall was above a row of shops, which can be seen in eighteenth-century views of its exterior. He

---

37 The examinations are printed in Galloway, ed. *Norwich, 1540–1642*, pp. 70–6.

38 The examinations are in the Shropshire Record Office, 3365/2218, and will be printed in my forthcoming REED: *Shropshire* volume.

39 Thomas Phillips, *The History and Antiquities of Shrewsbury* (Shrewsbury, 1774), p. 133.

betrays no affection for the old building, which was demolished in 1784; we are fortunate to have its dimensions to compare with other town halls and to tell us something about the location of the Lady Elizabeth's Men's performances.

I have put forward evidence that provincial tours followed established routes, with organized itineraries – they were not aimless provincial wanderings, and in many places the players' visit resulted in a 'season' of play performances. If we put ourselves in the position of actors planning such a tour, it is very likely that the company would have a pretty clear idea in advance of the physical conditions of playing in the various households, towns and cities to be visited; they could rely on their own and others' previous experiences. What were their expectations? To try as far as possible to put ourselves in their place it is helpful to create a census of playing places used by travelling professional actors between 1564 and 1642, identified in records printed in Malone Society or REED volumes either published or undergoing publication together with the date(s) of performance or other records that specify each playing place, and a brief note about our present knowledge of each site. In the following list I have not noted records that state that a play was performed 'before m*aste*r mayor' or some such wording; while these are most likely to have been given in the town's hall another place of entertainment may have been used, because sometimes a different place than the town hall is specified for such mayoral performances. I have described demolished and obliterated playing places as 'lost' and have used the phrase 'not identified' in cases where the location or description of the playing place has not yet been precisely determined, or where it is still uncertain if a present building was the one then in place:

Bristol: (plays 1563–4–1586–7, 1596–7; regulatory orders 1585–6, 1595–6); the Guildhall; lost; in Broad Street.
(plays 1605–25); the Play House in Wine Street; lost.[40]

Cambridge: (1599–1600); the Bear Inn; lost; the innyard presently serves as Market passage.

Chester: (regulatory order, 1615); the common hall; not identified.

Coventry: (1600); the Angel; not identified.

Leicester:[41] (regulatory orders, 1582–3, 1585–6, 1595–6; plays 1590–1, 1605–6); the Guildhall; survives.
(1583–4, 1589–90, 1599–1600); Inns, one named the Cross Keys; not identified.

Newcastle upon Tyne: (1565, 1566); the Merchant court; not identified.

Norwich: (1582–3); the yard of the Red Lion Inn; survives.[42]

York: (regulatory order, 1592); St Anthony Hall; not identified.
(regulatory orders, 1578, 1582, 1592, 1595; plays 1581, 1584, 1585, 1587, 1588, 1590, 1596, 1597, 1599, 1600, 1602, 1606); the Common Hall; replica constructed 1960; original hall destroyed by bombing in 1942.

Devon: Barnstaple (1592–3); the Guildhall; not identified.
Dartmouth (1569–70); the Church; not identified.
Plymouth (1575–6); the vicarage; survives.

Gloucestershire: Gloucester (1563–4, 1565–6,

[40] This remarkable permanent playhouse was the property of one Nicholas Wolfe and is known to have existed from 1605. In his will, dated 2 June 1614, Wolfe left a number of charitable bequests valid as long as the playhouse continued to be so used by visiting players or inhabitants of Bristol. These payments continued to be made until 1625. The complete evidence will be published in REED: *Bristol*, ed. Mark Pilkinton (forthcoming).

[41] I have omitted 'Mr Ludlam's house' (1623–4) from the Leicester listing, because the context of the record implies that the playing that took place there was local in origin, and may have been only musical.

[42] Another Norwich inn, the White Horse in Tombland, is mentioned as a proposed playing place on a number of occasions, but the mayor in each case intervened to prevent the performances. See Galloway, ed. *Norwich, 1540–1642*, pp. 117, 146–7, 151 and 181.

1575–6; 1602–3); the booth hall; lost; on the site of the present Shire Hall.[43]

Gloucester (1589–90); the college (cathedral) churchyard; survives.

Kent: Canterbury (1574–5, 1576–7, 1582–3, 1583–4, 1585–6, 1588–9, 1591–2, 1599–1600, 1607–8); the Court Hall; not identified.

Canterbury (1608–9); the Checker (presumably an inn); not identified.

Dover (1575–6); Sprytwells (presumably an inn); not identified.

Dover (1615–16); the Castle; ruined.

Faversham (1573–4, 1577–8); the Court Hall; not identified.

Maidstone (1587–88); the Star Inn; not identified.

Norfolk/Suffolk:[44] Aldeburgh (1573–4); the church; not identified.

Great Yarmouth (regulatory order, 1595–6); the Guildhall; not identified.

Ipswich (1563–4, 1566–7, 1571–2) the Hall; not identified.

Ipswich (1563–4); Mr Smart's house (an Inn?); not identified.

King's Lynn (regulatory order, 1594); Trinity Hall (the town hall), St George's Hall; not identified.

Shropshire: Bridgnorth (regulatory order, 1601) the Town Hall; lost; in the High Street outside the east gate of the town.

Ludlow (1566–7, 1567–8, 1575–6); the castle; ruined.

Ludlow (1582); the New House; lost; at the junction of Broad Street and Castle Street.

Ludlow (1627); Oldstreet et Galdfords; presumably an inn; lost; at the junction of the present Old Street and Galdford Street.

Shrewsbury (1613–14); the Booth Hall; lost; opposite the Market Hall, on the present site of the Nationwide Building Society.

Somerset: Bath (1616–17); the town hall, not identified.

Bridgewater (1575–6, 1581–2, 1583–4); the hall; lost; in Fore Street.

Chard (1617–19); the hall; not identified.

Crewkerne (1637–9); the parish house; not identified.

Somerton (1605–6, 1607–9, 1621–2); the church house; not identified.

Suffolk:[45] Sudbury (regulatory order, 1606–7); the Moot Hall; not identified.

Westmorland: Kendal (1592–3); the New Hall or Moot Hall; lost; at the southwest corner of the present Market Place.

Worcestershire: Worcester (1587–8) Trinity Hall; lost; in Trinity Street.

Worcester (regulatory order, 1622); Guildhall; lost; in the High Street.

In addition we can safely infer that players visiting a household would perform in the great hall of the house, but I have omitted reference to these unless the records specifically name the playing place. Similarly with a record such as the fine at Newcastle-under-Lyme, printed above, we cannot discover if Thomas Dale's house was an impressive building with a room large enough for performances, or else was an inn, where the actors might perform either indoors or in the yard. Usually we can only locate the site of a playing place that has been obliterated by later destruction and rebuilding, or worse, we can only guess at locations of buildings of which every trace has disappeared. This list of forty-two specifically named playing places seems a sparse return from over three thousand recorded visits, but at least we can point to solid evidence for all of them. Further research on the ground in the various localities will, I am sure, bring to light

43 A performance in the Booth Hall is described by R. Willis in *Mount Tabor, or Private Exercises of a Penitent Sinner* (1639), pp.110–14. See Audrey Douglas and Peter Greenfield, ed. *Cumberland/Westmorland/Gloucestershire*, Records of Early English Drama (Toronto, 1986), pp. 362–4.

44 The 'game place house' (1563–95) at Great Yarmouth and the 'game place' (1583–6) at Wymondham are not recorded as playing places for professional actors, and hence are excluded here.

45 The churchyard at Bungay appears to have been used only for local players, and is hence excluded here.

2 The interior of the Leicester Guildhall

additional details about locations, and perhaps additional early descriptions of the buildings in question.

When we are lucky, as at Leicester, the Guildhall or town hall in which plays took place survives to this day, so one can stand in it and envision how plays might have been staged there. The accompanying illustration is photographed from a little over halfway down the length of the hall, and shows its eastern end (Plate 2). The hall originally belonged to the Corpus Christi Guild and was purchased by the City in 1562–3; it was larger than the old town hall which it replaced. The large upper hall measures sixty-three by twenty feet and the pitched cruck-beam ceiling rises to twenty-seven feet at its peak. In its floor area, then, it was about the same size as the Booth Hall in Shrewsbury. If we assume that the players would require about twenty by twenty feet as an acting space, and if Andrew Gurr's calculation that each seated spectator required approximately eighteen by eighteen inches, or 324 square inches, we can estimate an audience size of 355, or 300 if we estimate more conservatively.[46] Evidence from Bristol, where on two occasions the great press of spectators damaged parts of the Guildhall there, suggests that audiences sometimes packed themselves in.[47] At its eastern end Leicester's hall has a gallery (although the present structure dates from the nineteenth century) and there is an upper room behind the gallery whose original purpose is a mystery. A stairway at the right side allows access, although the present staircase is modern. At the western end of the hall is a low dais, which is original. Notwithstanding the later internal renovations at the eastern end, one can easily realize that the Leicester Guildhall provided a commodious and comfortable venue in which to act.

Can we reach any general conclusions from the foregoing list? During the seventy-five years during which converted or purpose-built theatres were used in London, it is significant that in only nineteen of these years (1567–76 and 1590–1600) were outdoor unroofed theatres the only ones available to audiences. The history of theatre development in the period, as Andrew Gurr has suggested, was in the direction of indoor playing spaces. By 1642 only two companies, catering to lower-class audiences at the Red Bull and the Fortune, inhabited outdoor theatres all the time while three indoor theatres catered to audiences of other companies.[48] The provincial evidence is startlingly similar. Of the forty-two playing places listed above, thirty-three are definitely indoors and a further seven (the unidentified inns) may have provided indoor playing space.[49] Only two indisputably outdoor playing places are specified. Travelling players may have had to contend with rain and mire on the road, as did others,[50] but at least they acted, most often, in dry and warm conditions while on tour. This was one of the advantages of touring. There was, I think, another. As a final, admittedly speculative, suggestion, we may note that touring also offered the advantage to the actors of a temporary relief from the onerous and continuing task of rehearsal of new

---

46 Glynne Wickham, *Early English Stages*, 4 vols. (London, 1959–), vol. 2, pt 1, p. 99.

47 The records date from 1575–6 (the Lord Chamberlain's Men) and 1577–8 (Leicester's Men). They will appear in REED: *Bristol* (forthcoming).

48 Gurr, *Playgoing*, p. 31.

49 Glynne Wickham attempted the experiment of mounting a production in the yard of the New Inn at Gloucester (at the time being run as a steak restaurant); he concluded that theatrical productions would have caused too much disruption to the operation of a coaching inn, and hence that players would have used an indoor upper room when they played at an inn. See *Early English Stages*, vol. 2, pt 1, pp. 188–9. However, the Red Lion's inn-yard was definitely used at Norwich, and the Boar's Head in London was simultaneously an inn and a playhouse, so it is dangerous to generalize about performances at inns particularly since so few inn-keepers' records survive.

50 On one recorded occasion (at Stafford in 1617) King James had to endure a three-hour wait in his coach under a gateway for a downpour of rain to end so that his royal entry could be staged in the market square.

plays for the repertory, and the possibility that a new play might not be well received. Instead, a company could plan an itinerary and choose, from among its repertory of recent proven audience favourites, the ten or a dozen plays that they wished to take on their tour of provincial cities, boroughs and households.[51] We might think of such a tour as a working holiday, somewhat more pleasant than the enforced banishment to bucolic backwaters that touring has often been taken to be.

[51] Bentley, *Profession of Player*, p. 197, notes that the Salisbury Court players took fourteen of their play-scripts on tour in 1634.

WRITING FOR THE METROPOLIS: ILLEGITIMATE PERFORMANCES OF SHAKESPEARE IN EARLY NINETEENTH-CENTURY LONDON

JANE MOODY

'A kingdom for a stage, princes to act, / And monarchs to behold the swelling scene.'[1] Such was Shakespeare's description of the theatrical space in which he wished his plays to be performed. Or rather, so Thomas Morton, a reader of plays at Drury Lane, sought to defend the existing system of dramatic regulation in nineteenth-century London. Shakespeare's plays, he claimed, should be performed 'only in the noblest temples of the Muses'.[2]

Until 1843, theatrical legislation permitted only Drury Lane and Covent Garden (the 'patent' theatres) to perform Shakespeare within the metropolis.[3] This article discusses certain 'illegitimate' performances of Shakespeare which took place at the London 'minor' playhouses. These establishments included the Royal Circus/Surrey in Southwark, the theatre in Tottenham Street, the Pavilion and Garrick theatres in Whitechapel, and perhaps most importantly, the Coburg theatre, now the Old Vic. Often converted from other non-cultural uses – an old clothes factory, a shop or a disused chapel – these new playhouses attracted not only the local gentry, but also *petit bourgeois* and artisan spectators: butchers, shopkeepers, sugar bakers, tailors and mechanics as well as hackney coachmen, sweeps and dustmen.

The commercial survival of local playhouses depended on their ability to target the interests of spectators from the neighbourhood. Nevertheless, managers also wished to encourage the lucrative patronage of genteel theatre-goers from Westminster. What deterred such spectators were the unrespectable neighbourhoods in which the minor theatres were often situated, and the 'vulgar' social constituencies which attended them. Reviewers too perceived the world of Whitechapel or the New Cut as a theatrical *terra incognita*: distant, exotic, primitive, and sometimes threatening. If ever the English Emperor or Empress were to visit the Coburg, commented one, it would be necessary 'to imitate the Roman potentate, by drenching the audience with rose-water to neutralize certain vile odours arising from gin and tobacco, and bad ventilation'.[4]

Accounts of minor performances of Shakespeare often read like theatrical travelogues of native culture for the amusement of a genteel readership. Although certain reviewers admired these performances, others laughingly dismissed popular Shakespearian consumption. Their derision seems to mask a pervasive anxiety about this theatrical disintegration of

[1] *Henry V*, Prologue, 3–4.

[2] *Report and Minutes of the Select Committee on Dramatic Literature*, in Parliamentary Papers, *Reports from Committees*, 18 vols., vol. 7, para. 3897.

[3] The Little Theatre in the Haymarket was permitted to perform 'legitimate drama' in the summer months only. See further, Watson Nicholson, *The Struggle for a Free Stage in London* (London, 1906) and Dewey Ganzel, 'Patent Wrongs and Patent Theatres: Drama and the Law in the Early Nineteenth Century', *PMLA*, 76 (1961), 384–96.

[4] F. G. Tomlins, *A Brief View of the English Drama* (London, 1840), p. 60.

established cultural and social hierarchies. The presence and visibility of 'vulgar' spectators at these performances, and their capacity to influence the choice of dramatic repertoire, seemed to threaten the stability and the integrity of the cultural state.

In order to avoid prosecution, the minor theatres needed to circumvent the illegality of their Shakespearian productions. House playwrights were therefore hired to adapt and recast the plays in accordance with the regulations governing illegitimate performance. At the same time, these playwrights reinvented Shakespeare for popular dramatic constituencies. Critics have recently claimed that the early nineteenth century is the cultural moment when a 'populist' Shakespeare becomes politically unpalatable.[5] Illegitimate productions of Shakespeare offer a different perspective on these arguments. My exploration of how theatrical practice and cultural politics map on to each other seems to make possible a more eclectic description of Shakespeare's cultural capital in nineteenth-century London.

The most obvious ruse by which Shakespeare could be staged was by reinventing his plays as burlettas or melodramas.[6] Playbills therefore advertised a 'serious Melo-dramatic Burletta, founded on a favourite and popular Tragedy to be called *The Mantuan Lovers, or Romeo and Juliet*' or 'a new grand historical spectacle' entitled *The Death of Caesar; or, the Battle of Philippi*.[7] These compilations usually retained the 'principal incidents' of Shakespeare's play, often adding a few extra characters for a comic subplot. Reviewers interpreted these changes in terms of the theatrical interests of the spectators at a particular playhouse. An account of *The Death of Caesar* reported for example that the adapter had 'introduced something of his own, which is probably better understood by the Surrey audiences'.[8]

The geographical location of the East-End theatres ensured them some immunity from the litigious eyes of the patentees. On the south bank of the river, however, the Surrey and Coburg theatres ran a much greater risk of prosecution. Glossop, manager of the Coburg, was prosecuted and subsequently fined £50 for representing *Richard III*, starring the controversial tragedian Junius Brutus Booth.[9] In 1828, the Coburg was threatened with prosecution by Drury Lane for proposing to stage what seems to have been an unadulterated version of *Macbeth, King of Scotland! or the Weird Sisters*. On this occasion, the new manager was keen to avoid a confrontation. Having protested against 'so inordinate a Claim to the Intellectual Monopoly and Domination', he withdrew the piece and a version of *Hamlet* based on Jean-François Ducis's adaptation was staged instead.[10]

The Royal Circus *Macbeth* of 1809 carefully signposted its own illegitimacy.[11] The opening address, spoken by Elliston, wryly pointed out

---

5 See Annabel Patterson's discussion of Coleridge in *Shakespeare and the Popular Voice* (Oxford, 1989), pp. 5–7; John Collick, *Shakespeare, Cinema and Society* (Manchester, 1989), pp. 19–20.

6 Burletta had become an umbrella term for performances at the minor theatres which for legal purposes included five or six songs in each act. See Joseph Donohue, 'Burletta and the Early Nineteenth-Century English Theatre', *Nineteenth-Century Theatre Research*, 1 (1973), 29–51.

7 Surrey playbills, 4 March 1823; 26 December 1823. All playbills cited can be found in the collections of the Theatre Museum.

8 *Mirror of the Stage*, vol. 3, no. 12 (5 January 1824), p. 185.

9 Middlesex Sessions, 6 and 19 January 1820. See *Morning Chronicle*, 10 February 1820; *British Stage and Literary Cabinet*, vol. 4, no. 34 (March 1820), 140–1.

10 For the controversy over *Macbeth*, which was to have been staged on 15 and 16 February, see playbills for 11, 15 and 18 February 1828.

11 *The History, Murders, Life and Death of Macbeth* (London, 1809). The theatre was not prosecuted, but Elliston's interpretation of the law was raised at a meeting between Sheridan and the Lord Chamberlain. 'The Justice was in a fury. Much was said about the illegality of your Circus Macbeth, when Sheridan slily observed, the greatest violation was to the bard, in *your* attempting the impersonation!' See George Raymond, *Memoirs of Robert William Elliston*, 2 vols. (London, 1844), vol. 1, p. 437.

that the performers were 'not indulged with fullest pow'rs of speech'. Here, the manager cautiously set out the theatrical terms under which he proposed to negotiate the law and yet apparently keep within the terms of his licence. The play was staged in dumbshow, with occasional rhymed dialogue. Linen 'scrolls' or banners carried by the characters and bearing such announcements as 'Macbeth ordains a solemn Banquet' or 'Destruction to the Tyrant' (Macduff's banner at Birnam Wood) translated or supplemented the events narrated in dumbshow. What in the patent houses would have been communicated to the audience primarily by linguistic means was presented at the Royal Circus in a non-verbal affective code.

Music accompanied the stage action almost throughout. One notable exception was Act 1, Scene 7, after the retirement of Macbeth's guests, and Banquo's presentation of the ring to Macbeth. The next part of the play bears the specific stage direction, 'very solemnly and strikingly performed without music'. The music stops, as if to express the encroaching evil, and eerie silence, broken only by the sound of the bell tolling, prevails throughout a dumbshow version of the dagger scene:

Lady Macbeth descends and listens at Duncan's door, and finds all quiet, she then enters. Macbeth and attendant descend. Macbeth discharges him, and moves lightly about. Enter Lady Macbeth. A struggle between her and Macbeth, he being afraid to execute the deed. Lady Macbeth then leaves him. An illusion of a spirit holding a dagger appears, which he endeavours to seize, but it vanishes when he makes the attempt. A bell tolls.

MACBETH Hear not that Duncan; for it is a knell
That summons thee to Heav'n, or to hell.
[*Exit*]

By the 1820s, however, caution had been thrown to the winds, at least as far as banners were concerned. Nevertheless, the presence of musical accompaniment continued to provide a theoretical safeguard against prosecution as well as an important theatrical language in itself. We know that the Coburg production of *Richard III* in 1819–20 was accompanied by music because of the testimony provided by Doobey, an assistant in the Covent Garden box office who had been sent to spy on the performance. Doobey stated that the Coburg *Richard III* resembled the Covent Garden production with the exception of an occasional, and almost inaudible musical intrument. According to one reviewer, a Surrey production of *Othello* as late as 1831 was 'interspersed with melo-dramatic music, in order to render it legitimately illegitimate'.[12]

Managers employed their house dramatists to adapt or 'melodramatize' Shakespeare for a particular playhouse. My argument is that this process of adaptation began primarily as a legal safeguard but also provided an opportunity to translate Shakespeare for popular consumption. Glossop defended his production of *Richard III* on the grounds that he had employed Moncrieff to 'melodramatize' the play; he claimed that the production therefore came within the terms of the Coburg's licence. Indeed, the extant evidence would suggest that the Coburg play differed only in its penchant for gory sensation. Doobey remarked that the scene featuring the murder of the children in the Tower (which took place off stage at Covent Garden), was staged at the Coburg in full view of the audience, accompanied by music whose purpose Doobey conjectured was 'to drown the cries'.[13] Moncrieff's adaptation seems to have catered to the notorious taste of Coburg audiences for 'blood-tub' drama.

In the wake of this prosecution, the Coburg management exercised more caution, and not a little ingenuity, in their Shakespearian productions. One tactic was to stage a different version of the story altogether. Milner's adaptation of *Hamlet* – staged 'at the request of

12 *Figaro*, no. 7 (21 January, 1831), p. 82.

13 *British Stage*, p. 141. Compare the Surrey *Macbeth*, where Macduff's children were murdered 'very properly off the stage' (Act 2, Scene 6).

numerous Frequenters of the Theatre' – was therefore based on Ducis' version of Shakespeare's play. The playbill somewhat gleefully emphasized that the piece 'is neither founded on Shakespeare's admirable Tragedy of the same name, nor is it for one moment purposed to be thrust into a mad competition with that sublime production'. The story of *Hamlet*, it was announced, provided 'a multitude of powerful Situations, capable of being Melo-Dramatically treated'; the resulting melodrama would be 'as interesting, impressive, moral, and terrific, as was ever produced in a Minor Theatre'.[14]

Ducis had transformed Shakespeare's tragic plot into a gothic melodrama.[15] The hero whose prevaricating introspection seemed to epitomize a certain kind of Romantic idealism becomes a decisive military hero who has returned in triumph after his victory over the Norwegians. Having dispensed with the *confidantes* for Gertrude and Hamlet, introduced by Ducis in accordance with neo-classical convention, Milner closely followed the plot of the French play. At the 'SPLENDID BANQUET Given in honor of Hamlet's Victory', Hamlet presents his mother with the poisoned cup, ordering her to '*Pledge his Father's Memory*'; her horror convinces him that she is guilty. She later confesses her crime at the elder Hamlet's tomb; Hamlet is on the point of killing her when he is forbidden to do so by the ghost's 'SUDDEN APPEARANCE'. Finally, Hamlet is put on trial in the 'GRAND HALL OF AUDIENCE' for his father's murder, and the attempted murder of his mother. On the point of being condemned, he is absolved by the Queen's confession. The conspiracy of Claudius is '*defeated by the Zeal and Loyalty of Horatio*' and Hamlet is proclaimed King.

It is clear from the language of the playbill that the fear of prosecution lay behind the Coburg's decision to stage Ducis's version of *Hamlet* rather than Shakespeare's. Ducis provided Milner with a convenient theatrical short cut enabling the Coburg to stage a play which was both Shakespearian and not Shakespearian, legitimate and illegitimate. But the melodramatic framework of Ducis' play may also have appealed to the Coburg dramatist. For Ducis recasts Shakespeare's plot within that familiar moral economy where the good are rewarded, and the evil punished in a last-minute reversal. The French play reinvented *Hamlet* in such a way that it would dovetail neatly with the values and ideology of the Coburg's non-Shakespearian repertoire.

Magna Charta; or, The Eventful Reign of King John was Milner's most distinctive adaptation.[16] Here a popular melodramatic subplot was woven into a Shakespearian narrative. Comic subplots were frequently interpolated in performances at the London fairs in the eighteenth century.[17] What is distinctive about Milner's translation is that it makes a hero out of a lowly French servant. In addition, Magna Charta, an event scarcely mentioned in Shakespeare's account, is placed in Milner's play at the heart of the plot.

Milner's *Magna Charta* was grandiose in scale and visually spectacular. The 'splendid and characteristic scenery' included an 'exact Representation of the Arms, Armorial Bearings, and Warlike Accoutrements of those Ancient times (1215)' in the final scene; it had been painted for the occasion by Wilkins, Walker, Pitt and others. The play's attractions included 'a DESPERATE COMBAT between the French and English kings MOUNTED ON

14 Playbill for 28 January advertising a forthcoming performance on 4 February 1828.

15 J. F. Ducis, *Hamlet*, Tragédie en cinq actes (Paris, 1769, new edition, 1815).

16 My reading of the performance is based on a playbill for 5 May 1823 and a juvenile drama text published by Hodgson. It cannot be assumed that this play script is a faithful record of the Coburg production. Nevertheless, it does provide a textual skeleton from which we can to some extent reconstruct *Magna Charta*.

17 Stanley Wells discusses eighteenth-century booth adaptations of *The Winter's Tale* including the history of *Doratus and Fawnia* in 'A Shakespearean Droll?' *Theatre Notebook*, 15 (1961), 116–17.

SUPERB WAR HORSES' and a 'GORGEOUS banquet' 'embracing the entire extent of the Stage'.

In *Magna Charta*, a comic melodrama of mistaken identities involving two French couples – Celine and Henrique, Louise and Basil – is incorporated into the story of the barons' demand for a charter. The hero of Milner's play is Henrique, Baron Falconbridge's faithful French servant. Henrique is a loyal and patriotic character who vows to sell his cottage and garden and to shed 'the last drop of my blood' fighting for his country. It is Henrique and the Baron who try to prevent Arthur's death; in its aftermath Baron Falconbridge is responsible for the creation and signing of Magna Charta. Watched by all the barons, Falconbridge brings the dead Arthur out of the moat; the demand for a charter to protect their rights and liberties begins from the contemplation of Arthur's death:

> See this, ye noblemen of England, and lament for ever! – here is your lawful prince inhumanly murdered! – Follow me, brave Barons, and let us swear never to sheath our swords till John shall grant us a charter to secure our rights and liberties.[18]

At Runnymede, King John capitulates in desperation and signs the charter in a last-ditch attempt to hold on to his crown. But the disguised Henrique (rather than an anonymous monk) offers him a poisoned goblet: the King drinks and dies, having accepted the justice of his fate as melodramatic convention dictates. Milner thus makes a poor Frenchman the author of the gesture which transforms Britain into 'the land of liberty'.[19]

Popular subtexts sometimes took the form of miniature plots as in *Magna Charta*; in other performances the addition of a single character seems to introduce a kind of ideological change or disturbance. Consider a Coburg performance of a favourite Shakespearian plot: *The Battle of Bosworth Field; or, the Life and Death of Richard III*. The standard acting version of the play incorporated part of Rowe's tragedy, *Jane Shore*. In a Coburg playbill for 1827, Shore, in an 'EXTREMITY OF DISTRESS' is 'on the point of DYING with HUNGER in the Streets'. Here however, she is rescued by a 'BENEVOLENT BAKER', who is promptly arrested for his trouble.[20] It seems that the Coburg compiler suddenly detected an opportunity to include a tragic version of the melodramatic rescue formula starring a humble character with whose status and heroism a Coburg audience might readily identify.

I want to turn now from the adaptation of texts for performance to the broader context in which illegitimate productions of Shakespeare were being presented. The meanings and functions of these performances were varied and distinctive: rivalry with the patent establishments, defiant flouting of theatrical legislation, signs of cultural legitimacy. Certain benefit performances conspicuously deployed Shakespeare as a weapon in metropolitan theatrical politics. *Othello* was performed in support of the Bill 'to relieve the Minor Theatres from unjust oppression, and thus give the Public an opportunity of seeing the regular Drama performed at other than the Major Houses'.[21] John Kemble Chapman, the manager of the New City, also staged *Othello* in order to help pay the fine which he had incurred at the suit of the patentees for having illegally performed legitimate drama at the Tottenham Street theatre. Although commercial considerations were obviously paramount in the selection of repertoire for such a benefit, the choice of Shakespeare for these performances also drew public attention to the fact that, according to law, Shakespeare could not be represented at the minor playhouses.

Playbills announced that certain Shakespearian performances had been 'requested' by the

---

18 Act 2, Scene 12.

19 Chorus, Act 3, Scene 18.

20 See playbills for 29 January and 5 February 1827.

21 Surrey playbill, 27 January 1832.

audience. A Surrey bill for 1832 described the proprietor having been 'waited on by a Deputation of Gentlemen, and others' from the neighbourhood requesting the performance of 'some part of the NATIONAL DRAMA'.[22] A later bill emphasized that the chosen burletta 'interspersed with Melo-dramatic Music, founded on Shakespeare's Othello! TO BE CALLED *THE VENETIAN MOOR*' was to be staged 'solely in compliance with the above request, and not in opposition to the existing laws, which it is his HUMBLE PETITION, and that of HUNDREDS OF THOUSANDS of this vast and enlightened Metropolis, may be forthwith altered and amended'.[23] Were these tactics a democratic subterfuge for circumventing dramatic regulation, or simply an ingenious dramatic puff designed to emphasize the management's determination to please its consumers even if it meant staging illegal performances?

A Surrey playbill advertising the 'highly popular burletta founded upon *King Richard III*' announced the inclusion of an unusual interlude during the Battle of Bosworth Field:

> MR COOKE will (accoutred in a REAL) FRENCH CUIRASS, STRIPPED FROM A CUIRASSIER, ON **THE FIELD OF BATTLE AT WATERLOO**, and which bears the Indenture of SEVERAL MUSKET SHOT AND SABRE CUTS go thro' the Evolutions of the **Attack and Defence, with a Sword in each Hand!**[24]

Here, a Shakespearian battle becomes a sign of a war outside the playhouse; the performance of *Richard III* a patriotic event. By putting on a French cuirass, did Richard/Cooke (the archetypal representative of the British tar) become in the minds of the Surrey spectators a British soldier at Waterloo? The cuirass seems to be advertised not so much as a cue for patriotic display as an authentic, yet almost supernatural spoil of war. A visual sign of the war with France outside the theatre, the cuirass was also a piece of exotic booty.

Shakespearian performances were a crucial way of signalling a theatre's aspirations towards cultural legitimacy. Playbills cited the performance of Shakespeare and other legitimate playwrights as evidence of the theatrical 'march of intellect', and the substitution of 'decorum' for 'jingling doggerels . . . riot and confusion'.[25] When the Coburg was prosecuted for representing *Richard III*, the manager's defence hinged on the argument that the patentees were trying to suppress cultural improvement and theatrical respectability. Glossop argued that to force the theatre back to 'ribaldry, nonsense, scrolls, and orchestra tinklings' would be 'an outrage on the intellectual character of the nation, an injury to public order and christian morality'.[26] By linking the minor theatres' dramatic past with immorality and disorder, the manager cleverly insinuated that theatrical democracy and the performance of legitimate plays were necessary conditions for popular cooperation in the social order.

Staging Shakespeare with a famous patent performer like Junius Brutus Booth or Kean also challenged the supposed dramatic supremacy of the patent houses. The Regency theatre in Tottenham Street even had the audacity to invite the patent proprietors to a representation of *Othello* to witness the superiority of their own actor 'on the above extraordinary occasion'.[27] But the most notorious example of an attempt at cultural legitimacy which backfired was the engagement of Edmund Kean at the New City theatre in Milton Street, Finsbury, and the Coburg theatre in 1831.

---

[22] 16 January 1832.

[23] Surrey playbill, 30 January 1832.

[24] 11 September 1815. The bill added that the Cuirass belonged to 'a Gentleman just arrived from the Continent, who has kindly lent it to Mr Cooke FOR THIS NIGHT ONLY'.

[25] Surrey playbill, 15 September 1832.

[26] 'Attempt to Suppress the Minor Drama' in the *Theatrical Inquisitor*, vol. 16 (February 1820), 99–103, 102. See also the *Morning Chronicle* for 8 and 14 January 1820.

[27] *The Times*, 10 January 1815.

Kean's engagement was presented by these playhouses as an incontrovertible sign of their dramatic respectability. Davidge's playbill alluded to Southwark's glorious theatrical history and the manager's pride 'in reflecting that the Preference for the first Appearance of Mr KEAN on this side of the Water ("the side on which the olden Theatres once stood, where Shakspeare, Massinger and Ben Jonson wrote and acted") had been given to his Theatre'.[28] In order to capitalize on the profits anticipated during Kean's engagement, the Coburg redesigned its theatrical space so as to provide stall seats. The playbill promised that those who had seen Kean at the patent theatres would 'find their Admiration and Delight at his splendid powers tenfold increased by embracing the present opportunity of seeing them exerted in a Theatre of moderate Dimensions, allowing every Master Look and fine tone of the Artist to be distinctly heard and seen'. Ironically, Kean's performance as Othello at the Coburg was marked by disruption as spectators loyal to Cobham, a favourite local actor, expressed their disapproval that Kean had invaded the native performer's territory. The *Tatler* commented somewhat wryly that Davidge's 'laudable ambition' of introducing Shakespeare, 'and his present best interpreter, KEAN', at the Coburg was unlikely to be realized 'till his audiences learn to abate much of their boisterousness, and approach nearer to his own good taste in these matters'.[29]

Reviewers flocked to the New City and the Coburg partly in order to gloat at the contrast between Kean's once glorious career and his descent to what they regarded as a theatrical Hades. Both these playhouses were perceived as plebeian and therefore unrespectable cultural spaces. Their neighbourhoods offered a distinctive collection of social and cultural signs through which critics interpreted Kean's performances. As the *Satirist* remarked, Kean must surely realize 'it will be transportation to no one but himself to exhibit at such a place'.[30] And whilst 'by no means for monopoly . . . we certainly *do* consider Mr Kean's present itinerary derogatory to himself, and degrading to the drama at large'.[31]

What was the significance of Kean's performances? Several recent prosecutions had highlighted the precarious legal position of the minor playhouses; the campaign to abolish the theatrical monopoly was now gaining momentum. At the New City, Kean – whether out of conviction or as a politic dramatic role we cannot tell – explicitly supported the cause of the minor theatres. He alluded to the declining state of the patent houses and 'their monopolizing spirit' and announced his determination to make the New City 'the rival of the large ones in talent, though not in style'.[32] Kean's appearance might not have fulfilled its financial promise; it did however provide more incidental ammunition for the minor theatres' cause.

We can see from the comments surrounding Kean's engagement that the status and 'respectability' of these theatres dominated reviews. Just as the tastes of popular theatregoers were being incorporated into Shakespearian adaptations, so these consumers and their insalubrious neighbourhoods were relentlessly inscribed on critical descriptions of illegitimate Shakespearian performances. Both critics and playwrights were deploying Shakespeare to write for and about the nineteenth-century metropolis. Since

---

28 Coburg playbill, 1 July 1831. Cf. *Tatler*, no. 260 (4 July 1831), p. 11.

29 *Tatler*, no. 276 (22 July 1831), p. 80.

30 *Satirist*, vol. 1, no. 12 (26 June 1831), p. 94.

31 *Age* (3 July 1831), p. 213.

32 *Tatler*, no. 225 (24 May 1831), p. 900, signed 'F.F.'. Whilst engaged at the New City, Kean was asked to appear at Drury Lane. He accepted, but insisted, much to the amusement of reviewers and supporters of the minor theatres, that the Drury Lane playbill should mention his appearance at the patent house 'by kind permission of John Kemble Chapman'. According to the *Age* (12 June 1831), p. 189, the Drury Lane management instituted an inquiry into the inclusion of this reference.

the minor theatres continued to be regarded as artisan domains, the interpretation of these plays was inevitably preoccupied with questions of popular cultural consumption. Cast adrift from the familiar territory of Westminster, critics tried to come to terms with the changing configuration of urban and cultural space in London – and the apparently inexplicable sight of Whitechapel butchers watching Shakespeare.

On the one hand, some reviewers welcomed what they perceived as improvements in the repertoire and productions of the Surrey or the Pavilion theatres. For others, however, these productions violated not only established social and cultural hierarchies, but Shakespeare himself. The claim that *Hamlet* and *Macbeth* 'are but little calculated for the multitude' was simply a convenient way of displacing into liberal paternalism the more determinedly conservative argument that Shakespeare should not be available to the populace at all.[33] We can identify these concerns in the critical antipathy which greeted the Surrey *Macbeth* of 1809. One reviewer accused Elliston of having transformed Macbeth into 'a musical retailer of eight line verses' and the manager was indicted for 'administering to the ignorance or depravity of the multitude'.[34] The *Theatrical Inquisitor* called for the theatre to return to its former repertoire of ballets of action and pantomimes, which suggestion produced an indignant reply from a local theatregoer congratulating Elliston on behalf of the Surrey inhabitants for his improvements to the theatrical culture in the neighbourhood.[35]

Illegitimate Shakespearian productions provided genteel reviewers with comic and satirical ammunition. One critic remarked that Farrell's performance as Macduff at the Whitechapel Slaughter House (*alias* the Pavilion) resembled that of a Whitechapel butcher.[36] Reviewers alluded darkly to the 'murdering' of Shakespeare at certain minor theatres, or the 'conspiracy now going on at the Queen's against Shakespeare's immortality' in the presence of 'a selection from the Tottenham Court Road sweeps, and the Saint Giles' vagabonds'.[37]

Laughing at plebeian consumption of Shakespeare was another more oblique method of policing those social constituencies which had, or should have access to 'high' culture. The rhodomontades which posed as reviews of these performances allowed their writers to replay as comedy anxieties about the consequences of these cultural changes. Burlesquing minor Shakespeare, and its spectators in particular, provided a textual form for critics to express, and simultaneously to dismiss genteel fears about the social and political consequences of popular education and knowledge.

Reviewers drove an aesthetic wedge between a 'genuine' representation of Shakespeare, and the travesty they had condescended to patronize at the Surrey or the Pavilion in order to recover some ideological ground and to shore up their cultural élitism. Shakespeare's own authority provided a convenient weapon for these manoeuvres. An account of *King Lear* starring David Osbaldiston at the Surrey for example scored its pejorative critical goal by invoking Hamlet's instructions to the players:

> When he repeated 'This is not Lear', the whole house, or rather those who knew what *Lear* ought to be, bore evidence of the truth of the exclamation. Whatever approbation he might have elicited from the generous shopkeepers who knew no better, his whole performance had the effect of making the 'judicious grieve'.[38]

This account is founded upon the gap, half comic, half disturbing, between an 'authentic'

---

[33] *Theatrical Inquisitor*, vol. 5 (December 1814), p. 403.

[34] *Theatrical Inquisitor*, vol. 2 (April 1813) p. 136, signed 'H'. in vol. 16 (January 1820), p. 34; the journal concluded that Lawler 'broke SHAKESPEARE upon the wheel by versifying him, and Mr. ELLISTON gave him the *coup de grace* by performing his *Macbeth*'.

[35] *Theatrical Inquisitor*, vol. 1 (October 1812), 68–70, signed 'Veritas'.

[36] *Columbine*, no. 4 (25 July 1829), p. 30.

[37] *Figaro in London*, no. 90 (24 August 1833), p. 136.

[38] *Satirist*, vol. 1, no. 19 (14 August 1831), p. 150.

Shakespeare, and a popular travesty. The reviewer is of course alluding to Hamlet's objections about that style of acting which 'though it make the unskilful laugh, cannot but make the judicious grieve'.[39] Hamlet's distinction between a 'judicious' theatrical constituency and those groundlings to which a 'periwig-pated fellow' might play for cheap laughs, is seen to have its nineteenth-century parallel in the Surrey performance. Here, the spectators can be divided into the 'judicious' (who share with the reviewer the right to make critical judgements) and the 'generous' (who can never be culturally enfranchised). A popular Shakespearian event is neatly and conclusively dismissed.

That broader nineteenth-century debate about social and cultural hierarchy, the nature and function of cultural provision, often breaks through the cracks of these critical accounts. Watching Shakespeare at a minor theatre was an unfamiliar and jarring experience to reviewers precisely because these performances made visible the theatrical interests of 'generous shopkeepers'. These playhouses were neither unequivocally genteel nor unequivocally plebeian places. Illegitimate performance seemed to resist assimilation into either the language of moral and biological contagion in which the middle classes sought to characterize the social 'other', or indeed the emerging discourse of social respectability. The old moral topographies in which the metropolis had been defined were losing their authority, but new interpretive maps which might have made these cultural spaces legible and familiar had not yet replaced them. And what was threatening about theatres like the Coburg or the East-End playhouses was that they made available cultural capital to social groups which until now had been theatrically disenfranchised. That Shakespeare was popular, and even commercially successful at these playhouses challenged existing assumptions that, as Thomas Morton would have put it, princes acted, whilst monarchs beheld. The presence of mixed social groups watching these performances no doubt seemed all the more incomprehensible in view of the increasing segregation of domestic and cultural spaces by class taking place outside the theatre.

I have argued here that the iconographic conventions of minor Shakespeare – banners, music and song – originated from specific legal circumstances. However, it has been suggested that these various adaptations and translations of Shakespeare must also be interpreted in terms of the social identity of their consumers. Moncrieff and Milner adapted and reworked Shakespearian material for particular local audiences. Melodrama – the prevailing theatrical form in the minor repertoire – offered a set of theatrical conventions and moral values through which Shakespeare was mediated and transformed. The critical ambivalence surrounding these performances reveals the way in which theatrical practice, and in particular popular consumption, disturbed existing assumptions about the control, dissemination and patronage of dramatic culture in the metropolis.

---

[39] *Hamlet*, 3.2. 25–6.

THE PERISHABLE BODY OF THE UNPOETIC: A. C. BRADLEY PERFORMS *OTHELLO*

MARK GAUNTLETT

A. C. Bradley's influence on generations of critics and readers of Shakespeare has often been remarked, as has the mixture of notoriety and respectful indebtedness which makes up his critical reputation.[1] Part of the importance of Bradley's work to the task of assessing the uses and effects of Shakespeare lies in its timely incorporation of two of the most influential impulses in modern criticism. Bradley's monumental *Shakespearean Tragedy*,[2] published in the shadow of the Victorian era, brings together Romantic criticism's emphasis on imaginative engagement with Shakespeare's plays and the psychologism which had been developing throughout nineteenth-century Shakespearian criticism and which, in Bradley's work, emerges as a mode of character analysis whose unrelenting detail and literal-mindedness are unrivalled even in the work of those critics most obviously influenced by him.[3]

Bradley, inheritor and perpetuator of critical practices hostile to the theatrical nature of the plays and to the incorporation of an understanding of the Elizabethan theatrical conditions which shaped them, is a reader of Shakespeare speaking to and instructing other readers of Shakespeare.[4] Yet an analysis of Bradley's first lecture on *Othello* reveals the extent to which he is prone to reverse the polarity of reading and performance on which his critical practice is based. Indeed, this first lecture on *Othello* (*Tragedy*, pp. 142–68) is here considered as a site which exemplifies the extent to which notions of 'theatre' and 'performance' in fact serve to sustain but at the same time to destabilize certain literary critical approaches to dramatic texts.

What Terence Hawkes terms Bradley's 'theory of reading'[5] is concisely announced in the most widely quoted passage from the Introduction to *Shakespearean Tragedy*:

Our one object will be what, again in a restricted sense, may be called dramatic appreciation; to

---

1 Terence Hawkes remarks that *Shakespearean Tragedy* is 'one of the most influential texts of our century, one which by now ranks as almost synonymous with the study of "English" and which, despite earnest efforts to unseat it, remains a key, and vastly formative work', in *That Shakespeherian Rag: Essays on a Critical Process* (London and New York, 1986), p. 31. See also the remarks on Bradley's standing in G. K. Hunter, 'A. C. Bradley's *Shakespearean Tragedy*', *Essays and Studies*, 21 (1968), p. 101.

2 A. C. Bradley, *Shakespearean Tragedy* (London, 1976). References to this work will be included in the text of the essay, and indicated by the abbreviated title *Tragedy*.

3 See, for example, Irving Ribner, *Patterns in Shakespearian Tragedy* (London, 1960). Ribner begins by remarking that '[al]though I have written in opposition to A. C. Bradley's principal tenets in his influential *Shakespearean Tragedy*, my great indebtedness to him will be everywhere apparent' (p. xi).

4 Bradley's academic career necessarily made him a part of the process of the professionalization of literary studies, but in *Shakespearean Tragedy*, at least, Bradley positions himself in the sphere of 'public' criticism. On this point, see Hugh Grady, *The Modernist Shakespeare: Critical Texts in a Material World* (Oxford, 1991), p. 37.

5 Hawkes, *That Shakespeherian Rag*, p. 32.

> increase our understanding and enjoyment of these works as dramas; to learn to apprehend the action and some of the personages of each with a somewhat greater truth and intensity, so that they may assume in our imaginations a shape a little less unlike the shape they wore in the imagination of their creator.
> (*Tragedy*, p. xiii)

According to this theory, then, reading, which has 'a vivid and intent imagination' as its prime requisite, is a means to an end; the imaginative re-creation of the drama (*Tragedy*, p. xiv) via the imaginative rehearsal of the process of its composition. In the sense, then, that reading is an act of repetition, the Bradleian reader does 'perform' the drama, but in a special and peculiar sense. In the almost mystical reading programme Bradley outlines, the written word of the text is the medium which contacts the ideal or imaginative essence that is the play[6] and through which, ultimately, Shakespeare himself is 'performed': through reading Shakespeare's plays, the reader 'realizes' Shakespeare.

The Shakespeare play, which has its essential existence in the mind of the author (and specifically in the process of its composition), must, according to this theory, have the same or an equally essential existence in the mind of the reader. But this does not adequately resolve the problem of the way in which this essence and process are realized in the mind of the reader. Since Bradleian readers 'read a play more or less as if they were actors who had to study all the parts' (*Tragedy*, p. xiii), there is the suggestion that some kind of 'theatrical sensibility' is required. Immediately, though, a rider is placed: 'They do not need, of course, to imagine whereabouts the persons are to stand, or what gestures they ought to use' (*Tragedy*, p. xiii). It is clear, then, that 'action issuing from character, or . . . character issuing in action' (*Tragedy*, p. 7), the cornerstone of Bradley's model of Shakespearian tragedy, is not character in action in some theatre of the mind, let alone on the stage. Rather, in taking the parts, the reader contacts and realizes inwardly the dynamic of 'inner movements' (*Tragedy*, p. xiii) that is a character.

The inwardness of character, in Bradley's model of drama and of reading, is tied in this way to the inwardness of drama. It is a point taken up in Bradley's 1902 Oxford Lecture entitled 'Shakespeare's Theatre and Audience'.[7] In a section of this lecture dealing with the taste of the Elizabethan audience, Bradley catalogues some of the uses of music and other sound effects in Shakespeare's plays, and concludes that as well as having an appetite for songs and dance, the audience 'loved few things better than the explosion of fire-arms' ('Theatre', p. 371). And in *Hamlet*, according to Bradley, Shakespeare satisfied this taste while at the same time producing what is repeatedly called this 'most mysterious and inward of dramas':

> And yet out of this sensational material – not in spite of it, but out of it – he made the most mysterious and inward of his dramas, which leaves one haunted by thoughts beyond the reaches of our souls.
> ('Theatre', p. 372)

Bradley's argument about the taste of the Elizabethan audience, and Shakespeare's uncompromised but ambiguous relation to this audience, will be considered more fully later. The important point here is that Shakespeare could appeal to the popular audience while nevertheless transcending his theatrical environment and indeed his own time to produce works characterized by an 'inwardness' which is the end of both reading and drama:

> The essence of drama – and certainly of Shakespearean drama – lies in actions and words expressive of inward movements of human nature.
> ('Theatre', p. 388)

As the example from *Hamlet* suggests, this

---

6 Hawkes, *That Shakespeherian Rag*, p. 32.

7 *Oxford Lectures on Poetry* (London, 1959), pp. 361–93. Further references to this lecture will be included in the text of the essay, and indicated by the abbreviated title 'Theatre'.

hypostasizing of inwardness depends on Bradley's elevation of an imaginative engagement with the play's ideal essence over the other orders of the play's existence. Ironically, it is on this basis that Bradley in fact justifies his decision to consider Shakespeare's theatre and audience in his Oxford lecture. In the Introduction to *Shakespearean Tragedy*, as well, Bradley concedes that studies 'of literary history and the like . . . are useful and even in various degrees necessary', yet sees them as dispensable in the face of 'that habit of reading with an eager mind which make[s] many an unscholarly lover of Shakespeare a far better critic than many a Shakespeare scholar' (*Tragedy*, p. xiii). But it is in the early stages of 'Shakespeare's Theatre and Audience' where the case is most fully developed. Here Bradley confirms that ignorance of the conditions under which Shakespeare's plays were produced 'does not exclude us from the *soul* of Shakespearean drama' ('Theatre', p. 361):

> Everything I am going to speak of in this lecture is relatively unimportant for the appreciation of that which is most vital in Shakespeare: and if I were allowed my choice between an hour's inspection of a performance at the Globe and a glimpse straight into his mind when he was planning the *Tempest*, I should not hesitate which to choose.
>
> ('Theatre', pp. 361–2)

Bradley's problem is the impossibility of distinguishing between that which is essential and that which is trivial or unimportant, and the possibility that even the patently trivial might prevent the reader from failing to appreciate or indeed from misapprehending the soul of a play or scene ('Theatre', p. 362). And yet, as I have suggested, this concession is made even as Bradley affords supreme value to the 'essential' in Shakespeare:

> Nevertheless, to say nothing of the intrinsic interest of antiquarian knowledge, we cannot make a clear division between the soul and the body, or the eternal and the perishable in works of art. Nor can we lay the finger on a line which separates that which has poetic interest from that which has none.
>
> ('Theatre', p. 362)

Far from being merely metaphorical, the repression of the body in this series of oppositions serves to focus Bradley's idealist conception. That which is essential in Shakespeare is of the soul, is eternal and is poetic; it belongs to the realm of the ideal, the transhistorical and the spiritual. That which is not essential – that which is relatively unimportant (but which might save us from misapprehending the soul of Shakespearian drama) – is of the body, is perishable and is unpoetic; it is corporeal, ephemeral, mundane and worldly. Which is to say that it is of the theatre and of performance.

As Terence Hawkes has remarked,[8] Bradley in his *Hamlet* lecture scrupulously follows his own dictum on the centrality of character to Shakespearian tragedy by launching (after an excursion into the matter of 'Shakespeare's tragic period') into an analysis of Hamlet's character, on which, he argues, the story turns. In the *Othello* lectures, the analysis of the hero's character is equally a model of Bradleian criticism, since it attests to the transparency of the text by taking Othello at his own word. Indeed, it is so excellent an example of Bradley's idealist and idealizing practice that it provoked F. R. Leavis[9] not only to rail against Bradley's enduring potent and mischievous influence more than thirty years after the publication of *Shakespearean Tragedy*, but also to testify unwittingly to this very potency of influence by using essentially the same approach in order to oppose Bradley's version of the play. As Christopher Norris points out, Leavis's debunking project in fact involves him in a curious pattern of compulsive repetition.[10]

---

8 Hawkes, *That Shakespeherian Rag*, p. 34.

9 F. R. Leavis, 'Diabolic Intellect and the Noble Hero: Or the Sentimentalist's Othello', in *The Common Pursuit* (London, 1952), pp. 136–59.

10 Christopher Norris, 'Post-Structuralist Shakespeare: Text and Ideology', in *Alternative Shakespeares*, ed. John Drakakis (London and New York, 1985), p. 60.

What is significant here, though, is that Bradley's analysis of Othello's character is delayed until several pages into the lecture, until Bradley has dealt with what, for him, is one of the key effects of the reception of a Shakespeare play, the way it *impresses* itself upon a reader. The matter is an urgent one for Bradley, not just because the impression made by *Othello* is an extraordinarily powerful one, but because it is this distinctive impression itself which creates problems for the reading of the play. Bradley's strategy here is not, as it is in the *Hamlet* lecture, to overcome the problems he encounters by reading the silences or gaps in the text;[11] and neither is it to remain silent himself about those scenes or actions in *Othello* which might be understood as achieving their full power or meaning only in performance, as J. L. Styan argues.[12] Rather Bradley confronts directly those aspects of the play which he and (he assumes) his contemporary readers find difficult to swallow. But this boldness, it turns out, is itself a way of making the play more palatable.

The distinctive impression of *Othello* marks the reader in two ways. The first is a matter of immediate imaginative response, the sensations the play excites:

> Of all Shakespeare's tragedies, I would answer, not even excepting *King Lear*, *Othello* is the most painfully exciting and the most terrible. From the moment when the temptation of the hero begins, the reader's heart and mind are held in a vice, experiencing the extremes of pity and fear, sympathy and repulsion, sickening hope and dreadful expectation. (*Tragedy*, p. 143)

The second is the sense of the play's imaginative atmosphere, which turns out to be far from merely metaphorical when Bradley comes to make his rationalizing appeal to an idea of the performance of the play:

> He [the reader] seems to breathe an atmosphere as fateful as that of *King Lear*, but more confined and oppressive, the darkness not of night but of a close-shut murderous room. (*Tragedy*, p. 143)

What is registered throughout Bradley's discussion of the distinctive impression of the play is its unpleasantness and painfulness. The result is that Bradley arrives at, or finds himself pushed towards a point where he must, having recorded the impression of the play, resist it by invoking a decorous resolution:

> it is marvellous that, before the tragedy is over, Shakespeare should have succeeded in toning down this impression [here, specifically, of the fatefulness of the course of the play] into harmony with others more solemn and serene. (*Tragedy*, p. 148)

But Bradley, anxious rather than serene at this point in his argument, proceeds immediately to question this desired view of the play. The passage which this questioning initiates is worth quoting at length, because it anticipates the moves Bradley will make to allay this anxiety:

> But has he wholly succeeded? Or is there some justification for the fact – a fact it certainly is – that some readers, while acknowledging, of course, the immense power of *Othello*, and even admitting that it is dramatically perhaps Shakespeare's greatest triumph, still regard it with a certain distaste, or, at any rate, hardly allow it a place in their minds beside *Hamlet*, *King Lear* and *Macbeth*.
>
> The distaste to which I refer is due chiefly to two causes. First, to many readers in our time, men as well as women, the subject of sexual jealousy, treated with Elizabethan fullness and frankness, is not merely painful but so repulsive that not even the intense tragic emotions which the story generates can overcome this repulsion. But while it is easy to understand a dislike of *Othello* thus caused, it does not seem necessary to discuss it, for it may fairly be called personal or subjective. It would become more than this, and would amount to a criticism of the play, only if those who feel it maintained that the fullness and frankness which are disagreeable to them are also needless from a dramatic point of view, or betray a design of appealing to unpoetic feelings in the audience. But I do not think that this is maintained, or that such a view would be plausible. (*Tragedy*, pp. 148–9)

---

[11] Hawkes, *That Shakespeherian Rag*, pp. 38–42.

[12] J. L. Styan, *The Shakespeare Revolution: Criticism and Performance in the Twentieth Century* (Cambridge, 1977), pp. 39–40.

If the distinctive impression of *Othello* is overwhelmingly unpleasant and even repulsive, how can this be made acceptable to an audience of readers who respond with distaste? At the end of this section, Bradley does take the step which seems logically to follow from his model of reading: he resolves that the distinctive impression of *Othello* leaves us with the impression that we are somehow 'not in contact with the whole of Shakespeare' (*Tragedy*, p. 151). Yet the alternative, that the impression of the play is not in fact the 'real' impression of the 'real' play, is registered in the appeals for a more forceful imaginative engagement with the play which recur throughout this section:

> All we can profitably do is consider narrowly our experience, and to ask ourselves this question: If we feel these objections, do we feel them when we are reading the play with all our force, or only when we are reading it in a half-hearted manner? For, however matters may stand in the former case, in the latter case evidently the fault is ours and not Shakespeare's. (*Tragedy*, p. 149)

But the acknowledgement of his own audience, 'readers of our time', and of the matter of their (dis)taste, confronts Bradley with the fact of the historical situatedness of reading itself. And a whole sense of historical difference follows from this. Paradoxically enough, Bradley is thus enabled to register this difference even as he promotes a reading practice whose sheer forcefulness would dissolve it: an appropriately intent reading of the play contacts its inwardness, he argues, and so absorbs the sensations which in fact define the impression the play leaves into an altogether more decorous tragic effect. In the same way, while the mere reference to the 'Elizabethan fullness and frankness' of the play's treatment of the theme of sexual jealousy locates the play historically but also theatrically, Bradley can use the available evidence of Elizabethan staging in an effort to override and in fact to censor those aspects of the play which actually define its distinctive impression.

If repetition is a sign of anxiety, then it is clear that Bradley's concern is focused on three actions in the play. These three actions – the striking of Desdemona, the treatment of her as a whore, and her murder – are identified, along with the sexual jealousy of the hero from which they spring, as major sources of the 'special effect of this tragedy' (*Tragedy*, p. 145). And in discussing the problems his contemporary readers have with this special effect or distinctive impression, Bradley again refers to these actions:

> To some readers, again, parts of *Othello* appear shocking or even horrible. They think – if I may formulate their objection – that in these parts Shakespeare has sinned against the canons of art, by representing on stage a violence or brutality the effect of which is unnecessarily painful and rather sensational than tragic. The passages which thus give offence are probably those already referred to, – that where Othello strikes Desdemona (4.1.251), that where he affects to treat her as an inmate of a house of ill-fame (4.2), and finally the scene of her death. (*Tragedy*, p. 149)

The way Bradley finally deals with these three actions involves reference in each case to a historical understanding of Elizabethan theatre practice and conditions. The effect of these references is anticipated in the curious and revealing note which accompanies the first mention of these actions:

> The whole force of the passages referred to can be felt only by a reader. The Othello of our stage can never be Shakespeare's Othello, any more than the Cleopatra of our stage can be his Cleopatra. (*Tragedy*, p. 145 n.)

The ambivalence of Bradley, a keen theatregoer, to the productions of Shakespeare's plays on the nineteenth-century stage is recorded regularly in *Shakespearean Tragedy* (as it is in 'Shakespeare's Theatre and Audience'). But it is important to note that Bradley does not set the 'Othello of our stage' against the Othello of the Elizabethan stage. Rather he sets contemporary representation against the essential Othello possessed by and realized through Shakespeare himself. Which is as much as to say that this 'real' Othello (or for that matter *Othello*) could not be realized on the stage of Shakespeare's time either. But in dealing with the three problematic actions, Bradley does use his historical understanding of the conditions and practices of the Elizabethan stage in order that these actions can in effect be largely explained away. The historical understanding he possesses is employed to argue that actions have their 'whole force', their real abstract expression, only when their 'inwardness' is realized through reading – only, in fact, when they need not appear at all. And so it is that Bradley can use his historical understanding to promote a reading practice which, if sufficiently engaged and forceful, does not need or benefit from this understanding.

It is more than convenient for Bradley that the first of these actions, the striking of Desdemona, can be rated as the 'least important' of the three, because it is the effect of this action which he has the most difficulty in ameliorating. Indeed, he is moved to confess that 'do what I will, I cannot reconcile myself with it' (*Tragedy*, p. 149); the reason being, he argues, that there is not sufficient of the necessary 'tragic feeling' (*Tragedy*, p. 149) to absorb the sensations excited by the passage in order to make it bearable. 'Tragic feeling' is a mysterious effect of the mysterious process of reading, achieved through the application of sufficient force in this process. But the suggestion that in such a passage Shakespeare 'has sinned against the canons of art, by representing on the stage a violence or brutality the effect of which is unnecessarily painful and sensational rather than tragic', that in such a passage Shakespeare has 'betray[ed] a design of appealing to unpoetic feelings in the audience' (*Tragedy*, p. 149), makes it clear that the matter of tragic feeling cannot be separated from the question of decorum. Indeed, the ability of the stage to accommodate the decorous at all is brought into question here, since that which is 'unpoetic', or which appeals to the 'unpoetic', is necessarily of the theatre in Bradley's formulation.

I want to take up the important question of decorum and of its relation to taste by returning to Bradley's discussion of *Hamlet* in 'Shakespeare's Theatre and Audience'. In a section which traces the circular case which would have it that the prevalence of noise and other 'sources of inartistic joy' ('Theatre', p. 364) in Shakespeare's plays reflects the demands of the popular audience, and that the popular audience can be defined by its liking for certain inartistic elements which recur in the plays of the period, Bradley makes this point:

> In *Hamlet* Shakespeare gave the public plenty that they could not understand, but he made it up to them in explosions. ('Theatre', p. 371)

If Shakespeare was not in the end writing only for himself, then both he and Bradley project an absent audience whose taste and understanding are above those of what Bradley reminds us were punningly referred to as the men of understanding and indeed of the rest of the audience. In the history of literary recuperations of Shakespeare, this is not an unfamiliar image: it is of the playwright divorced from his own creations, yet speaking through them to an absent audience to whom he is eternally present.

Yet the point must be made that in the first part of 'Shakespeare's Theatre and Audience', which deals at some length with the taste of Shakespeare's audience, the image of this audience is not nearly as clear as Bradley's throwaway line about *Hamlet* might suggest. Indeed, in the name of using the historical in order to save his readers from misapprehending the soul of a Shakespearian drama, Bradley generates an image of Shakespeare's relationship to his audience which is confused and inconsistent. After the highly qualified announcement that Shakespeare 'wrote, mainly at least, for the more popular kind of audience, and that, within certain limits, he conformed to its tastes' ('Theatre', p. 363), Bradley seems to equate 'popular' with 'public', involving the distinction between the public and private theatres. In this sense the whole of the audience is a popular one, whether they are 'Elizabethan nobility and gentry' or 'the mob' ('Theatre', p. 364). But within this generalized popular a distinction is drawn between the larger popular audience and the more popular section in it. This more popular section exerted the most obvious pressure on Shakespeare to write 'poor stuff' ('Theatre', p. 365); indeed, this section 'doubtless loved what we should despise', even as it 'appears also to have admired what we admire' ('Theatre', p. 364). Yet since this more popular section is distinguished from the larger audience only by the degree of its indifference to the classical unities and of its liking for excitement, violence and noise ('Theatre', p. 364), the whole of Shakespeare's audience, like the Elizabethan stage itself later in the lecture, is implicated in the blemishing of Shakespeare's work.

In the movement of Bradley's argument, the responsibility for the 'unpoetic' imperfections in Shakespeare's work lies ultimately with the Elizabethan theatre and its audience, although as a measure of the difficulty Bradley has in articulating this case it is worth noting that he does obviously worry over the question of Shakespeare's relationship to his audience. In a long note, Bradley sets out some reasons 'for at least diminishing the proportion of defect attributable to a conscious sacrifice of art to the tastes of the audience', yet in the same note he does have it that 'the question whether, or how far, [Shakespeare] knowingly "wrote down to" his audience, in the sense of giving it what he despised, seems to me very difficult, if not impossible to answer' ('Theatre', pp. 366–7 n.). Elsewhere, Shakespeare is characterized as a writer who 'neither resisted the wishes of his audience nor gratified them without reserve' ('Theatre', p. 365), but also as a writer who 'never needed to think of his audience, but wrote what pleased his own imagination, which, like theirs, was not only dramatic but, in the best sense, theatrical' ('Theatre', p. 392 n.). In tackling directly the matter of the 'poor stuff' in the plays, Bradley, as advocate, presents Shakespeare as answerable to a court of universal values on a charge that would ultimately be dismissed:

> I imagine that (unless perhaps in his early days) he knew clearly what he was doing, did it deliberately, and, when he gave the audience poor stuff, would not seriously have defended himself.
>
> ('Theatre', p. 365)

Shakespeare's taste is thus in clear distinction from that of his audience. Where these tastes intersected – where the audience happened to admire 'what we admire' – Shakespeare was in the fortunate position of being able to write what he wanted to write; where they didn't, Shakespeare was either writing down to his audience or writing for an absent audience whose taste he shared. This absent audience is of course Bradley and his assumed readers, whose taste is in accord with the 'canons of art' – as, in the end, is Shakespeare's.

So in the striking of Desdemona the Bradleian reader encounters the unavoidable 'poor stuff'. By appealing in this passage to the unpoetic feelings and demands of his audience, Shakespeare sins against the canons of art. But while in these terms Bradley can explain the unnecessarily sensational effect of the passage, the fact of its performance remains, a fact he seems to confront (even as he implicates the Elizabethan theatre in the barbarousness of the passage) when he bluntly reminds his readers that the action must occur on the open stage (*Tragedy*, p. 149). The second of the three actions, the treatment of Desdemona as a whore, must also occur on the open stage. But this must be assumed, since there is no direct discussion of the staging of the scene, or in fact of the scene itself. Instead, in an appeal which introduces the treatment of both the 'bewhoring' and the murder of Desdemona, Bradley urges his readers to apply sufficient force in the process of reading, to 'fully imagine the inward tragedy in the souls of the persons as we read' (*Tragedy*, pp.149–50). In the case of this 'bewhoring', then, it is *through* the passage that the reader contacts the whole of Shakespeare or the 'real' play, rather than *in spite* of the passage, as is the case with the striking of Desdemona. If, Bradley argues, the reader works hard enough in not misapprehending this second action, 'the more obvious and almost physical sensations of pain or horror do not appear in their own likeness' (*Tragedy*, p. 150). Bradleian reading in this case makes the apparent, the physical, disappear, or at least to appear as something different, more acceptable. This transformation affects not just the sensations excited by the scene, but also the scene itself. By way of this process, the scene seems to be figured as appearing as something other than itself on the stage, and is made, in effect, to disappear from the discussion. If Bradley's discomfort with the striking of Desdemona seems to be confronted directly, what can be understood as his greater discomfort with the treatment of her as a whore is registered in a silence which is masked by the appeal to 'tragic feeling', an effect whose sufficiency absorbs the painful and unacceptable impression of the scene.

Earlier, in the discussion of the striking of Desdemona, Bradley seems to acknowledge the power of Elizabethan open staging when the crowning dismissal of this 'unpoetic' scene comes in the reminder that the scene must occur on the open stage. But the limited application of this earlier admission becomes apparent when Bradley refers to the staging of Desdemona's murder in order to discolour the brutality of the scene. In this case the defence of the passage against the charge that it represents 'poor stuff' is mounted not just in terms of the absorption of the scene's unpleasantness into tragic feeling, but also in light of the understanding that the killing was not in fact openly staged on the open stage:

> Whether this would be so in the murder-scene if Desdemona had to be imagined as dragged about the open stage (as in some modern performances) may be doubtful; but there is absolutely no warrant in the text for imagining this, and it is also quite clear that the bed where she is stifled was within the curtains, and so, presumably, in part, concealed.
>
> (*Tragedy*, p. 150)

For the striking of Desdemona, then, the Elizabethan stage is implicated in the unpoetic repulsiveness of the scene due to its inability to mask horror or unpleasantness in something other than its own likeness, while for Desdemona's murder it is figured as a stage which enables action to conceal rather than disclose its own likeness.

To achieve this, Bradley mobilizes a reconstruction of the Shakespearian stage which involves what he calls the 'back stage', an area towards the back of the platform which could be curtained off to represent a room, tent, cave, cell, or the like ('Theatre', p. 378). This theory of Elizabethan staging is opposed to, but develops and works off the same realist assumptions as the theory of the 'inner stage' which had particular currency in the late nineteenth century. Bradley's reconstruction of the Elizabethan stage in these terms in fact anticipates its reformulation in the 1940s and 1950s when the 'booth theory', as it became known,[13] was held to be superior to the theory of an inner stage on the grounds that the use of an inner stage (or discovery space) demanded the withdrawal of the action into a cramped space within the façade of the tiring-house. Notwithstanding the increasing recognition that the booth theory, as much as the theory of the inner stage, rested on the realist assumption of the framing of action, framing effected in the realist theatre by the proscenium arch, the booth theory was applied to a reconstruction of the last scene of *Othello* as late as 1961 when Lawrence J. Ross[14] argued that it was preferable to inner stage theories

---

[13] See, for example, George F. Reynolds, *The Staging of Elizabethan Plays at the Red Bull Theatre* (New York, 1940), C. Walter Hodges, *The Globe Restored* (London, 1953) and A. M. Nagler, *Shakespeare's Stage* (New Haven, 1958).

[14] Lawrence J. Ross, 'The Use of a "Fit-Up" Booth in *Othello*', *Shakespeare Quarterly*, 12 (1961), 359–70.

because it enabled superior visibility and audience contact.

Yet it is on the grounds of invisibility, rather than visibility, that Bradley calls on the booth theory to rehabilitate the scene of Desdemona's murder. For one thing, the drawing of the curtains which separated the back stage from the main part of the platform – which Bradley takes to be the action called for by Lodovico's 'Let it be hid' (5.2.366) – allows 'the dead actors [to withdraw] into the tiring-house unseen, while the living went off openly' ('Theatre', p. 379). However, the illusionism of concealing the exit of the 'dead' actors is questioned in Bradley's own note on this point, wherein he recognizes that a complete curtaining off of the back stage – to the sides as well as the front – which would be necessary to achieve this illusionistic effect, would in fact prevent many spectators from witnessing the scene at all. In his note, then, Bradley concedes that '[t]he Elizabethans probably would not have been troubled by seeing dead bodies get up and go into the tiring-house when a play or even a scene was over' ('Theatre', p. 379 n.). So for Bradley, the framing and subsequent total concealment of the action by curtains is effective only for that part of the audience front-on to the tiring house, which amounts to an odd privileging of the groundlings who are elsewhere so much to blame for the 'poor stuff' in Shakespeare.

For Bradley, the real effectiveness of the curtaining of the back part of the stage lies in the fact that it conceals as much as it frames and reveals the scene of Desdemona's murder. As a move designed to dampen the 'sensations of pain or horror' excited by the scene, Bradley's reconstruction taps into a well-established tradition of scandalized response to the ending of *Othello*. Taking as his cue Dr Johnson's relief at having completed his revision of the scene – 'it is not to be endured' – Michael Neill detects an 'anxiety evident almost everywhere in the play's history – a sense of scandal that informs the textual strategies of editors and theatrical producers as much as it does the disturbed reactions of audiences and critics'.[15] Avoiding either the assault on the audience's sensibilities 'if Desdemona had to be imagined as dragged about the open stage (as in some modern productions)' (*Tragedy*, p. 150), or the total obscuring of the action by having the murder screened from the audience by closing the curtains upon the bed (as in some nineteenth-century productions),[16] Bradley's reconstruction doubly frames the scene by having it played within the booth curtains and, presumably, within the curtains of the bed. But since Bradley's reconstruction therefore figures the Shakespearian stage as a perspective stage, with (implicitly) a single, ideal position from which to witness the action, through the two frames, this very framing serves to focus as well as partly to conceal the scene. Like the pictorial tradition of epitomizing the play in the representation of the murder scene,[17] and, ironically, like the nineteenth-century theatre's effacement of the bed as the scene of the action, Bradley's reconstruction serves in the end 'to foreground not merely the perverse eroticism of the scene but its aspect of forbidden disclosure'.[18] Just as the pictorial tradition offered a 'voyeuristic manipulation' of the parted curtains, and just as the theatrical tradition intensified the audience's 'scandalized fascination' with the scene,[19] so the partial concealment of the action proposed in Bradley's reconstruction can be understood as actually heightening rather than dampening the sensations excited by the scene.

For Bradley and his readers, these are not merely the 'almost physical sensations of pain

---

15 Michael Neill, 'Unproper Beds: Race, Adultery, and the Hideous in *Othello*', *Shakespeare Quarterly*, 40 (1989), p. 384.

16 James R. Siemon, '"Nay, that's not next": *Othello*, v.ii in Performance, 1760–1900', *Shakespeare Quarterly*, 37 (1986), p. 46.

17 Neill, 'Unproper Beds', pp. 384–5.

18 Ibid., p. 385.

19 Ibid., p. 385.

or horror' which the process of reading must absorb into tragic feeling. They are in fact sensations which have as their focus the marriage bed – that key site of the conjunction of racial and sexual anxieties, whose presentation is for so long deferred in the play. This becomes clear if we return to Bradley's analysis of the distinctive impression of *Othello*. In that section which first lists the three actions which require special attention, Bradley links them to a major cause of the 'special effect of this tragedy', sexual jealousy (*Tragedy*, pp. 144–5; all quotations in this section are from this passage). For Bradley, sexual jealousy is, to adapt Michael Neill's phrase,[20] an ambiguous excitement. It is a 'painful' subject, which brings with it 'a sense of shame and humiliation'. But it is also 'engrossing'; 'there is no subject more exciting than sexual jealousy rising to a pitch of passion'. In what I can only understand as a displaced image of the black Othello's sexual violation of Desdemona, sexual jealousy works on Othello in a way which sees 'the animal in man forcing itself into his consciousness in naked grossness, and he writhing before it but powerless to deny it entrance, gasping inarticulate images of pollution, and finding relief only in a bestial thirst for blood'. This image not only displays the mixture of excitement and revulsion which makes up Bradley's attitude to the subject. It also suggests that his ambivalence at the *idea* of sexual jealousy is inseparable from his arousal at the *sight* of the fruits of that jealousy. It is indeed remarkable – in a discussion which insists on the primacy of the reading of Shakespeare's plays – how many times Bradley refers to the *spectacle* of jealousy: 'there can hardly be any spectacle at once so engrossing and so painful . . .'; 'What spectacle can be more painful . . .?'; 'This is what we have to witness . . .' It is, Bradley reminds his readers, 'generally hidden; if we perceive it we ourselves are ashamed and turn our eyes away'. But Bradley's eyes are drawn ineluctably back to it, and most particularly to its object: according to Bradley, the suffering of Desdemona is 'the most nearly intolerable spectacle that Shakespeare offers us'. We 'watch Desdemona with . . . unmitigated distress', but 'the sight of her suffering [is] exquisitely painful'.

What becomes clear is that when it comes to the scene of Desdemona's murder, Bradley's notion of Shakespearian staging has as its major effect the partial concealment of that which the imagination – which is both applied to and fired by the act of reading – must see. In this sense, Bradley here reverses the polarity of reading and performance which is the basis of his critical practice. For in this case it is the stage itself which masks that which, Bradley assumes for his readers, the imagination must look upon. In this case it is, ironically, the stage itself which makes poetic that which is unpoetic: it is the stage which renders decorous the 'real' play, the play which is enacted in the reader's imaginative rehearsal of the process of its composition. To rehearse the process of the play's composition – to read the play – is to inhabit its 'imaginative atmosphere', the fateful, confined, oppressive, darkened, 'close-shut murderous room' (*Tragedy*, p. 143). In this imaginative 'seeing' of the play, the reader cannot escape, and must witness that which is 'generally hidden', that from which, generally, 'we turn our eyes away'. Bradley's reconstruction of the 'seeing' of the scene in the Elizabethan theatre rehabilitates the scene by partly concealing it. But this reconstruction actually literalizes the image of the close-shut murderous room, and can be understood as having the effect of unleashing rather than harnessing the imaginative powers of both the notional Elizabethan spectator and the Bradleian reader for whom it is reconstructed. For in this formulation, the stage can reveal the 'real' play to the imagination even as it conceals it from sight.

---

[20] Ibid., p. 391.

PLAYING PLACES FOR SHAKESPEARE: THE MADDERMARKET THEATRE, NORWICH

FRANKLIN J. HILDY

In 1599, while the first Globe playhouse began opening its doors to the London public, Shakespeare's fellow actor, Will Kemp, set out on his 'Nine-days Wonder' morris-dance to what was then England's second most important city, Norwich. Fittingly, it was near the spot where Kemp ended his dance in Norwich that the Maddermarket Theatre, the first permanent Elizabethan-style theatre to be built in modern times, was opened on 26 September 1921. The Maddermarket Theatre was built by W. Nugent Monck, who was arguably the most accomplished and influential of the generation of directors who passed on the legacy of William Poel. By 1933, when Monck completed the Shakespeare canon – making him the first producer known to have done so – he was one of the most highly regarded Shakespearian producers in England and his Maddermarket Theatre among the best-known 'Little Theatres' in the world. Today, with the International Shakespeare Globe Centre building its new Globe near the site of the 1599 original, it seems especially appropriate to revisit the Maddermarket experiment and the work Nugent Monck did there.

Nugent Monck was twenty-four when he joined William Poel's highly influential revival of the medieval classic, *Everyman*, in 1902.[1] Monck played the part of Fellowship and for the next ten years he acted in Poel's productions and served regularly as his stage manager. Monck was able to observe Poel's methods in meticulous detail and seems to have grasped both the great potential and the serious limitations of Poel's approach. At the same time, Monck was developing a considerable reputation as a director in his own right, staging medieval and Renaissance dramas in what would now be called London's fringe theatres. By 1910 he was in the provinces staging outdoor productions of Shakespeare with his young assistant, W. Bridges-Adams. There, in the Norfolk county town of Norwich, he helped to found an amateur theatre group that is now one of the oldest continuously operating community theatre organizations in England and almost certainly the first such group to have worked from its inception with a professional director. They called themselves the Guild of the Norwich Players and over the next three and a half years, from 1911 to mid 1914, Monck juggled the task of staging productions for them with his regular work for William Poel and a new position as head of the Abbey Theatre School of Acting in Dublin.

Monck had been brought to the soon-to-be-famous Abbey Theatre by W. B. Yeats, who had seen his work and was impressed by his ability to teach actors to speak verse. Yeats wanted him to train a young group of actors to perform the verse dramas Yeats envisioned for

[1] For the full documentation of Monck's career see my *Shakespeare at the Maddermarket: Nugent Monck and the Norwich Players* (Ann Arbor: UMI Research Press, 1986).

the Irish Players. While there, Monck introduced the Abbey to direct lighting (lighting from the auditorium onto the stage) and to the thrust stage. He also managed the main company's second tour of the United States. In the midst of all this activity Monck still found time to stage the Mancroft Pageant, one of the large-scale historic spectacles for which he was later to become widely known.[2] But more importantly he visited the full-scale Globe playhouse reconstruction that England's leading architect, Edwin Lutyens, had designed for the Earl's Court Exhibition of 1912. Lutyens' Globe was intended to raise money for the building of a permanent Shakespearian theatre in London in time for the Shakespeare Tercentenary in 1916 but it inspired Monck to start planning for a small-scale theatre of his own.[3] Unfortunately, with the outbreak of war in August 1914, both projects had to be put aside. Monck joined the Royal Army Medical Corps, finding himself working as an orderly in Egypt when the Tercentenary arrived. Undaunted, Monck formed the '15th General Hospital's Music and Drama Society' and began staging Shakespeare and modern dramas in the Elizabethan tradition, with all-male casts. The society was so successful it ran for three years.

By the time he was discharged Monck was forty years old and had acquired a remarkable range of experience in directing. He had staged every type of drama from medieval moralities to the most contemporary plays and he had worked with small casts, large casts, all-male casts and all-female casts. From this experience he was developing an approach to directing that combined the clear quick flow of action championed by Poel with Monck's own strong visual sense and ability to communicate effectively with actors – two areas in which Poel had generally been found lacking. With the war's end he returned to Norwich and to the plans he had for a theatre of his own.

Just before the war Monck had settled the Norwich Players in the upper room of an ancient Norwich building called the Old Music House. There he had set up an end-stage theatre not unlike a small Tudor masquing hall. Upon returning to Norwich he ran two very successful seasons in that space before setting out to find more appropriate quarters for the style of production he was perfecting. Monck had been irresistibly attracted to William Poel's ideas concerning Shakespearian staging. He fully integrated into his own work Poel's notion that Shakespeare's lines should be given a rapid, almost musical, delivery and he was noted for his ability to teach actors to do this. He was also committed to the idea that scenes in Shakespeare's plays ought to flow from one to another without pausing except when a pause would have a clear dramatic purpose.[4] Finally, he shared Poel's conviction that to achieve the proper flow of action, the plays must be as unencumbered by scenery as possible. But whereas Poel, a trained architect, came to focus more and more on the vocal scoring of Shakespeare's plays, treating each voice like a musical instrument, Monck, a trained musician, was a Pre-Raphaelite at heart and focused on the visual beauty that could be created through minimal means. The wide platform stage thrust

[2] Monck's contributions to civic pageantry can be found in my doctoral dissertation *Reviving Shakespeare's Stagecraft: Nugent Monck and the Maddermarket Theatre, Norwich, England.* (Northwestern University, Ann Arbor: UMI, 1980), pp. 103–5, 277–9, 312–17.

[3] The 1912 Globe is discussed by Marion F. O'Connor 'Theatre and Empire: "Shakespeare's England" at Earl's Court, 1912' in Jean E. Howard and Marion F. O'Connor, *Shakespeare Reproduced* (New York: Methuen, 1987), pp. 68–98 and by me in 'Reconstructing Shakespeare's Theatre', *New Issues in the Reconstruction of Shakespeare's Theatre*, ed. Franklin J. Hildy (New York: Peter Lang, 1990), 1–37; pp. 18–25. The object of this enterprise, 'to erect, equip, and endow adequately a theatre as a living monument, commemorative of the Shakespeare tercentenary', was announced in *The Times* (17 January 1912), p. 9.

[4] Poel did not leave a concise statement concerning his goals for the Elizabethan Revival but Lewis Casson provided a clear six-point summary of Poel's approach in 'William Poel and the Modern Theatre', *The Listener* (10 January 1952), p. 56.

out into the audience, and backed by a permanent architectural set containing a small alcove and overhanging balcony, which Poel had so eloquently argued for, was therefore more important to Monck's work than it had been to Poel's own. Monck had learned that such a stage worked well for a wide range of drama. The economy of means it inspired suited the aesthetics of 'The New Stagecraft'. And the fact that such productions were ultimately less expensive was a great advantage for an industry that Monck knew would be in ever greater competition with cinema. Seeing Jacques Copeau's experimental Théâtre du Vieux-Colombier in Paris in 1920 convinced him that this was not mere antiquarianism; it was the wave of the future.

Monck found the space he needed in a disused Roman Catholic chapel in St John's Maddermarket Alley. The alley led from one of the numerous medieval flint stone churches, for which Norwich is famous, down to the square where madder root had been sold as dye to merchants in the wool trade. The chapel had been built in 1794 when Roman Catholicism was still ostensibly illegal in England so it was a modest structure, measuring 42 feet wide by 52 feet long on the outside and only 40 feet by 46 feet on the inside, and it had been unobtrusively set back in a courtyard half way down the alley's length. But the chapel had a high barrel vaulted ceiling which gave it excellent acoustics and, what was more important for Monck's purposes, it had galleries on three walls, 12 feet above the floor. This gave the building a ground plan not unlike the one conjectured for the Blackfriars Playhouse by W. J. Lawrence.[5] The galleries on the side walls were 10 feet deep but the one at the rear had a depth of 12 feet. This left a central open area that measured just 20 feet wide by 34 feet in length.

Within this space Monck built a remarkably large stage. It seems to have been modelled after the portable 'Old Fortune Stage' – also called the 'Fortune fit-up' – which Poel originally had built for a production of *Measure for Measure* at the Royalty Theatre in 1893.[6] The height of Poel's portable stage probably varied depending on where it was used but Monck set 3 feet as the stage height at the Maddermarket. Poel's stage measured 30 feet across the front and tapered to 16 feet at the rear. Monck's stage was wider at the front, measuring 32 feet, but slightly narrower across the back where it measured just under 15 feet. Both stages had an alcove at the rear surmounted by a matching stage balcony at 8 feet above. This was not a tiring house, however; there was no space for the actors behind it (Plate 3). Projecting out at oblique angles on to the stage from each side of this alcove/balcony structure were two stage doors, a feature not found on Poel's 1893 stage. The idea for these oblique doors originated with the Archer/Godfrey reconstruction of the Fortune in 1907 and had become a common feature of reconstructions by 1921. But Monck added lattice windows above those doors, a feature that does not appear on scholarly reconstructions until after the Maddermarket was built.[7] The alcove/balcony rear wall with the oblique doors on each side filled the 20 foot space between the overhanging side galleries of the building, but this still left 6 feet of stage under the galleries on each side with nothing behind it to complete the picture. To solve this problem Monck had another set of doors added along the same oblique angles as the first set,

5 *The Elizabethan Playhouse and Other Studies*, 2 vols. (Stratford-upon-Avon: Shakespeare Head, 1912–13), vol. 1, pp. 20–1.

6 Poel's stage is described in Arthur J. Harris, 'William Poel's Elizabethan Stage: The First Experiment', *Theatre Notebook* (Summer, 1963), 111–14. Further information is provided by Marion O'Connor in 'William Poel's Staging of *The Alchemist*: Some Corrections', *Theatre Notebook*, 46 (1992), 95–104, who points out that the fit-up does not seem to have been used after 1900 so it is unlikely that Monck actually worked on it.

7 The idea for these windows undoubtedly came from T. J. Lawrence who had written on the subject in 'Windows on the Pre-Restoration Stage', *Anglia*, 36 (November, 1912), 450–78.

3 The Maddermarket Theatre stage

thereby carrying the façade under the galleries out to the edges of the stage. Having two doors on each side of the central alcove gave the Maddermarket stage a pattern of exits and entrances much like those shown in the well-known Inigo Jones drawing of the Cockpit at Court. It also gave it a rear wall with a shape remarkably similar to that found at the excavations carried out on the Rose Playhouse in 1988.

Monck's stage had an overall depth of 20 feet which made it 4 feet shallower than Poel's stage had been. In both cases the overall depth included the small alcove discovery space or inner stage at the back. The open platform in front of the alcove had a depth of just over 15 feet at the Maddermarket and about 19 feet on Poel's Fortune fit-up. These stage depths compare quite favourably to the 16 feet 5 inches depth determined by the archaeologists for the stage of the 1587 Rose Playhouse or the 18 feet 4 inches depth calculated for the renovated Rose stage of 1592.[8]

Since 1832 when Collier first interpreted, or possibly misinterpreted, the Fortune contract, a

[8] The dimensions of the Rose excavations are taken from Julian M. C. Bowsher and Simon Blatherwick, 'The Structure of the Rose' in *New Issues*, ed. Franklin J. Hildy, pp. 55–78; pp. 63 and 70.

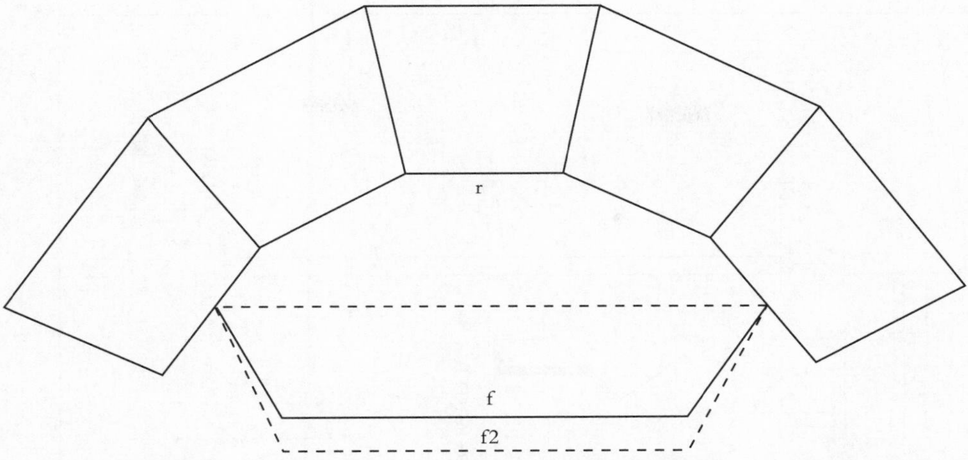

Fig. 3 The 1587 Rose stage divided into lower and upper trapezoids. This stage has equal focal points at f on the lower stage and at r on the upper stage. The primary focal point on the 1592 renovation was at f2

depth of 27 feet 6 inches had been used as a standard for all reconstructions of Elizabethan playhouses.[9] Poel had been forced by the architecture of the Royalty Theatre to make his 1893 stage shallower than this standard but by 1926 he was arguing in favour of an Elizabethan stage with a depth of not just 27 feet 6 inches but of as much as 40 feet.[10] Monck undoubtedly settled on his shallow stage at the Maddermarket for economic reasons. For every two feet of increase in the depth he would have lost an entire row of seats in the audience, his only source of income. But Monck staged multiple productions of every Shakespeare play except *Henry VIII* on this stage along with hundreds of other plays from the most ancient to the most modern. He never felt unduly restricted by this space and no reviewer ever commented that any of the productions seemed cramped or that they might have benefited from a greater stage depth. Monck's experience, supplemented by the Rose discoveries, must seriously call into question any notion that Elizabethan plays required deep stages. In 1990 the Norwich Players added 7 feet 6 inches to the front of Monck's stage. Partly this was to give the stage a forward taper like that found on the front of the Rose stage and partly it was to provide their modern directors with more space in front of the stage posts. Ironically, while this produced a Rose-like stage shape, it eliminated the shallow depth that is such a striking feature of the Rose discoveries. It has also disturbed the visual balance of the building's architecture. It remains to be seen whether this experiment has clear benefits for performance.

The similarity of size between the Maddermarket stage and the one discovered by the Rose excavations makes an analysis of the Maddermarket stage more valuable than has been previously considered. The Rose stage has been described as an elongated hexagon in shape but it may be more useful to think of it as two trapezoids joined together along their longest side (Figure 3). The trapezoidal section thrust out into the yard at the Rose measured roughly 27 feet across the front and widens to nearly 37 feet on its long side where the stage intersects the playhouse frame. From that 37 foot line the stage tapers back sharply, in a 'roughly' trape-

[9] I have argued this in 'Reconstructing Shakespeare's Theatre', *New Issues*, p. 6.

[10] Robert Speaight, *William Poel and the Elizabethan Revival* (Cambridge, MA: HUP, 1954), p. 247.

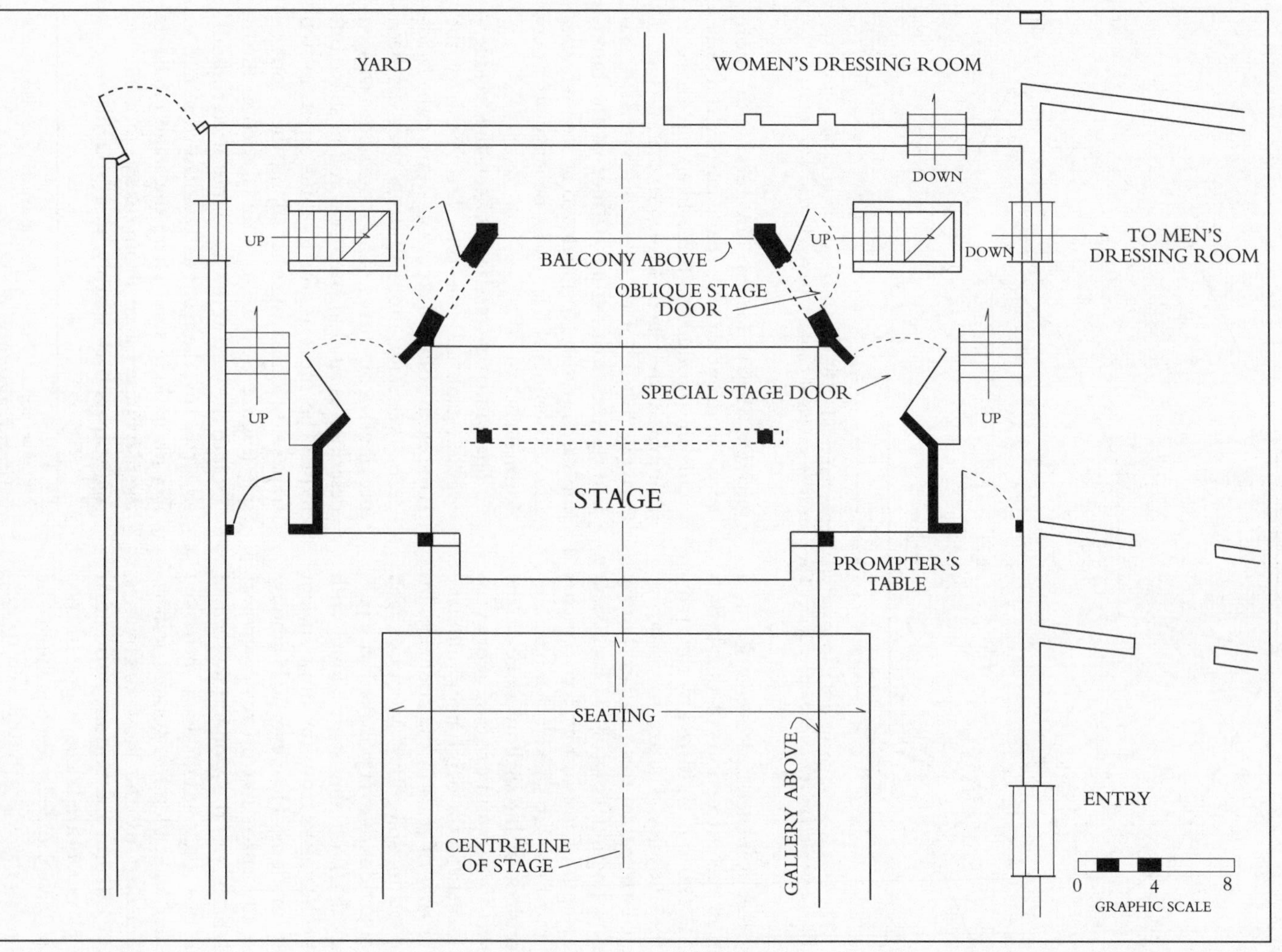

Fig. 4 Plan of the Maddermarket stage

zoidal form, to a short side of only between 10 feet 6 inches and 12 feet. In the 1587 Rose these two trapezoids are nearly equal in depth, just over 8 feet each. This is important because a trapezoidal shape tends to draw the viewer's eye towards the centre of the short side. This means that on the first Rose stage there was almost equal emphasis put on the front and rear centre positions. But in the Rose renovation of 1592 the front trapezoid is markedly deeper than the rear one, giving a greater focus to the front centre point on the stage. Monck's Maddermarket stage on the other hand was a single trapezoid measuring 27 feet across the front and tapering to 14 feet across the back (Figure 4). This made the Maddermarket stage somewhat smaller than the stage of the 1587 Rose and substantially smaller than the 1592 renovation. But it also significantly altered the point of focus, putting it at the rear centre. While this can be useful in drawing the audience into a scene, it can also take focus away from action near the front of the stage. In order to shift the audience's focus further forward, the Maddermarket stage made use of the stage posts and several sets of traverse curtains.

Poel's experiments had essentially divided the Elizabethan platform stage into foreground, middle ground and background. The foreground was the lower stage or apron, the open section of stage from the front edge back to the stage posts. The middle ground was the part of the stage that extended from the stage posts back to the tiring house. Since this space was up-stage of the posts in our modern stage geography, it was referred to as the 'upper stage'.[11] The alcove at the back, which later came to be known as the inner stage, made up the background division. On Poel's stage the lower stage (the foreground) was 12 feet deep ending with the two posts standing 16 feet apart at centre stage. These posts supported a false canopy. The depths of the upper stage (middle ground) and inner stage (background) are not documented but seem most likely to have been 7 feet and 5 feet respectively though it is possible that they divided this half of the stage depth into two equal parts of 6 feet each. At the Maddermarket a different geometry was applied. Here an attempt was made to give the stage more visual balance by placing the stage posts 9 feet out from the alcove/balcony background, a distance equal to one half the posts' height.[12] These posts were spaced just under 14 feet apart making them closer together, as well as being closer to the front of the stage than the posts on Poel's stage had been. The upper stage (the middle ground) at the Maddermarket was, therefore, two feet deeper than the upper stage used by Poel. But because the overall Maddermarket stage was 4 feet shallower than Poel's, Monck ended up with a lower stage (foreground) only 6 feet deep, half the size of Poel's. The major advantage of the stage posts was that they created a visual frame that could be used to isolate individuals or small groups so that they did not appear lost on the large open platform when alone on stage. By putting the posts so far down stage Monck was able to bring the focal point of these scenes to within 6 feet of his audience.

The division of the platform stage into lower and upper parts was the result of a suggestion by Karal Gaedertz, who had discovered the Swan drawing in 1888, that the pillars shown

[11] The terminology used for the divisions of the Elizabethan platform stage was admittedly confused in the early years of this century. The divisions used here were most clearly explained by Edward Everett Hale Jr in 'The Influence of Theatrical Conditions on Shakespeare', *Modern Philology*, 1 (1903), p. 173, but George Pierce Baker in *The Development of Shakespeare as a Dramatist* (New York: Macmillan, 1907), p. 220, called these three areas the outer stage, the inner stage and the rear stage, respectively.

[12] It should also be noted that the stage posts at the Maddermarket support a real canopy, the underside of which was used for attaching curtains and lighting equipment as well as providing a good reflective surface for the voices of the actors. The room required for this equipment may have been an important factor in Monck's decision to move his posts further down stage than Poel had done.

there must have been used to hide traverse curtains. These curtains could be drawn from time to time, it was thought, to cover changes of large properties like thrones and beds. Poel used his posts for exactly this purpose but Monck, seeking better proportions for his architecture, had left himself too little space on the lower stage to be able to make much use of curtains in this position. Lutyens had encountered the same problem when designing his full-scale Globe reconstruction in 1912. He simply moved the traverse curtains so they would divide the stage into lower and upper sections on a line several feet behind the posts, not between them. This was the solution Monck adopted.

The use of the traverse curtains, like the use of the posts as a framing device, helped shift the focus further forward on the stage. But these curtains create a flat plane and their regular use becomes repetitive and predictable. Monck was keenly aware of the problem and to compensate he added two more sets of curtains in the middle stage area. The first set drew in an arching line behind the posts while the second set formed a v shape. These two sets of curtains, in combination with the traverse curtains and two additional sets which closed off the alcove and balcony, could be opened and closed in remarkably varied combinations. And the opening and closing of these curtains became an integral part of the action in the productions. Actors manipulated the curtains in character, in full view of the audience. In Monck's 1925 production of *Romeo and Juliet*, for example, Benvolio and Mercutio entered in front of the closed traverse curtain searching for Romeo after the dance. As they exited Romeo entered through the centre of the traverse just in time to watch them go. As he spoke 'He jests at scars that never felt a wound' Romeo flung open the stage-right curtain. He then crossed and opened the stage-left curtain revealing Juliet on her balcony.[13] In this way the curtains could be used like a cinematic dissolve from one scene to the next. But they could also be moved with one single quick gesture giving a firm punctuation to the end of a scene or a startling opening to another. No matter how they were opened or closed the shape of the stage space was altered each time they were moved and the background was transformed with no break in the flow of the action. The manipulation of these curtains, furthermore, gave a very metatheatrical twist to the relationship of the actors to the characters they portrayed. Certainly the use of five different sets of curtains to move from scene to scene was not Elizabethan and Monck knew it, but it was bold and imaginative and by all accounts extremely effective.

The method of laying out the stage into three parts adopted by both Poel and Monck had a long tradition that predated even the discovery of the Swan drawing. Edward Capell had described the Elizabethan platform stage as being 'double: the hinder or back part of it rising some little matter above the front', as early as 1774.[14] But what could he have meant by this? If he was thinking that the stage was raked, as the stages of his own day were, what did he think divided the platform stage front and back? The Fortune contract had not even been discovered yet. If he was thinking in terms of a step up to an upper level, as Evert Sprinchorn has proposed in his discussions of the meaning of the phrase 'crossing over the stage', this would be our earliest suggestion for such a possibility and again it is difficult to imagine what physical evidence would have suggested the idea to him.[15] The third division of the stage, the background, came with Malone's conjecture of a rear balcony in the 1790s to which Tieck added an inner stage in a novel he

---

13 This scene is described by Norman Marshall in 'The Production of Shakespeare's Plays Today', *The Bookman* (April 1932), p. 63.

14 Quoted by Leslie Hotson in *Shakespeare's Wooden O* (New York: Macmillan, 1960), p. 100.

15 Evert Sprinchorn, 'An Intermediate Stage Level in the Elizabethan Theatre', *Theatre Notebook*, 46 (1992), 73–94.

4 The Maddermarket stage with its full complement of stage curtains. *Othello*, 1923

wrote in 1836. Tieck's inner stage was the only one of these features that was not validated by the Swan drawing, but, by the time of the Maddermarket's construction, it was a generally accepted part of the Elizabethan stage and Monck made effective, though judicious, use of it.

There is little disagreement with the proposition that there are a few scenes in Elizabethan drama that seem to require a space in which something can be revealed. The problem with proposing an inner stage to provide for such scenes is that, as G. F. Reynolds has pointed out, 'if we assume a permanent rear stage, our natural tendency is to look for scenes in which to use it, and try so far as possible for modern convention and realism'.[16] Monck avoided this tendency and used his inner stage sparingly, quickly letting the action spill out onto the full platform. He never fell into the trap of equating the use of the inner stage with realism in establishing the location of a scene. When Monck used the inner stage he used it for scenes that benefited from some distancing of the audience from the action. Othello might kill Desdemona on a bed within the inner stage (Plate 4 shows the setting for this scene in Monck's 1923 production) but Romeo and Juliet would never commit mutual suicide there. When Monck staged the ending of *Romeo and Juliet* in 1925, he used a moveable staircase to connect the balcony with the platform.[17] The existence of moveable stairs on

[16] George Fullmer Reynolds, *The Staging of Elizabethan Plays: At the Red Bull Theatre, 1605–1625* (New York: MLA, 1940), p. 133.

[17] This scene is documented in a review in *The Nation* (17 January 1925).

Spanish stages had long been known but their existence on the Elizabethan stage was not considered by scholars until two years after this production.[18] Monck's choosing to use one, therefore, was a matter of his intuitive sense of how a platform stage needed to be handled and predated any scholarship on the matter. With the stairway in place the stage balcony became ground level and the platform stage became the underground tomb. Juliet was on a slab centred on the lower stage with her head toward the audience while Tybalt's slab was off to one side. When Romeo entered to join Juliet he was therefore able to give his most impassioned speeches while facing an audience that was less than 6 feet away. But the formal declaration given by the Prince at the end of the play was delivered from the top of the stairs on the balcony stage. As the Prince withdrew the assembled characters filed up the stairs and exited the stage. By all accounts this staging was emotionally compelling and visually stunning.

There were a great many such moments in Monck's productions throughout his life; his most important work, however, was over by 1933. By that time, Monck's work was known world-wide and a long list of notable directors and critics were making their way regularly to Norwich to see the successful application of principles they had first associated with William Poel. Robert Atkins, W. Bridges-Adams, Harley Granville-Barker, Nigel Playfair, Barry Jackson, Harcourt Williams, Hugh Hunt, Donald Wolfit, and Tyrone Guthrie are just a few of the distinguished directors who made that trip and found their own work influenced by what they saw on the Maddermarket stage. When Monck was invited to stage *Cymbeline* and *Pericles* at the Shakespeare Memorial Theatre for the 1946–7 seasons his productions were well received but it was clear that his directorial brilliance had long since begun to fade. Those productions outshone the efforts of the Festival's youngest director, Peter Brook, but it would soon be obvious that the next generation of directors was going to carry the work on to another level, making Monck's efforts seem pedestrian and lacking in innovation by contrast. By the time Monck came to write his own comments on his work for *Shakespeare Survey 12*, the legacy he and others had passed on from William Poel had become so fully integrated into general theatre practice that few people realized how influential Monck had been in its formation. But the Maddermarket theatre and its Elizabethan platform stage was a remarkable achievement. It offers rare insights into the possibilities of staging in the Shakespearian private playhouses and it has been an unheralded asset in the development of our modern approaches to Shakespearian staging.

---

18 The idea was first raised by William John Lawrence, *Pre-Restoration Stage Studies* (Cambridge, MA: Harvard UP, 1927) pp. 16–23, and was later taken up by T. J. King, *Shakespearian Staging, 1599–1642* (Cambridge, MA: Harvard UP, 1971), p. 37. I have discussed this issue in relation to the Spanish stages in '"Think when we talk of horses, that you see them"; Comparative Techniques of Production in the Elizabethan and Spanish Golden Age Playhouses', *Text and Presentation*, 11 (1991), p. 65.

'A FAIRLY AVERAGE SORT OF PLACE': SHAKESPEARE IN NORTHAMPTON, 1927–1987

RICHARD FOULKES

The Globe, Covent Garden, Drury Lane, the Lyceum, Her Majesty's, the Old Vic, the Shakespeare Memorial Theatre, the National Theatre – these are the theatres which resonate through the annals of theatre history, the places where actors – and latterly directors – have sought the stamp of contemporary acclaim and a passport to immortality. But for Shakespeare's plays there has always been 'a world elsewhere': the stock companies, the London 'minor' theatres, the touring circuit and the repertory theatres. Quantitatively these alternative places have outstripped the patent and national theatres in their output of Shakespeare; qualitatively they have achieved standards at least high enough to sustain Shakespeare in their repertoires, but, with rare exceptions, their work has been overlooked. No doubt this is partly because of the relatively scant records available – no lengthy reviews in the national press, few memoirs by or biographies of the performers, little memorabilia beyond programmes, rarely a promptbook or stage design, only occasional glimpses through the photographer's lens. And yet the endeavours of these Shakespearians are worthy of attention; indeed to echo Linda Loman, in Arthur Miller's *Death of a Salesman*, 'attention must be paid'.

In no sphere is this truer than the repertory movement, which from Miss Horniman's pioneering work at the Gaiety Theatre, Manchester (1908), transformed the nature of the nation's theatre outside London and remains its foundation to this day. Shakespeare's plays were always fundamental to repertory, but, Barry Jackson at the Birmingham Rep apart,[1] attention has not been paid to their achievements. To rectify this omission on a comprehensive scale would be an overwhelming undertaking, but a start can be made on individual theatres. What place did Shakespeare occupy in a repertory theatre's repertoire and what effect did such a place have on the staging of his plays?

In his foreword to Aubrey Dyas' *Adventure in Repertory*, published in 1948, J. B. Priestley described Northampton as 'a town that is neither very large nor very rich – a fairly average sort of place', but asserted that the view that a history of its repertory theatre was 'of no great matter, except to people living in that town and its neighbourhood . . . would be . . . mistaken'.[2] An historic country town, some seventy miles north of London, Northampton has some proprietorial claim on Shakespeare since it was at Abington Abbey (now within the town's boundary) that Elizabeth Barnard, Shakespeare's grand-daughter and last descendant, lived and was buried. David Garrick planted a mulberry tree near to the adjacent church, but Northampton's status was not such

1 Claire Cochrane, *Shakespeare and the Birmingham Repertory Company* (London, 1994).

2 Aubrey Dyas, *Adventure in Repertory Northampton Repertory Theatre 1927–48* (Northampton, 1948), p. 5. See also Richard Foulkes, *Repertory at the Royal. Sixty-five Years of Theatre in Northampton 1927–92* (Northampton, 1992).

as to attract first-rank actors to its theatres. In 1884 the Royal Theatre and Opera House, designed like so many metropolitan and provincial theatres of its day by C. J. Phipps, opened as a touring house. Squeezed into a cramped site, affording a proscenium width of barely twenty-one feet, it was and remains, with its intimate red-plush auditorium, a quintessential Victorian theatre. The resemblance between the Royal and Shakespeare's Globe extends only to the essentials of all theatres, yet it was built with the expectation that Shakespeare's plays would be performed there regularly. Indeed the very first performance was of *Twelfth Night* by Edward Compton's Comedy Company and afterwards the theatre's general manager Mr Isaac Tarry pronounced that: 'We intend to cater not for a class but for all classes. There shall be Shakespeare for those who admire him – and who does not?'[3]

During its days as a touring theatre the Royal regularly hosted Shakespeare companies: Osmond Tearle, Charles Doran and, inevitably, Frank Benson, who presented as many as seven different plays in a week. It was the desire to control the theatrical repertoire that led to the foundation of the Northampton Repertory Players, who took up residence at the Royal Theatre in January 1927.

It was not until December 1927 that the fledgling company spread its wings with Shakespeare. Faced with the selection of a seasonal offering, the producer Rupert Harvey took 'an exceedingly bold step in producing for their Christmas show a Shakespeare work, in preference to a back-slang [sic], and possibly vulgar, pantomime'.[4] He escaped the strait-jacket of the customary twice-nightly performances by giving evening performances at 7.45 p.m. plus several matinees and doubled the run to two weeks. Although built as a touring theatre the Royal was complete with its own paint-shop with a drop-frame, which is still in active service today. In 1927 this was the preserve of Charles Maynard whose designs for *A Midsummer Night's Dream* were eagerly discussed in the local press. Maynard and Harvey were determined 'to get away from tradition . . . The traditional white costumes with gold key pattern is [sic] being thrown to the four winds and will be replaced by costumes of the most delightful colours.' Maynard established the tradition of 'also designing the costumes, shoes and wigs, not forgetting the Ass's Head to be worn by Bottom'. For Puck, 'an old Peter Pan', Maynard produced a costume giving 'the appearance that he had just been cut from an old oak tree'.[5] Accordingly the visual impact was 'extremely modern in treatment, the blend of colour and the futuristic touch of both scenery and costumes, at once strike the visitor'.[6]

Lighting was an important feature: 'really wonderful effects have been secured, that representing dawn in the wood being the masterpiece'.[7] More traditionally the music played by 'The AUGMENTED ORCHESTRA' featured Grieg and Mendelssohn together with 'Philomel' specially composed by Harvey.[8] In the true spirit of repertory no one performance was allowed to dominate: 'When one comes to individual performances, differentiation is impossible, so high is the general standard', though in retrospect James Hayter, then described as 'something of an athlete', as Puck stands out as fine casting.[9]

From the outset therefore repertory Shakespeare was different from touring. The designs, produced and executed in house, were 'extremely modern in treatment'; the acting company was an ensemble, affording regular patrons the opportunity to see familiar actors rise to the challenge of Shakespeare.

Rupert Harvey was succeeded by Herbert

---

[3] *Era*, 10 May 1884.
[4] *Northampton Independent*, 10 December 1927.
[5] *Northampton Independent*, 17 December 1927.
[6] *Northampton Independent*, 31 December 1927.
[7] Ibid.
[8] Theatre programme, 24 December 1927.
[9] *Northampton Independent*, 17 December 1927.

Prentice, who was inexplicably lured to Northampton from Cambridge where he had run Terence Gray's enterprising Festival Theatre. Prentice was obliged to adopt a much more cautious policy in his new post and the only incursion into Shakespeare was 'The Hubert and Arthur Scene' from *King John*, a play with local associations. Strongly cast 'the power and beauty of one of the finest passages in Shakespeare' became 'a triumph of artistry for Miss Vivienne Bennett as Arthur and Mr Godfrey Kenton as Hubert'. The bill was completed with Shaw's *Fanny's First Play*: 'there is teamwork about the whole production'.[10]

In 1932 Prentice moved on to the Birmingham Rep and his place at Northampton was taken by Robert Young, until recently a Labour MP and a founder member of Equity. Cecil Chisholm wrote of Young: 'Few repertory producers have experience of doing poetic drama on the grand scale. Robert Young of Northampton is an exception, since he has spent much of his stage life on Shakespeare work.'[11] Chisholm considered Northampton to be one of only four repertory theatres (alongside Birmingham, Bristol and Liverpool) capable of staging Shakespeare successfully. Young staged three Shakespeare plays: *Twelfth Night* in February 1933, the success of which encouraged him to present *The Merchant of Venice* in April; and *Othello* in 1934. All three productions were rehearsed and performed within the relentless routine of twice-nightly weekly repertory.

From early in 1928 the strength of the Northampton Repertory Players had been augmented by the considerable talents of Tom Osborne Robinson in the scenic department. Born in Northampton in 1904 Robinson had been determined to become a scene and costume designer after seeing Diaghilev's Russian Ballet in *The Sleeping Prince* (featuring decor by Bakst) at London's Alhambra's Theatre in 1921.[12] Robinson had trained at Northampton School of Art, but had been obliged to earn his living in printing; his association with the Royal Theatre continued until his death in 1976. The designs for Young's three Shakespeare revivals indicate that Robinson's early work was innovative introducing contemporary styles on to the stage of the small Victorian theatre. *Twelfth Night* was presented in three acts comprising fourteen scenes and happily the boldly geometric design for 'A City in Illyria' has survived, having been chosen by Cecil Chisholm for the dust-jacket of his book *Repertory: An Outline of the Modern Movement* (1934), an early indication of Robinson's growing reputation (Plate 5). Modern though the set designs were, the costumes were 'correct period dress'. Osborne Robinson was to return to *The Merchant of Venice*, and indeed Venice itself, throughout his life, but sadly no record survives of his first encounter with the play. His designs for *Othello* were described as 'in semi-expressionistic fashion' and surviving photographs of Desdemona's chamber show a bed canopied in modern-style fabric, with powerful, non-naturalistic light pouring in from a window at the back.[13]

Unlike touring actors who spent months, years even, in a stable repertoire or just one popular play, repertory actors had to encompass the whole dramatic canon week by week. For young actors this provided a thorough training in the repertoire and equipped them with the ability to master a role quickly. Important though repertory was as a training ground only a small proportion of aspirants went on to stardom; for many repertory was to become a lifelong occupation. Amongst the senior ranks certain actors achieved the status of 'repertory star', capable of giving bravura

---

10 *Daily Echo* (Northampton), 27 May 1930.

11 Cecil Chisholm, *Repertory An Outline of the Modern Theatre Movement* (London, 1934), pp. 130–1.

12 *Patron Extraordinaire A Tribute to Osborne Robinson O.B.E.* (Northampton, 1976) and Colin Robinson, *Thomas Osborne Robinson O.B.E.: Beginnings* (Northampton, 1977).

13 *Northampton Independent*, 3 March 1934.

5 *Twelfth Night*, 1933. 'A City in Illyria'

performances in recent West End successes and in Shakespeare. The most productive conjunction was that between a talented newcomer and an established actor, the former's performance being lifted by the latter's experience.

Young assembled a company with the right balance. Oswald Dale Roberts, a clergyman's son educated at Shrewsbury School and Exeter College, Oxford, was about forty years old at the time. His career, which had included three years with Frank Benson, had been spent entirely in the provinces and he was a great favourite in Northampton. As Sir Toby Belch 'he was absolutely in the right environment';[14] his Shylock was 'marked by excellence. His clever facial expression is convincing and subtle';[15] and as Iago, 'One gets tired of handing out bouquets to Mr Dale Roberts, but his Iago, one must again record, is a triumph in which every point is made, every emphasis correct.'[16]

In *Twelfth Night* the young Lois Obee (later Sonia Dresdel) was acclaimed as 'a born Shakespearean actress' as Viola;[17] she was 'a charmingly vivacious Portia. She enters into the scheme to masquerade as the youthful advocate with a girlish enthusiasm that is delightful, and her deportment and delivery of her lines in the trial scene are especially good'.[18] Lois Obee left

[14] *Chronicle and Echo* (Northampton), 28 February 1933.
[15] *Era*, 6 April 1933.
[16] *Chronicle and Echo*, 5 March 1934.
[17] *Chronicle and Echo*, 28 February 1933.
[18] *Era*, 6 April 1933.

the company before the production of *Othello*, but in Freda Jackson, Young had a major actress in the making; she was 'an ideal Desdemona', sharing 'the honours of the evening' with Dale Roberts.[19]

The importance of a permanent company is indicated by the continuity between Young's three Shakespeare productions. Noel Howlett: Orsino, Bassanio; Peter Rosser: A Sea Captain/ Fabian, Antonio and Othello; Sheila Millar: Olivia, Nerissa and Bianca; Stringer Davis: Malvolio and Morocco; Joan Kemp-Welch: Maria and Jessica. For *Othello* Errol Flynn had joined the company, playing First Senator and Lodovico, not, as he later claimed, Othello.[20] The credit for assembling and harnessing these talents was, of course, Robert Young's and he was repeatedly commended for his excellent work. Not only was Northampton creating its own Shakespeare, but 'in each instance they have played to good houses – much larger than touring companies have done'.[21]

Bladon Peake, who took over as producer in 1935, had experience in both the amateur and professional theatre, including a spell at the Abbey Theatre, Dublin. Remission of entertainment tax for 'educational plays' reinforced Peake's inclination towards a more adventurous repertoire – he introduced an annual Dryden Festival – but his experience showed that play selection must be matched by acting talent skilfully deployed.

The burgeoning talent of Tom Osborne Robinson was at Peake's disposal. For *The Taming of the Shrew* Robinson supplied 'some inspired treatments', using modern hangings, stylized arches and bright lighting, but again period (Elizabethan) costume.[22] His *Macbeth* designs were in 'a symbolised style . . . with an almost entire disregard of the conventional'.[23] The set featured 'two pillars (symbolising Macbeth and his wife) which dominate every scene and through whose cleverly concealed transparence the "spirits" of the murderous couple are often visible in a most arresting fashion'.[24] Other features included: 'The gradual unfolding of the trees into three witches' and, later, 'the shadows of the dread spectres seem to rise out of the cauldron'; and 'the array of giant battle-spears before Dunsinane'.[25] This time the costumes were in a stylized convention. With *Macbeth* Robinson had indulged himself rather than put his talents to the service of the play.

Furthermore the acting strength of the company was inadequate to counter these scenic distractions. Oswald Dale Roberts provided ballast as Baptista, but left the company soon afterwards. Alastair MacIntyre, though equal to Petruchio, was woefully o'er parted as Macbeth. Instead of casting Olga Murgatroyd, who had been a spirited Bianca, as Lady Macbeth Peake wasted her on Fleance, entrusting Lady Macbeth to Betty Larke-Smith, whose only previous Shakespearian credit was the Widow in *The Taming of the Shrew* and who suffered from 'her natural disadvantage (in this case) of a charming personality'.[26] Peake had previously produced *Macbeth* at the Abbey Theatre and Osborne Robinson went on to design (in a much simpler style) Ben Iden Payne's 1938 Stratford production, but neither man enhanced his reputation with the Northampton production.

The board dispensed with Peake's services in 1937 and so precarious were its finances that the prospect of further Shakespeare was uncertain. By May 1938 the theatre had marshalled its resources sufficiently to stage *Romeo and Juliet*. In the meantime Osborne Robinson had seen *Romeo e Giulietta* in Venice in 1937: 'The vast

[19] *Stage*, 8 March 1934.

[20] Errol Flynn, *My Wicked, Wicked Ways* (New York 1959, 17th edn, New York, 1985), p. 162: 'I played the title role in *Othello*. My performance is still remembered; it was said I made the worst Othello in the history of the English stage.'

[21] *Stage*, 8 March 1934.

[22] *Northampton Independent*, 29 November 1935.

[23] *Northampton Independent*, 20 March 1936.

[24] Ibid.

[25] *Chronicle and Echo*, 17 March 1936.

[26] Ibid.

stage, built on the scale of a film set, provided for almost continuous action' – how different from the confines of the Royal Theatre.[27] Robinson's own sets were 'as realistic as possible', but required frequent changes for the eighteen scenes (in five acts) and inevitably the 'outstandingly effective' frontcloth was used continuously, even though with 'the play . . . being performed twice nightly . . . whole scenes will have to be left out'.[28] The casting of Sarah Churchill as Juliet attracted attention founded more on her famous father and her much publicized marriage (to the comedian Vic Oliver) than her own acting ability. Arthur Lawrence was a manly Romeo, but the production (by William Sherwood) relied on the supporting cast for its acting strength. This was emphatically not the case when *Romeo and Juliet* was given a reprise in October 1939 with guest appearances by Godfrey Kenton ('a brilliant interpretation of Romeo') and Vivienne Bennett ('a clever characterisation' of Juliet).[29] Black-out restrictions now enforced once-nightly performances, thereby alleviating the savagery of the cuts enforced by twice-nightly repertory.

The pre-war experience of the Northampton Repertory Players yields some precepts about Shakespeare in 'a fairly average sort of place'. The actual quantity of Shakespeare available was on average less (certainly in terms of plays and generally also in playing weeks) than under the touring system. However with repertory Northampton could develop its own style. The Victorian theatre was not inimical to experimental design (semi-expressionistic; 'symbolised') and the main snare was the designer over-reaching himself. A good permanent company was capable of impressive individual performances and team-work, but the choice of play and the casting were crucial if strengths rather than weaknesses were to be to the fore. There was no audience resistance to Shakespeare as such, indeed if the company had won patrons' confidence the prospect of seeing them in Shakespeare was an added inducement.

There was no Shakespeare during the war. The difficulties of assembling a sufficiently large and well-balanced company were too great and with clothing materials rationed it would have been impossible to produce costumes in house. In March 1948 Alex Reeve staged *Twelfth Night*, with sets and costumes (made in the theatre wardrobe by the long-serving wardrobe mistress Emily Tuckley) by Osborne Robinson to lighten the mood of post-war austerity: 'It is rightly played with a minimum of scene and the maximum use of lighting plot taking as its theme for set and costume the note "high fantastical."' The action was 'unimpeded by the modern convention of curtain'.[30] The Malvolio Lionel Hamilton, then in his late thirties, had joined the company in 1946 and was to remain its mainstay for many years. He presented 'a commendably restrained and melancholy Malvolio', but 'the honours' were 'almost equally shared'.[31] Despite this success six years (during three of which the company also performed in Kettering) were to elapse before Shakespeare returned and then it was under the direction of Professor Joseph Wright of Vanderbilt University Tennessee, who was sharing a Ford Foundation exchange with Alex Reeve.

Wright turned to *Much Ado About Nothing* for his farewell production, by which time he had got the measure of weekly rep: 'I had never produced a play in five three-hour rehearsals. I learned fast. The actors were most helpful. They knew each other's strengths and weaknesses, and they were skilful in capitalising on the former and hiding the latter.'[32] That the result was judged to be 'at about the level of a modern pot-boiler'[33] may sound demeaning to

---

27 Theatre programme, 16 March 1938.
28 *Chronicle and Echo*, 24 May 1938.
29 *Stage*, 5 October 1939.
30 *Chronicle and Echo*, 8 March 1948.
31 Ibid.
32 Correspondence from Professor Wright.
33 *Chronicle and Echo*, 24 March 1954.

Shakespeare, but it does show that a well-tuned repertory company could deliver an assured and entertaining production albeit one that left the play's subtleties and profundities largely unexplored. Lionel Hamilton was a competent Benedick, partnered by Evangeline Banks as Beatrice. Other members of the cast formed the core of a company which was to remain stable for many years: Tenniel Evans (Claudio), Donald Churchill (Borachio), Arthur Pentelow (Dogberry) and Anne Jameson (Margaret). Osborne Robinson consolidated his post-war style with a colourful permanent set and costumes to match.

The 1950s were not propitious times for repertory (many companies closed down). Audiences were sapped away by the novelty of television and state subsidy had yet to come on stream. Shakespeare in an old-fashioned theatre posed a double disincentive. For *As You Like It* in 1955 1,100 out of the 1,800 permanent seat holders cancelled their seats and in the first week attendance fell from the customary 4,000-plus to 3,653. Fortunately the production had been scheduled for two weeks and by the second 'there was quite a rush on the box office as the success of the production "got around"'.[34]

A Midsummer Night's Dream in 1956 provided Osborne Robinson with the opportunity to indulge his 'high fantastical style', which reached its annual apogee in the seasonal pantomime. Indeed his Shakespearian designs in the 1950s had more than a little of his pantomime style about them.

The company for *As You Like It* and *A Midsummer Night's Dream* (both produced by Reeve) was fairly constant: Evangeline Banks: Audrey and Hippolyta; Tenniel Evans: Touchstone and Theseus; Arthur Pentelow: the Banished Duke and Bottom; Anne Jameson for Celia and Lionel Hamilton for Jaques. Mary Kenton (Godfrey's second wife) played Rosalind and Titania and the young Nigel Hawthorne was a 'sturdy likeable' Orlando and a Lysander 'with a pleasant sense of humour'.[35] In later life Hawthorne testified to the excellent training he gained in repertory and how well it served him in the medium of television. He recalled that 'the standard achieved [in repertory] was quite high'.[36] Certainly *A Midsummer Night's Dream* was a creditable piece of work: 'It is imaginatively directed, extremely well acted, and magnificently dressed . . . essentially a piece of team-work and a splendid team it is'.[37]

In 1957 Lionel Hamilton, now the company's producer and established as a 'repertory star' appeared as Shylock in his own staging of *The Merchant of Venice*. He gave 'a memorable performance, full of force and fire, yet losing none of the pathetic aspects of the Jew's character. In the trial scene especially he achieves some moments of rare intensity.'[38] Anne Ford's Portia was scarcely his match, but Tenniel Evans (Antonio) and Arthur Pentelow (Morocco and the Duke of Venice) were still in the company to lend strong support. Osborne Robinson (who can be seen adorning his set for the trial scene – Plate 6) provided designs which were 'simple though far from austere, and by the drawing of a curtain he transplants one effectively from Venetian courtyard to Belmont interior'.[39]

Peter Wyatt, whose fate in *The Merchant of Venice* had been Solanio, was propelled into prominence as Hamlet the next year, with Alan Brown, a long serving member of the company and later a staff director at the National Theatre, experiencing a similar elevation from Arragon to Claudius. Osborne Robinson, who had achieved the pinnacle of his career as designer of the Guthrie/Olivier Old Vic/Elsinore *Hamlet*, experimented with vaguely

[34] *Northampton Independent*, 15 March 1955.

[35] *Northampton Independent*, 18 March 1955 and *Northampton Independent*, 16 March 1956.

[36] Correspondence from Nigel Hawthorne C.B.E.

[37] *Chronicle and Echo*, 14 March 1956.

[38] *Chronicle and Echo*, 13 March 1957.

[39] *Chronicle and Echo*, 13 March 1957.

6 *The Merchant of Venice*, 1957. Lionel Hamilton as Shylock, Arthur Pentelow as the Duke and Anne Ford as Portia. Scenic designer Tom Osborne Robinson can be seen making a rare stage appearance on the Duke's right

Ruritanian costumes. No repertory Hamlet is likely to scale the heights, but Wyatt acquitted himself creditably and vindicated the policy of promoting a young actor to the most celebrated role in the theatre.

Twelfth Night, Northampton's favourite Shakespeare play, was the natural choice to celebrate (in 1959) the Royal Theatre's seventy-fifth anniversary and its refurbishment by its new owners, Northampton Borough Council. Lionel Hamilton combined producing with playing a poignant Malvolio. He introduced two visiting actresses: Jennie Goossens as Viola and Ruth Trouncer as Olivia, a tempting and not unsuccessful expediency, but basically at odds with the principles of repertory.

The seven Shakespeare productions between 1954 and 1961 had all been designed by Osborne Robinson, who had settled into a simple style of setting and colourful costume. Robinson's work had lost the innovatory quality of the 1930s and its 'fantastical' effect was becoming predictable, but at least Northampton audiences could be assured that their Shakespeare would be a visual delight. Two-week runs for Shakespeare (though not for other plays) had become the norm. Although this allowed a production to settle and mature the schedule usually only allowed a week's rehearsal. Most important of all the company was used to working together as a team and the pattern of an annual Shakespeare production (from

1954 to 1959) meant that they could build on past performances and develop the particular skills required.

Like most repertory companies Northampton rose to the challenge of Shakespeare's quatercentenary in 1964, by which time Peter Hall's innovations at the Royal Shakespeare Theatre were permeating through to less prestigious theatres, as was state subsidy on a much more modest scale. Northampton's choice of *King John*, the only history play to be performed by the company, may have been influenced by Hall's 'The Wars of the Roses', as well as its local associations; certainly Osborne Robinson's sets were more innovatory than they had been for a quarter of a century. Under the direction of Keith Andrews, Robinson introduced an Elizabethan-style staging, a bold step for a Victorian theatre, but there was the example of the National Theatre recently installed at the Old Vic:

> The stage is enlarged with an Elizabethan apron and the players hold the audience with power and strength and the costumes, some of which come from Stratford itself are a riot of glorious colour. Osborne Robinson excels his own consistently high standards with these 'King John' settings.[40]

Bright colours, which were not a feature of Stratford productions in the early sixties, must have been Robinson's touch.

Kenneth Gilbert was a forceful King John and Anthony Brown a brashly self-confident Bastard ('a gentleman / Born in Northamptonshire'), but it was Pauline Letts, specially engaged as Constance, who scored 'a personal triumph':

> Her bursts of agony as she cried aloud for 'her boy, her joy, her life, her widow's comfort and her sorrow's cure' was the most moving expression of a mother's sorrow that I have ever seen.[41]

Commendations were unstinting: 'all excelled to produce a rare and impressive performance – an evening to remember'; 'It is a thousand pities that this notable production should be running for less than a fortnight.'[42]

Buoyed up by this success Andrews staged *King Lear*, an ambitious choice for a repertory company, in the following March, again using 'an apron stage extended over the orchestra pit . . . [giving] a skilfully lit, spacious set'.[43] Kenneth Gilbert, following his success as King John, was an excellent, if somewhat under-age, Lear; John Ringrose 'gave depth of feeling and sensitivity to his part of Gloucester' (Plate 7);[44] as the Fool James Wellman was 'outstanding, just the right composition of wisdom and comedy'. Beth Harris and Judy Dickson were well differentiated as Goneril and Regan and Angela Down played Cordelia 'with understanding and compassion', but it was 'teamwork' – that indispensable ingredient of repertory success – that made 'this production one to be remembered'.[45] The respected critic Gareth Lloyd Evans, whose familiarity with the Royal Shakespeare Company's work gave him a benchmark by which to judge other productions, proclaimed: 'At Northampton "King Lear" is triumphantly Shakespearean . . . first-class.'[46]

Keith Andrews had the benefit of two weeks' rehearsal, as well as a two-week run, but this alone does not account for his achievement. Valuable though time is, Robert Young had shown that it was not the most significant ingredient in repertory Shakespeare. Like Young, Andrews assembled a talented company and deployed them well in challenging, but well-chosen, plays. He spurred Osborne Robinson on to create designs in a contemporary style.

Willard Stoker, a generation older than Andrews and already a veteran of several repertory companies when he came to Northampton,

---

40 *Stage*, 14 May 1964.
41 *Chronicle and Echo*, 7 May 1964.
42 *Stage*, 14 May 1964.
43 *Stage*, 18 March 1965.
44 Ibid.
45 Ibid.
46 *Manchester Guardian*, 15 March 1965.

7 *King Lear*, 1965. Kenneth Gilbert as Lear and John Ringrose as Gloucester

maintained Shakespeare's place in the repertoire from 1967 to 1975. During that time the dominance of the Royal Shakespeare Company and the National Theatre increased, as did that of 'director's theatre', but Stoker's style was characterized by 'an ancient simplicity . . . [he] nobly resisted the temptation towards the trendy and directed in a manner so admirably straight-forward as to invite comment from the avant-garde'.[47] Thus of his *Much Ado About Nothing*: 'Willard Stoker's direction makes Shakespeare as lively as any West End comedy.'[48] Stoker essentially treated Shakespeare as another repertory author and refused to be overawed by his work.

Osborne Robinson's sets reverted to the more fantastical, but the installation of a revolving stage gave him more scope on the small stage. For, yet another, *Romeo and Juliet*: 'Tom Osborne Robinson added much to the swift movement of the play with an ingeniously constructed set, which used the revolving stage to full advantage. Six sets were built as one and as the stage revolved each set was revealed.'[49] Costumes remained colourful, generally in a somewhat exaggerated period style, except in *Much Ado About Nothing* when they were late-Victorian.

The principle of a permanent company was upheld, but without the season to season continuity of the 1950s – for actors lucky enough to

47 *Mercury and Herald* (Northampton), 17 April 1975 of *As You Like It*.

48 *Chronicle and Echo*, 28 February 1973.

49 *Mercury and Herald*, 28 October 1971.

get it, television work was a priority. One such was twenty-three year old Michael Harbour, who returned to the company to play Iago in 1959. His Othello was guest artiste Keith Grenville. The theatre's readiness to exploit media celebrities was illustrated by the engagement of pop singer Adam Faith to play Feste for which he received predictably deferential praise. *Romeo and Juliet*, mistakenly regarded as an ideal repertory play in which to display young talent, found the supposed leads under par and 'secondary characters with scene-stealing potential milk[ing] their roles for all their worth'[50] – the fruitful interaction of youth and experience was not realized. The same problem arose with *The Tempest*: 'the occasional dominance of actors in smaller roles, with more experience of Shakespeare, over younger actors with more of a burden to shoulder'.[51]

Willard Stoker's approach to Shakespeare was workmanlike, he knew how to stage Shakespeare competently in two weeks' rehearsal, but the new generation of actors was less accomplished in the practices of repertory. His regime was something of a throwback and with the appointment – in 1975 – of Christopher Denys, still in his thirties, a more progressive policy was introduced. Denys staged *A Midsummer Night's Dream* in his first season, bringing in a new designer Helen Wilkinson with whom he had worked elsewhere. Denys and Wilkinson took their cue from the theatre itself:

> Our particular theatre is very different from the one in which Shakespeare's plays were first presented and this, of course, is bound to influence one's style of presentation.
> Here we have a beautiful Victorian Opera House, and I have tried to reflect, in the production, the atmosphere of the theatre.[52]

Accordingly the costumes were Victorian and the interior scenes reflected the red-plush auditorium: 'the Victorian costume and setting harmonizes cosily with the theatre'. For the wood Helen Wilkinson created 'a splendid setting of rustling trees and sound of a waterfall'.[53]

With the impact of Peter Brook's mould-breaking production of *A Midsummer Night's Dream* still fresh Denys' Victorianism might have seemed retrograde, but he did follow Brook in doubling Theseus/Oberon (Gilbert Wynne) and Hippolyta/Titania (Wanda Moore): 'four characters as variations of . . . the two sides – the light and the darker – of human nature'.[54] The suggestion that 'the director . . . had Victoria and Albert in mind' was understandable, if over-literal. Gilbert Wynne, monocled as Theseus and bare-chested as Oberon, delivered his speeches 'with an eloquence worthy of Stratford' – a significant comparison to invoke.[55] The mechanicals were treated with indulgence, engaging in a good deal of vintage ham-acting in 'Pyramus and Thisbe'.

Denys had introduced a much stronger directorial concept than Northampton was accustomed to, but he had responded to the ambiance of the theatre with a warm, joyous and decorative production which appealed to local audiences. The same could not be said of his *Macbeth* in May 1976. The company had changed almost completely in the interim and not for the better. Denys 'approached *Macbeth* as a thriller . . . a blood and thunder melodrama'.[56] Linal Haft was a physically powerful Macbeth and Alice Fraser's Lady Macbeth was capable of venom, but their verse-speaking was badly deficient:

> Indeed very few members of the cast seem to have grasped even dimly the principles of rhythm and cadence. Linal Haft as Macbeth must stand forth as the main offender . . . he delivers the magnificent and moving eulogy for his wife as if it were a grocery list.[57]

---

50 *Chronicle and Echo*, 27 October 1971.
51 *Chronicle and Echo*, 3 May 1967.
52 Theatre programme 14 October 1975. The advent of director's programme notes was a sign of the times.
53 *Chronicle and Echo*, 15 October 1975.
54 Theatre programme.
55 *Chronicle and Echo*, 15 October 1975.
56 *Chronicle and Echo*, 12 May 1976.
57 *Mercury and Herald*, 13 May 1976.

The actors were not helped by Ray Lett's set of logs and ladders on the revolving stage; it was 'abominably self-conscious. Like a Percy Thrower nightmare it abounds with wooden lattice-work cunningly devised to entrap the actor rash enough to attempt free movement of his skin beset costume.'[58]

Twelfth Night was the traditional choice to celebrate the Northampton Repertory Players' golden jubilee in 1977. The new artistic director David Kelsey explained his choice of setting:

> I have chosen some echoes and influences largely inspired by the Pre-Raphaelite movement . . . an evocative retreat into an age of classical grandeur and romanticism. There is also a minor parallel between Olivia's loss of her brother and Queen Victoria and Prince Albert – hence we may be forgiven for giving Feste a slight touch of John Brown . . . And Malvolio too may resemble a Prime Minister – noted for his supercilious arrogance and snobbery . . . As for the lovers – they are eternal –[59]

Ray Lett's set evoked 'the Pre-Raphaelite sense of idyllic beauty . . . on the revolving stage – a garden replete with pillars and statuary';[60] Martin Waddington, who appeared as 'Curio, a harpist', composed period music. In all this was a diverting production, but one which relied more on the director's period transplant than on the traditional values of repertory Shakespeare.

Kelsey's choice of *Hamlet* in 1979 upheld the repertory principle of promoting a young actor to prominence:

> In choosing the play I had to be sure we had an actor who possessed the skill and merit to take on this demanding role. SIMON TEMPLEMAN has been with the company for over twelve months. In that time he has gained considerable confidence in the first year of his professional career as well as having captured the interest of our regular patrons in a series of performances.[61]

Templeman, at twenty-four, looked the part, handled the verse competently and radiated sincerity: 'he is the sole possessor of sanity in a lunatic court'.[62] His strongest scene was that in Gertrude's bedchamber where the interplay with the experienced Clare Welch resulted in a powerful emotional charge (Plate 8).

Templeman's straightforward Prince was surrounded by a number of rather wayward performances,[63] but at least Ray Lett's set was unpretentious: 'steps on both sides of the stage, platforms at several levels, and an imposing backcloth of clouded sky [it] is functional and atmospheric'.[64]

Kelsey's approach to the play had been coloured by the imminent general election ('Hamlet takes to the Hustings'), but whether his injunctions to 'recognize our moral obligations' really facilitated either the cast's or the audience's understanding of *Hamlet* is doubtful.[65] His insistence that 'The proper delivery of the verse isn't the first thing a director of *Hamlet* has to worry about . . . After the roles are interpreted the verse will fall into place' was probably over-optimistic,[66] but in any case in repertory he would have been better advised to concentrate on the performances rather than a directorial interpretation. Templeman went on to join the Royal Shakespeare Company.

Michael Napier Brown's 1982 *Romeo and Juliet* fell victim to the same trap as previous productions. He cast 'two inexperienced young actors . . . Jonathan Dockar-Drysdale (25) and Yolande Vazquez (21) . . . hired this season as assistant stage managers in the title roles,[67] only to find them eclipsed by experienced actors in subsidiary roles: Vilma Hollingbery as the Nurse, Kim Wall as Mercutio and Lionel

---

58 Ibid.

59 Theatre programme, 6 April 1977.

60 *Stage*, 14 April 1977.

61 Theatre programme, 28 February 1979.

62 *Mercury and Herald*, 29 March 1979.

63 Ibid. A Claudius (Anthony Linford) reminiscent of Edward Heath; Ophelia (Jane Egan), 'an over-painted tart in dementia'; and a disembodied Ghost (Kelsey himself).

64 *Stage*, 5 April 1979.

65 Theatre programme.

66 *Chronicle and Echo*, 13 April 1979.

67 *Northants Evening Telegraph*, 7 October 1982.

8 *Hamlet*, 1979. Simon Templeman as Hamlet, Clare Welch as Gertrude

Hamilton as Escalus, Prince of Verona. Ray Lett's 'expensive set' did succeed in giving a sense of space to the small stage and the costumes were faithful Elizabethan, but 'this production is unremittingly pedestrian'.[68]

Napier Brown took up the cudgels again with *Macbeth* in 1987. He and his designer Ray Lett were not as co-ordinated in their approach as they should have been. This time Lett's set resembled 'a vast revolving salad bowl',[69] but he maintained that:

> It hasn't been used as well as intended. I wanted the set to add more to the dramatic element of the play, but Michael Napier Brown said it was not technically possible.[70]

Directorial effects were ill-advised: 'the play began with the sound of a liquid, presumably blood growing from a trickle to a flood';[71] Banquo's ghost was nothing more than a bright light; and the final fight between Macbeth and Macduff was played on the revolving stage with the witches screaming. The costumes looked as though they had come 'from the local Oxfam shop'.[72]

By now the principle of a permanent company had lapsed, though some 'through-casting' took place. Michael Irving had played Macbeth previously at Sheffield, but, although he remarked on the better acoustics in the Northampton theatre: 'he seldom forced himself beyond a stifled whimper'.[73] His Lady Macbeth, Liz Crowther had enjoyed successes in contemporary plays in Northampton, but she pitched her Shakespearian performance in too low a key. Blank verse eluded most of the cast, save James Hornby as Macduff.

The collective experience – between 1975 and 1987 – of Denys, Kelsey and Napier Brown was discouraging to repertory Shakespeare – Denys' *A Midsummer Night's Dream* excepted. The effect of the demise of the permanent company showed how fundamental that was to repertory team-work in Shakespeare. Importing an actor, who has played his role elsewhere, is no substitute. Although attendance at drama school had become the standard means of entering the profession actors were less well equipped in speaking blank verse than in the old days. Longer runs (and rehearsals – three weeks for Napier Brown's *Macbeth*) were no panacea. The fashion of 'director's theatre' was ill-suited to repertory, distracting the cast from vital essentials – characterization and verse-speaking. Despite limited success (*Hamlet*) Ray Lett had not shown Osborne Robinson's consistent mastery of the small stage and costumes had ranged from the eccentric to the dowdy. It is not surprising that Michael Napier Brown has no intention of re-introducing Shakespeare to the Northampton repertoire. His budget is probably inadequate, though that is not an over-riding reason. More significant are the shortage of suitable actors and the demise of the permanent company. Increasingly Shakespeare is seen as the preserve of specialist companies: the Royal Shakespeare Company (with Stratford only one-hour's drive away) and the English Shakespeare Company, who performed *The Tempest* at Derngate (adjacent to the Royal Theatre) in 1993. In Northampton Shakespeare is no longer a repertory dramatist.

Taking an over-view of repertory Shakespeare in Northampton in the sixty years from 1927 to 1987 various conclusions emerge. Only fourteen different plays have been performed, leaving vast areas of the canon unexplored. The romantic comedies have been staged recurrently, with *Twelfth Night* notching up five performances. Its other qualities apart, *Twelfth Night* does provide a range of evenly balanced roles well-suited to a repertory company – an opportunity for team-work, which is reper-

68 *Northants Post*, 16 October 1982. Ray Lett had a budget of £900 for the sets plus £1,000 for costumes.

69 *Post Midweek* (Northampton), 28 September 1987.

70 *Chronicle and Echo*, 29 September 1987.

71 *Mercury and Herald*, 25 September 1987.

72 Transcript of YOUR CHANNEL radio broadcast 13 September 1987.

73 *Post Midweek*, 23 September 1987.

tory's greatest strength. Certainly matching the play to the talents of the acting company is a fundamental requirement. *The Merchant of Venice* succeeds when an established 'repertory star' as Shylock is paired with an emerging talent as Portia. Despite its popularity *Romeo and Juliet* is likely to be an ill-advised choice, with inexperienced leads overshadowed by senior actors in smaller roles. Of the tragedies *Hamlet* offers the opportunity to a young actor to scale the dramatic heights and his efforts are likely to be sympathetically received. *Macbeth*, attractive because of its relative brevity, is best avoided, though its reputation as an unlucky play seems to owe more to the misguided approach of successive producers than to superstition. With the exception of *King John* the histories have been a closed book.

This may be partly because the histories seem ill-suited to Northampton's Victorian theatre, but in practice the small stage has not proved to be an obstacle to varying styles of design from semi-expressionist to 'symbolised' and quasi-Elizabethan (apron stage). The installation of a revolve has provided more scope, but like the stage itself it requires skilful deployment. For over forty years Osborne Robinson showed himself to be the master of the Royal Theatre stage, which he adorned with his sets and distinctive costumes.

It is difficult, of course, to make comparisons between productions separated by decades, but the evidence is that Robert Young in the 1930s achieved standards, within the rigour of twice-nightly weekly rep, which his successors, with more generous time at their disposal, have rarely matched. It is arguable that the working conditions in Young's day were actually close to those in Shakespeare's – an accomplished permanent company, used to working together as a team, adept at mastering a role quickly and creating an unpretentious, but effective performance. It is unlikely that Shakespeare's actors had the inclination or opportunity to indulge in a soul-searching interpretation of the ideas in the play or their concept of it. Aping the style of 'director's theatre' (fruitful though that may be for companies such as the Royal Shakespeare Company) has not served repertory theatres well.

If Shakespeare is to survive in repertory theatres a return to their traditional strengths would be well-advised: a permanent company, blending youth and experience; team-work; good verse-speaking; not too much straining after the depths of interpretation; restrained, but not necessarily neutral, sets; striking costumes; and the rejection of 'director's theatre'. A repertory company bold enough to uphold these principles, even in a Victorian theatre, would be producing Shakespeare with a degree of authenticity of which they could be proud and to which audiences would surely respond.

Audience attitudes to Shakespeare in Northampton have varied, from enthusiasm in the 1930s to ennui in the 1950s and deference to Stratford from the mid-1960s, but there is no evidence of inherent resistance, provided the standard is good.

Whether, in terms of repertory Shakespeare, Northampton is 'a fairly average sort of place', as J. B. Priestley claimed, will have to await the results of work on other towns and cities, but hopefully this article will provide a modest touchstone when the attention, that 'must be paid', is paid to repertory Shakespeare.

Shakespearian Productions by the Northampton Repertory Players

		Director	Designer
24.12.1927	*A Midsummer Night's Dream*	Rupert Harvey	Charles Maynard
26. 5.1930	Scene from *King John*	Herbert Prentice	Herbert Prentice & Osborne Robinson
17. 2.1933	*Twelfth Night*	Robert Young	Osborne Robinson
3. 4.1933	*The Merchant of Venice*	Robert Young	Osborne Robinson
5. 3.1934	*Othello*	Robert Young	Osborne Robinson
25.11.1935	*The Taming of the Shrew*	Bladon Peake	Osborne Robinson
16. 3.1936	*Macbeth*	Bladon Peake	Osborne Robinson
23. 5.1938	*Romeo and Juliet*	William Sherwood	Osborne Robinson
2.10.1939	*Romeo and Juliet*	William Sherwood	Osborne Robinson
8. 3.1948	*Twelfth Night*	Alex Reeve	Osborne Robinson
23. 3.1954	*Much Ado About Nothing*	Joseph E. Wright	Osborne Robinson
15. 3.1955	*As You Like It*	Alex Reeve	Osborne Robinson
13. 3.1956	*A Midsummer Night's Dream*	Alex Reeve	Osborne Robinson
12. 3.1957	*The Merchant of Venice*	Lionel Hamilton	Osborne Robinson
11. 3.1958	*Hamlet*	Lionel Hamilton	Osborne Robinson
5. 5.1959	*Twelfth Night*	Lionel Hamilton	Osborne Robinson
14. 3.1961	*The Merry Wives of Windsor*	Lionel Hamilton	Osborne Robinson
6. 5.1964	*King John*	Keith Andrews	Osborne Robinson
9. 3.1965	*King Lear*	Keith Andrews	Osborne Robinson
2. 5.1967	*The Tempest*	Willard Stoker	Osborne Robinson
19. 3.1968	*The Merchant of Venice*	Willard Stoker	Osborne Robinson
4. 3.1969	*Othello*	Willard Stoker	Osborne Robinson
3. 3.1970	*Twelfth Night*	Willard Stoker	Alan Miller Bunford
26.10.1971	*Romeo and Juliet*	Willard Stoker	Osborne Robinson
27. 2.1973	*Much Ado About Nothing*	Willard Stoker	Osborne Robinson
15. 4.1975	*As You Like It*	Willard Stoker	Osborne Robinson
14.10.1975	*A Midsummer Night's Dream*	Christopher Denys	Helen Wilkinson
11. 5.1976	*Macbeth*	Christopher Denys	Ray Lett
6. 4.1977	*Twelfth Night*	David Kelsey	Ray Lett
21. 3.1979	*Hamlet*	David Kelsey	Ray Lett
7.10.1982	*Romeo and Juliet*	Michael Napier Brown	Ray Lett
17. 9.1987	*Macbeth*	Michael Napier Brown	Ray Lett

THE LIVING MONUMENT: SELF AND STAGE IN THE CRITICISM AND SCHOLARSHIP OF M. C. BRADBROOK

J. R. MULRYNE

'Elizabethan drama', Muriel Bradbrook wrote in 1962, 'was . . . an embodied art, and existed for performance. To treat it as book art is to do it great violence.'[1] The belief that interpretation of Elizabethan theatre must derive from an informed and flexible sense of its staging remained central to Bradbrook's writing throughout a long career, until her death in June 1993. A discussion of her criticism of Shakespeare and the Elizabethan drama, the main but by no means the exclusive focus of her scholarly work, together with some account of its personal origins, will serve as implicit commentary on developments in critical practice and theatre performance over the last sixty years.

Muriel Bradbrook's first published book (out of an eventual total of more than twenty) was her Harness Prize Essay of 1931, *Elizabethan Stage Conditions*. The work of a Cambridge graduate student of twenty-two, the book exhibits at the outset the essential characteristics, and charts the essential convictions, that mark her work throughout. With, for a novice, extraordinary imperturbability Bradbrook runs through the critics of the past and finds them wanting as commentators on Shakespeare's stage. Hazlitt, for example, 'though he was interested in the virtuosity of the actor' failed as critic due to his general mistrust of theatre; Coleridge, on the other hand, won't do because 'his historical knowledge was neither detailed nor extensive'.[2] Such limitations are for Bradbrook significant and symptomatic. The crippling outcome for Shakespeare studies, she asserted, was that 'so far was Shakespeare separated from the stage that much of the inferior criticism was only a kind of mental performance of each play by the critic, at which the reader attended' (p. 15). Something more rigorous, more scholarly, and more robustly in touch with theatre was required. There were of course oases in the critical desert. Chambers was exempted from the charge of a want of critical faculty, but 'it is difficult to believe the same of all historic investigators' (pp. 3–4). Too often, historical scholarship had deteriorated into the aberrations of biographical enquiry: 'As Steevens and Malone had called up the forger Ireland from the vasty deep, the inevitable response of supply to demand, so the Baconians and Oxfordians appeared, followed by those minor eccentrics who merely wished to prove that Shakespeare was a cripple, or a lawyer, or a soldier, or a bee-keeper at some period of his existence' (p. 16). These last, especially from today's perspective, seem easy targets, but the need to identify fruitful objectives for critical scholarship was for Bradbrook in 1931 an essential task. There were new methods to contemplate. C. Bodmeier, a now obscure

[1] M. C. Bradbrook, *The Rise of the Common Player: A Study of Actor and Society in Shakespeare's England* (London, 1962), p. 38.

[2] M. C. Bradbrook, *Elizabethan Stage Conditions: A Study of their Place in the Interpretation of Shakespeare's Plays* (Cambridge, 1932), pp. 13, 14.

interpreter, is discussed as one who 'admirably illustrates the danger of applying scientific methods in the expectancy of discovering scientific facts, a procedure about as logical as digging with a silver spade in the hope of striking a vein of silver' (p. 19). American scholarship of the day attracted its own swipe of the tiger's paw: '*Shakespeare's Plots* (Fleming, 1902) and *Shakespeare's Soliloquies* (Arnold, 1911) are typical of the Ph.D. theses regularly turned out, with perhaps more industry than wit, from the American Universities' (p. 21). The grander literary figures are by no means exempt: Shaw, a formidable presence when the book appeared, is chastised for his 'offensive popularization' of the notion that Shakespeare was no more than a jobbing playwright, 'a shifty dramatist cadging lines . . . with snobbery and bumptiousness as his dominating characteristics' (p. 22). Even Bradley, though admired, is admonished because of a failure in theatrical understanding: his precision, detail and thoroughness 'was in a sense its own *reductio ad absurdum*, for the number of inconsistencies and irrelevancies that were revealed showed the incongruity of judging Shakespeare by the standards of the novel or the drama of the Shaw–Galsworthy kind, i.e. through consistency of motivation and character, and the logical articulation of the plot' (p. 26). Lesser but yet significant figures are put down: 'Schücking's difficulties arise from his extreme literal-mindedness' (p. 90); Stoll, more admired, is nevertheless misled by 'his New England conscience' (p. 99). Bradbrook's conclusion takes pleasure in what she discerns as the main direction of recent criticism, which she regards as 'healthy'; but the true spirit of her work shows itself when she exults that 'ferocity has returned to Shakespearean criticism' (p. 144); Schücking and Robertson, though limited, she says, 'sharpen the wits, rouse up the spirits, and have most of the virtues of Falstaff's sherris sack' (p. 144). There is something here of youthful exuberance, something of the combativeness of her own critical moment and something too of the flavour of the young discipline of English literature making its way at condescending Cambridge. But there are solid virtues too that predict future achievement, especially in regard to the necessary combination of knowledge and imagination.

Elizabethan Stage Conditions is by no means all ground-clearing. The book offers a remarkable set of observations about the whole range of Shakespeare's work, together with references to Elizabethan plays, well-known and obscure – all of it delivered in the staccato Bradbrookian prose, with the Bradbrookian impatience with qualification. Characteristically, the method is one of cross-reference and comparison, with a readiness to appeal to modern examples: Shakespeare's theatre, she urges, 'was very near to the cinema in technique: his trick of showing a series of short separate actions, each one cut off before it is finished (for example the battle scenes of *Julius Caesar*) which gives a sense of merged and continuous waves of action, is a common habit of Eisenstein and Pudovkin' (p. 49). Already, the play in performance is held to be the test of quality, so that knowledge and experience not only of the Elizabethan theatre but of the modern stage become essential qualifications for the academic critic. Claiming that 'the modern theatre approximates more nearly to the Elizabethan theatre than to any other' (p. 114) she nevertheless urges discriminations. Much later judgements by others are anticipated when the modern director (or 'producer') gets a stern wigging for presuming to consider his limited role as a kind of creative art: 'The rise of this very new and very belligerent art means that its rights are asserted with the noisiness of a Suffragette' (p. 120). Celebrated modern playwrights suffer by comparison with the Elizabethans: '*The Emperor Jones* produces a powerful abdominal response, as much akin to literature as the feeling of going up in a lift' (p. 125); Pinero and his apologist William Archer are acidly put down; even Ibsen seems pretentious beside the best of the Elizabethans: 'When scenery is used symbolically in prose, it gives one an unpleasant effect of having been jerked on to a Higher Plane, as in Ibsen's use of the mountains in *Brand, Little Eyolf* and *The Master Builder*' (p. 130). Some critics, she believes, have like Bradley misled by paying undue attention to the wrong kind of modern theatrical conventions: Dover Wilson for example is chastised for stage directions in his 'New Shakespeare' edition which show 'traces of nineteenth-century realist staging' (pp. 136–7). Yet 'playing Shakespeare in a vital tradition rather than by archaeological reconstructions' (p. 115) is the essential prerequisite to a genuine understanding of his achievement, even if there is a price to be paid: 'on the whole an occasional travesty is preferable to a level mediocrity' (p. 115). Never given to theory, Bradbrook nevertheless raises in this early book a series of questions about classical texts and revivals, authenticity and theatrical style, which in various forms have challenged later and more theoretically minded students of the Elizabethan theatre.

Something of the quality of Bradbrook's early achievement, and something of its temper, can be measured from her own retrospective account of these years in *That Infidel Place: A Short History of Girton College*.[3] The pioneering note in the book's account of university education for women is qualified by a typically Bradbrookian sense of the comic. Her own undergraduate and research years, the late twenties and early thirties, are described almost without personal reference, but the ambience comes through deliciously:

> On arrival we grouped into small parties known as 'college families', who sat together in hall, sharing amusements, small tasks, special tastes and jokes . . . The chaperon rules, which survived in vestigial form, were relaxed and were unofficially ignored by many of the students . . . the fire brigade still rose to its early drills, and games were played vigorously . . . at the end of the Lent term, we all rose early to pick violets in the College garden; in the summer the freshers served early teas to those sitting the Tripos, and raised a faint feminine cheer as the College bus rumbled off from the College gate; on return there were Tripos teas in the Honeysuckle Walk.
>
> (pp. 72, 73)

No doubt these phrases represent a sophisticated later assessment: the idyll is coloured with all the affection of memory, but placed too by a more worldly wise sensibility.

The strong-minded note of Bradbrook's early criticism reflects in part, one supposes, the combative stance embodied in that symbolic bus rumbling off with its cargo of eager heroines to challenge the male-dominated tripos; though Bradbrook it has to be said was never 'faintly feminine'. But it reflects too the critical era of *Scrutiny*, a periodical to which Bradbrook briefly contributed. Her essay 'Notes on the Style of Mrs Woolf' appeared in *Scrutiny*'s first issue, and serves as instance of that capacity for sympathetic identification she never lost, here in the form of a (presumably unconscious) pastiche of a critical manner not her own. 'In reading any of the later novels of Mrs Woolf', she begins, 'a curious and persistent trick of style obtrudes itself on the attention.'[4] Almost exactly fifty years later she was to write an obituary notice of Queenie Leavis for *The Cambridge Review* (November 1981), barbed, sometimes, and censorious where in Bradbrook's view Queenie had acted indefensibly, but brought to a conclusion by a plea for recognition of the 'late-achieved power' of a woman who had been, all those years before, her awkward undergraduate neighbour. The obituary attacks the Leavisite habit of 'the oblique thrust and the haughty sniff' instancing '"the corollary . . . does not need stating explicitly" or "there is no need to enlarge upon" or "It is not for nothing that" – all the complicities of Minority' (p. 127). Yet in her own early essay just this idiom appears: 'The

---

[3] M. C. Bradbrook, *That Infidel Place: A Short History of Girton College* (Cambridge, 1969, rev. edn, 1984).

[4] M. C. Bradbrook, *Collected Papers II: Women and Literature 1779–1982* (Brighton, Sussex, 1982), p. 152.

connection of this with the refusal to assent to a statement absolutely is too obvious to need any stressing' (p. 154). The essay's attack on Virginia Woolf adopts the very language of Leavisism: 'Without any connections of a vital sort between them, with no plot in the Aristotelian sense, the sensations are not interesting' (p. 155). But the 'singularly fruitful lack of single-mindedness', which Inga-Stina Ewbank celebrates as a dominant trait of Bradbrook's sensibility,[5] not only leads in the first instance to this act of mimicry, but leads also to the context in which it latterly appears, in Bradbrook's 1982 reprinting of both the Leavisite essay and the Leavis obituary. Rejecting suppression, Bradbrook prints with the essay Virginia Woolf's half-admiring response: 'She is young, Cambridge, ardent': not a put-down, exactly, but a 'placing'. Several times elsewhere Bradbrook recounts the incident when Woolf came to supper at Girton and compared the food unfavourably with lunch at King's.[6] Bradbrook defends Girton's reputation by explaining that Woolf was late (for admirably aesthetic reasons: she was appreciating sunset on the Backs), and by declaring that the King's meal was a special occasion: 'even the most opulent men's college does not serve *crême brûlée* every day'. Embedded in all this one may find the origins and the qualifying conditions of a critical temper that never lost its edge, its loyalty and generosity, its feminist affiliations, its independence of mind, its robust sense of the actual and its sheer pleasure in drama and the dramatic.[7]

It is enticing, but would be impractical, to follow Bradbrook's critical career throughout its sixty years. The recurrent topics characterize her essential interests: theatre as text and theatre as performance; the 'triple bond' of author, actor, and audience; theatre spaces; the inheritance of Elizabethan theatre from pageant and public display; the 'conservative' nature of the Elizabethan drama; women and theatre; religious procession and religious belief. Throughout, the methodology remains constant: encyclopaedic knowledge of Elizabethan playtexts and their detailed study ('I know no substitute for laminating the text into one's mind in a variety of moods and settings, the equivalent of the actor's study and rehearsal')[8] alongside a constantly renewed command of Elizabethan theatrical scholarship and tireless attendance at play performances of all kinds and in many places. Together, these provide the context within which the plays are interpreted. No one could call her work theoretically rigorous, but in its kaleidoscopic variety and magpie opportunism it offers a map of Elizabethan drama animated by knowledge, an extraordinary power of making connections, and a youthful eagerness she never lost.

Bradbrook's late *John Webster: Citizen and Dramatist* (1980) offers a characteristic example of her critical practice, while illustrating the furthest reach of her contextualizing method. Webster's plays are situated within a set of allusions and analogues that take in the playing place (he was most comfortable writing for the indoor theatre) the acting company (Richard Perkins had the expertise to play 'a character divided within itself . . . like Flamineo or Bosola'),[9] the familiar experience of the audience (the *Duchess of Malfi* recollects 'the tolling of the great bell of St Sepulchre's on nights before executions' (p. 14)), contemporary political events (the funeral of Prince Henry and the marriage rites of Princess Elizabeth that in their juxtaposition illuminate the inverted ritual

5 In her Foreword to *Collected Papers II*, p. vii.

6 See e.g. *That Infidel Place*, p. 16.

7 Bradbrook returned from time to time to her *Scrutiny* experiences, rarely in a wholly benevolent frame. In *Literature and Action: Studies in Continental and Commonwealth Society* (London, 1972), she roguishly comments that 'his [Leavis's] formula "This is so – is it not?" seldom expected the answer "No, it isn't" but was none the less an invitation to respond' (p. 37).

8 M. C. Bradbrook, *Collected Papers I: The Artist and Society in Shakespeare's England* (Brighton, Sussex, 1982), p. 4.

9 M. C. Bradbrook, *John Webster: Citizen and Dramatist* (London, 1980), p. 9.

of the death of Brachiano), and a sweeping cultural setting that in its contradictions ('the deep ambiguities, the beauty and deformity, the misery and splendour of the great' (p. 51)) complements the paradoxes of the tragedies. The biography the book maps out of Lady Penelope Rich serves as model for the theatre-experience of *The White Devil* and *The Duchess of Malfi*: 'if there can and should be no crude and direct identification here, of the kind which invites decoding, the story of the Lady of St Bartholomew's demonstrates that the paradoxes of these tragedies could be matched from the tragedian's own neighbourhood. It is presented as part of Webster's London' (p. 51). Equally, the colourful narrative of Antonio Pérez, spy and political victim in Spain, France and England, offers a contextualizing parallel for Webster's writing; moreover 'deeper than any analogues is the "absurdist" attitude, the belief that the world does not make sense, which underlies the fantastic conceits of Pérez and the tragedy of Webster' (p. 87).

Repeatedly in her published criticism, Bradbrook is scornful of tying plays to topical references: in *The Living Monument* (1976), for example, she dismisses Glynne Wickham and Frances Yates on the Last Plays: 'in spite of the temptations they seem to offer', these plays are *not* 'built on cryptograms about Henry Prince of Wales or the Princess Elizabeth, or the belated placing of the body of James's mother among the royal tombs of Westminster Abbey'.[10] In her work on Webster, Bradbrook defends her own contextualizing practice by asserting that the evoked context is 'neither theoretical nor descriptive but demonstrative' (p. 2). It could be objected that the very selection of analogues, no less than the language in which they are evoked, and the manner of their presentation, are in themselves acts not of demonstration but interpretation. What cannot be denied is the plausibility of the working circumstances she creates for the dramatist himself, a form of attention rarely paid by literary interpreters. The discussion of the Red Bull, 'a neighbourhood theatre' with its actors 'respectable local people' (p. 120) (in contrast to the thoroughly professionalized companies elsewhere) avoids the familiar stereotypes and brings the reader close to those active if ephemeral pressures that characterize the trade of playing, then and now; Webster's risky (and doomed) impulse was to give an ambitious play to this less-than-fully professional company, so allowing them 'to "trade up" – to move, as it were, from the Charing Cross Road to Savile Row, with this scion of the Merchant Taylors' (p. 120). Bradbrook's style of interpretation shares a good deal with impressionistic criticism, of a kind now regarded as discredited by the newer – and not so new – orthodoxies. As an aid to study of Elizabethan drama, it is vindicated, it may be thought, by the scope and practised awareness of the imagination that conceived it. Writing of this matter in 1982 ('I am still learning') she claims: 'The magisterial work of Fernand Braudel supports me here.'[11] It is, characteristically, a bold analogy, but one that many readers may consider defensible.

Historical contextualizing was one side of Bradbrook's work; another drew on the play in the theatre now. More than once Bradbrook returned to the issue of the director in the modern theatre. Writing in 1964, she took delight that 'drama today is full of experiment' but she cautioned that 'the claim of the playwright must be maintained, against the modern counterclaims of the "director"';[12] 'when Jan Kott', she commented, 'can praise *Titus Andronicus* as great Shakespearian theatre . . . it may be seen how far the theories of Artaud could influence the reading of a great dramatist' (pp. 19–20). Michael Bogdanov's *Romeo and Juliet* (1986) received less than admiring comment for its ruthless way with the text ('Friar

[10] M. C. Bradbrook, *The Living Monument* (Cambridge, 1976), p. 115.

[11] Bradbrook, *Artist and Society*, p.14.

[12] M. C. Bradbrook, *English Dramatic Form* (London, 1965), p. vii.

Lawrence, a modernist cleric with a cigarette hanging out of his mouth, and the horseplay with the Nurse, were very much that of a stage from which the Lord Chamberlain had abdicated control.')[13] Bradbrook coupled this Royal Shakespeare Company production with a Cambridge student production a few months later (characteristically at seventy-seven she found the energy, and the interest, to take in student productions) where 'Romeo saw Juliet not at a window but in a bath and in the nude' (CP IV p. 72). Her comment is crushing – even students must be responsible to Shakespeare's script – 'This is what in the Sixties used to be called "relevance" – making up, as one group said, for the banality of the text' (p. 72). Yet hers was no reactionary refusal to perceive the play as a living organism that transforms itself through time. Re-interpretations are 'valid in terms of an original invitation extended to the audience to "work, work your thoughts"'.[14] 'Some modern productions have succeeded as no archaeologically "correct" play could do, because they respond to the open form which is inherent in the Jacobean drama itself' (p. 121). Even the Marowitz *Hamlet* or *An Othello* has, Bradbrook considers, its part to play in the evolving and comprehensive biography of the play-text. More surprisingly, perhaps, 'I hold the greatest modern version [of *Lear*] to be the Russian film of Grigori Kozintsev' (p. 143); *Throne of Blood* attracts her praise; the Zulu *Umabatha* and the West Indian *Macbeth* make the play available to the modern audience because they are presented by 'people who still know what [witchcraft] means' (p. 130). Peter Brook's *A Midsummer Night's Dream* can claim to be true to its original because 'there was no attempt at illusion, yet the spirit of gaiety and of carnival presided in all the slightly dangerous wildness that the Elizabethans associated with summer festivities, whether Mayday or Midsummer . . . the spirit denounced by Stubbes in his attack on May games'.[15] What seems to emerge across the range of Bradbrook's critical writing is an informal theory of play presentation that will be responsive to current interests while understanding these as mutations of the past. 'As well as listening to the multiplicity of voices in the present', she writes, ' – and even trying to meet the very different kinds of audience at their different levels honestly – it is necessary constantly to replenish the sense of Shakespeare who is *not* our contemporary'.[16]

This formulation of her views appeared in 1982, but as far back as one of her earliest books, *The Growth and Structure of Elizabethan Comedy* (1955), Bradbrook was insisting on the need for criticism to be embodied in, and tested by, production: 'Drama is the co-operative creation of author, actors and audience . . . Criticism which is embodied in production, like that response of the audience which kindles and transforms the actors, is too evanescent to be captured or repeated, for all performances are different; yet it is only in such moments that the special richness, the living fullness of drama is displayed' (p. 11). The theme is one that reaches its culmination in *The Living Monument* of 1976. There Bradbrook rebukes John Arthos for a romantically effusive discussion of Marina which fails to see that in performance 'she may be presented either as the bright angel Daphne Slater made of her at Stratford in 1947, or the sunburnt Greek girl, reacting to her trials with energy, and with hot resentment, presented by Susan Fleetwood twenty-two years later in 1969' (p. 192). Typically, drawing on a lifetime of scholarship and theatregoing, she offers a view of Elizabethan playing conditions that is, simultaneously, a judgement on the play on the modern stage. In a discussion of *Cymbeline* she writes:

> Imogen is here the one fully realised character. In terms of the King's Men, this means that a boy took the lead. There is really no part of any substance for

13 M. C. Bradbrook, *Collected Papers IV: Shakespeare in his Context* (Brighton, Sussex, 1989), pp. 71–2.

14 *The Living Monument*, p. 121.

15 M. C. Bradbrook, *The Growth and Structure of Elizabethan Comedy* (Cambridge, new edn, 1973), p. 211.

16 Bradbrook, *Artist and Society*, p. 13.

Burbage . . . This was a most unusual experiment for Shakespeare. Although the Roman plays of *Coriolanus* and *Antony and Cleopatra* have leading parts for women, these are mature and masculine roles; and I think, like other parts for older women, they were probably taken by men. Cleopatra could speak of some 'squeaking Cleopatra' boying her greatness because she was not played by any such. Imogen, however, is designed for a slighter, delicate artifice, and to put such a part at the centre lightens the whole tone of the play. (p. 195)

The extended quotation is necessary because Bradbrook's method depends on the interweaving of (sometimes unorthodox) scholarship, an acute sense for the Elizabethan play and a sensitivity to the potentialities of modern performance. Raymond Williams has called Bradbrook's work 'defining and pre-eminent' in 'the history and analysis of dramatic forms and their conditions of performance';[17] it is precisely in the freedom and scope of her attention to theatre that this pre-eminence is demonstrated.

Bradbrook's originality as a critic of Elizabethan theatre is well illustrated by the attention she gives to that theatre's inheritance from its own past, a topic canvassed by others, but in Bradbrook's case with a particularly keen sense of playing practices in Shakespeare's England and before. *Shakespeare the Craftsman*, based on the Clark lectures for 1968, emphasizes continuity in theatrical performance: 'at least two hundred years' pageantry lay behind the great English gild cycles, and two hundred years more of the gild cycles lay behind the Elizabethan theatre'.[18] Shakespeare and his contemporaries, she claims, 'were not, after all, founding a drama, but living in the ruins of a great gild tradition that needed refounding' (p. 13). Such a perspective alters her assessment of the work of Shakespeare and others: Shakespeare's histories did not only derive, as Tillyard and Dover Wilson seemed to assert, from 'the clerkly and argumentative morality plays'[19] but from a far richer theatrical tradition of pageants and shows woven into the cultural experience of the nation. Marlowe's work is similarly full of icons that recall, or invert, symbolisms familiar from pageants and processions. George Peele, as a producer of shows from City and Court, is recuperated as a dramatist worthy of a place in the tradition. Robert Greene's quip about the upstart Crow 'is no allusion to Horace's Crow or Aesop's Crow, as the learned would have it; Greene is remembering the pageants and "the sudden appearance of a fabricated Being made of wood and cloth, entirely invented, corresponding to nothing in Nature"' (p. 15). Elsewhere, Bradbrook interprets *Macbeth* as assimilating the shows of James's coronation together with the profound shock of the Gunpowder outrage. Shakespeare, clad in his scarlet livery, took part in the Royal entry of March 1604, she reminds us, with its themes of Britannia Rediviva and the restoration of Troynovant. 'When, superimposed on this triumph, came the Gunpowder Plot, the fair day and the foul day rushed together in his mind.'[20]

The heuristic value of a knowledge of performances outside the established theatres is not confined to gild pageants or country shows. Bradbrook also underlines the interaction of plays with Lord Mayors' processions, commenting, for instance, on the politics of Spanish opposition, from 1617 on, that is common to both forms.[21] The masque, in particular under James, becomes a focus of attention, not only for its intrinsic interest, but as implicit commentary on plays for the theatre: 'The variety, the uncertainty, the *trompe l'oeil* of this play [*Antony and Cleopatra*], seems to transmute the

[17] Marie Axton and Raymond Williams, eds., *English Drama: Forms and Development. Essays in Honour of Muriel Clara Bradbrook* (Cambridge, 1977), p. ix.

[18] M. C. Bradbrook, *Shakespeare the Craftsman: The Clark Lecture for 1968* (London, 1969), p. 7.

[19] p. 13; nor from Holinshed and Hall, merely. See *The Living Monument* p. 39 for expansion on this point.

[20] Bradbrook, *The Living Monument*, p. 135.

[21] Bradbrook, *Shakespeare in his Context*, 'The Politics of Pageantry', pp. 95–109.

splendour of a courtly masque . . . Having explored its effects, having accepted that it was not for him, Shakespeare has here fully digested the masque, brought it into relation with his works as they were to develop over the remaining four or five years of his working life.'[22] For Bradbrook, the theatrical context of Shakespeare's plays was never merely that; exploring alternative theatres, assimilating (and rejecting) their aesthetic and their implicit moral stances, was in her view one of the animating impulses of Shakespeare's work as craftsman.

In retrospect, Bradbrook in 1982 traces her scholarship on pageantry to the foundation of the Warburg in 1934, with its interest in 'all forms of Renaissance display, especially the politically tinged forms of masque, tourney and royal entry'.[23] The tribute is a generous one, but her engagement with pageantry springs also from another and more personal source. Characteristically, her discussion of the medieval gilds and mayoral processions leads directly to discussion of Holy Week processions at Seville, or Easter shows at Santa Cruz de Tenerife. In Bradbrook's writing, theatre has a value that goes well beyond entertainment, both for the individual and the community. Since theatre, she wrote, is a communal art, 'response to a play can strengthen inner freedom and balance'[24] among both actors and audience. Commenting on an Easter procession at Seville, she writes: 'The [image of the] Son is Human, agonized; the Mother is Divine, her grief transmuted into supernatural glory; while His crown of thorns stabs like the darts in the neck of the bull' (p. 42). 'All this tide of feeling', she goes on, 'beating on the image and rolling back in reflected power, animates the community in veneration; and the communal veneration of the image generates a dynamic akin to drama' (p. 43). At Santa Cruz, the Easter pageant culminates in the processing of the Host: 'the shock of removal from past and future, to here, now and always, from play and game to truth, leads everyone into the Play beyond the Play'.[25] The conscious echo of Eliot, a kinship that is credal as well as literary, represents an underlying view of the essentially religious nature of theatre, one that declares itself only infrequently on the surface of her work, but which is implicitly present throughout.

The conclusions of Bradbrook's *The Rise of the Common Player* (1962) will now surprise no one, largely because the book itself has been so influential. Rooted in her unfailing conviction that 'Elizabethan drama was . . . an embodied art, and existed for performance' (p. 38), Bradbrook saw the need to provide what she called 'the social envelope' (p. v) within which the plays were made, both in terms of the actors' social experience and the esteem in which theatre-performance as cultural activity was held. The Act for Restraining Vagabonds of 1572, superficially demeaning to players, proved, Bradbrook shows, a significant step on the path that led to James's Letters Patent, directed to Shakespeare and eight of his fellows, requesting all and sundry 'to allow them such former Courtesies as hath been given to men of their place and quality' (quoted p. 64). No doubt this legal language is routine and the social advancement easy to oversimplify and misrepresent, yet Bradbrook's sense of the increasing socio-cultural influence of theatre is both persuasive and uncomfortably consistent with a developing political and social role, for subversion as well as consensus, which Bradbrook herself would be disinclined to admit. For her, the main implications of social advancement and influence are understood in terms personal to the players and playwrights (the 'last and greatest usurpation of the poor players was to produce a poet of their own, a man who, however skilled and well-mannered,

22 Bradbrook, *The Living Monument*, pp. 177–8.

23 Bradbrook, *The Artist and Society*, p. 2.

24 Bradbrook, *English Dramatic Form*, p. 31.

25 Bradbrook, *Shakespeare the Craftsman*, p. 8.

had *not* enjoyed the privilege of spending his youthful years as an out-at-elbows poor scholar' (pp. 82–3)) and in terms of the audience, who 'gradually realized that the offering was addressed to them all . . . It must have been an intoxicating feeling for the humbler man' (p. 100). The book is full of vivid glimpses of Elizabethan playing, especially in its interpretation of Laneham's Letter as 'the sole surviving product from the first great company of actors, founders of the Theatre, Leicester's Men' (p. v), and in its evocation of Tarlton's clowning before 'his noisy and familiar admirers [who] were still an assembly rather than an audience' (p. 176). Bradbrook's commentary on the rise of the player remains anecdotal, with the strengths and limitations this implies; scarcely sociology, though she uses the term, but a living portrait nonetheless, and one that provides another and necessary dimension in the definition of Elizabethan playing.

Bradbrook's achievement as a critic rests initially on her *Themes and Conventions of Elizabethan Tragedy* (1935, second edition 1980) and its companion *The Growth and Structure of Elizabethan Comedy* (1955, new edn with additional chapter, 1973). But the core of her work is arguably found in *The Living Monument* (1976). Resuming familiar interests and arguments, she deals in Part I with 'the actor-audience relationships . . . and their effect on plays and playwrights' (p. 7), a topic 'more elusive and conjectural' (p. 7) as she says, than the mere 'archaeology' of the playhouse. The book is stocked with brilliant thumbnail sketches of writers, actors and theatre-occasions, and with brief and more extended interpretation of the plays. True to her sense of the stage as a current and living organism, responding to the theatrical as to the moral and political pressures of the moment, she reads *King Lear* as 'a reversion to that old countrified form of drama which Shakespeare saw being superseded by the London stage . . . It brought into the modern theatre with its new techniques of acting some of the old breadth and humanity – instinctive pieties and rough jesting come as if from the humble who never look for justice' (p. 158). There's a conservative note here, that consorts with Bradbrook's central conviction, widely challenged in recent years, that 'drama was an integrative force in the reigns of Elizabeth and James . . . the theatre could absorb, reflect and attempt to reconcile very different social levels, which were being ever more rapidly stratified by social change' (p. 7). Social (and political) tension is acknowledged, but the main function of theatre is, according to Bradbrook, reconciliation; even in 1600–13 the playhouse was to 'draw into itself all the interests of an age where new conflicts were developing between different systems of religious and political thought' (p. 10). Jonson is seen, in his early masques, as one who 'drew together masquers and audience in homage to the throne' (p. 59), though even he was to find by 1621 (or perhaps a few years earlier) that 'the image of harmony and unity was becoming impossible to sustain' (p. 75). Bradbrook interprets Jonson's comedies as offering 'a powerful image of the unified city' (p. 84), a debatable proposition, surely, given that the plays are populated by sharpers, con-men and merchants avid for their own, not for a common interest. Temperamentally, Bradbrook is drawn to consensus, accord, conciliation, taking theatre as their social expression. It is a stance that underpins all her writing on theatre from first to last.

Bradbrook's understanding of theatre-practice is at odds with a critical climate which favours a view of theatre as characterized by subversion and contestation. Remarkably she has come under very little overt criticism from proponents of more recent critical fashions, perhaps because her work is so various, so idiosyncratic, so formidably knowledgeable, and so open-minded as to evade narrowly focused attack. Her view of the place of Shakespeare in contemporary culture is at once sophisticated and elusive:

> The electronic revolution means that Shakespeare attracts more attention than ever, because paradoxically he provides, if not a fixed centre, a uniquely complex variable – the stabilizing (if Protean) feature in a weightless free-floating cultural dream-world.[26]

It is not a view compatible with recent studies of 'Shakespeare' as social construct, but represents a typically adroit implicit rejoinder to the more simplifying tactics of some of these studies. Bradbrook's own contribution remains that of the wonderfully informed scholar who is at the same time the avid play-goer, eternally youthful and responsive, valuing Shakespeare and his fellow dramatists, his actors and audiences, as voices in that dialogue with the modern theatre which incorporates, for her as for us, a living heritage.

---

[26] Bradbrook, *Artist and Society*, p. 2.

STRATFORD STAGES: TWO INTERVIEWS

PETER HOLLAND

MICHAEL REARDON AND TIM FURBY

The architects Michael Reardon and Tim Furby have worked on all three of the RSC's theatres in Stratford, designing the Swan Theatre and the new Other Place and undertaking a number of alterations to the Royal Shakespeare Theatre including, in 1993, a major refurbishing of the auditorium.

PETER HOLLAND How did you first become involved in working for the Royal Shakespeare Company?

MICHAEL REARDON It began very modestly. David Brierley, the company's General Manager, asked us to develop a modest scheme to seat about 140 people in the converted rehearsal studio, the Conference Hall at the rear of the Royal Shakespeare Theatre, created in the shell of the old theatre which burned down in 1926. John Napier, a stage-designer with the RSC, had sketched a scheme, similar to the Pit in the Barbican, with metal tiered seating, facing in the opposite direction to the current shape of the Swan. David Brierley already had a sense that it would not work and would not meet the complex regulations controlling theatres.

We then talked to Trevor Nunn about spaces and performances in a rather vague way. I had previously tried to convince him that he ought to be doing some of his work not in theatres but in galleried churches like Birmingham Cathedral. I always thought theatres limiting and that people ought to take more theatre into liturgical spaces because Renaissance and Baroque churches are very theatrical.

PH Michael, your architecture is rooted in your work on cathedrals and historic houses whereas, Tim, your background is in stage design.

TIM FURBY I could see the problems from the other side. Given the confines of the site, the theatre had to be designed to make a virtue of the very little space left over when the audience space and acting space were accounted for.

MR We went to look at Christ's Hospital in Horsham, where Trevor Nunn had worked. This had a gallery within a hall, but it was much too flaccid, far too wide from gallery to gallery so that there was no contact between them. I had worked with Chris Morley on the 'wooden O' season in the Main House in 1976, when part of the audience were placed behind the stage in timber galleries. Certainly the thinking about balconies that season did make sense of the whole space in the Main House and probably made the RSC think again about how they could use the Conference Hall. That design never integrated the two audiences, whereas the connection between the sides and gallery is crucial to the Swan. But Trevor

Nunn made the point very early on that he wanted a space in which the audience and actors were inhabitants of the same space, living in the same world; I think this is true of great medieval buildings and of great rooms of state. People say of such buildings that the architecture dominates people but it can in fact pull people together.

PH Bob Crowley has said that 'I always come away with this image of the Swan overriding the memory of the production.'[1] Does that worry you about work in the Swan?

MR But that is because some designers fight it. Our brief was to make a strong space within which directors would work and it was Trevor Nunn's firm view that the designer would play a secondary role. Once the Swan opened, designers tried to play a very major role, not understanding what Trevor was trying to achieve, and instead trying to turn the Swan into the background for a set. Trevor's view was that he did not want any sets in the Swan at all; he just wanted the space for the play.

TF I can see how designers would think that the basic timber structure of the Swan is too much of a burden, that they are now stuck with a framework which they cannot escape and which therefore does not allow them to make a statement – and therefore continue their career – as if anyone would think that there were not limitations on the other stages, or that the Barbican gave them everything that they wanted. It is a curious notion that, because the statement was there before you arrived, it is somehow oppressive. It is no more oppressive than the brick walls of the auditorium of the Main House or the square box of the new Other Place.

MR A group of architects visiting the Swan complained that it was not high-tech enough, that we had missed the opportunity to use this or that piece of modern technology. I have also often been asked why, in a theatre specifically designed for the performance of Renaissance drama, we did not design a classical building using elements derived from Renaissance architectural theory. But this would place a historicist emphasis on the theatre and on productions, making plays 'costume drama'. I believe that the more limited the means, the more meaning the architect can command from the architecture; the Swan's rather minimalist architectural language, its rhythm of post and beam, avoids this constricting historicism. The Swan is a space created as a framework to be decked out, not by the scene painter, but by the transformation of verbal images into visual ones. Neither a high-tech theatre nor a historicist one could possibly ever keep pace with the rapidity of that process in Renaissance plays.

PH The Other Place had a tradition of leaving an open space. Do you feel that responses to the new Other Place have been to over-design?

TF Definitely. The use of The Other Place has changed; it is almost as if they are trying to live up to it. It is partly the accident of the theatre being the starting-up point for the RSC's annual tour to towns without theatres, so that they are building a touring set that has to go and look wonderful in a warehouse without any help. But it is also that, both in The Other Place and on the Main House stage, audiences can no longer accept five actors on a stage in black pullovers saying the words. Because people see more television shows, more films, more West-End glitz, they expect more. It is hard to know how you stop throwing money at sets, except by producing stunning theatre with very little.

We always knew that once the RSC tinkered with The Other Place people would want it to be different. Therefore the first design was a

1 Ronnie Mulryne and Margaret Shewring, *This Golden Round: the Royal Shakespeare Company at the Swan* (Stratford-upon-Avon, 1989), p. 86.

glitzy small repertory theatre, holding up to 300. It was far away from the original intention, which is, after all, a floor on which you play, in which the audience are allowed to come in and sit down quietly and watch. It is almost a televised rehearsal which you are watching; that is the voyeuristic sense of The Other Place. We are partly responsible for the loss because we have given the audience slightly more comfortable seats, given them a bit more space, so that they do not feel quite so much on the edge as before.

PH That sense of 'being on the edge' is clearly a motif for all the work you have done at Stratford.

TF But isn't that the excitement that happens when the three spaces work? At the Swan, you should be out of your seat leaning over the balcony, wanting something to happen just in front of you, somebody about to cut your ear off with a sword. The Swan is as far as it can be from television where you sit back and let it happen in front of you. The Main House has always the problem that you are sitting back in comfortable seats and the performance goes on without you; it is a spectacle.

PH Actors entering or exiting through the audience in the Main House have always looked very forced and awkward, because the audience feels the actors should be up there where they belong, behind the proscenium arch.

MR That is an unalterable feature of that building. One of the important things about the old Other Place was that it was like a little house in which audience and actors came in through the same front door. Now, actors tend to make their own entrances from other points. We have lost something by losing the shared door.

There is a different problem in the Swan. One of its weaknesses is the lack of an axial entrance point for the actors. It is intended for Renaissance theatre and I think that in all Renaissance buildings the axial entrance is important. In medieval buildings, apart from cathedrals, doorways are never important. When the Swan was being designed we discussed whether we should have a major axial entrance, opposite the stage, with a central gangway; I am sorry that in the end we decided not to on the grounds that it would have divided the audience into two.

PH One of the effects at the moment is that the two entrances down through the audience have also become places for actors to park themselves, when they are trying to distribute themselves around the stage. An axial entrance is a demand of tension between stage and the possibility of the stage extending through the audience. But there is also the failure of actors and some directors to recognize the fluidity of the space you have given them.

TF The actors tend to get stuck at the edge of the stage, imagining that, if they stood at an entrance point, they would not be part of the action. The more people play out in the space the better the whole space will be.

PH There were early complaints from some members of the audience that they felt squeezed.

TF You still hear people saying, 'there isn't a lot of room, is there?', because they wanted a comfortable armchair. We always were of the opinion that they should have to fight a little, they should have to be a bit uncomfortable.

PH Which productions in the Swan seem to you to have real strengths and which have extended your own perception of the building you created?

TF Deborah Warner's *Titus Andronicus* is possibly the most powerful use of the space, partly because of the strength of the acting and direction, but also because the set had nothing and did nothing. We feel that the focus of the three Stratford spaces is in terms of a camera: that the Main House will always be the spectacular, wide-screen movie, that the Swan will always be the actor as television, from waist to top of head, and that in The Other Place it is the head.

PH Your work in the Main House has been to try to rethink the auditorium.

MR Before our remodelling in 1993, actors often said that the Main House was very intimidating because they have nothing to respond to; they are talking into a great black void and cannot even see where it ends. We have tried to make visible the architecture which defines the space by adding lights on the walls and stressing doors, both to divide the stage and the auditorium and to give the space human scale, because doors are always the key to the human scale of a building. It is now an easier space to play in because it is not an infinite blackness but a finite room.

PH One of the effects which is so marked in the Swan is that, as the light bounces off the wood, the audience is aware of each other and actors must be aware of the audience. Do you think that is crucial for playing Renaissance texts, because the environment they stemmed from was one in which the audience was intensely visible, with daylight productions in public theatres or candlelight in private theatres?

MR In a black void you see the play as an individual. In the Swan the audience is a body, rather like a congregation or a dinner party. Whenever you are looking at an actor you are always looking at somebody beyond. There is a pleasing sense of conspiracy.

TF The configuration of the Main House is unalterably like a cinema. That is what you are paying for: the luxury seat and the single view of the wide screen. In some ways that is an old-fashioned style, that the theatre is about 'going out' – but we tried to put that back. That then frees stage designers completely to create spectacle, to tackle the stage head-on. They could, for instance, exhume the hydraulics put in long ago for the 'Roman' season, because they are part of the spectacular theatre the Main House must be. I think you should use all the tricks of the trade and every modern illusion. It has to be a modern house but it has not gone on innovating. It is stuck in a 'sixties style of playing.

It was very noticeable when the Swan Theatre first opened that the RST style of delivery and acting was simply being transferred to the Swan, where of course it did not work. But equally, the virtues of the Swan do not belong in the Main House. From an actor's point of view, it appears to be easier in the Swan because you do not have the delivery problem whereas in the Main House you are always aware of the timing, the delivery, that it takes ages for an actor to get on stage. It is almost as if everything you learn about playing in the Swan, you must unlearn to go back in the Main House – except that you have to find some way of reaching the audience.

PH Let us suppose the RSC was given a large blank cheque for rebuilding the Main House in Stratford: what would you aim to provide, if you were given the brief of a big house for Shakespeare?

MR But theatres never turn out to be what they began by being in the design process. They develop. It is odd how we now invent reasons why we did things. Buildings of all sorts appear at the time they are due to appear and the reasons for their appearing have to be found later. I think the time for the Swan had come: it is a theatre of its time and it will one day seem dated. I have no idea what we would do in the Main House; it would be a bad idea if we knew.

TF I think we would want to address the major problem of how the audience relates to the stage, but that does not solve the problem of an epic stage for, in some ways, the opera house stage on that scale is impossible to make intimate. There was a style for it and unfortunately the style has gone.

MR I wish we could hear how Shakespeare was delivered in the eighteenth and nineteenth centuries. We would both like to see somebody do an eighteenth-century production of *Hamlet* complete with the Turkish Dances, just to see what it was like. It would be artificial, but it would be an interesting and illuminating experience. But will that epic style ever come back or does it belong to a whole past view of social organization? Apart from commercial considerations, do we really need a large theatre for Shakespeare?

SAM MENDES

Sam Mendes has been widely recognized as one of the most promising young directors in England. He is Artistic Director of the Donmar Warehouse and has directed four productions for the RSC: *Troilus and Cressida* (1990), *The Alchemist* (1991), *Richard III* (1992) and *The Tempest* (1993).

PETER HOLLAND Your first production at Stratford was *Troilus and Cressida* at the Swan Theatre. How did you first become involved with the Royal Shakespeare Company?

SAM MENDES Genista McIntosh, who was then Associate Producer, and Terry Hands scouted me out and we talked, as is normal with the RSC, about a handful of plays, all of which had not been done for some time and some of which had never been done at all. It had also seemed obvious from the start that it was going to be the Swan Theatre where I was going to make my debut; the Main House was considered to be too big a risk and The Other Place was closed for rebuilding. That limited my choice of plays because at that stage the Swan brief was Jacobean plays and 'minor Shakespeares', if there is such a thing.

I had also seen much of the work in the Swan over the two previous years and it had made me think this was a very good idea. Deborah Warner's production of *Titus Andronicus*, Di Trevis's production of *The Revenger's Tragedy* and Terry Hands' production of *Singer* used the space in different ways, and were all successful.

PH But why choose *Troilus and Cressida*, hardly a 'minor Shakespeare' and one which the RSC has frequently produced? What did the Swan Theatre offer that play?

SM It's a play in which many shifting and colliding perspectives exist; the play speaks through the dissonance of its various tones, moving very swiftly from high comedy to political scenes and then into tragedy at the end. There is something about the Swan which I have never experienced in any other theatre. It allows you to achieve the fluid and simple technique of shifting from one world to another, to be both epic and domestic. So it's the ideal theatre in which one can move from the inside of a tent onto the battle plains of Troy, and then back into a man's mind. It is really the ideal classical theatre: it is not an illusory space, it's a very honest space, but it is a space which fires the imagination of the audience as well as performers.

The fluidity of the Swan has something to do with the depth of its thrust stage, so much deeper than it is wide. It can give you this tremendous sense of people approaching from a distance. But you can also store up a world behind what is effectively a sort of proscenium, the space under the galleries; I used a set of curtains there which could then be opened to release actors and energize the space. With these entrances way upstage and also the entrances through the audience, it meant that the world could exist in opposition to the audience, as a separate world, and yet could also be a debating chamber, a place in which the audience is implicated in the action. For instance, I played the scene when the Greeks meet the Trojans for the first time with people around the audience so that the audience felt implicated in it. You can also have what I directed as an intensely private, very dark scene – the Helen scene –

which took place almost by candlelight. A disturbing, haunting scene, yet staged on the same near-empty stage.

PH In the first Cressida scene, you used a very elaborate stage prop, a pond in which first Pandarus and Cressida paddled their feet and which then became the site of ritual cleansing for the returning warriors. That was a transition from domesticity to grandeur, the heroic, with the same object in the same position on the stage.

SM We used a subtle lighting change to switch the light from a very domestic, front-on, comforting light, to much more dynamic backlighting, which came from underneath the gallery and put the figures' faces into shadow, as they bent down to perform their ritual. The pond became something metaphorical and imagistic, having been something naturalistic. It was just what the audience wanted it to be and that is the single great feature of that stage.

It is very difficult to find a unified space which can be everything and yet is always itself. The obvious example of that was Peter Brook's production of *A Midsummer Night's Dream*: it released the imaginations of the audience yet was absolutely true to its own nature. The Swan makes this problem much easier to solve because many of the difficult decisions are simply taken away from you.

PH Your second Shakespeare at Stratford was *Richard III* which went first into The Other Place before its tour and later returned to the Swan. Which of these three phases in the production's life was most important?

SM What happens when a building is reproduced, as in the transition from the old Other Place to the new one, is that subtly the aesthetic changes. The old Other Place, with its nooks and crannies and dusty corners which pushed you into a certain way of thinking about the place, no longer existed. So The Other Place became less like the Swan: you could not depend on the empty space to give a sense of atmosphere because it had become more impersonal. It seemed to need a set far more. We came up with a very simple grey wooden set with a series of doors at the back and just a simple grey wooden floor, which at the end opened up to reveal earth. These things worked. But the massive image of Simon Russell Beale behind the doors simply did not work. It did not sit as we thought it was going to and was not visible to much of the audience sitting at the sides.

When you are directing or designing a production for a new theatre, you go and sit in the empty theatre and you look around the space to sense its dynamic. You find where the most dramatic points on stage are, its focus and atmosphere. You sit in all the seats; you register the fact that the audience has to lean over the balcony if the action is further than halfway downstage. What we did not feel we had in the new Other Place was something that asked any more to be used as itself. We felt that we needed to dress it up. I think that this will go in time – it was because it was a new building – and the new brick that went behind the actors was particularly oppressive and heavy.

There are foolish things which influence you: the large number of exit doors and exit lights which suddenly made it feel rather formal as a space. It had lost the ability to have the audience sitting on cushions on the floor as in Adrian Noble's production of *Antony and Cleopatra* which I saw while still at school. It was an overwhelming experience – and not just because Helen Mirren was wearing a diaphanous gown, although I am sure that had a lot to do with it! But it now seemed to have lost that sense in which one trusted it to be itself as one does with the Swan.

But I also had an eye on the production going to the Swan and wanted to recreate certain elements of the Swan, partly because I felt very attached to it after *Troilus*. That took the action away from naturalism.

PH But isn't it also intrinsic to *Richard III*, a play that cannot be acted to an audience seated on cushions?

SM The production I wanted to do certainly could not have been. The play is a formal piece of early Shakespeare, a history play. I did feel that the audience needed to be drawn in in the early scenes. But there are also those enormously stylized scenes, with the three queens or three citizens, phases where the play needed to be presented in a much more formal, almost Greek way. I was being drawn towards something which was more Greek, more to do with retribution; that is why I kept bringing Margaret back. It was also connected with the fact that I was doing it on its own, out of the context of the Wars of the Roses.

PH I was surprised that Simon Russell Beale as Richard did not work off the audience in quite the way that I might have expected, given the small nature of The Other Place space.

SM That was not a permanent feature of the production, because something very different happened to it in the Swan. It was to do with the space: in The Other Place, the audience is too close for that sort of response. Simon wanted and needed a more unified reaction. Unless you are upstage centre in The Other Place, you can never speak to the audience as a unit; in this it subtly and crucially differs from the Swan which is also a three-sided stage, and yet is one where the audience is unified wherever an actor is standing.

When we went into the Swan, the production came into its own. Reactions I had expected but which never worked in The Other Place, the early comedy or the reaction of horror to the Elizabeth scene, were all provoked in the Swan. At the start of the play, in Simon's soliloquy, people felt freer to laugh. In The Other Place they were too close to laugh, as if they would be complying with him. In the Swan that slight distance was all that was needed; they went on the journey that that play asks of the audience, from the complicity with the murderers at the start to an absolute horror at his actions at the end.

PH What about the performances on tour at the Tokyo Globe?

SM The Tokyo Globe was reported to be a reproduction of Shakespeare's Globe, but it is not at all. It's a bizarre hybrid of a shallow, broad thrust stage and very broad auditorium. The production was thrilling on that stage, but in a totally different way to the Swan since it was not an involving space, being much closer to a proscenium stage with a big apron. We were just performing on this apron and the characters were caught and held in that space by Paul Pyant's wonderful lighting. The Margaret scenes were at their most dreamlike and ritualistic in Japan. They were slightly divorced from the audience and thus were strengthened, but of course it made Richard's scenes more difficult.

The shape of the Tokyo Globe pushes you towards a kind of linear staging, using width not depth, and not staging in diagonals but pushing people downstage and being very symmetrical. I tend to be very symmetrical anyway.

PH You had already done that in *Troilus and Cressida*, forming a frieze of warriors for the battle scenes at the end; that suggested a much wider and flatter stage than the Swan's.

SM I think that the Tokyo Globe would have suited that scene magnificently but nevertheless in the Swan I was delighted with what that line gave, the controlled power and the simple arrangement of bodies giving it real epic quality. The Swan does have that sense of latent power, of a space beyond the gallery that can explode at any minute with static or mobile figures, or an image.

PH So, after doing three shows in Stratford, two in the Swan and one in The Other Place, Adrian Noble had your arm twisted somewhere high up under your shoulder blades and said you were going to have to do a show in the Main House the next year.

SM I suppose the expectation after *Troilus and Cressida* was that I would move into the Main House, almost the expectation I had of myself. I prevented myself from doing that, partly because I had loved so much working in the Swan: it had released my own style for the first time. I had never felt at home with a proscenium stage and I felt that the Royal Shakespeare Theatre was the mother of all prosceniums.

It is a very big house and very difficult to manage because of the relationship of the stalls to stage, the vast distance from the front of the balcony to the stage, indeed from the front of the balcony to the back of the balcony; in other words the enormous distance over which you have to communicate. There is also a strange flatness to the proscenium: it lacks the feeling which you find in those Victorian theatres which possess boxes, that the audience is almost encroaching on the edges of the stage and enveloping, embracing the action. That is not the sense you get in Stratford with its flat stalls and squared-off apron stage. It is a very cold and unforgiving space when a production does not work. It is also a divided space: a forestage and a space behind the proscenium arch. Adrian Noble is the master at using it. I believe Trevor Nunn and John Napier brought the stage much further out into the auditorium, creating a greater sense of warmth between the audience and stage, but either way in the end I think it is a stage for classical theatre. It is suited to oratory, to public speaking; it just demands that the size of the emotions on display have to match the size of the space.

While I was resisting working in the Main House and doing *The Alchemist* in the Swan followed by *Richard III*, I watched much more in the Main House and by a process of osmosis I tried to learn where the strong points on stage were. Adrian Noble, for instance, staged ninety per cent of his superb production of *The Winter's Tale* on the forestage and very skilfully never drew attention to the fact. Terry Hands not only did that but most of the time characters in his productions were speaking out front, abandoning any attempt at naturalism.

PH Adrian Noble has often, in effect, divided the stage into two, creating pictures upstage and action downstage, as far down onto the apron as he can manage. But in *The Tempest* you created a unified space. You argue that the Main House is a space for oratory and public speaking, yet the play that you chose for your Main House debut was *The Tempest*, a play hardly exactly full of oratory and public speaking.

SM I would love to see *The Tempest* in the Swan. However, the reason I did *The Tempest* in the Main House was that the production I had in my head was a Main House production, a production which had to do with playing on the world of illusion and theatrical artifice that is somehow hinted at in the text. Anthony Ward, the designer of *The Tempest*, and I tried to take a Swan aesthetic into the Main House: to create a unified space in which the object that sat in the space had a succession of meanings, whichever you wanted to put on it.

Our objects for *The Tempest* were a wicker skip and a simple screen. Now that is the language of the Swan. We also put down a wooden floor with eight traps through which people either visibly or invisibly appeared. I wanted things in a space which was empty and somehow resonant beyond itself; so we created a kind of blue room, but it was not a room because you were not sure whether it was backed with a cyclorama or a wall. It had sand in it but it also had a wooden floor. It also had a door which you did not really see until the end. So it was both room and beach, the inside of Prospero's mind or whatever you wanted it to be. That is a difficult balance to strike; I found it in the Swan and I was attempting to do it in the Main House. That is very different from what Adrian Noble does; he's more pictorial and storyboards his productions. His great skill is of setting an impressive and resonant image and a very intimate and highly thought-through scene in counterpoint. But that is not the way I work; the images for me have to be part of the action. You could ask 'what has a wicker basket got to do with where Caliban lives? Surely, he lives in a rock: "here you sty me / In this hard rock"'. I expected that to get a laugh on the first night but it never has.

Of course one gets tempted by the trappings of the Main House, by the ability it gives one to be pictorially ravishing. And indeed I wanted to do someting suitably visually impressive with the storm, with the masque, with the banquet. These are the big set pieces and you have to meet their challenge. You cannot use a wind-up gramophone for the masque and you cannot use a picnic hamper for the banquet, although it nearly was a picnic hamper at one point in rehearsal. But the challenge was to make these things exist in a space which never changed, so that although the masque did take place in a giant Victorian toy theatre, the room surrounding it was identical.

But there is a problem in the transfer from Swan to Main House: you do not question the skip in the Swan in the same way as you question it in the proscenium. You ask objects to be more literal on a big stage and accept them as more imagistic in the Swan, as it has a less specific environment. Do what you want on the Main House stage in the way of trying to make it like a Swan-type stage, but you cannot prevent the audience from noticing that there are three walls on stage and therefore the focus is changed. The two spaces make the same object look different. And it is not you as an individual relating to the space but you as part of an audience with its own sense of shared focus.

PH Is part of the threat that the Main House offers, the sense that one is watching a film?

SM The Main House indeed has elements of cinema, particularly the architectural detail which is very 'thirties Odeon. But its depth makes it crucially different. What theatre has over cinema, I suppose, is its three-dimensionality. I wanted to use the space in a very three-dimensional way; there are, for instance, many moments when actors are placed upstage to give the audience this tremendous sense of depth. I like this space very much now.

PH You have now decided that you are not going to direct at Stratford in 1994. That gives you carte blanche to fantasize. Which Shakespeare plays would you ideally do in which space?

SM Being a born fantasist, as one must be if one is even to exist as a director, I do have an answer to that question: I would like to do *Henry IV Parts I* and *II* and *Henry V* in the Swan because I think that those plays and that space would be ideally matched. It is an idea which will probably never happen because I think that the plays are considered to be too major to be put on such a small stage. But the Swan is ideal because it is both an epic and domestic space and that is crucial for those plays which exist on those two planes. I think that kaleidoscopic vision is simply and deftly achievable on that stage in a way it simply cannot be in any other theatre in the country. It is a marriage of play and space which I would love to see achieved.

As Adrian Noble has proved, the epic elements of those pieces are eminently achievable in the Main House. But there is something about that extraordinary contraction, that rapid focusing in like an iris on a camera, and the speed with which that iris opens and closes which would be wonderful in the Swan. The sense of an entire country running parallel with somebody who cannot sleep at night, alone in his room, musing on the state of the nation – those two could be superbly married.

PH You have also talked of directing *Macbeth* at the Donmar Warehouse where you are artistic director. When the Donmar was first used by the RSC, it was The Other Place transfer house. Would your *Macbeth* be an 'Other Place production' in the Donmar?

SM I had a hand in redesigning the Donmar and I had learnt a great deal from working in the Swan and The Other Place; I introduced certain elements of what I felt was successful about the Swan into the Donmar. So I think the Donmar is now closer to the Swan; it is a more epic space.

PH If you did *Macbeth*, wouldn't you be fighting audience's memories of Trevor Nunn's production?

SM I do not think one is fighting it: I would relish the chance to do a 'nineties production of that same play following in his footsteps. But it will be a different production. When you work for the RSC you get used to embracing the fact that you are working within a tradition of classical theatre. You are constantly being met by images of past productions of the play that you are doing. With *Richard III* there was the enormous success of Bill Alexander's production with Tony Sher to contend with. But I relish that. One should not have to say that the way my *Macbeth* is going to differ from Trevor Nunn's is because I am doing it in a green box or in a blue swimming pool. The fact is that, wherever and whichever the theatre, the moment the lines start to be spoken it will be different by dint of every inflection, every emphasis, every piece of interpretation and of course every actor.

I am immensely grateful to Karen Courtier for transcribing the tapes of the original interviews.

DIS-COVERING THE FEMALE BODY EROTIC EXPLORATION IN ELIZABETHAN POETRY

WERNER VON KOPPENFELS

Yet Ovid's wanton Muse did not offend:
He is the fountain whence my streams do flow;
Forgive me if I speak as I was taught . . .
(Thomas Nashe, *The Choice of Valentines*)

I

The first and, arguably, greatest Elizabethan 'bed-scene' takes place in the last hundred lines of Marlowe's *Hero and Leander* (2.235–334).[1] By physically staging the drama of lust-in-action, the great literary pioneer engages in a highly original dialogue with classical tradition, and in a feat of poetic trail-blazing. Surprisingly enough, the literary origins and techniques of this memorable scene, as well as its impact on the Elizabethan erotic imagination, do not seem to have aroused much critical interest. Judging from this neglect, the representation of the body in sensuously inviting intimacy appears to be a more disreputable topic in Renaissance literature than in the fine arts of the period. Thus in what is probably the most influential treatment of *Hero and Leander*, the corruption of 'the Greek maiden of Musaeus' by the 'fleshliness of the *Amores*' is being emphatically deplored: 'One wonders what miracle Marlowe might have achieved if he had been able to approach Musaeus directly.'[2] One wonders.

Unlike Renaissance painting, Elizabethan poetry in the 1580s had not yet discovered the lure of the body. It was Marlowe who led the way, and in doing so he proved the brilliantly gifted pupil of his *magister amoris* Ovid, whose love poems he had formerly translated line by line. Marlowe's lover hero reaches the goal whose permanent denial was the raison d'être of the Petrarchan love relationship (even though motifs like the *basium*, the *blason* of the lady's bodily charms or the love dream might impart a certain sensuous warmth to some sonnet sequences): Leander is finally admitted

The following is a free English version of – and partly an addition to – ch. 2 ('*Lust in Action*: Elisabethanische Metamorphosen Ovids') of my book *Bild und Metamorphose*, Darmstadt 1991. It was written for the 1993 'Colloque du GERB' in Bordeaux.

[1] Marlowe, *The Complete Poems and Translations*, ed. S. Orgel (Harmondsworth, 1971), pp. 37–40.

[2] D. Bush, *Mythology and the Renaissance Tradition in English Poetry*, New York, 2nd edn, 1957, pp. 128 and 138; cf. ibid., p. 132: 'the Greek maiden of Musaeus does not emerge unsullied from association with Corinna'. In the case of Nashe's (admittedly more scandalous) *Choice of Valentines* we find McKerrow relegating this 'wanton elegy' to the limbo of Nashe's 'Doubtful Works', though he had few doubts as to his authorship: 'There can, *I fear*, be little doubt that this poem is the work of Nashe' (*Works*, vol. 5, Oxford, 2nd edn, 1958, p. 141; my italics). Elizabethan adaptations of Ovid include amazing transpositions of key. While Nashe intensifies the Ovidian note of sexual cynicism with a vengeance, Marlowe turns some of the corrupt advice the bawd Dipsas gave to Corinna (*Amores* 1.8.49–53) into Leander's wooing speech, 'full of simplicity and naked truth' (1.225–42); to Hero's question 'Who taught thee rhetoric to deceive a maid?' (1.338), Leander should, strictly speaking, have answered: 'Ovid'. Marlowe's 'innocent' Ovidian images reappear in Donne's provocative plea for promiscuity, 'Confined Love' – enriched by a few motifs from the incestuous love story of Myrrha (*Metamorphoses*, 10.320 ff.).

to the full visual and bodily enjoyment of his beloved.

After crossing the Hellespont he embarks on a second voyage of discovery, where again all his manly strength and cunning are needed to guide him to the desired port. The scene of this nocturnal enterprise is the bedchamber of Hero's tower – and this tower in turn symbolizes the 'beauteous fort' of her virginal body, almost ready to yield itself to his siege. (On his previous visit Leander found the door of the tower auspiciously 'Wide open'; 2.19.) If the story's overall structure is one of gradual 'rapprochement' between the lovers, the same is true – only more so – of its last, and truly climactic, movement. In Marlowe's two classical sources, the joining of Hero and Leander was handled briefly and discreetly. Musaeus has an extremely short scene, enacted in complete darkness and silence; and in Ovid's *Heroides* Leander passes over the great moment in retrospect with the line: 'Cetera nox et nos et turris conscia novit' (18.105: 'For the rest – night knows of it, and ourselves, and the tower that shares our secret'; Loeb translation). In Marlowe, however, the lovers play a slow-motion scene of erotic hide-and-seek, consisting of a sham flight and pursuit, and culminating in a mock battle and victory without defeat.

When Leander knocks at the door of Hero's tower, presumably rather wet and in need of warmth after his Byronic swimming feat, Hero, 'drunk with gladness', rises in her night-gown to open, but 'seeing a naked man, she screeched for fear', and 'ran into the dark, herself to hide' (2.237 ff.) – the tone of sexual comedy is unmistakable. But the luminous beauty of her body, shining through the thin texture, betrays her to his sight.

> The nearer that he came, the more she fled,
> And seeking refuge, slipped into her bed.
>
> (2.243 f.)

This of course is the unsafest of all hiding places. Leander, for his part, presses every advantage by word and action. At first he pleads loss of body heat through excess of swimming; she charitably yields him her 'lukewarm place' and retreats into the lower portion of the bed (almost certainly a curtained-off four-poster), turning her blanket into a tent, into an ultimate recess of privacy within her Chinese-box-like enclosure of tower, room and bed: the 'tent' serves her as a bed within the bed, and to her modesty as a night within the night.

While Hero half-heartedly tries to defend this last stand (here the fortress imagery returns with a vengeance), Leander in a daring thrust scales 'the rising ivory mount' (273), that is, touches her breast, whereupon her renewed resistance forces him to parley, use delaying tactics, and conclude a kissing truce; which he breaks almost immediately – there is a final bold advance, and the fort is taken, to the satisfaction of both parties. In a characteristic coda to the scene, Hero tries to slip out of the bed before dawn, is held back by her lover, and stands before him, illumined by her own fiery blush, in a 'kind of twilight' and 'false morn', which anticipates and no doubt surpasses the actual sunrise:

> So Hero's ruddy cheek Hero betrayed,
> And her all naked to his sight displayed,
> Whence his admiring eyes more pleasure took,
> Than Dis on heaps of gold fixing his look.
>
> (323 ff.)

The *false morn* conceit is clearly a 'reprise' and variation of the light shed by Hero's bright body through night-gown and darkness at the beginning of the love encounter. Self-betrayal seems to be the tenor of the whole scene; as the narrator knowingly comments at the height of the mock battle:

> Treason was in her thought,
> And cunningly to yield herself she sought.
> Seeming not won, yet won she was at length,
> In such wars women use but half their strength.
>
> (293 ff.)

There is a male perspective throughout, a game of concealment and discovery, of veiling and unveiling the object of desire, a drawing closer, whose stages constitute the crescendo of 'lust in action'. The narrator's note of worldly cynicism, turning the reader into an accomplice, contrasts with the lovers' half-ingenuousness (on an earlier occasion they both behaved like Daphnis and Chloe – before Daphnis received his private love lesson from a third party). Leander, this time, is led on by nature – and by Hero herself; though she is nominally a vestal, her status as 'Venus' nun' (1.45) has been a paradoxical one from the beginning. So the love fight appears as a sham, staged for decorum's sake, and in order to heighten the sense of erotic enjoyment – a comedy acting out the standard male and female parts in a mood of light-hearted irony.

Yet the Hero and Leander myth is a tragic one. Though the comic mode prevails in Marlowe's final scene, an ominous note is by no means absent. Thus some of the mythological references seem distinctly to jar with the worldly wise and frivolous narrative voice. This is especially true for the moments of visual revelation, where the possessive discovery of the female body imparts to both lover and reader a sense of voyeuristic thrill, a mingling of guilt and delight. Hero, with Leander moving closer, is compared to 'chaste Diana when Actaeon spied her, / Being suddenly betrayed . . .' (261 f.); Leander enjoying the full view of her naked body is likened to Dis, the 'Rich One', God of Hades, gloating over his riches. These images, though plausible enough in a context of playful stylistic exuberance, suggest with great narrative tact an undercurrent of violence, nemesis and death (the metamorphosis and killing of Actaeon; the rape of Proserpine). This becomes most obvious in Marlowe's use of predatory imagery at the very moment of Hero's surrender:

> she alas
> (Poor silly maiden) at his mercy was.
> Love is not full of pity (as men say)
> But deaf and cruel, where he means to prey.
> Even as a bird, which in our hands we wring,
> Forth plunges, and oft flutters with her wing,
> She trembling strove . . . (285 ff.)

Obviously there is betrayal as well as self-betrayal in this elaborate presentation of physical love-making. The verb 'wring' contains a rather grim ambiguity: is the bird just being caught in the hand, or is the hand actually about to wring its neck?[3]

II

There can be no doubt that in composing the first Elizabethan 'bed-scene' Marlowe was resolutely moving beyond Petrarchism, and that his main inspiration was the classical love elegy or, to be more precise, Ovid's *Amores*. The closest analogue is the famous erotic siesta (1.5), whose Latin title, at the top of Marlowe's own English version, reads *Corinnae concubitus*. The lively spontaneity of this highly dramatic scene is the result of an extremely careful verbal arrangement. There is a strong sense of time, place and of pleasurable expectation, a climactic course of events free from all irrelevant details, and the male point of view of the frivolously witty first-person narrator: moreover, there is a dual perspective, since the speaker also plays the part of the protagonist. This time it is the girl who approaches the man resting on his couch. Because of the midday heat the room is half-darkened, an atmosphere favourable to amorous overtures.

Ecce Corinna venit (lo! Corinna comes): The girl makes her dramatic appearance in a 'loose gown' (*tunica recincta*), that is to say in a rather intimate garment, extremely thin and transparent at that (*rara*) – propitious signs for the

[3] The latter reading is Shakespeare's; cf. his *Rape of Lucrece*, v. 457: 'Like to a new-killed bird she trembling lies.' J. B. Steane in his reading of the Marlovian scene stresses an underlying 'element of fierceness and destructiveness' (*Marlowe: A Critical Study*, Cambridge, 1964, ch. 9, p. 331). This hint is taken up by W. Keach, in his study *Elizabethan Erotic Narratives* (New Brunswick, 1977); but though Keach mentions the *Metamorphoses* in connection with Neptune's attempted seduction of Leander (p. 106), his Ovidian perspective of the final love chase is essentially derived from the elegies (cf. p. 111).

lover: this dress code reflects a heat other than just the noonday temperature. The lover at once gets hold of the flimsy texture, and a mock battle ensues (Marlowe's version):

> I snatched her gown: being thin, the harm was small,
> Yet strived she to be covered therewithal,
> And striving thus as one that would be cast,
> Betrayed herself, and yielded at the last. (13 ff.)

In the Ovidian model the contemplation of the girl's nakedness (which takes place *après coup* in *Hero and Leander*) leads up to the supreme moment, and is the episode's true centre of interest. The fact that this is the last stage but one of the lovers' bodily 'rapprochement' makes it both the anticipation and equivalent of the love act itself, which Ovid refuses to describe. The male eye registers the manifold female charms in a characteristic downward movement, thus expressing a voyeuristic perspective and a mounting rhythm of desire, and imposing both on the reader. (Here, as elsewhere, there is a certain coarsening of effect in Marlowe's version, as can be seen in his rendering of *posito velamine*, unveiled, by 'stark naked'.)

> Stark naked now she stood before mine eye,
> Not one wen in her body could I spy.
> What arms and shoulders did I touch and see,
> How apt her breasts were to be pressed by me!
> How smooth a belly under her waist saw I,
> How large a leg, and what a lusty thigh! (17 ff.)

This verbal strip-tease obviously caught – and enflamed – the imagination of Elizabethan readers and poets. When Marston in his *Pygmalion* (1598) made his artist hero ecstatically gaze at the details of his just-created marble beauty, about to be transformed into flesh and blood, the Ovidian reminiscence turns up as a matter of course:

> But when the faire proportion of her thigh
> Began appeare, O *Ouid* would he cry,
> Did ere *Corinna* show such Iuorie
> When she appear'd in *Venus* liuorie? [i.e. naked][4]

To state that, whenever female thighs and breasts are revealed in Elizabethan literature, there is a distinct (and slightly apologetic) reference to the Ovidian prototype would only be a slight exaggeration.[5] At any rate, the most notoriously out-spoken poems of sexual revelation, Nashe's *Choice of Valentines* and Donne's elegies 'Love's Progress' and 'To his Mistress Going to Bed' can be seen to be directly inspired by *Amores* 1.5, and by the Elizabethan *Ovidius redivivus* Marlowe.

But there exists yet another, and entirely different Ovidian perspective of desire, derived from the mythical *furor* of love in the *Metamorphoses*. At its extreme, this dark and destructive drive leads to a rape of the love object, as in the story of Tereus and Philomela, which left such a lasting impression on the Elizabethan mind. Here the sham fight of the elegy is transformed into a deadly struggle, the half-serious resistance of feigned modesty turns into a brutal forcing of purest innocence by absolute guilt, and the male visual and anticipatory enjoyment of the female body fully displayed becomes the rapist's sadistic gloating over his helpless victim. The possession of the desired body is equivalent to – and sometimes symbolized by – an act of mutilation. Its dramatic and

---

[4] J. Marston, *The Poetical Works*, ed. A. Davenport (Liverpool, 1961), p. 54.

[5] Cf. Sidney's poetic description of Philoclea's beauty, one of the most outspoken and influential *blasons* in Elizabethan literature: 'Yet never shall my song omitte / Thighes, for *Ovids* song more fitte . . .' (*The Countesse of Pembrokes Arcadia*, ed. A. Feuillerat, Cambridge, 2nd edn, 1962, p. 220). Marlowe's punning version of *Amores* 1.5.20: 'Forma papillarum quam fuit apta premi' – 'How apt her breasts were to be pressed by me' gained wide currency; Sir John Harington as translator of Ariosto introduced it into the description of Alcina the temptress' 'due pome acerbe' (*Orlando Furioso* VII, xiv): 'Two ivory apples seemèd there to grow / Tender and smooth and fittest to be pressed'. I owe this reference, as well as other suggestions, to H. Klein, *Das weibliche Portrait in der Versdichtung der englischen Renaissance* (Diss. Munich, 1969, p. 345).

climactic movement, as well as its male perspective and disturbing voyeurism (though the narrative voice expresses pity and indignation in strongest terms) link this type of 'lust in action' with *Amores* 1.5. While the elegy's sense of transgression in making the normally removed and veiled female body both visible and available is merely titillating, this infringement of decency becomes profoundly shocking in the story of Tereus, and in such Elizabethan – as well as Roman/Italian – rapes as those of Lucrece, of Lavinia in *Titus Andronicus*, or of Heraclide in *The Unfortunate Traveller*. In these cases, proverbial 'Italian' villainy is made an excuse for presenting the unpresentable.

There are distinct traces of this second Ovidian tradition in the final love scene of *Hero and Leander*. The allusions to Actaeon and Dis are not the only references to the fatal *eros* of the *Metamorphoses*. In the striking image of Hero's 'silver body' diving down into the bed in order to escape Leander's hands there may well be an echo of the famous watery love chase between Salmacis and Hermaphroditus. In this case the man is pursued by the nymph for a change, and while swimming in the 'water cleare / . . . his body faire and white doth glistringly appeare'.[6] Predatory love imagery (which proves the clearest indication for the presence of the destructive Ovidian *eros* in Marlowe's copulation scene) is applied to the helpless Hermaphroditus in the grasp of his nymphomaniac nymph: he is a snake writhing in the talons of an eagle, or a fish locked in the embrace of an octopus (*Met.* 4.362 ff.). Similarly Tereus in his sexual aggression is successively compared to an eagle with a stricken hare at his mercy (6.518: 'nulla fuga est capto, spectat sua praemia raptor'; Golding, 76r: 'The rauening fowle with greedie eyes upon his pray doth gape'), with a wolf facing a half-killed lamb, and with a dove caught by a bird of prey (*Met.* 6.527 ff.). What Marlowe in fact does, is to turn Hero's surrender for one disturbing moment into a rape situation. Immediately afterwards the mythological reference changes again, and Leander enters the orchard of the Hesperides to pluck the golden apples of sensual bliss.

III

Shakespeare for one clearly realized the presence of the two contradictory yet related Ovids in Marlowe's famous love scene. His *Rape of Lucrece*, much neglected by criticism, retranslates Marlowe's predominantly 'elegiac' erotic encounter into the darker key of the *Metamorphoses*.[7] The ravisher's gradual approach to the sacrosanct chamber, bed and body is described as a crescendo of fatal attraction and fascinated transgression, whose voyeuristic interest is not at all covered up by the narrator's righteous indignation. There is the Marlovian passing of more and more intimate spatial limits: Tarquin crosses one room after another, and finally opens the door of Lucrece's bedchamber with a characteristic gesture anticipating his deed –

[6] *Metamorphoses*, 4.340 ff.; in A. Golding, *The xv Bookes . . . entytuled Metamorphosis*, facs. edn, Amsterdam: 1977, 48^{v}, line 15 f.

[7] Though his 'official' source is Livy, and Ovid's account in *Fasti* 2.721–852. The critics do not seem to have followed up D. Bush's wholesale observation of 'many obvious parallels' between *Hero and Leander* and *Lucrece* (*Mythology*, p. 125). There is an isolated note on *Lucrece*, v. 407, in the New Arden Edition, but not a word in the New Penguin Shakespeare (1971) or in the detailed source discussion of the recent New Cambridge edition (1992); the same applies to T. W. Baldwin, *On the Literary Genetics of Shakespeare's Poems* (1950), to F. P. Wilson, *Marlowe and the Early Shakespeare* (1953), to G. Bullough, *Narrative and Dramatic Sources*, vol. 1 (1975), as well as to the more substantial recent readings of *Lucrece* (N. Vickers, '"The blazon of sweet beauty's best": Shakespeare's *Lucrece*', in P. Parker/G. Hartmann, eds., *Shakespeare and the Question of Theory*, London, 1985, pp. 95–115; H. Dubrow, *Captive Victors*, Ithaca, 1987, ch. 2).

his guilty hand plucked up the latch,
And with his knee the door he opens wide.
(358 f.)[8]

The opening of the bed-curtains, the possessive placing of his hand on her breast (after *Fasti* II.804: 'tunc primum externa pectora tacta manu', with a touch of fortress metaphorics from *Hero and Leander*: 'Rude ram, to batter such an ivory wall'; v.464), finally the brutal tearing of her nightgown in order to gag her – these are increasingly sacrilegious irruptions into the stronghold of innocence. The Ovidian type of predatory imagery is much in evidence, even from the moment of Tarquin's rapt and anticipatory contemplation of his unsuspecting victim (cf. Tereus in *Met.* 6.513 ff.)

As the grim lion fawneth o'er his prey,
Sharp hunger by the conquest satisfied,
So o'er this sleeping soul doth Tarquin stay,
His rage of lust by gazing qualified . . . (421 ff.)

On being roused from innocent sleep by the rude touch of his hand, 'Like to a new-killed bird she trembling lies' (457; an echo from Marlowe: cf. note 3); under his phallic 'falchion'[9] she lies like a fowl beneath a falcon's wings (505 ff.), and under his deadly eye she is 'Like a white hind under the gripe's sharp claws' (543); finally 'The wolf hath seized his prey, the poor lamb cries', till her voice is stifled 'with her own white fleece' (677 f.).

Compared with Marlowe, Shakespeare has slowed down the rhythm of the scene even further. He seems to aim at surpassing his model through amplification and extravagance of description. Tarquin's visual progress through the various standard items of the beauty catalogue – hair, (closed) eyes, hands, breasts etc. – is painstakingly systematic; the central Marlovian conceit of the fortress assaulted is considerably extended and carried over into the 'parley' (which turns into a long-drawn-out *débat*): 'I come to scale / Thy never-conquered fort . . .'[10] The motif of self-betrayal is used, too, but in a different sense: 'The fault is thine, / For those thine eyes betray thee unto mine' (482 f.). Finally both Hero and Lucrece are ashamed of the morning light, though for different reasons:

For much it grieved her that the bright daylight
Should know the pleasure of this blessed night
. . . (*Hero and Leander*, 303 f.)

She prays she never may behold the day.
'For day', quoth she, 'night's scapes doth open
lay . . .' (*Lucrece*, 746 f.)

These words introduce what is to be Lucrece's nine-stanza apostrophe to Night, imploring her as the accomplice of dark deeds to hide the crushing shame, which the innocent rape victim is bound to experience, according to the sexual code of the time.[11] Night offers protection to the lovers, but it also favours the ravisher, who quenches his torch at the decisive moment with a final symbolic gesture proleptic of his crime, 'For light and lust are deadly enemies' (674).

---

8 Cf. Thomas Nashe, *The Unfortunate Traveller and Other Works*, ed. J. B. Steane (Harmondsworth, 1972), p. 336: 'he . . . used his knee as an iron ram to beat ope the two-leaved gate of her chastity'.

9 The 'falchion' or sword raised in menace functions as symbol of sexual aggression within the iconography of the scene both in painting and literature. Cf. *Unfortunate Traveller*, p. 335: 'Therewith he flew upon her and threatened her with his sword, but it was not that he meant to wound her with.' The fully dressed and armed Tarquin is implicitly contrasted with 'naked' (i.e. unclothed/unarmed) Leander. Renaissance paintings of the rape as compared with the suicide of Lucretia reveal the iconographic pattern of inversion: his dishonouring sword versus her sword of 'honour restored'.

10 v. 481 f.; cf. *Hero and Leander* 2.16: 'As he had hope to scale the beauteous fort'. Shakespeare carries this imagery on into the lengthy *ecphrasis* describing the Fall of Troy (1366–1582).

11 The coming of daylight in Marlowe's final lines ('his flaring beams mocked ugly night, / Till she . . . / Danged down to hell her loathsome carriage') are obviously echoed in Shakespeare's lines 1081 ff.: 'And solemn night with slow sad gait descended / To ugly hell . . .' The ritual cursing of the morning ultimately derives from the *alba*-like imprecations against dawn in *Amores* 1.13.

Thus Shakespeare's reading of Marlowe has fully realized the potential of 'Murder, rape, war, lust and treachery' (*Hero and Leander* 1.457) subliminally present in the model. There are disturbingly grim elements present in the Marlovian sexual comedy, and there are some rather comic touches to its tragic counterpart in Shakespeare. Tarquin in post-coital low spirits –

> With lank and lean discoloured cheek,
> With heavy eye, knit brow and strengthless pace (708 f.)

– is the very mirror-image of Tomalin leaving the brothel in Nashe's *Choice of Valentines*:

> I pay our hostess scot and lot a most,
> And I look as lean and lank as any ghost.[12]

In Nashe's *Unfortunate Traveller* the rape of Heraclide is a tragically styled inset in a dominantly burlesque narrative. The picaresque narrator Jack Wilton watches the gruesome scene 'through a cranny in my upper chamber', where he has been locked up by the ravisher. Given Nashe's often-voiced admiration for Aretino, it is more than likely that this situation was suggested by the first chapter of the *Ragionamenti*. (There the sexual novice, who has just entered a nunnery, watches through several chinks in the wall of her room the various copulations between clerics and nuns taking place in the neighbouring cells.) Nashe seems to have transferred this act of voyeurism from an openly pornographic to an allegedly tragic context. The invitation to voyeurism, undoubtedly present in Renaissance pictorial treatments of such highly moral themes as 'The Rape of Lucrece' or 'Susannah and the Elders', is no less alien to Shakespeare's little epic than to Nashe's sensational narrative.[13] Both appeared in the same year, and were dedicated to the same young aristocrat, the Earl of Southampton – a gentleman not particularly noted for the strictness of his morals.

IV

At one point in his trend-setting metamorphosis of Ovid Marlowe uses a conceit seemingly at odds with the prevalent military imagery of Hero and Leander's amorous scuffle:

> . . . the rising ivory mount he scaled,
> Which is with azure circling lines empaled,
> Much like a globe (a globe I may term this,
> By which love sails to regions full of bliss) . . .
> (273 ff.)

Here the erotic siege and conquest have all of a sudden, and parenthetically, been transformed into a voyage of discovery. The moment of semantic transition can be located in the verb *empale*, which means (1) to render pale (hence more white, and more beautiful); (2) to enclose and fortify troops for defence; (3) to encircle (a globe by meridians). Its intimate and lust-provoking beauty turns Hero's bastion of defence into a nautical chart that will send Leander to the Isles of Bliss.[14]

Again we can tell exactly how Shakespeare

---

[12] Nashe, *Unfortunate Traveller* etc., p. 467 (v. 309 f.).

[13] Cf. *Unfortunate Traveller*, pp. 332–9; ibid., pp. 309–11, for Wilton's (and Nashe's) ecomium of Aretino, suspiciously confined to the latter's more edifying works. (An Italian edition of the *Ragionamenti* came out in London in 1584. With regard to Nashe's possible knowledge of this erotic masterpiece criticism seems to have stopped short at McKerrow's questionable verdict that direct influence was unproved and therefore unlikely to have occurred; cf. his Nashe, *Works*, vol. 5, pp. 128 f.). In lamenting her sad fate, and before committing her Lucrece-like suicide, Nashe's Heraclide quotes a line from the *Metamorphoses* (2.447: the rape of Callisto) in Latin! (p. 338). For the 'invitation to voyeurism' of Lucretia paintings by Titian, Tiepolo and others, cf. I. Donaldson, *The Rapes of Lucretia* (Oxford, 1982), p. 20.

[14] Sidney, in his *blason* of Philoclea (cf. n. 5), gives an anorganic turn to the erotic topos of the blue-veined breasts: 'Like pomels round of Marble cleere: / Where azurde veines well mixt appeere, / With dearest tops of porphyrie' (*Arcadia*, p. 220). B. Barnes, who freely introduces erotic motifs into his sonnet sequence, *Parthenophil*, puts Marlowe's globe conceit to strange use in

read this passage. Without actually using Marlowe's polysemantic verb, he employs all three meanings, within his own tragic context, for the desecration of Lucrece's breast.

> Her breasts like ivory globes circled with blue,
> A pair of maiden worlds unconquerèd . . .
> (407 f.)

This is how the breasts appear as crowning items of the beauty catalogue – as worlds of purity about to be invaded by force. At the first act of assault Marlowe's dual image of pallor and a garrison fortified reappears in the form of an extravagant conceit:

> [His hand] . . . march'd on, to make his stand
> On her bare breast, the heart of all her land,
> Whose ranks of blue veins, as his hand did scale,
> Left their round turrets destitute and pale.
> (437 ff.)

The battered fortress, the sacked city, the rifled mansion – Shakespeare is not to be diverted from his central metaphorics by Marlovian frivolity; the pallor of Lucrece will contrast later on with Lucrece's own blood restoring both her purity and the perfect red and white as the true *blason* of beauty. Marlowe's globe conceit, however, will father a different, and less reputable, offspring. It appears to have inspired a whole Elizabethan geography of desire by turning the discovery or uncovering of the desired female body into an adventurous journey of exploration, conquest, and Eldorado -like gratification:

> O my America, my new found land,
> My kingdom, safeliest when with one man
> manned,
> My mine of precious stones, my empery,
> How blessed I am in this discovering thee![15]

In Donne's famous lines the globe conceit has all but disappeared, as have the items of the beauty catalogue: this body in the process of undressing, and the rising tide of desire it calls forth, are only reflected in the rhythm of the garments shed; the voyeurism is of a refined kind, even compared with the ultimate model, *Amores* 1.5. But in the final hymenic celebration of 'full nakedness', the wordplay on 'discovering' is ubiquitous; and it is repeated, and carried further, by means of a blasphemous pun on 'revelation' in the literal and physical sense of 'unveiling':

> [Women] are mystic books, which only we
> Whom their imputed grace will dignify
> Must see revealed. (41 ff.)[16]

The occasional note of worldly cynicism, by no means absent from Ovid and Marlowe, and clearly marked in the sexual wit of this poem, becomes the predominant mode in the most notorious of Donne's elegies, 'Love's Progress'. This poem outrageously preaches the shortest way to the 'centric part' of the female body as the 'right true end' of love. In this case there is no specific and dramatic love scene as in Ovid, Marlowe and Donne's own 'Going to Bed': only a paradoxical argument that parodies the traditional items of the beauty catalogue as aberrations of an erotic voyage likely never to reach its desired goal, 'her India . . . where thou wouldst be embayed' (i.e. harboured) (65 ff.). This erotico-satyricon is a kind of *Carte du Tendre à rebours*, for it turns both the traditional downward progress and all its laudatory *blasons*

---

one of his extravagant *blasons*: 'Her neck, that curious axletree, / Pure ivory like, which doth support / The Globe of my Cosmography'; at an earlier place he had applied Charles V's motto *plus ultra* to the lady's breasts, as re-christened Pillars of Hercules to be passed in his imaginary voyage of erotic discovery. (*Elizabethan Sonnets*, ed. S. Lee, Westminster, 1904, vol. 1, pp. 299 and 295.)

15 J. Donne, 'To his Mistress Going to Bed', in *The Complete English Poems*, ed. A. J. Smith (Harmondsworth, 1971), p. 125.

16 Cf. Marlowe's use of erotic book metaphorics in his version of *Amores* 3.13.44 (usually 3.14 in modern editions), where he renders the line 'Et fuerint oculis probra videnda meis' (Loeb translation: '[if] my eyes perforce shall have looked upon your shame') by 'Though . . . / . . . I see when you ope the two-leaved book.' As translator of Ovid, Marlowe likes to add his own little frivolous puns and points.

upside down. All the individual bodily charms are listed as so many mantraps – not for the usual moral reasons, but for the unusual and cynical one that they divert the sexual explorer from instant gratification. Those who erroneously 'set out at the face' (40) are either shipwrecked or lulled into a lotophagean forgetfulness of their true mission.

Though Donne does not actually use the globe conceit for the lady's breasts, his voyager leaves an unmistakable homage to Marlowe's mythological lovers in calling these dangerous straits

> the strait Hellespont between
> The Sestos and Abydos of her breasts . . . (60 f.)

Like the lover, the reader expecting to embark on a voyage of sexual discovery is led on a wild-goose chase: the chase was 'Misspent by thy beginning at the face' (72). Though the brief final section pretends to teach other and more direct ways, beginning at the foot, yet there is no voyeurist revelation; the shock of cynical argument remains paramount. And the conclusion, in its brutal image for those who refuse to take the southern itinerary –

> He which doth not, his error is as great,
> As who by clyster gave the stomach meat

– is positively anaphrodisiac in effect. After the Ovid of the *Amores* and the *Metamorphoses*, enter the author of the *Remedia Amoris*.

In Donne's poetry, desire for, and loathing of, the female body can exist side by side. In this particular poem, the 'right true end of love' is not so much celebrated as demonized. In a rather ambiguous simile Marlowe had compared Leander's rapturous contemplation of Hero's nakedness with Dis (or Pluto) enjoying the sight of his gold. Donne enlarges upon this theme when he calls Cupid 'an infernal god, and underground / With Pluto dwells, where gold and fire abound' (29 f.). Clearly the India for which his strange love-vessel is bound, is not the India of 'spice' but rather of 'mine', the American Eldorado. The all-important 'centric part' as the only true object of worship and desire is located at the bottom of mineshafts (v. 32: 'pits and holes'). This imagery indicates that here the creed of mere carnality reaches almost the point of sexual disenchantment and disgust envisaged in Donne's 'Love's Alchemy' by the same metaphoric means:

> Some that have deeper digged love's mine than I,
> Say, where his centric happiness doth lie . . .[17]

The shortest way to the centric part leads to the experience of 'mummy, possessed' (ibid., v. 24); it is a descent into infernal regions: India, the Hesperides and Earthly Paradise alike transformed into Hades. The centric part reached without further ado tends to become a hell of sexual disillusion, as the Shakespeare of the Dark Lady Sonnets knew so well.[18]

Its ultimately bleak outlook sets 'Love's Progress' miles apart from Marlowe's bed-scene and from its own second (presumable) source, Nashe's *Choice of Valentines*, which seems to have had some private circulation in manuscript. Like 'Love's Progress', Nashe's voyage of exploration is not a downward but an upward one. Tomalin, the first-person narrator, who has entered a 'house of venery' and joined an old favourite of his, Mistress Francis, straightaway starts lifting her 'rattling silks' (v. 78) with great zest. There is no defence, however spurious, and the progress of love is quick and unchecked – up to a point:

> I come, I come, sweet lining, by thy leave,[19]
> Softly my finger up these curtains heave
> And make me happy stealing by degrees.
> First bare her legs, then creep up to her knees,
> From thence ascend unto her manly thigh[20]
> (A pox on lingering when I am so nigh).
> Smock, climb apace, that I may see my joys:
> Oh, heaven and paradise . . . (5.99 ff.)[21]

---

17 Donne, *Poems*, p. 65.

18 Cf. Sonnets 129 and 144.

19 The text has: 'be thy leave'.

20 Ovid's 'iuvenale femur' from *Amores*, 1.5; 'manly' in the sense of 'upright' or 'strong'; Marlowe renders 'iuvenale' by 'lusty'.

21 Nashe, *Unfortunate Traveller*, p. 461.

This paradise is lovingly described in terms of erotic scenery as a *locus amoenus*:

> A pretty rising womb without a weam[22]
> That shone as bright as any silver stream . . .

At one point during the exploration of these enticing nether regions the Marlovian model is alluded to, for purposes of inversion. The part of the female body 'with azure lines empaled' is (for obvious reasons) not the breast, and its touch does not guide the lover to the Hesperides in order to pick the golden apples – on the contrary:

> A lofty buttock barr'd with azure veins,
> Whose comely swelling, when my hand distrains,
> Or wanton checketh with a harmless stripe,[23]
> It makes the fruits of love eftsoon be ripe,
> And pleasure pluck'd too timely from the stem
> . . . (115 ff.)

Here the comic motif of the lover's temporary impotence is introduced from *Amores* 3.7[24] and expressly alluded to (123 f.). Thanks to Mistress Francis' expertise, Tomalin – unlike Ovid's lover – overcomes his weakness: his belated but impressive performance is detailed for some sixty lines, whereas in *Amores* 1.5 it was passed over with the tactful formula *Cetera qui nescit?* Obviously, and in spite of its authorial label of 'wanton elegy', Nashe's poem belongs to a different genre, which might be termed Elizabethan 'soft porn'. This fact is finally brought home to the reader when the insatiable courtesan, stimulated but not satisfied by her lover's exertions, reaches her own climax by using a dildo or artificial phallus. This seems to be another voyeurist motif suggested to Nashe by the 'nunnery chapter' of Aretino's *Ragionamenti*. In spite of their common reductionism of erotic experience, 'Love's Progress' and the *Choice of Valentines* mark opposite poles of the Elizabethan–Ovidian spectrum: blasphemic and radically subversive wit versus voyeuristic sexual comedy. In both cases the tragic potential of lust-in-action has been sacrificed at a price.

V

The dramatic as well as the tragic aspect of the Elizabethan exposure of the female body to male desire (in view and action) had been exploited by Shakespeare in *Titus Andronicus*, his earliest attempt at tragedy.[25] Much later, and in a context of 'comedy', he returned to the theme in order to give it a fascinatingly new and original turn which may serve as fitting conclusion to my sketch of this complex, intertextual and hitherto rather uncharted field. In *Cymbeline* the dual nature of the theme is being dramatized, and the male voyeuristic gaze is translated into an imaginary loss of innocence on the part of the body gazed at; if, on a psychological level, the first stage of this process amounts almost to an Ovidian rape, it is afterwards restyled, with abysmal cynicism, as an Ovidian sexual comedy.

In *Cymbeline* 2.2 Giacomo (Jachimo), the Italian villain and rapist of the mind, creeps out of his hiding place, draws the bed-curtains and takes a far from disinterested inventory of Innogen's (Imogen's) sleeping beauty helplessly exposed to his sacrilegious eyes. Many of the familiar topoi are present: the allusion to Philomel and Tarquin, the nightly and stealthy

[22] Cf. Marlowe's translation *Amores*, 1.5.18: 'Not one wen in her body'.

[23] The text has 'stype', duly glossed by the editor as 'Unknown'.

[24] *Elegies*, 3.6, in Marlowe's count.

[25] The rape of sacrosanct innocence serves as a symbolic concept of great power in some of the later tragedies. The 'Tarquinian' forcing of King Duncan's chamber, bed and body has often been commented on: Macbeth's evil lust, like Tarquin's, is denied any real satisfaction. But it should be noted that the deadly 'bed-scene' at the end of *Othello* has also a distinctly Lucretian quality in the sequence of its phases: nocturnal approach, drawing of the bed-curtains, address and extinction of the torch, rapt contemplation, awakening, plea and repartee, brute physical violence. Desdemona's emblematism of innocence withdrawn into deathlike immobility ('smooth as monumental alabaster') clearly links her back to Lucrece (cf. *Lucrece*, 391; 419).

approach to the sacrosanct bed, the anticipatory and possessive look, the blasphemous *blason*: skin, lips, closed eyes are dwelt on and metaphorically praised – especially the eyelids 'white and azure-laced / With blue of heaven's own tinct' (22 f.); here the abject voyeur, *malgré lui*, turns the blue veins of erotic geography into heavenly emblems of innocence and sanctity. There is the intruder's overwhelming urge to touch and kiss what he sees, and his consciousness of having broken into a *sanctum*. His eye commits the act and stains the purity of the body at his mercy (in its state of deathlike withdrawal) by discovering a little mole at an intimate place: 'On her left breast / A mole, cinque-spotted' (37 f.).

This is an innocent enough variation of *Amores* 1.5.18: 'Not one wen in her body could I spy',[26] put to diabolic uses by the *voyeur*. Later on Giacomo's Iago-like imagination and Machiavellian rhetoric will turn this harmless mole into the foul stain of sexual betrayal. In doing so, he translates the visual rape committed on sleeping Innogen into a frivolous scene of Ovidian lust-in-action, adjudging himself the double part of erotic hero and wittily cynical commentator:

> GIACOMO. . . under her breast –
> Worthy the pressing – lies a mole, right proud
> Of that most delicate lodging. By my life,
> I kissed it, and it gave me present hunger
> To feed again, though full. You do remember
> This stain upon her?
> POSTHUMUS Ay, and it doth confirm
> Another stain, as big as hell can hold . . .
> (2.4.134 ff.)

In this outrageously fictitious – and for that very reason obscene – 'love's progress' the touch of the breast is again the *plus ultra* of desire, a whetting of the sexual appetite for the 'full meal'; and with a shift of perspective the 'right true end of love' appears as the hell of sexual disillusion. In this case the most telling evidence of the Ovid–Marlowe filiation, which – as I have tried to show – essentially shaped the Elizabethan discovery of the female body in literature, is the formula in parenthesis, an obvious, though hitherto uncommented, echo of *Amores* 1.5.20: 'How apt her breasts were to be pressed by me.' Giacomo boldly changes Innogen's unwittingly Ovidian role from Philomel to Corinna. Shakespeare, like other authors of his generation, read Marlowe's Ovidian *erotica* at an impressionable age, and the impression stayed with him, for multiple uses.

26 Marlowe's 'wen' (Elizabethan variants are *weam* or *wem*) translates Ovid's 'menda' (stain or spot).

THESEUS' SHADOWS IN *A MIDSUMMER NIGHT'S DREAM*

PETER HOLLAND

As I was going up the stair
I met a man who wasn't there,
He wasn't there again today.
I wish, I wish he'd stay away.[1]

It is often noted that *A Midsummer Night's Dream* shares with *Love's Labour's Lost* and *The Tempest* a common lack of a clearly defined adequate narrative source. As Stanley Wells remarks in his essay 'Shakespeare without Sources',

> We are accustomed to the study of Shakespeare's plays by way of his sources. It is a common, and often rewarding, critical technique. But there are a few plays in which Shakespeare did not adapt existing sources . . . Other plays might almost be included in this list, and even these three show the influence of his reading, though in them the influence is local rather than pervasive. But in these three plays Shakespeare seems himself to have been responsible for the main story line, however much he may have drawn on his reading for points of detail.[2]

That seems unexceptionable and my summary of it in my phrase 'clearly defined adequate narrative source' perhaps equally so. There are no sources for *A Midsummer Night's Dream* sufficient to identify *all* the elements of the action – Theseus, lovers, fairies and workers – nor even any three of the list. There are, though, many ways of rethinking this view in relation to the play. One could argue that across a remarkable number of features Chaucer's 'Knight's Tale' constitutes a sufficient narrative source for at least much of *A Midsummer Night's Dream*, more than the framework of Theseus and his marriage. The homecoming of the triumphant Theseus with his bride Ypolita in Chaucer modulates into a series of disruptions, by three mourning ladies, rather than Egeus and his complaint, and the triangle of lovers, Palamon–Arcite–Emelye, with the men conspicuously interchangeable, is simply and neatly squared in *Dream* with four lovers, rather than three, making the notion of interchangeability all the more complicatedly and comically explored. This might then be an 'existing source', providing an adequate version of the main story line. There is plainly much about 'The Knight's Tale' in particular and other work by Chaucer that influences many aspects of the creation of *A Midsummer Night's Dream*. Warring fairies, mortals in love with fairy-queens, visions in May and the story of Pyramus and Thisbe all come from or were available in Chaucer, to a greater or lesser extent, from poems as diverse as *The Legend of Good Women*, 'The Merchant's Tale' and 'Sir Thopas'.[3]

[1] Hughes Mearns, 'The Psychoed' in *The Oxford Dictionary of Quotations* (2nd edn, 1953), p. 335.

[2] Stanley Wells, 'Shakespeare without Sources' in *Shakespearian Comedy*, eds. Malcolm Bradbury and David Palmer (Stratford-upon-Avon Studies, 14, 1972), p. 58.

[3] See, for example, John S. Mebane, 'Structure, Source, and Meaning in *A Midsummer Night's Dream*', *Texas Studies in Literature and Language*, 24 (1982), 255–70; E. Talbot Donaldson, *The Swan at the Well* (New Haven, 1985); Ann Thompson, *Shakespeare's Chaucer* (Liverpool, 1978).

Rather more to the point the influence of Shakespeare's reading may – and I will be arguing did – go far beyond what Wells calls 'local rather than pervasive . . . points of local detail' for *Dream*. But scholars have looked far and unsuccessfully for a source as close, say, as Cinthio's tale for *Othello* or Greene's *Pandosto* for *The Winter's Tale*. The result has been the generation of a remarkable plethora of sources for the play and more arrive every year; another tale from Cinthio's *Hecatommithi* for instance has recently been offered as a reasonably plausible source for the action involving the lovers, another version of a conventional romance action of confusion and cross-wooing, one significantly more like the action of *A Midsummer Night's Dream* than any other so far proposed.[4]

But the proposals for *local* influence of Shakespeare's reading raise the central problems of the treatment of sources: the extraordinary weakness in our *conventional* critical use of the term and consideration of its meaning and function. What, after all, is the point of a source? Is it simply a scholar's recognition of material lying behind and transmuted in the process of the writing? Or is it also, often or occasionally, an evocation by the play of other narratives, other modes of perception, other possibilities of meaning that are available for the audience, in differing ways, to differing degrees, to use and make functional? Is the source read or heard alongside and within, an informing presence in Shakespeare's text that is not directly there but is transmuted, an evoked presence discernible in many of its crucial features only in its partial and significant absences, a man on the stair who will not go away? As we have learned to talk with greater apparent sophistication about cultural contexts and the possibilities of intertextuality, this presence has been rendered problematic. Of course any 'source' can now be seen as intertextually present, present simply because evoked. But the question of theatrical presence, the looming quality of a source as it works in conjunction with the text on the audience's perception still seems to me unclear. Some of the 'sources' for *A Midsummer Night's Dream* raise this acutely. Let me take first the problem of Seneca.

In his Arden edition, Harold Brooks argues for Shakespeare's substantial use of Seneca's *Medea*, *Hippolytus* and *Oedipus*.[5] It has long been known, of course, that Bottom's enthusiastic speech on the raging rocks and shivering shocks (1.2.27–34) is a parody of two passages in John Studley's translation of Seneca's *Hercules Oetaeus*, though the two passages are much more widely separated in the translation than editions have ever indicated, making its presence as source much less immediately apparent. Studley's translation is part of that great edition of Seneca in English prepared by Thomas Newton and others and published in its completed form in 1581.[6] It was a collection Shakespeare knew well and had already used by the time of *A Midsummer Night's Dream*. Given its presence as a source for the parody of bombastic tragic diction at this point in the play, Shakespeare is, one supposes, quite likely to have at least dipped elsewhere in the volume. When R. A. Foakes carefully says, in his New Cambridge edition, that the echoes Brooks traces 'perhaps reflect again Shakespeare's absorption of images and motifs into his capacious memory and transforming imagination, rather than a conscious use of Seneca as source',[7] I want to wonder rather hard what the difference is that lies behind his separation here of *absorption* and *source*, whether the latter is held to have some greater informing power of meaning through its presence than the accidental local reminiscence and transformation.

---

4 Hugh M. Richmond, 'Shaping *A Dream*', *Shakespeare Studies*, 17 (1985), 49–60.

5 W. Shakespeare, *A Midsummer Night's Dream*, ed. Harold Brooks (1979), pp. lxii–lxiii and 139–45.

6 Thomas Newton et al., *Seneca His Tenne Tragedies, Translated Into Englysh* (1581).

7 W. Shakespeare, *A Midsummer Night's Dream*, ed. R. A. Foakes (Cambridge, 1984), p. 145.

I will need to spend some time going over Brooks' suggestions. The use of Seneca's *Oedipus* is the slightest: the lengthy description of the plague of Thebes at the beginning of the play describes many of the disasters that are part of Titania's description of the disorder of the seasons in 2.1: fogs, failed harvests, dying cattle. Brooks' quotation from the 150 lines of Seneca is acknowledgedly selective but the result is, perhaps, a little misleading. Can a line like 'What shall I say? all things (alas) are writhen out of course' really be held to affect in *any* imaginative and creative way Titania's account of the distortions of the seasons, as Brooks suggests, and can it really be separated from the other banal half of its couplet, which Brooks does not quote: 'And, as they seeme to me, are lyke, to fare still worse and worse' (fol. 80v), a line that Quince might well have used in 'Pyramus and Thisbe'? Perhaps Oedipus' description of the 'black and hellike hue' which has 'overshaded all the Skyes, whence deadly mists ensue' (fol. 79r) does have a link to Titania's 'Contagious fogs' (2.1.90) but I cannot see it and not every reference to the moon can be held to link straight back to the play, however pleasing Oedipus' couplet may be: 'The Moone with clowds quight ouer cast, all sadly forth she glides, / And dolefull darksom shades of night, the whole worlde overhides' (fol. 79r). The problem of the usefulness of a passage like this is that there is ample material in much more likely sources, particularly Golding's Ovid, that more self-evidently lie behind the speech and, though I would be the last to suggest that Shakespeare was incapable of using more than one source at a time, this passage does not seem to me to be operating clearly here. One could, in the wake of Brooks' suggestions, construct a plausible argument of similarity: seeing the plague in *Oedipus* and the cosmic disorder in *Dream* as equally the result of sexual transgression and disruption of the marriage-bond (at least if one takes Oberon's view of what Titania has been doing);[8] but the effect is laboured and I end up feeling that such similarities can always be constructed, irrespective of their immanency, that they are not vitally created by a strong presence.

The same argument, the lack of necessity to see unremarkable details as recalled from precisely this text rather than many others, holds for Brooks' proposal that Shakespeare made use of Seneca's *Medea*, specifically Medea's invocation to Hecate and her account of the cosmic disorder her work has created – indeed, the more sources that are suggested for Titania's speech (and Brooks adds in numerous echoes of Spenser's *Shepheardes Calendar* as well) the less any of them seem to be sufficient or necessary.

The *Medea* at least offers a closer direct connection to *A Midsummer Night's Dream* since Hecate is invoked directly in the play, in Robin's association of the fairies with 'the triple Hecate's team' (5.2.14) at the end of the play; the tripleness of Hecate, the complex multi-named multi-personed god also appears with immense power and significance throughout *A Midsummer Night's Dream* as both Diana, god of chastity and hunting and Cynthia, god of change and the moon. The whole theomachia of the play, a structure of warring and opposed divinities, a form of organizing principle that Shakespeare might well have found in another familiar 'source' – if that is what it should be called – the plays of Lyly, depends crucially on the nature of triple Hecate.

But the *Medea* passage's link to Titania's speech is too tenuous. 'Triple Hecate' is entirely conventional as a phrase: Shakespeare had no need of Seneca or Golding's Ovid for the concept.[9] Can one, as Brooks proposes, really move at all profitably from Studley's version of the wish that Hecate might 'the heart of people smyght / Wyth agonies of suddeyne dread' (fol. 135r) to Titania's account of the 'mazèd

[8] See, for example, Larry Langford, '*The Story Shall be Changed*: The Senecan Sources of *A Midsummer Night's Dream*', *Cahiers Elisabéthains*, 25 (1984), 37–52.

[9] See James Sledd, 'A Note on the use of Renaissance Dictionaries', *MP*, 49 (1951), 10–15.

world' (2.1.113), a phrase so rich in its association with the mazes and amazement that permeate the play? These, if present at all, *are* no more than local details, absorption of images from his reading. There is nothing here to justify seeing Oberon as a Medea-figure because of his jealousy over his wife's affections for another.

But it is the last of the Seneca plays, the one Brooks argues is most used, that is most intriguing, the *Hippolytus*. Brooks proposes that it is used at four specific points: that Hippolytus' directions to his huntsman at the start of the play affect the language for the discussion of hounds and hunting between Theseus and Hippolyta in 4.1; that a series of passages about the activities of Cupid informed the construction of Oberon's image of the flying Cupid shooting at the vestal in 2.1; that Phaedra's resolve to pursue Hippolytus, resulting from what Brooks rather trivializes by calling her desire 'infatuated' (p. 141), influences Helena's pursuit of Demetrius, also the result of a doting, perhaps obsessive love; and that Phaedra's Nurse's petition to Diana to change Hippolytus' disdain to love affects the change that happens to Demetrius. The first two are fairly plausible: though the range of language for expressing hunting is comparatively narrow and one would expect many passages to be similar; the same is true for descriptions of Cupid and his arrows. But there are enough shared details to make the case reasonably reasonable. Prayers to Diana are also likely to associate her with 'forestes wyld and groues' (fol. 62v), a specific verbal echo Brooks notes.

At this point one might reasonably feel that none of this source-hunting adds up to very much or is adequately or significantly convincing. But Brooks suggests that Phaedra's nurse prays that

> three-formed Hecate . . . will ensnare the mind of Hippolytus so that he may turn back into the fealty of love. In a play which makes its supernatural agents runners beside the triple Hecate's team, Demetrius . . . is turned back into the fealty of his original love for Helena by having his mind supernaturally ensnared. (p. lxiii)

In such a statement the source is no longer a matter of local detail and absorption but instead appears to be offered as a deliberately invoked difference, a source demanding to be noticed and contrasted by an audience made up, I assume, of Elizabethan theatre-goers not Arden editors. Seeing Helena as a version of Phaedra or Demetrius as a version of Hippolytus is both to see the comedy of *A Midsummer Night's Dream* as a deliberate transformation of the tragedy of the *Hippolytus* and to see the transformation as one placed for observation by the audience.

When a critic working with Brooks' proposals, moving to the interpretative use of 'local influence', suggests that the play is full of 'Senecan figures, waiting in the shadows of the Athenian forest . . . for a cue that . . . never comes'[10] he is clearly envisaging an active and informing principle for the Seneca, the source now defined as what we might want to call allusion, an allusion deliberately unfulfilled. M. C. Bradbrook in a fine phrase described *A Midsummer Night's Dream* as a play in which 'the marvellous elbows out the sinister'; others have sought to make the Senecan passages the precise source of that sinister world. But my initial response is to see these shadows as inadequately delineated, the linguistic echoes too faint, too imprecise, the process too hopeful on the critics' parts. For the comedy of Helena's difference from Phaedra, the recognition that this sexual desire is not incestuous but socially acceptable and realizable, depends on the recognition of Phaedra's language lying behind Helena's. Similarly the perception of Demetrius as a successful Hippolytus, a man who can find love, who can recreate that full expression of affect that Hippolytus cannot, depends on seeing the parallel Brooks finds, as actively present, for audience as well as Shakespeare –

[10] Langford, p. 50.

otherwise we are in the presence of some private Shakespearian joke, a joke of the author never available to the audience, a wry smile in his contemplation of his own game of metamorphosis of which the playing with the Senecan passages echoed in *A Midsummer Night's Dream* is a part.

If there are echoes of Seneca, the variations and transformations are operative only as a residue of possibility, the infinite analogousness of text, the pleasurable joys of intertextuality in the rarefied world of the scholar. I enjoy, for instance, the implication that the forest in *A Midsummer Night's Dream* is a world freed from conventional social patterns of sexual and gender restraint in contrast to the forest's normal identification with the chaste world of Diana and hunting. But such a difference, amply explored through the play's evocation of Diana, does not need Hippolytus' preference for hunting when the play is so full of Diana and Actaeon.[11] Nor does it seem to me that the comedy of ungovernable sexual desire has anything very much to do with Hippolytus' problems with his stepmother.

Indeed my interest in Seneca as a source might stop here with a verdict of 'not proven', were it not for the whole problem of Hippolytus himself, a problem that makes me wish that the Senecan play were more directly and convincingly present. For Shakespeare, in following Chaucer and naming Theseus' bride as Hippolyta, rejected, in effect, the preference carefully set out in balanced terms in North's translation of Plutarch's life of Theseus, a work we know Shakespeare read. North's Plutarch states that only one historiographer believes that the name of the Amazon Theseus married was Hippolyta, a result of her making peace between the Amazons and the Athenians after the Amazon invasion of Athens, when they camped right inside the city itself.[12] Others went even further, envisioning not a Theseus who captured Hippolyta but a Hippolyta who defeated Theseus: Anthony Gibson suggested that '*Hippolita* dissipated the troupes of great *Theseus*, dismounting himselfe in the fight, yet afterwards (on meere grace) made him her husband'.[13] North offers rather more evidence that the name of the Amazon-bride was Antiopa, whose name is conjured into brief existence in *Dream* as one of the women that Oberon accuses Titania of helping Theseus to seduce (2.1.80).

A Midsummer Night's Dream leaves entirely open the question of what the issue or outcome of this marriage of Athenian and Amazon will be, describing and blessing the future without directly stating what might or rather *will* happen (*will* because it is already accomplished, already fixed unalterably in the Theseus mythography). In any version of the Theseus story Theseus does not stay with his Amazon bride, be she Hippolyta or Antiopa, and the next person on the Theseus list of seduced, raped and abandoned women seems usually to have been Phaedra – indeed North's Plutarch repeats the suggestion that the Amazon wars were the result of this: 'the Amazones made warres with *Theseus* to reuenge the injurie he dyd to their Queene *Antiopa*, refusing her, to marye with *Phædra*' (p. 15).

When Oberon describes the future for the four lovers, 'And back to Athens shall the lovers wend / With league whose date till death shall never end' (3.3.373–4), this seems ironically different from what the audience could reasonably be assumed to know would happen to Theseus and Hippolyta. When Theseus in the first scene anticipates 'The sealing day betwixt my love and me / For everlasting bond of fellowship' (1.1.84–5) the bond is one that he will, outside the play but within the world of 'antique fables' (5.1.3) to which he indissolubly belongs, prove to make very briefly finite, very far from everlasting.

---

11 See Leonard Barkan, 'Diana and Actaeon: the Myth as Synthesis', *ELR*, 10 (1980), 317–59.

12 Plutarch, *The Lives of the Noble Grecians and Romanes Compared*, translated by Sir Thomas North (1579), p. 15.

13 Anthony Gibson, *A Womans Woorth* (1599), fol. 5r.

Again, in all versions that I know the issue of the bride-bed of Theseus and Amazon, what Oberon describes as 'the issue there create' (5.2.35), is certainly, as Oberon promises, handsome but equally certainly not, as he says, someone who 'Ever shall be fortunate' (36). For the only child of Theseus and an Amazon was Hippolytus, the child whose name is so shadowily close to Chaucer's and Shakespeare's use of Hippolyta as the name for Theseus' Amazon-bride; indeed since Hippolytus means 'destroyed by horses' and therefore is a name directly derived from the mode of Hippolytus' death, his mother's name is a back-formation, a name passed back from son to mother. The tight connection of one to other is all the more emphatically present. Oberon's careful listing of the 'blots of nature's hand' which 'Shall not in their issue stand' (39–40) was right: 'Never mole, harelip, nor scar, / Nor mark prodigious, such as are / Despisèd in nativity / Shall upon their children be' (41–4), for Hippolytus was unquestionably a stereotypically gorgeous macho man. But the result of this physical beauty is Phaedra's sexual obsession with him and Theseus' responsibility for his own son's death, a demonstration of paternal power over child analogous to that which Egeus claims over Hermia. Even Plutarch, sceptical as ever, accepts that since none of the historiographers disagree with the poets 'we must needes take it to be so, as we finde it written in the tragedies' (p. 15).

Whether or not Seneca's *Hippolytus* was an active source, the shadowy presence of Hippolytus is undeniably a man on the stair, a character who both is and is not there, a shadow, an unavoidable future for the marriage so richly, lengthily and apparently gloriously celebrated at the end of a play which deliberately, though only momentarily, invokes Theseus' promiscuity and his brutality towards his lovers. There is no reason, of course, to think that Oberon's accusations about Titania's part in Theseus' actions are right – she after all calls them the 'forgeries of jealousy' (2.1.81). But the lines summon into being and cannot then eliminate that other Theseus so substantially different from the one seen in the play, the vicious ravisher who balances in Plutarch the heroic warrior and ruler, someone, says North, whose 'faults touching women and ravishements . . . had the lesse shadowe and culler of honestie. Bicause *Theseus* dyd attempt it very often' (p. 43). The very frequency of the rapes and seductions is part of the indictment; what is more they are not the product of warlike conquest, as with Hippolyta in *A Midsummer Night's Dream*, won with his sword, but of something creeping, deceitful and thief-like, dark and vicious deeds of the night, so unlike the activities of the moonlit night of the play's wood:

> How canst thou thus for shame, Titania,
> Glance at my credit with Hippolyta,
> Knowing I know thy love to Theseus?
> Didst thou not lead him through the
>   glimmering night
> From Perigouna whom he ravishèd,
> And make him with fair Aegles break his faith,
> With Ariadne and Antiopa? (2.1.74–80)

Above all, the passage evokes not the ravishing itself but the aftermath, the creeping away, *from* Perigouna, not towards her, breaking faith not promising it, fracturing supposedly everlasting bonds of fellowship. Titania is not accused of helping the rape but aiding and abetting the abandonment, helping Theseus add to that long series of abandoned women that led Plutarch to say that it 'dyd geve men occasion to suspect that his womannishenes was rather to satisfie lust, then of any great love' (p. 43). Chaucer suppresses this Theseus in the Knight's Tale; Shakespeare includes him in *A Midsummer Night's Dream*. The triumphant ending of the play, the overwhelming celebration of marriage and blessing that the end of *A Midsummer Night's Dream* so fully evokes is set in relation to an individual for whom marriage-vows are transient devices for satisfying lust and whose career of broken marriages is a pattern of male dominance and oppression carried to extreme.

The success of the marriages at the end of *A Midsummer Night's Dream* is dependent not on the fairies' blessing, not on the benign approval of a supernatural world but on the faithfulness – or rather faithlessness – of men, something which Hermia states, however much she may be saying it with wry and teasing mockery, at the start of the play, and which she will find in the dream to be painfully if accidentally true:

> My good Lysander,
> I swear to thee by Cupid's strongest bow . . .
> And by that fire which burned the Carthage queen
> When the false Trojan under sail was seen;
> By all the vows that ever men have broke –
> In number more than ever women spoke –
> (1.1.168–76)

It is an odd oath, a summoning up of an abandoned woman who kills herself as her lover sails away (though in the wood, Hermia abandoned by Lysander does not kill herself – *A Midsummer Night's Dream* is comedy, not tragedy). Aeneas, a man who broke his vow, at least did so on divine instruction; Theseus has no such excuse. Hippolytus is the hidden threat to the play's ending, the unborn child whose implicit silence is undermining.

Hippolytus cannot be ignored, but does that mean he should be noticed? The extent to which he is, to which we remember or recall his future presence, may make us wish he would *stay* away, remain unborn, and yet know that he will not go away, cannot be wished away. Once remembered, Hippolytus doggedly refuses to be forgotten.

In Euripides' *Hippolytus* opaquely and in Seneca's *Hippolytus* clearly, Theseus' father is Poseidon (Neptune). Seneca's Theseus calls explicitly on his father to kill his own grandson; in Studley's version:

> thou knowest that Neptune great
> My Syre who flotes on floudes, and waves, with forked Mace doth beat
> Geve licence freely unto me three boones to chuse and crave, . . .
> All for the Fathers wrathful rage the cursed child downe smight,
> To waile among the ghastly sprites o Father bend thy might,
> To give (alas) this lothsome ayde unto thy needy Sonne. (fol. 69r–v)

Everywhere else Theseus' father is named Egeus. As editions of *A Midsummer Night's Dream* have long made clear, Shakespeare could have found the name for Hermia's father conveniently to hand in Chaucer in a passage after the death of Arcite:

> No man myghte gladen Theseus,
> Savynge his olde fader Egeus,
> That knew this worldes transmutacioun,
> As he hadde seyn it chaunge both up and doun,
> Joye after wo, and wo after gladnesse,
> And shewed hem ensamples and likenesse.[14]

Oddly, no one seems to have thought this fragment at all interesting but I want to emphasize Chaucer's use of 'transmutacioun', a word that seems particularly appropriate to a play like *A Midsummer Night's Dream* so full of transmutations and metamorphoses. Brooks' note in his edition also refers to the passage in Golding's translation of Ovid's *Metamorphoses* dealing with Theseus' father in Book 7.

The story Ovid uses there is the tail-end of a narrative outlined at much greater length by Plutarch. Let me use North as a convenient summary, since the story is, in my experience, unfamiliar to modern readers: '*AEgeus* desiring (as they say) to know how he might have children, went unto the city of DELPHES to the oracle of *Apollo*: where by *Apolloes* Nunne that notable prophecy was geven him for an aunswer. The which did forbid him to touch or know any woman, untill he was returned againe to ATHENS.' The enigmatic prophecy confused Aegeus who visited Troezen and was tricked by Pitheus who 'cunningly by some

[14] 'The Knight's Tale', lines 2837–42 in Geoffrey Chaucer, *The Works*, ed. F. N. Robinson (2nd edn, Boston, 1957).

devyse deceived him in such sorte, that he made him to lye with his daughter called *AEthra*'. She became pregnant and he left her with a sword and, improbably enough, a pair of shoes, which were put under a rock as a test of strength. Theseus, when he had grown up, removed the rock and set off to find his father, clutching the sword and, I suppose, wearing the shoes, deciding to go by land rather than sea in order to do great deeds like his kinsman Hercules. The city when he finally reached it was 'turmoyled with seditions, factions, and divisions, and perticularly the house of *AEgeus* in very ill termes also' (p. 6) because Medea had turned up, married Aegeus and was using 'medicines to make him to get children'. Medea, unlike Egeus, recognized Theseus and persuaded Egeus to invite him to a feast to poison him. I turn to Golding:

> The King by egging of his Queene
> Did reach his sonne this bane as if he had his enmie beene.
> And *Thesey* of this treason wrought not knowing ought, had tane
> The Goblet at his fathers hand which helde his deadly bane:
> When sodenly by the Ivorie hilts that were upon his sword
> *Aegeus* knew he was his sonne: and rising from the borde
> Did strike the mischiefe from his mouth.[15]

And they all lived happily ever after.

Except of course that the one story about Theseus' father that modern readers know is that, when Theseus was sailing back from killing the minotaur, 'they were so ioyfull', as North put it, 'he and his master, that they forgate to set up their white sayle, by which they shoulde have geven knowledge of their healthe and safetie to *AEgeus*. Who seeinge the blacke sayle a farre of, being out of all hope evermore to see his sonne againe, tooke suche a griefe at his harte, that he threw him selfe headlong from the top of a clyffe, and killed him selfe' (p. 11).

Naming Hermia's father Egeus cannot then be a completely innocent act; it is not up to Shakespeare to decide how much of this baggage should be present – it is simply carried into the play with the name for the audience or, now, critic, to use. Whether the Elizabethan theatre audience did notice such implications is irrecoverable but knowledge of the Theseus myths was hardly a prerogative of the well-educated; the early stages of grammar-school education would have easily provided the information on which my argument is based. Shakespeare may have wanted the creative freedom with myths that the rapidity of theatre performance makes possible, the possibility of the audience *not* noticing changes and alterations, but he cannot have controlled the audience's ability to observe what he was doing. Sources in this sense come to be context, an indissoluble tying of the words to their origins. The name cannot choose whether to be allusive. Conjuring up Egeus in the play is to invoke his history, his antique fables.

The mythography of Theseus contains a surprising number of family murders, of parents *and* children. Theseus, directly responsible for the murder of Hippolytus, was also indirectly the cause of his own father's death. Plutarch states that Theseus because of his negligence in forgetting about the sail, 'cannot be cleared of parricide, howe eloquent an oration soever could be made for his excuse' (p. 42). Egeus, even more significantly for *A Midsummer Night's Dream*, was nearly responsible for the death of his son. The crucial change at the banquet is a recognition of identity: to know your son is not to kill him. To know the step-son, for Medea, is to want to kill him. The power of the parent over life and death is exerted here only in ignorance and is transformed into joy when the child is recognized. Only in ignorance could Egeus *want* to kill Theseus. Egeus in *A Midsummer Night's Dream* of course knows perfectly well who his child is

---

15 Arthur Golding, *The .xv. Bookes of P. Ovidius Naso, entytuled Metamorphosis* (1567), fol. 87r.

and is still willing to have his daughter killed simply for going against his wishes and consent, thwarting him – and the Athenian law allows it:

> I beg the ancient privilege of Athens:
> As she is mine, I may dispose of her,
> Which shall be either to this gentleman
> Or to her death, according to our law
> Immediately provided in that case. (1.1.41–5)

Lysander makes clear, and no one contradicts him, that there is nothing to choose between the two men in terms of social status:

> I am, my lord, as well derived as he,
> As well possessed. My love is more than his,
> My fortunes every way as fairly ranked,
> If not with vantage, as Demetrius (1.1.99–102)

There is no apparent reason for Egeus' objection, no socially explicable cause. It is simply, coldly and absolutely a matter of power and control, aided and abetted in its insubstantiality by the substantial and effective indistinguishability of Demetrius and Lysander as far as the audience is concerned at this stage.

There is, as Leo Salingar has pointed out, an echo here of Arthur Brooke, in his *Tragicall Historye of Romeus and Juliet*, who describes at length the power of parents in Rome where, 'if children did rebell, / The parentes had the power, of lyfe and sodayn death',[16] an echo that might support the priority of Shakespeare's *Romeo* over *A Midsummer Night's Dream*. Let me add another resource: George Sandys' translation of Ovid's *Metamorphoses* was published well after *A Midsummer Night's Dream* but made extensive use, in his totally unoriginal notes, of the long series of commentaries on Ovid, the *Ovide Moralisé* tradition; Sandys comments of Pyramus and Thisbe in Book 4 of *Metamorphoses* 'whose wretched ends upbraid those parents, who measure their childrens by their own out-worne and deaded affections; in forcing them to serve their avarice or ambition in their fatall marriages . . . more cruell therein to their owne, then either the malice of foes or fortune . . . [n]ot considering that riches cannot purchase love; nor threats or violence either force or restraine it'.[17] While Pyramus and Thisbe in *A Midsummer Night's Dream* are not strongly identified as being kept apart by parents, even though the wall comes down that, as Bottom says, 'parted their fathers' (5.1.345–6), Sandys' moral could easily be applied to Hermia's Egeus.

It is, of course, part of the careful structure of power that Shakespeare outlines in Act 1 that the choice between marriage to Demetrius and death are not in fact the only options to Hermia. Significantly, it is not Egeus who mentions another possibility: '*Either* to die the death, *or* to abjure / For ever the society of men' (1.1.65–6), becoming a nun. Equally significantly Theseus himself does not mention it until he is directly asked by Hermia 'The worst that may befall me in this case / If I refuse to wed Demetrius' (63–4). It is worth considering whether Egeus knows of this other avenue and has deliberately suppressed it as part of his expression of complete paternal power or whether Theseus' announcement is news to him: it is a choice actors might want to consider. Theseus' first response to Egeus' complaint creates the image of the father altering his daughter's appearance, physically transforming her body:

> To you your father should be as a god,
> One that composed your beauties, yea, and one
> To whom you are but as a form in wax,
> By him imprinted, and within his power
> To leave the figure or disfigure it. (47–51)

This image of a wax impression distorted and disfigured hints at something violent and horrific: it does not suggest death so much as disfigurement, some brutal and callous maiming. If

---

[16] Leo Salingar, *Shakespeare and the Traditions of Comedy* (Cambridge, 1974), p. 313.

[17] George Sandys, *Ovid's Metamorphosis Englished, Mythologized, and Represented in Figures*, ed. Karl K. Hulley and Stanley T. Vandersall (Lincoln, Nebraska, 1970), p. 202.

'disfigure' can mean nothing more than 'alter' (OED *v.*2), as with sealing wax, the word cannot quite here lose its primary sense of 'mar, destroy the beauty of' someone (OED *v.*1). Theseus is complicit in this act of cruelty, helping this father to destroy his child until, like Theseus at the feast at Athens in Ovid and Plutarch, this child demands recognition, with a boldness that, as Hermia makes clear, may go beyond the normal limits of female behaviour:

> I know not by what power I am made bold,
> Nor how it may concern my modesty
> In such a presence here to plead my thoughts
> (59–61).

It is part of the play's modulation from the threats of Act 1 that similar comments later in the play, particularly in relation to Helena, about the dangers of immodesty, now appear comic rather than genuinely dangerous. When Demetrius warns her, 'You do impeach your modesty too much, / To leave the city and commit yourself / Into the hands of one that loves you not' (2.1.214–16), we do not really imagine for a moment that he is likely to rape her. His reference to the place and time, 'the opportunity of night, / And the ill counsel of a desert place' (217–18), seems no more threatening as the wood endlessly and fluidly transforms from desert to rich bank, and from deserted to being equally richly populated.

Egeus' reappearance in Act 4 is no less antagonistic, no less violent, the rhythms of his anger as breathless and impatient in their characteristic repetitions:

> Enough, enough, my lord, you have enough.
> I beg the law, the law upon his head. –
> They would have stol'n away, they would, Demetrius,
> Thereby to have defeated you and me –
> You of your wife, and me of my consent,
> Of my consent that she should be your wife.
> (4.1.153–8)

Frederick Reynolds' extremely successful version of the play in 1816 was so anxious about the problem Egeus faces in Act 4 that it included lengthy speeches showing Egeus' dilemma before the lovers reappear – they enter in his version wide awake, rather than being discovered asleep. After Theseus reminds Egeus what day it is he replies:

> EGEUS It is, my Liege – and, ah! for her sake, and for mine,
> 'Pray Heaven she chuse Demetrius for her lord! –
> He hath my sacred pledge; my honour's bound!
> Else, Oh, my Sovereign! Nature struggling with duty, I fear,
> I should indulge a fond, fond father's weakness!
>
> THESEUS
> What if Demetrius should resign her hand,
> And chuse fair Helena?
>
> EGEUS
> In vain; he loves but Hermia, who, till of late,
> Bore such resemblance to her mother!
> So watch'd – so nurs'd me! But lo! Demetrius
> Comes to claim my promise –
> 'Tis well – and I must claim our stern
> Athenian law![18]

Much as this Egeus would otherwise he is forced to 'beg the law':

> since a parent's sacred word is pledg'd,
> Though life should in the contest cease, I claim
> Your sentence, Sire! – I, her father, claim it.
> (p. 55)

Hermia approaches Egeus:

> Father! what say you?
> May I love Lysander? (*Kneels.*) Oh, pardon! pardon!

Egeus duly forgives and seems to shift some of the blame neatly on Demetrius:

> My blessings on thee! (*Raising and embracing her.*)
> Take her, Lysander; and for thee, Demetrius,
> The busy phantoms of thy brain dispers'd,
> May all be happiness and love! (p. 55)

---

[18] *A Midsummer Night's Dream*, adapted by Frederick Reynolds (1816), p. 54.

In the Quarto text of *A Midsummer Night's Dream* Egeus has nothing further to say after he begs the law upon Lysander's head and exits, later in the scene, overruled by Theseus; though Egeus' emotions on his exit are inevitably opaque in the text's silence, in production he can appear begrudgingly reconciled to Theseus' will or, perhaps marginally more likely, angry and unforgiving. In the Folio text Egeus takes over Philostrate's lines in Act 5, making visible and audible his incorporation in Athenian society at the end of the play. But the text does not prescribe his attitude. He may be truculent, obstinate or irritable. His silence towards his daughter and her new husband may be a significant cold-shouldering or it could be a happy silence because there is no need for words. His silence now matches Hermia. It is perfectly possible, using the Quarto text, to show Egeus reconciled; productions do not need any more words to show an Egeus now happy with the new state of affairs than an Egeus still angry and unaltered.[19]

Like it or not, Egeus has to accept that his will has been overborne, that the power of the father has limits, that his demands are not compatible either with the operation of ducal power in Theseus, whimsical though that might appear to be, or with the operation of the ending of comedy. Egeus, Theseus' father, who chose not to kill his son becomes Egeus, Hermia's father, who finds he cannot choose whether to kill his child. It is as if Theseus in *A Midsummer Night's Dream* takes over his father's functions in North and Golding, creating the social recognition of the child, acknowledging the lovers as Egeus there acknowledged him, but also perhaps allowing the marriages almost solely as a pleasing accompaniment to his own: 'for in the temple by and by with us / These couples shall eternally be knit', putting into effect, unknowingly, Oberon's promise.

I have one more shadowy figure, a man on the stair, briefly to add, or rather half a man, the minotaur. There is of course no direct reference in the play to the minotaur, no direct link to the killing of a monster at the heart of the Cretan labyrinth. Everything here works, if it works at all, by evocative difference. Titania mentions mazes but the 'quaint mazes in the wanton green' (2.1.99) are turf mazes, patterns found quite widely in England, often linked to fairies and, by distortion of a Welsh word, to Troy. These were unicursal mazes, mazes without false turnings and confusions, and led directly to their own centres, a maze in which one does not need an Ariadne's assistance with a ball of thread, or as Caxton has it in his translation of *Aeneid*, a 'botome of threde'. The labyrinth designed by Daedalus was multicursal, a puzzle maze – though, for reasons I do not at all understand, all Renaissance representations of the Cretan labyrinth show a unicursal maze, one, that is, in which Ariadne's help would have been unnecessary. This makes nonsense of the story but suggests the extent to which the process is inevitable: there is no route for Theseus that does not bring him to the minotaur.

Ariadne, mentioned in *A Midsummer Night's Dream*, is not there connected with the labyrinth in the reference, her abandonment on Naxos more important than her help in Crete, as it had been in Julia's description, in *The Two Gentlemen of Verona*, of performing

> a lamentable part.
> Madam, 'twas Ariadne, passioning
> For Theseus' perjury and unjust flight.
> (4.4.163–5)[20]

But Ariadne is part of a complex of family

[19] See Barbara Hodgdon, 'Gaining a Father: the Role of Egeus in the Quarto and the Folio', *RES*, n.s., 37 (1986), 534–42 and Philip C. McGuire, 'Egeus and the Implications of Silence', in Marvin and Ruth Thompson, eds., *Shakespeare and the Sense of Performance*, (Newark, 1989), pp. 103–15 and his 'Intentions, Options, and Greatness: An Example from *A Midsummer Night's Dream*' in Sidney Homan, ed., *Shakespeare and the Triple Play* (Lewisburg, 1988), pp. 177–86.

[20] Presumably she performed a version of Ovid's *Heroides*, Bk 10, Ariadne's letter of complaint to Theseus.

relationships in the Theseus myth: she is the daughter of Minos and Pasiphae, and the sister of Phaedra, later Theseus' wife. Pasiphae is, of course, the mother of the minotaur.

The journey through the wood in *A Midsummer Night's Dream* leads the lovers through a maze and then out again and, if their experience is of having been in a puzzle maze, it is one that is always beyond their control as they are made to take false paths, false turnings, false patterns of desire until the true pattern can be found and reinforced. This maze in which the people are 'mazed' gives the audience a superior and secure perspective on those wandering within it.

If the wood is a maze then the only half-man, half-animal the play can offer at the centre of the maze is half-ass, not half-bull: Bottom. Though his transformation is the play's structural centre, emphasized by every device Shakespeare conventionally uses to achieve it, particularly the subsequent expository dialogue between Oberon and Robin at the start of 3.2, it does not follow that he is the kind of thematic centre that accounts of the minotaur in the play have tended to suggest.[21] This metamorphosed man is not to be murdered but loved and laughed at: like the suggested metamorphosis of Phaedra into Helena, this is comedy not tragedy.

Invoking the minotaur, even for a sensitive critic, is to see the myth itself paradoxically and perhaps mockingly transformed: hence M. E. Lamb's suggestion that 'the substitution of Bottom for a minotaur represents the transmutation of the elements of tragedy into comedy'[22] and that 'Bottom is both the monster of this labyrinth and the thread leading the way out of it',[23] thereby turning Bottom into both the minotaur *and* Ariadne. If Quince and presumably the others see him as 'monstrous' when 'translated' (3.1.99, 113), the audience does not. The ass-head is never anything but funny. There is no threat of death here, no terror and destructiveness. Bottom is always benign and harmless, roaring but never hurting, or perhaps singing and hee-hawing. Even the terror of the labyrinth itself is only superficially similar to the wood, a maze which is beneficial to those who enter it, a maze that exacts no tribute from its young Athenians, a labyrinth now located just outside the walls of Athens rather than across the seas in Crete.

In Apuleius' *The Golden Ass*, Lucius, transformed *completely* into an ass, is taken to bed by, as William Adlington describes her in his wonderful Elizabethan translation, 'a noble and riche Matron'.[24] Lucius is reminded, both in her desire for the ass and in the physical problem of her accommodating his large ass's penis, of the minotaur's conception: 'she was amorous of me, and could finde no remedie to her passions and disordinate appetite, but continually desired to have her pleasure with me, as Pasiphae had with a Bull' (fol. 109r–v) and later she 'had her pleasure with me, whereby I thought the mother of Minotaurus, did not causelesse quenche her inordinat desier with a Bull' (fol. 110r). The minotaur is repeatedly defined as an emblem of lust; as Golding puts it intemperately in Book 8 of *Metamorphoses*, 'and now appeared more / The mothers filthie whoredome by the monster that she bore / Of double shape, an ugly thing' (fol. 98r). Apuleius is, obviously, a major source for Bottom's transformation. But Bottom, if he does indeed have sex with Titania, an activity in which he seems to show no particular interest, being much more concerned to munch hay, does not face Lucius' problem here: as William Empson characteristically puts it, 'if the genital action is in view, nobody denies that the genitals of Bottom remained human'.[25] All that Robin

[21] See, for example, M. E. Lamb, '*A Midsummer Night's Dream*: The Myth of Theseus and the Minotaur', *Texas Studies in Literature and Language*, 21 (1979), 478–91 and David Ormerod, '*A Midsummer Night's Dream*: The Monster in the Labyrinth', *Shakespeare Studies*, 11 (1978), 39–52.

[22] Lamb, p. 486.

[23] Ibid., p. 481.

[24] Lucius Apuleius, *The .xi. Bookes of the Golden Asse*, translated William Adlington (1566), fol. 109r.

[25] William Empson, *Essays on Shakespeare* (Cambridge, 1986), p. 229.

has done, as modern productions seem inclined to forget, is to put an ass's head on Bottom; the rest of him stays irredeemably human. Titania is not Pasiphae, Bottom no bull, the outcome will be no minotaur.

In that sense, Bottom is paradoxically close to a separate strand of classical and Renaissance thinking about the minotaur, a strand exemplified in North's Plutarch. For alongside the fascinated disgust at the notion of the woman having sex with a bull goes a second sceptical rationalization. Pasiphae's lover became not *taurus*, the bull, but a man named Taurus, one of Minos' captains, 'a churlishe, and naughtie natured man of condition' as North calls him (p. 8). Theseus defeated him in a set of games, much to Minos' delight. The labyrinth becomes a prison and there is no semi-human figure. In such a light one could perhaps see Bottom as an even more rationalist version of semi-human transformation, the man temporarily, harmlessly and comically transformed. Plutarch's scepticism denies the monstrous as the product of lust. Bottom is similarly non-productive.

If, though, the more conventional version of the minotaur is a shadow, a vicious image cast by the play's transformation, it is one that is explicitly and repeatedly marginalized. To think of the minotaur, to summon him (it?) up is to recognize how little place he has in *A Midsummer Night's Dream*. If the thought cannot be suppressed it is always controlled. This man on the stair has gone away; he makes no threat of return. Our wish to make him go is fully acceded to by the play: 'I wish, I wish he'd stay away.'

My shadows may seem small-scale ones but they are only examples of a large problem. The mere presence of Theseus in *A Midsummer Night's Dream* makes the whole of the Theseus myth available. Very little has to be done, indeed very little *is* done, by the play to bring specific parts of that rich store of narratives and motifs into the play-world, the context of allusive action that the drama represents. What is more the play, very largely, cannot confidently choose how those aspects are controlled. It can choose what is invoked but it cannot easily choose what else that invocation will carry. Theseus, much more than Seneca, constitutes a major source for *A Midsummer Night's Dream*, a source of allusion, opposition and difference, a source of threat and terror, a source that the play, for all its wonderful assuredness in its happy ending, cannot really eliminate. Theseus leaves his shadows over the play.

There is of course the next stage, the parallel problems in virtually every Shakespeare play, the same difficulty of dealing with referential context, the same need to define the implications of uncontrollable presences. If such patterns are a regular part of our critical vocabulary, we do not seem to know what we mean when we move from source to allusion, from local detail to informing presence. The world of such shadows is as dark as the night in the wood.

'TIME FOR SUCH A WORD' VERBAL ECHOING IN *MACBETH*

GEORGE WALTON WILLIAMS

It is a critical commonplace that Macbeth's opening line – 'So foul and fair a day I have not seen' (1.3.36), whatever its particular referents may be[1] – is singularly important to Macbeth's character, echoing as it does the enigmatic and ominous chant of the Witches as they conclude their first appearance: 'Fair is foul, and foul is fair' (1.1.10). That the play begins with the witches strikingly adumbrates their immanent presence throughout the play; that they are the first to mention the name of the hero confirms their importance. The play and the character both will live under the shadow and the menace of these opening lines – the shortest first scene in the canon. The scene includes this gnomic utterance that destroys 'the distinction [between] . . . *foul* and *fair*'; with it the Witches verbalize their position, standing for 'those who have said "Evil, be thou my good."'[2] Their contrasting adjectives occur often in proverbial contexts in English, but the paradox here suggested is unusual, though not unique, in the tradition.[3] 'Fair without but foul within', says the proverb; the Witches say that fairness and foulness are the same, a point that Shakespeare had expressed with extraordinary foreshadowing in *Love's Labour's Lost*: '"Fair" in "all hail" is foul, as I conceive' (5.2.340).[4]

By repeating the adjectives and reversing their sequence in the second half of the Witches' line, Shakespeare calls particular attention to these words, invests them with mystery, and fixes them in our minds so that when Macbeth speaks them just over one hundred lines later, his echo of the Witches' diction comes in with an eerie, *secondary* force (independently of the speaker's presumed intention). Macbeth intends, presumably, little more than a reference to a mixed sort of day – the uncertain tide of the battle, the dubious nature of the weather – but his use of the Witches' terms, linking the Witches and the speaker in vocabulary, intimates that there is a bond between them and

---

1 See Marvin Rosenberg, *The Masks of Macbeth* (Berkeley, 1978), pp. 35–6, for some of the suggestiveness.

2 Bernard Groom, ed. *Macbeth* (New Clarendon edn, 1939), p. 117.

3 Nicholas Brooke, ed. *Macbeth* (Oxford edn, 1990). See Tilley, *Dictionary*, F29 (and Dent F29); the pair occurs in *The Faerie Queen*, 4.8.32, and in *Much Ado*, 4.1.101.

4 Rosenberg, p. 114. In addition to the uses of these two adjectives, cited here in conjunction, each occurs twice in the play used singly. *Fair* occurs in the King's description of Lady Macbeth as 'Fair and noble hostess' (1.6.24) and in the Messenger's description of Lady Macduff as 'Fair dame' (4.2.66). We might argue that only one of these ladies is truly fair. The King's observation is inadequate; he himself acknowledges that he cannot find the mind's construction in the face. (The King's sons, however, have the ability that their father lacked: Malcolm's extended testing of Macduff (4.3.1–126) demonstrates his corrective to his father's inadequacy, and even Donalbain recognizes that a smile may conceal a dagger (2.3.139).) *Foul* occurs in what might almost be a gloss on these two disparate references to *fair*: 'Though all things foul would wear the brows of grace, / Yet grace must still look so' (4.3.24–5, Malcolm's perceptive observation). And the Scots Doctor observes that 'Foul whisp'rings are abroad. Unnatural deeds / Do breed unnatural troubles' (5.1.68–9), the only issue of the Macbeths' generating.

him,[5] more significant than mere repetition of diction. He is ready to receive them when they come to him. Macbeth did not hear the Witches, but he knows how they speak and so knows how they think; speaking their words, he speaks their thoughts.[6]

A comparable echoing of a word not heard occurs in Scene 5 of the first Act, as Lady Macbeth reads and reacts to her husband's letter.[7] That letter brings her the sense and the spirit of the encounter with the Witches and gives Lady Macbeth some seven words of their vocabulary, five that she repeats, commenting to herself – 'Cawdor', 'shalt be', 'promised', 'great[ness]', 'mortal'[8] – and two others that she addresses to Macbeth – 'all-hail', 'ignorant' (1.5.14–56). Three of these words appear together at the end of Macbeth's letter: 'that thou . . . [mightst not be] *ignorant* of what *great*ness is *promised* thee' (11–13; emphasis mine).[9] The three words spring from love; Macbeth uses them to her, '[his] dearest partner of greatness', as a demonstration of his affection for her. Lady Macbeth, reconceiving them, turns two of them back on him, thinking how 'great' he is and what has been 'promised' (17, 15, 21) to him. He wanted her to be not 'ignorant' of the future; she turns that third word also, using it with supreme contempt to describe the moment as 'This ignorant present' (line 56) – 'The language forces the two to converge.'[10]

Powerful as these terms may be in their dialogue, one word she uses was, significantly, not in the letter: 'hereafter'; she greets Macbeth: 'Greater than both by the all hail hereafter!' (54). The Third Witch had said: 'All hail, Macbeth, that shalt be king hereafter!' (1.3.48); but the letter had said: they 'all-hailed me Thane of Cawdor' and 'Hail, King that shalt be!'[11] (1.5.6–9). Lady Macbeth's phrase is a fusion of these messages, using the 'all hail' that describes the present thaneship to confirm the 'hereafter' that describes the future kingship. Forcing the instant to control the future. It is her way. Lady Macbeth's phrase, 'all-hail hereafter', adopting the 'time word' that will 'ring powerfully later',[12] is a brief abstract of the Witch's salutation, a collapsing or foreshortening of time, 'a shorthand reprise of the Sisters' greeting'.[13] W. A. Wright observed that 'Lady Macbeth speaks as if she had heard the words as spoken by the witch'; and John Upton, the noted textual scholar of the eighteenth century, finding the presence of the word in Lady Macbeth's speech so jarring with its absence in Macbeth's letter, supposed that the text of the letter was defective, should have had 'hereafter' in it, 'for this word she uses emphatically when she greets Macbeth . . . being the [word] of the Witch'.[14]

---

5 Cp. Roy Walker, *The Time is Free* (London, 1949), p. 11.

6 Cp. G. K. Hunter, ed. *Macbeth* (New Penguin edn, 1967), p. 37.

7 For interesting observations of another kind on Lady Macbeth's reception of the letter see Mark Taylor, 'Letters and Readers in *Macbeth*, *King Lear*, and *Twelfth Night*', *Philological Quarterly*, 69 (1990), 31–53. The letter functions in the play 'chiefly as a way of revealing something about the motives and proclivities of the [person who reads it]' (p. 31). 'What Macbeth puts into his letter is not, for the most part, what Lady Macbeth reads out of it' (p. 35).

8 Macbeth's phrase in the letter, 'more . . . than mortal knowledge' – he seems to have investigated their credentials – becomes Lady Macbeth's 'mortal thoughts'. And the spirits – the 'weird sisters' – 'tend on' those thoughts of mortality. Her destructive 'tend on' of line 40 mocks her considerate 'Give him tending' in line 36.

9 These written words of Macbeth's constitute the only reference in the play to Lady Macbeth's becoming a queen; the Lady herself never mentions any desire on her own part for queenship. The absence of any such expression is the more remarkable since in Holinshed she is 'verie ambitious' in her personal lust for a crown (*Chronicles of Scotland*, p. 171).

10 Rosenberg, p. 115. These two instances of the word 'ignorant', both spoken by Lady Macbeth, are the only two in the play.

11 As customarily in Shakespeare, the quoting of an earlier speech is inexact, but the intent is sufficiently clear to Lady Macbeth.

12 Ibid., p. 234.

13 Ibid.

14 Wright, ed. *Macbeth* (Clarendon edn, 1869), p. 94; Upton, *Critical Observations on Shakespeare* (1748), p. 204.

It is the word of the Witch, first used in the play by the Third Witch (1.3.48), that tantalizes Macbeth with the hope that will lead to his destruction. It appears again, properly used, we may say, by the rightful monarch to suggest his rightful control of the future: 'Malcolm, whom we name hereafter / The Prince of Cumberland' (1.4.38–9). Having heard the word from the Witch in Scene 3, interpreting it as a temptation, Macbeth hears it again (140 lines later) from his King in Scene 4 in a context to which he says he will give his full allegiance (1.4.22–7) – but which he immediately rejects (48–53): 'The Prince of Cumberland – that is a step / On which I must fall down or else o'erleap' (48–9).[15]

The vacillation in Macbeth's response to the word is terminated by Lady Macbeth's use of it in Scene 5, a scant 73 lines further on (1.5.54). This trio of uses – three times in three consecutive scenes within 217 lines – offers a set of references to the future that will have impressed Macbeth's mind in three different ways, the last way, Lady Macbeth's way, being the final and dominant one. To ensure the 'promised' hereafter, Lady Macbeth will 'feel now / The future in the instant' (1.5.56–7). The relationship that the two Macbeths have to time, one uncertain and one assertive, is perfectly and concisely represented in the collocation between them just after Duncan's murder:

MACBETH

When?

LADY MACBETH

Now. (2.2.16)

In order to remove the question and to make the future in the instant, now, Lady Macbeth proposes to 'beguile the time' (1.5.62); Macbeth accepts that way of life, echoing her idea (though not her term) in his 'mock the time' (1.7.81). This echo speaks the crucial change in Macbeth's attitude to time; he has forgotten his normative attitude towards the movement of time with which he properly concluded his response to the Witches' prophecies: 'Come what come may, / Time and the hour runs through the roughest day' (1.3.145–6).[16] Thanks to the encouragement and threats of his wife, however, he now is 'settled, and bend[s] up / Each corporal agent to this terrible feat' (1.7.79–80).[17] No longer will he allow that 'chance may crown me / Without my stir' (1.3.142–3). He begins to stir.

The word of the Witch resonates powerfully in these three early scenes of the play. Its presence in Lady Macbeth's speech[18] invites the question: how came she by that word? Since no editor has seen fit to accept Upton's textual explanation by adding the 'omitted' word to Macbeth's letter, we may seek an explanation within the existing text. We may argue that just as Macbeth has adopted the phrase of the Witch that he never heard, so Lady Macbeth here adopts the word of the Witch that she never read.

'Come, you spirits', she says (1.5.39). Can there be any doubt but that they will come? What spirit could resist so charming an invitation to such an interesting programme of activity and entertainment? The play is a play of hospitality perverted, its great central scene

[15] Macbeth echoes himself in the use of the word 'o'erleap' in his later soliloquy (1.7.27), in both instances perverting a normal process of ascent – climbing a set of stairs, mounting a horse – by an action inappropriate or inept that causes him to 'fall' (1.4.51; 7.28). I owe to a former student the insight that Macbeth here, depersonalizing, transmutes a human into a thing.

[16] And, we may be confident, the roughest night – 2.3.60.

[17] As 'bend up' signifies Macbeth's commitment in the first part of the play, leading on to the crisis of 3.4, so 'I am bent to know' (3.4.133) signifies his commitment in the second part of the play, leading on to the catastrophe of 5.10.

[18] The Variorum edition (p. 60) quotes Mrs Jameson's excited response to hearing this word on the stage (vol. II, p. 324): 'those who have heard Mrs Siddons pronounce the word *hereafter*, cannot forget the look, the tone, which seemed to give her auditors a glimpse of that awful *future*, which she, in her prophetic fury, beholds upon the instant'. Another powerful lady, Mrs Dorothy Dunnett, has used the word to conjure up a grandly imaginative account of Macbeth and Lady Macbeth in *King Hereafter* (1982).

(3.4) the banquet in which Macbeth particularly wishes to establish order (line 1) and to promote health (line 38) (in both which efforts he fails, being no true King – lines 109, 118, 119). To this banquet he specifically invites Banquo (3.1.15, 29). Can there be any doubt but that he will accept? As Banquo, coming from his realm of the supernatural, accepts Macbeth's invitation, so, we may argue, the Witches, coming from theirs, accept Lady Macbeth's. One of the proofs of their presence is the fact that Lady Macbeth in both action and word seems to have become unsexed, seems to have become mannish. Confirmation of their presence in her body is the presence of their word 'hereafter' in her vocabulary.

The word of the Witch becomes Lady Macbeth's word; its fourth and final use in the play is spoken by Macbeth at her death: 'She should have died hereafter' (5.5.16). It is Macbeth's epitaph for his wife; it is all that he has to give her. In the hereafter that they thought they would have, there would have been time for a longer epitaph than this, but 'now' there is no time. Those who mocked the time have no time. They sought the future in the instant; they secured it. As might, therefore, have been expected, when the normal calendrical future comes, there is nothing there. 'Naught's had, all's spent' (3.2.6), says she; and he discovers that their life has been one 'Signifying nothing' (5.5.27). Lady Macbeth's use of the word 'hereafter' deranged the regular sequence of time; his use restores it. But it is too late. Discovering the futility of the theory of time that he has espoused, Macbeth returns, after the brief epitaph for his wife, to thoughts of himself and to his original understanding of the sequence of time – 'Tomorrow, and tomorrow, and tomorrow / Creeps in this petty pace from day to day' (5.5.18–19) – though it is an understanding tempered now with sad experience that proved the Witches right, that what seemed fair was foul and that what offered 'fairest show' has proven to be most foul.

That lesson, we may say, Banquo understands from the beginning, having heard his partner link fairness and foulness in his opening speech. At the salutations of the Witches, Macbeth, as Banquo tells us, 'start[s] and seem[s] to fear / Things that do sound so fair' (1.3.49–50).[19] Banquo is the first to use the word *fear* in the play, introducing here a series of more instances of this word than are to be found in any other of Shakespeare's plays: *Macbeth* is the most fear-filled play of the canon. Macbeth's response, then, is correct: in this play things that sound fair are to be feared, and perhaps Banquo's cautious self apprehends the fact that things that sound fair are to be feared because they are, in the proof, foul. 'The fear–fair sound-pun mirrors fair–foul; something dark shadows this golden promise.'[20] Banquo links the two near homonyms *fair* and *fear* in consecutive lines and repeats one of them eight lines later (line 58).[21] Though the two words may

[19] Richard J. Jaarsma, in 'The Tragedy of Banquo', *Literature and Psychology*, 17 (1967), 87–94, suggests that Banquo at 2.1.6–9 'for the first time . . . recognizes, as Macbeth did not, the Witches' evil intent' (p. 91); the recognition may have come sooner.

[20] Rosenberg, p. 116.

[21] Helge Kökeritz, *Shakespeare's Pronunciation* (New Haven, 1953), identified these two words as homonyms – they 'were often pronounced alike' (p. 106); but Fausto Cercignano, *Shakespeare's Works and Elizabethan Pronunciation* (Oxford, 1981) finds that in this passage 'word-play is based on antithesis not identity' (p. 235). Nevertheless, he gives examples of passages in which *fair* and *fear*, though never rhyming to one another, rhyme to the same words: *fair* : *air* : *ear* : *appear* : *there* : *bear* : *fear* (pp. 80, 167, 238). Though the two words are, and could be sounded as, phonologically distinct, it is clear that they were not always sounded so. Various speakers used variant soundings in varying contexts. Professor Ronald Butters, to whom I am obliged in this matter, notes that 'there has been much interaction/interchange between the *-ear* and *-air* vowels in the history of English, and [the distinction] was very much in flux in Shakespeare's day' (Correspondence, 31 March 1993). The trio of homonymic words in this passage (1.3.49–58) is exactly balanced in *Venus and Adonis*, 1083–6. In both works, Shakespeare is playing with the echo; if the words are inexact homonyms to the ear, their sounds are sufficiently close to provide an echo to the mind.

not sound with a phonic identity to some natural ears, they resound with a suggestive echo in the ear of memory, even as the mind disambiguates their significations.

It is no doubt too much to claim that Banquo, echoing one of the two key words of the Witches, has shown a susceptibility to the Witches of a lesser degree but not of a different kind from that of Macbeth; but it is certainly true that, immediately after he has used one of 'their' words, 'fair'/'fear', the Witches speak to him as they spoke to Macbeth after Macbeth had used their vocabulary. The dauntless temper of Banquo's mind, however, protects him. When the Witches vanish mysteriously, he associates them with the basest element, their natural element, the earth; he is disposed to think ill of them. Macbeth, on the other hand, disposed to think well of them, supposes they have returned upward to their natural element, the air (1.3.79–80), a pleasing hope that he repeats in the letter to his wife. Banquo is rightly seen in this first encounter as setting the standard of integrity and probity from which Macbeth is later to fall off, but it should be noted in Macbeth's defence that his final response to the blandishments of the Witches is, like Banquo's, that he shall not be tempted. We learn later that Macbeth and his Lady have previously (several times?) considered taking action to secure the crown for Macbeth (1.7.47–52); each time the idea has arisen, however, Macbeth has rejected it. The latest and last rejection is before us: 'We will proceed no further in this business' (1.7.31). His record is beyond reproach – indeed his integrity, we may say, is stronger than Banquo's: it has been tested and found firm. Banquo's probity has not before now been tested.

Such testing is soon to come. Banquo is suddenly made aware of his unique and privileged position. Before the meeting of the thanes held after the death of Duncan, Banquo speaks his mind:

let us meet
And question this most bloody piece of work,
To know it further. Fears and scruples shake us.
In the great hand of God I stand, and thence
Against the undivulged pretence I fight
Of treasonous malice. (2.3.126–31)[22]

Banquo's shift from the plural that includes all the thanes to the singular – himself only – marks his recognition that he is a privileged witness: he has information that no one else has about the death of Duncan. Here he vows before God to fight against the treason and malice so far undivulged. He makes this statement suspecting, we must suppose, that the pretence is on the part of his friend: he must suspect Macbeth. We know that Banquo has dreams of the Witches: 'I dreamt last night of the three weird sisters' (2.1.19), and that in his nightmares or his sleepless state he has 'cursèd thoughts' (2.1.8). What those may have been he does not say, but they were so seriously threatening as to drive Banquo to pray to the 'Merciful powers' that those thoughts be restrained – natural though they were – or that he be restrained in thinking them (2.1.7–8).

What then, in this condition, is he to make of Macbeth's proposal to 'cleave to [his] consent, when 'tis' (2.1.24)?[23] 'When 'tis' occurred a few hours later, at the meeting of the thanes in the hall after the death of Duncan. At that moment, standing in the hand of God, Banquo had his test. He failed. He said nothing. He had vowed that he would fight against pretence and malice; instead, when his test came, he held his peace and, in so doing, clove to Macbeth's consent. He said nothing; it is not unreasonable to suppose that had he disclosed the knowledge he had in his privileged position, the election would not have fallen on Macbeth (2.4.29–32).

---

22 Though Banquo begins this speech with the straightforward statement that the thanes should dress in proper and decent attire before they reassemble (line 125), when Macbeth echoes the metaphor in line 132, the same image suggests a covering over of hypocrisy and deceit (Jaarsma, p. 92).

23 Walker notices that Macbeth's insinuating 'cleave' echoes Banquo's harmless use in 1.3.144.

He might have kept silent from timidity, or from an unwillingness to speculate, or from a reluctance to stand in the way of his good friend's advancement; he might have kept silent because he was greedy for the 'honour' – the greatness promised to him by Macbeth (2.1.25). It is more likely, however, that he kept silent because he realized that until Macbeth was king and the Witches' royal prophecy had been fulfilled, his own children would be unlikely to reign in their turn (3.1.5–10). He wishes the prophecies to be 'truth' (line 6), though he knows that 'The instruments of darkness tell us truths, / Win us with honest trifles to betray's / In deepest consequence' (1.3.122–4). As Macbeth needed the 'truth' of the advancement to Cawdor to make him especially vulnerable to the gaining of the kingship, so Banquo needed the 'truth' of Macbeth's advancement to the kingship to make him especially vulnerable to the temptation of the advancement of his children.[24] Macbeth's third 'truth' was the happy prologue to set up Banquo's swelling 'hope' of the imperial theme for his children (1.3.126–8; 3.1.10). Banquo knows in his heart that Macbeth has done the thing which he ought not to have done; he is not fully aware that at the meeting of the thanes he himself has left undone the thing he ought to have done. There is no health in either of them. Banquo's silence is the tie that knits him indissolubly to Macbeth (3.1.16–18); his 'advice', as Macbeth terms it, has been 'both grave and prosperous' (3.1.21–2). Prosperous for Macbeth, grave for Banquo.

The deterioration in Banquo's character is represented by the deterioration in Banquo's diction. It has been intimated that he has used – three times, in fact – one of the words of the Witch or its homonym: he now uses the other; and he uses the two words in conjunction, just as Macbeth had done before:

> Thou hast it now: King, Cawdor, Glamis, all
> As the weird women promised;[25] and I fear
> Thou played'st most foully for't.[26] (3.1.1–3)

The fair promise was to be feared because it was foul.[27] Banquo, like Macbeth, has echoed the crucial words of the Witches.

Shakespeare sharpens the significance of this passage by one of the instances of ironic juxtaposition for which this compact play is famous.[28] At the end of the preceding scene, the Old Man, the embodiment of wisdom, addressing himself first to Ross, prays in the concluding couplet:

---

24 Noted also by Jaarsma (p. 93).

25 'Promised' is itself a word interesting in its associations. It is used four times in the play, thrice by the Macbeths and here finally by Banquo. Macbeth uses it first to describe the predictions of the Witches (1.3.118) because he wishes to persuade himself that the fore-tellings pertaining to himself are in fact binding commitments promised. In his letter, as we have seen, he transfers the word (1.5.12) to his wife, who uses it with a positiveness and a determination keener than those of her husband: 'and [thou] shalt be / What thou art promised' (1.5.14–15). When Banquo uses the word here in its final appearance, he does so with the same assurance that marked the Macbeths' uses; though he speaks of the predictions as 'hope' (1.3.54; 3.1.10), here his 'promised' that defines Macbeth's future suggests that he regards his children's future as promised also. He has appropriated the word of the Macbeths and their attitude to it. Too late, however, Macbeth discovers that though the Witches 'keep the word of promise to our ear / [They] break it to our hope' (5.10.21–2).

26 *Fear–foully* will surely recall the pun that Banquo made when he first used *fear* and *fair* in 1.3.49–50, as they recall also Macbeth's *fair* and *foul*. Furthermore, Banquo's supposition that Macbeth '[played] most foully' echoes Lady Macbeth's assumption that he '[would] not play false' (1.5.20). But, at her urging, Macbeth does play false, assuming a 'false face' to hide 'what the false heart doth know' (1.7.82) (that false face does not deceive Malcolm (2.3.135–6); see also note 4 above). Later, Macbeth falsely '[plays] the humble host' (3.4.4), though a murderer.

27 Though, as has been noted, *fair* and *foul* are often linked in the proverbial and literary traditions, *fear* and *foul* are not; but *fair*, *fear*, and *foul* are linked in a work that Shakespeare knew intimately, *Tamberlaine*: 'Ah fair Zenocrate, divine Zenocrate, / Fair is too foul an epithet for thee, / That in thy passion for thy country's love, / And fear to see thy kingly father's harm . . .' etc. (Part 1, 5.1.135–8).

28 Each of the three major characters has an entrance that ironically comments on the line of the preceding speaker: Macbeth's occurs at 1.4.14, after Duncan's lines 13–14; Lady Macbeth's is at 1.7.28, after Macbeth's line 25; Banquo's is here.

God's benison go with you, and with those
That would make good of bad, and friends of
foes. (2.4.41–2)

'*Enter Banquo*' – the only character who had indeed the knowledge that might have made good of bad and friends of foes.[29] He chose not to use it; he remained silent. The first words he speaks after that failure to speak are the words of the Witches. Banquo speaks these words to characterize Macbeth and Macbeth's guilt, not himself and his own. That is not surprising: we need no bubbles come from the earth to tell us that humans in their frailty see in others those sins which they are unable to see in themselves.

Long ago Bradley recognized the deterioration of Banquo's character;[30] Granville-Barker, Richard J. Jaarsma, and Marvin Rosenberg have argued in support of Bradley's view, still not generally accepted. Banquo's language suggests that Bradley was right. Like Macbeth, like Lady Macbeth, Banquo has chosen to speak the language of the Witches. Lady Macbeth deliberately and with manly resolve placed herself under the control of the Witches; Macbeth rejected that control firmly (1.7.31) as he unmanly and weakly submitted to the control of his wife; Banquo negligently allowed himself to be seduced by them. These three central characters, in ways peculiar to their personalities and defining of those personalities, labour to work out their own damnations.

---

[29] Walker proposes that 'the first phrase is for Ross and the rest spoken after the retreating . . . Macduff' (p. 82), and Rosenberg concurs. I would suggest that Macduff 'retreats' after his last line (39), marking his solo exit from the stage with a rhymed couplet. Ross then addresses the Old Man, whose reply, also a rhymed couplet, includes a blessing specifically on Ross, who leaves now (41) (not in company with Macduff who earlier headed off to Fife), and another of 'those' unspecified persons who would make good of bad. The first such person, ironically, is Banquo, who arrives now. Prior critics have been misled by the traditional 'act break' – in reality no more than a scene break, as we now know.

[30] A. C. Bradley, *Shakespearean Tragedy* (London, 1904), pp. 384–5.

SHAKESPEARE'S KNOWLEDGE OF ITALIAN

NASEEB SHAHEEN

The question of whether Shakespeare could read Italian remains uncertain although the plots of many of his plays were based on Italian sources. *Othello*, *The Merchant of Venice*, and *Measure for Measure* were based either wholly or in part on Italian narratives written by Cinthio, Bandello, Ser Giovanni Fiorentino and others. *Twelfth Night* and *The Merry Wives of Windsor* were heavily indebted to the anonymous Italian play *Gl'Ingannati* and Ser Giovanni Fiorentino's *Il Pecorone*. Many other Italian sources were used to a lesser extent in other plays.

Did Shakespeare read these sources in Italian, or did he have to rely on English and French translations of these works? Nothing certain is known. The claim that Shakespeare's knowledge of Latin enabled him to read Italian cannot be supported. The differences in the two languages are so great that even one versed in classical Latin cannot necessarily read Italian. For Shakespeare to have known Italian so as to be able to read the *novelle* of Cinthio and Bandello, he would have had to make some study of Italian as a separate language.

John Florio, well known in London's intellectual circles and Italian tutor in Southampton's household, published two Italian–English manuals, *Firste Fruites* in 1578, and *Second Frvtes* in 1591 (*STC* 11096–7). These were manuals of polite conversation as well as textbooks for teaching Italian to Englishmen and English to Italians. They also come within the courtesy book tradition with their discussions of fencing, tennis, polite conversation, hunting, hawking, and other activities suitable for a gentleman. *Firste Fruites* includes a lengthy appendix of 108 pages entitled 'Necessarie Rules, for Englishmen to learne to reade, speake, and write true Italian', which surveys Italian grammar and pronunciation for those unacquainted with Italian. The manual itself presupposes that the reader has some knowledge of Italian since the first chapter includes not only everyday greetings, but also advanced conversation that would hardly be suitable for someone with no knowledge of Italian. The first page of the manual includes the following dialogue:

Vi piacciono le Comedie à voi?
Signor, si la festa.
Mi piacciono anche a me, ma
i predicatori non le vogliono
acconsentire.

Doo Comedies like you wel?
Yea sir, on holy dayes.
They please me also wel, but the
preachers wyll not allowe
them.

Io credo che si faccia di molte
furfanterie a queste Come-
die, che credete voi?
Cosi credo anche io.

I beleeue there is much knaue-
rie vsed at those Comedies:
what thinke you?
So beleeue I also. (sig. A.i.^{r})

Research for this study was supported by a grant from the Marcus W. Orr Center for the Humanities at Memphis State University.

What is significant for our purpose is that Shakespeare seems to have been acquainted with Florio's language manuals. He seems to have progressed beyond *Firste Fruites*, and mastered both it and *Second Frvtes*, as can be seen from the following borrowings from Florio. Chapter 7 of *Second Frvtes* deals with 'ciuill, familiar, and pleasant entertainments betweene two Gentlemen . . . [as] they talk of armes . . . fencing, and of many other things'. The Italian–English dialogue in *Second Frvtes* is presented on facing pages rather than in parallel columns, as in *Firste Fruites*, and chapter 7 begins thus:

G *Perche state cosi scoperto? v.s. si fa torto.*
E *Perdonimi v.s. io lo faccio per mio agio.*
G *Copriteui di gratia, voi sete troppo cerimonioso.*
E *Io stò tanto bene, che mi par d'esser in paradiso.*
G *Deh metteteui il cappello, se mi volete bene.*
E *Io lo farò per vbidir v.s. non gia per voglia ch'io n'habbia.* (110)

G Why do you stand barehedded? you do your self wrong.
E Pardon me good sir, I doe it for my ease.
G I pray you be couered, you are too ceremonious.
E I am so well, that me thinks I am in heauen.
G If you loue me, put on your hat.
E I will doe it to obay you, not for any plesure that I take in it. (111)

Compare these lines with the Osric scene, *Hamlet* 5.2.92–105:

HAMLET
. . . Put your bonnet to his right use, 'tis for the head.
OSRIC I thank your lordship, it is very hot.
HAMLET I beseech you remember.
[*Hamlet moves him to put on his hat.*]
OSRIC Nay, good my lord, for my ease.[1]

Although this putting on and taking off of the hat seems to have been an old joke and had been used by other writers, it appears safe to conclude that chapter 7 of *Second Frvtes* was the model for these lines in *Hamlet* (compare 'for my ease' in both Shakespeare and Florio), and that Shakespeare had gone through Florio's manual at least up to that chapter, page 111 of the manual.

Another resemblance to *Second Frvtes* occurs in *Othello*. The passage in question is in chapter 12, the final chapter of the manual. The Italian–English dialogue appears thus:

**Le donne sono il purgatorio della borsa, il paradiso del corpo, & l'inferno della anima.*
**Le donne sono Sante in chiesa, Angele in strada, Diauole in casa, Sirene alla fenestra, Gazze alla porta, e Capre ne' giardini.*

Women are the purgatory of mens purses, the Paradise of mens bodies, and the hell of mens souls.
Women are in churches, Saints: abroad, Angels: at home deuills: at windowes Syrens: at doores, pyes: and in gardens, Goates. (174–5)

Compare these passages with Iago's cynical description of women:

. . . you are pictures out a' doors,
Bells in your parlors, wild-cats in your kitchens,
Saints in your injuries, devils being offended,
Players in your huswifery, and huswives in your beds. (*Othello* 2.1.109–12)

Although cited by Tilley as a proverb (W702)[2] with parallels from other works, Florio is one of the most likely sources from which Shakespeare could have borrowed these lines.

A third parallel with Florio occurs in *The Taming of the Shrew*. In chapter 19 of *Firste Fruites* Florio has:

Lombardia è il giardino del mondo.

Lombardie is the garden of the world. (31^{v})

The same proverb is repeated in *Second Frvtes* (106–7). Compare *The Taming of the Shrew* 1.1.3–4: 'I am arriv'd for fruitful Lombardy, /

[1] References to Shakespeare's plays are to *The Riverside Shakespeare*, ed. G. Blakemore Evans (Boston, 1974).

[2] Tilley, Morris Palmer, *A Dictionary of the Proverbs in England in the Sixteenth and Seventeenth Centuries* (Ann Arbor, Mich., 1950).

The pleasant garden of great Italy'. Tilley lists 'Lombardy is the garden of the world (Italy)' as a proverb (L414) and cites Heywood's use of the proverb in *The Four Prentices of London*, written *c.* 1592–4, around the same time as Shakespeare's play (*c.* 1591–2). But of all the works cited by Tilley in which the proverb appears, Florio was Shakespeare's most likely source.

It is possible, of course, that Shakespeare's use of Florio's language manuals was limited to the English portions of the manuals, and that his main interest in them was not to learn Italian but to tap them for the many English proverbs and quotations they contain. The title page of *Firste Fruites* proclaims it to be a storehouse of apt quotations: 'FLORIO His firste Fruites: which yeelde familiar speech, merie Prouerbes, wittie Sentences, and golden sayings.' The title page of *Second Frvtes* reads: 'FLORIOS SECOND FRVTES, To be gathered of twelue Trees, of diuers but delightsome tastes to the tongues of Italians and Englishmen. To which is annexed his GARDINE OF RECREATION yeelding six thousand Italian Prouerbs.' From this point of view, Shakespeare's use of Florio's works would be parallel to his reading of any English book prior to writing a play, and borrowing from Florio's English text whatever he found useful for his plays.

While that is entirely possible, we have at least one indication which dictates against it and reveals that Shakespeare had his eye on more than just the English portion of Florio's books. In *Love's Labour's Lost* 4.2.97–8, as the pedant Holofernes seeks to display his knowledge of foreign languages, he quotes a proverb that appears in chapter 19 of Florio's *Firste Fruites*, the chapter entitled 'Prouerbes'. These are described as 'certaine prouerbes that commonly are vsed as wel in Italie, as in Englande' (26^{v}; misnumbered 28^{v}). Among the more than 270 proverbs listed by Florio, the following proverb appears at the top of page 34:

Venetia, chi non ti vede, non ti pretia.

Venise, woo seeth thee not, praiseth thee not. (34^{r})

In Shakespeare's play, Holofernes' Italian appears as: '*Venechia, Venechia, / Che non te vede, che non te prechia.*' The Quarto edition of the play (1598), which abounds in misprints, has: '*vemchie, vencha, que non te vnde, que non te perreche*' (sig. E1^{v}).[3] The reading of the First Folio is identical, it being printed from a copy of the Quarto. The same proverb is repeated in chapter 6 of *Second Frvtes*, again in a long series of proverbs, and appears on the same pages (106–7) as the proverb 'Lombardy is the garden of the world', referred to above. While there were other works in which Shakespeare could have found this proverb praising Venice, and Tilley also lists it as a proverb (V26), the fact that Shakespeare quotes the proverb in Italian rather than English strongly suggests that Florio's manuals were his source. It appears likely, therefore, that Shakespeare's acquaintance with Florio was not limited to the English portions of his works, but that he learned or at least increased his knowledge of Italian by means of Florio's two conversation manuals.[4]

The best evidence that Shakespeare could read Italian, however, comes from the close adherence of his plays to his Italian sources. For some plays, those Italian sources had not been translated into any other language, and the only logical conclusion is that Shakespeare must have read the source in Italian. In other instances, although the Italian source had been translated into French or English, Shakespeare's play is

[3] References to the Quarto editions of Shakespeare's plays are to *Shakespeare's Plays in Quarto: A Facsimile Edition of Copies Primarily from the Henry E. Huntington Library*, ed. Michael J. B. Allen and Kenneth Muir (Berkeley and Los Angeles, 1981). References to the Folio are to *The Norton Facsimile. The First Folio of Shakespeare*, ed. Charlton Hinman (New York, 1968).

[4] The longest Italian passage in Shakespeare's plays occurs in *The Taming of the Shrew* 1.2.24–6, and most of the phrases in that passage (*con tutto il core*; *ben trovato*; *ben venuto*) occur in the opening chapters of *Firste Fruites*. See Mario Praz, 'Shakespeare's Italy', *Shakespeare Survey 7* (1954), pp. 95–106, p. 105.

often closer to the Italian original than to the translations or adaptations of the original. At times, there is also a verbal similarity which adds to the evidence that Shakespeare had read the original Italian.

Consider *Othello*. Shakespeare's main source was Giraldi Cinthio's *Hecatommithi*, first published in Venice in 1565, which contains 110 tales about love and marriage. The introduction contains ten short tales, and then follow ten decades of ten stories each. For *Othello*, Shakespeare borrowed the story in decade 3, story 7, the account of the valiant Moor and Disdemona.

Cinthio's *Hecatommithi* was translated into French by Gabriel Chappuys in 1584. His was a close translation that, with a few exceptions, faithfully followed Cinthio's text. No English translation of Cinthio appeared until 1753.

Shakespeare followed Cinthio's plot closely throughout most of *Othello*. For the murder scene, however, he turned to a completely different story by Matteo Bandello, the account of an Albanian captain who killed his beautiful wife lest anyone should enjoy her after his death. Bandello's *Novelle* first appeared in 1554, were translated into French by Belleforest in 1561, and Belleforest, in turn, was translated into English by Geoffrey Fenton in 1567. Neither of these were close translations. Fenton greatly expanded Belleforest, even as Belleforest had expanded Bandello, so that Bandello's 2,200-word account became 10,500 words in Fenton's tediously moralizing version.[5]

The murder scene in *Othello* is the strongest evidence that Shakespeare read Bandello in the original Italian. The sensational device that Shakespeare uses of having Desdemona momentarily revive and exonerate Othello after having been apparently killed by him (5.2.80–125) is to be found only in Bandello. Only in Bandello does the maid (like Emilia) call for help. Only in Bandello do the neighbours break in and find the dead husband lying face downwards on his almost dead wife. These events occur in neither Belleforest nor Fenton. Bandello, however, relates how

> the ferocious wife-murderer gave himself a thrust right through his heart and drove out his vile criminal soul to the house of a hundred thousand devils; while his unhappy wife remained more dead than alive.
>
> The maid who had heard an unaccountable noise had gone to her master's room, and heard the sounds of the villain's blows. Being unable to enter, she had gone to a window and called to the neighbours for help. Some of them came and broke down the door of the room, and having lights with them they perceived the treacherous husband lying face downward on the almost lifeless body of his unhappy wife. They realized at once that she was not quite dead . . .
>
> The wife, returning somewhat to consciousness . . . made confession, pardoning her husband with all her heart, not being willing to let anyone speak ill of him, but accusing nobody but her own misfortune. She made her will and left everything to her daughter by her first husband and, dying, asked to be buried in the Barza tomb . . .[6]

Shakespeare followed this pattern of the murder. In both Belleforest and Fenton, the husband kills himself at the end of the tale, and the wife has barely enough breath to pray and ask to be buried with her first husband. There is no revival by the wife after having (almost) died, and no pardoning of her husband. No outsiders enter the bedchamber to witness what had happened. These incidents occur only in Bandello and indicate that Shakespeare must have read Bandello's account in Italian. Nor is there a revival after apparent death in Cinthio's account, which Shakespeare followed throughout most of the play up to the scene of the murder. Cinthio's ending is completely different. In Cinthio, the Moor and the Ensign kill Disdemona with a sand-filled stocking, break her skull, and then cause part of the ceiling to fall on her to make it appear that the

---

[5] Geoffrey Bullough, *Narrative and Dramatic Sources of Shakespeare*, vol. 7 (London, 1975), p. 202.

[6] Bullough, vol. 7, pp. 261–2.

fallen rafters had killed her. In Cinthio, the Moor is accused of the murder by the treacherous Ensign, is arrested, brought to Venice where he is tried, tortured, and banished to perpetual exile. Only later is the Moor finally slain by Disdemona's relatives. Shakespeare's account of the murder is clearly based on Bandello's Italian narrative.

Several verbal parallels exist between *Othello* and Shakespeare's Italian sources which reinforce the conclusion that Shakespeare could read Italian. Two of these verbal parallels are with Cinthio's *Hecatommithi*, which Shakespeare followed throughout most of the play. The first is Othello's demand to Iago, 'Give me the ocular proof' of the truth of what you have told me (3.3.360). Cinthio's Italian narrative has

se non mi fai, disse, vedere cogl' occhi quello . . .[7]

('if you do not make me see with my own eyes what . . .'). Shakespeare's choice of the word 'ocular' seems to have been inspired by the Italian word for 'eyes' in Cinthio. It was not borrowed from the French translation of Gabriel Chappuys, since his translation has,

Si tu ne me fais voir ce que tu m'as dit . . .[8]

The Italian word for 'eyes' also occurs a few lines earlier in Cinthio's text,

vi hà così appannati gli occhi, . . .

'[if she] has so blinded your eyes', and Cinthio's Italian text is most likely the source of Shakespeare's 'ocular proof'. This is the only occurrence of 'ocular' in Shakespeare.

Another verbal borrowing from Cinthio's Italian narrative occurs at 1.3.347–9: 'The food that to him now is as luscious as locusts, shall be to him shortly as acerb as the coloquintida.' Although the Folio changed 'acerb' to 'bitter', Shakespeare's use of 'acerb' seems to be based on Cinthio, who says that the love of the Ensign for Disdemona turned into the bitterest hatred, 'in acerbissimo odio'.[9] The corresponding passage in Chappuys contains the French word *haine*, 'hatred', and not *acerbité*: 'et changea l'amour qu'il portoit à la femme, en une très-grande haine'.[10] Shakespeare's 'acerb' was probably borrowed from Cinthio's Italian text.

There may be a verbal borrowing from Ariosto when Othello describes the handkerchief he had given Desdemona: 'A sibyl . . . / In her prophetic fury sew'd the work' (3.4.70–2). The expression 'prophetic fury' also occurs in stanza 80 of the last canto of Ariosto's *Orlando Furioso*:

Vna donzella della Terra d'Ilia,
C'hauea il furor profetico congiunto,
Con studio di gran tempo, e con vigilia
Lo fece di sua man di tutto punto.[11]

The words 'prophetic fury' do not occur in Sir John Harington's free translation of 1591 (*STC* 746), which at times is but a paraphrase and occasionally omits some long passages. The corresponding stanza (65) in Harington is:

The worthyest wight that eu'r man did behold,
That should proceed forth of his noble line,
She here portrayd, in worke of silke and gold,
Of precious substance, and of cullor fine:
Also the time and season was foretold,
Both of his birth, and of his praise deuine:
Hector of this her gift great count did make,
Both for the worke, and for the workers sake.[12]

If it is true that Shakespeare had read Ariosto and borrowed *furor profetico* from Ariosto and

7 *Othello*. A New Variorum Edition of Shakespeare, ed. Horace Howard Furness (1886; reprinted New York, 1965); p. 381.

8 Chappuys' French translation of Cinthio's tale is seldom published, but it can be found in Victor Hugo's edition of Shakespeare, *Oeuvres Complètes de W. Shakespeare*, vol. 5, part 2 (Paris, 1860), pp. 430–45. The quotation is from page 437.

9 *Othello*, ed. Horace Howard Furness, p. 379.

10 *Oeuvres Complètes de W. Shakespeare*, vol. 5, part 2, p. 434.

11 M. Lodovico Ariosto, *Orlando Furioso* (Venice, 1556), canto 46, stanza 80. Stanza 80 falls on p. 560 of these unnumbered stanzas.

12 *Orlando Fvrioso in English Heroical Verse, by Iohn Harington* (1591; Amsterdam and New York, 1970), canto 46, stanza 65.

not from some other source, then his knowledge of Italian was hardly superficial, confined to a few proverbs and everyday expressions. A person able to read Ariosto would be able to read not only the prose narratives of Cinthio and Bandello, but also the much more difficult and highly structured poetry of one of Italy's greatest poets. But until other verbal echoes of Ariosto are pointed out, this must remain a moot point. Nonetheless, even without any of the above verbal similarities, the evidence from *Othello* that Shakespeare had read Bandello's account in Italian is substantial.[13]

Another play for which there is strong evidence that Shakespeare read an Italian source is *The Merchant of Venice*. There were many stories in Shakespeare's day about greedy moneylenders who demanded their debtor's flesh, making it difficult to determine how many of these he used. Some stories have been lost. Of the extant sources, the most important for Shakespeare was *Il Pecorone*, a collection of prose tales by Ser Giovanni Fiorentino (Ser Giovanni of Florence), published in Italian in 1558 and not translated into any other language when Shakespeare wrote his play. *Il Pecorone* may have been Shakespeare's main source. No other source that has come down to us corresponds in so many details.

A summary of Ser Giovanni's tale (day 4, tale 1) will reveal that although Shakespeare made many alterations, he followed its main outline.

Ansaldo (who corresponds to Antonio), a wealthy merchant of Venice, adopts his godson, Giannetto (Shakespeare's Bassanio). Giannetto tries on two separate voyages to win the lady of Belmont (Portia), a rich widow who agrees to marry the first man who enjoys her. Should the suitor fail, however, he would forfeit all his wealth. Giannetto fails on both occasions since he is given drugged wine and falls asleep without possessing the lady. Ashamed, he tells his godfather Ansaldo that he had been twice shipwrecked. In order to equip a third ship for Giannetto, Ansaldo borrows 10,000 ducats from a Jew on condition that if the loan is not repaid by St John's Day, the following June, Ansaldo would forfeit a pound of flesh from any part of his body that the Jew wished. In Belmont, Giannetto is warned by a maid not to drink the wine, enjoys the lady, marries her, and becomes king of Belmont to the delight of all its inhabitants. To his dismay he forgets about Ansaldo's bargain until it is too late and when his wife learns why he is so sad, she sends him to Venice with 100,000 ducats and follows him disguised as a lawyer. The Jew refuses the ducats, but the disguised lawyer arrives and makes a proclamation that she will settle any dispute. Giannetto and the Jew go before the lawyer, but when the Jew adamantly refuses her advice to accept the 100,000 ducats, she tells him to take his pound of flesh. The Jew orders Ansaldo be stripped naked and when he is about to satisfy his bond with Ansaldo's flesh, the lawyer warns him that if he takes more than a pound or sheds a drop of blood, off goes his head. The Jew asks for the money but is refused. Giannetto offers the 100,000 ducats to the lawyer, but she requests his ring as payment. When he returns to Belmont with Ansaldo, his wife accuses him of having given the ring to a former mistress, but later explains everything to him. Ansaldo ends up marrying the lady who had warned Giannetto not to drink the drugged wine, even as in Shakespeare's play Bassanio's friend Gratiano marries Nerissa, Portia's waiting woman.[14]

For other elements in the play – particularly the choice of caskets and Jessica's elopement –

---

13 A few other verbal links with Cinthio's Italian text have been pointed out by other scholars, but they are too marginal. See, for example, E. A. J. Honigmann, '*Othello*, Chappuys and Cinthio', *Notes and Queries*, 211 (1966), 136–7; Kenneth Muir, *The Sources of Shakespeare's Plays* (London, 1977), pp. 183, 305 n. 4.

14 The full text of Ser Giovanni's tale can be found in Bullough, vol. 1 (London, 1977), pp. 463–76.

Shakespeare borrowed from other sources. These include Marlowe's *Jew of Malta*, Anthony Munday's *Zelauto or The Fountaine of Fame*, Richard Robinson's translation of the *Gesta Romanorum*, and others, but none of them corresponds so closely and in so many details with Shakespeare's play as does Ser Giovanni's tale. Only Ser Giovanni uses Venice as the setting for the merchant, and Belmont as the city of the lady whom many suitors sought to win. Only Ser Giovanni has the lady disguise herself as a lawyer and turn the tables on the greedy Jewish moneylender. Only Ser Giovanni has the episode of the ring which Shakespeare followed closely. And only in Ser Giovanni's tale does the merchant's friend marry the Lady of Belmont's waiting woman. These correspondences make it clear that *Il Pecorone* was one of Shakespeare's main sources, perhaps his main source, and it was available to him only in Italian.[15]

Measure for Measure offers additional evidence that Shakespeare read at least one of his sources for that play in Italian. Its main source was George Whetstone's two-part play *Promos and Cassandra* (1578), which has a plot strikingly similar to Shakespeare's. Promos and Cassandra are the equivalent of Angelo and Isabella in *Measure for Measure*. When Whetstone was unable to have his crude, awkward play performed ('but yet neuer presented vpon stage'),[16] he made a prose version of the story and published it in his collection of stories called *An Heptameron of Civill Discovrses* in 1582. Shakespeare read both versions. His most important changes were the introduction of the bed trick and making the story much more complex.

But Shakespeare also knew Cinthio's 'Story of Epitia', decade 8, story 5 of the *Hecatommithi*, first published in 1565. Cinthio later took his tale and transformed it into a drama, *Epitia*, published posthumously in 1583. There is strong evidence that Shakespeare knew Cinthio's play, which he must have read in Italian, since it was not available in any other language. He could have read the *Hecatommithi* either in the original Italian or in the French translation by Gabriel Chappuys, 1584. There were many other sources that Shakespeare could have borrowed from since there were many stories about the unjust governor and the woman who had to sacrifice her chastity in order to save the life of someone she loved; about the Disguised Ruler who circulated among his subjects in order to learn what was going on in the realm; and about the 'bed trick' or substitution in the dark. But it is safe to conclude that the above four works by Whetstone and Cinthio were Shakespeare's main sources.

Shakespeare's use of an Italian source centres not so much on Cinthio's 'Story of Epitia' in the *Hecatommithi* (although the *Hecatommithi* was his main source for *Othello*), as on his use of Cinthio's play, *Epitia*. Especially the verbal similarities between Shakespeare's play and *Epitia* make it clear that Shakespeare had read *Epitia*, as the following examples will show.

In Shakespeare's play, when the Duke disguised as a friar tells Isabella that Claudio has been executed, she exclaims,

---

15 Some critics think that for Jessica's elopement with much of her father's wealth, Shakespeare borrowed not only from Marlowe's *Jew of Malta*, but also from the fourteenth tale in *Il Novellino* by Masuccio di Salerno about the daughter of a miser who escapes with her father's jewels and joins the gentleman she loves. Bullough even gives the text of Salerno's tale (vol. 1, pp. 497–505). If Shakespeare borrowed from *Il Novellino*, then he must have read the tale in Italian, since it does not seem to have been translated into English in his day. But Kenneth Muir thinks 'it is unlikely that Shakespeare knew this tale' (*The Sources of Shakespeare's Plays*, pp. 89, 298 n. 10).

16 George Whetstone, *An Heptameron of Civill Discovrses*, in the New Variorum Edition of *Measure for Measure*, edited by Mark Eccles (New York, 1980), p. 370. Whetstone's prose version of Promos and Cassandra, published in the *Heptameron*, is not included by Bullough in *Sources*, vol. 2, but it appears in the Variorum edition of *Measure for Measure*, hereafter referred to as Variorum.

> O, I will to him, and pluck out his eyes! (4.3.119)

So also in *Epitia*, when Angela, the deputy's sister, learns that her brother has executed Vico (who corresponds to Claudio) rather than release him, she cries,

> Male ne hò detto à Iuriste, & poco meno
> Che non gli habbia cacciati ambiduo gli occhi
> ...[17] (III.ii; p. 55)

Although the speaker is Angela rather than Epitia, the occasion is the same – anger at the supposed execution of Claudio/Vico – and *Epitia* was no doubt Shakespeare's source for Isabella's wish to pluck out Angelo's eyes. It occurs in none of the other sources.

An even closer verbal similarity occurs in Isabella's next words,

> Unhappy Claudio! Wretched Isabel!
> Injurious world! Most damned Angelo!
> (4.3.121–2)

Isabella's cries were no doubt patterned on Cinthio. When Epitia's maid hears of Vico's 'execution', she cries out,

> O scelerato, ò traditore Iuriste,
> Ò dolorosa Epitia, ò miserella.[18] (III.I; p. 50)

Compare also the message which Angelo sent to the Provost concerning Claudio's execution when a pardon was expected,

> Whatsoever you may hear to the contrary, let Claudio be executed by four of the clock. (4.2.120–1)

So also in *Epitia*, just when a reprieve was expected for Vico,

> Andai al Podesta ratto, ei mostromme
> Lettra di man d'Iuriste, & del sigillo
> Di lui segnata, che gli commetteua
> Che, senza vdir cosa, che fusse detta,
> Leuar gli fesse il capo.[19] (III.I; p. 50)

Later in the same scene in *Epitia* (III.I; p. 51) we have another reference to the seal of Juriste, 'Lettra, segnata del maggior Sigillo'. Likewise in *Measure for Measure*, when the Duke in the habit of a friar seeks to allay the fears of the Provost over not executing Claudio as ordered, the Duke says, 'here is the hand and seal of the Duke; you know the ... signet' (4.2.192–3). When we consider that all these elements in *Measure for Measure* – the hand and seal of the Duke, the messenger who comes to the prison with the execution order when pardon is expected, the specific order to disregard any contrary expectations – are peculiar only to Shakespeare's play and *Epitia*, it seems clear that Shakespeare had read Cinthio's play in Italian and borrowed these ideas from it.

When Epitia complains to the Emperor about her injuries, the Emperor asks whether all this was true: '[E] questo è uero?' To which Epitia replies, 'Più uer, che il uero' ('More true than truth itself'; IV.iii; p. 79). So also in *Measure for Measure* Isabella tells the Duke,

> ... this is all as true as it is strange;
> Nay, it is ten times true, for truth is truth.
> (5.1.44–5)

A few lines later Isabella again says: 'O that it were as like as it is true!' (5.1.104) The closest parallel in Shakespeare's other sources occurs in Whetstone's *Promos and Cassandra* when the King says, after hearing Cassandra's charges, 'If this be true ...'. Promos readily admits his guilt and says: 'I doe confesse this tale is true'

17 'I have cursed Juriste, a little less (fiercely) / Than if I had thrust out both his eyes'. *Epitia* is quoted from the first edition, *Le Tragedie di M. Gio. Battista Giraldi Cinthio* (Venice, 1583). Page numbers from the 1583 edition are provided after the act and scene numbers, since there are no line numbers in the play. Cinthio's text is reproduced exactly as printed in 1583, following the original typography, although inconsistencies are occasionally evident.

18 'O villain, O treacherous Juriste, / O wretched Epitia, O miserable one'.

19 'Swiftly I went to the Podestà, who showed me
A letter in Juriste's hand, impressed
With his own seal, which commanded
That, without hearing anything to the contrary,
He should be beheaded.'

(Bullough 2.499). But Shakespeare's primary source was probably *Epitia*. Isabella's words 'for truth is truth' are considerably closer to Cinthio's 'Più uer, che il uero' ('More true than truth itself') than to Whetstone's 'If this be true . . .'.

In addition to verbal borrowings, Shakespeare seems to have borrowed the name Angelo from Cinthio's play. In *Epitia*, the deputy's sister is named Angela. In Shakespeare's play the deputy has no sister, but he himself is named Angelo. Just as the name Isabella was probably borrowed from the name of the lady who narrates the story in Whetstone's *Heptameron* ('The rare Historie of Promos and Cassandra, reported by Madam Isabella'),[20] so also Angelo's name was probably inspired by that of the deputy's sister *Angela*. There are no similar names in the *Hecatommithi* or in either of Whetstone's versions. It is also likely that the name of Shakespeare's fantastic, Lucio, was inspired by the name of Juriste's counsellor, Lucillo, in *Epitia*.

Several other plays provide similar evidence that Shakespeare could read Italian. *Twelfth Night* is one example. Although there were many works with plots similar to *Twelfth Night* which Shakespeare could have drawn on, his two main sources were probably Riche's story of Apolonius and Silla (1581), and the anonymous Italian play *Gl'Ingannati* ('The Deceived'), published in 1537. The latter was a seminal influence for later stories about a young lady with an almost identical twin brother who disguises herself and takes service as a page with the man she loves. *Gl'Ingannati* gave rise to many translations and adaptations, both dramatic and narrative. Shakespeare seems to have taken the title *Twelfth Night* from *Gl'Ingannati*, and it was available to him only in Italian. It also provided him with a few verbal echoes, including 'accost' at 1.3.49–59, 'Accost, Sir Andrew, accost . . .'. *Gl'Ingannati* has *accostare, s'accostan molto*, and *accostatevi* (Bullough, vol. 2, pp. 298, 307).

Shakespeare's choice of the name Cesario for Viola disguised as a page may have been taken from Curzio Gonzaga's play *Gl'Inganni* (1592), one of several plays based on *Gl'Ingannati*. In Gonzaga's play, the disguised sister uses the name 'Cesare'. If Shakespeare's choice of the name Cesario was borrowed from Gonzaga's play, then Shakespeare must also have read that play in Italian.

It seems clear, therefore, from plays which have an Italian source that Shakespeare could read Italian, and that for a surprising number of plays he read those sources in Italian.

---

20 Variorum, pp. 370, 373.

TAMBURLAINE AND EDWARD ALLEYN'S RING

S. P. CERASANO

Before Edward Alleyn died on 25 November 1626 he made some very careful arrangements. In his will he provided detailed instructions for bequests to his wife and servants, for the maintenance of the poor parishioners in St Giles Cripplegate (the parish in which he built the Fortune Playhouse), and for the future administration of the College of God's Gift at Dulwich (now Dulwich College). He left his personal papers – from which we derive the nucleus of our knowledge concerning theatrical management in the English Renaissance – to the College as well. And in his characteristically precise manner he concluded:

> I give and bequeath to the Corporation of God's Gift College aforesaid, these goods and implements following, that is to say: first my seal ring with my arms, to be worn by the Master and his successors. Next I appoint that a common seal shall be made for the said College, at the charge of my executors, which said two seals shall be repaired by the College as often as need shall require.[1]

Not surprisingly, some of Alleyn's bequests have disappeared over the years, including his collection of playbooks and the copy of Shakespeare's *Sonnets* he purchased for 5*d* when it was first printed in 1609. But fortunately, Alleyn's ring, his seal, and his silver-gilt chalice survive, and are today the only known personal effects that belonged to a Renaissance actor. For theatre historians interested in Marlowe's plays and Alleyn's acting style, Alleyn's ring is perhaps the most important piece of evidence to emerge in many decades. The size of Alleyn's ring allows us to make some assessments of his physical stature; and this, in turn, suggests a more historically accurate sense of the roles of the Marlovian ranters that were written for Alleyn. Moreover, the evidence provided by Alleyn's signet ring, combined with recent archaeological excavations of the Rose Playhouse, indicates that Alleyn probably looked like a giant to his audiences at the Rose. Although he was probably shorter than his full-length portrait would suggest, the self-willed passion and bombast usually associated with the roles Alleyn played seem to have been accurately described by those contemporary accounts which emphasize his powerful voice and the sheer force of his physical presence.

Alleyn began his professional career as a player, probably performing early on with Worcester's Men in 1583. At a later date he joined the Lord Admiral's Men, gradually becoming one of the company's most accomplished actors. By the early 1590s Alleyn had already become well known for his depictions of the lead roles in Christopher Marlowe's plays, particularly Tamburlaine and Doctor Faustus. (Doubtless he also played other parts, but the ambitious Marlovian heroes were favoured by contemporary audiences.) By the 1590s he had become a leader and a shareholder in the Lord Admiral's Men; and in October

[1] Alleyn's will (dated 13 November 1626) is PRO, PCC PROB11/150, fols. 291v–293r.

1592 Alleyn married Joan Woodward, the step-daughter of Philip Henslowe who owned the Rose Playhouse. Together Henslowe and Alleyn formed the most lucrative theatrical partnership of the period. Over time they came to own the Rose Playhouse (built in 1587 and later enlarged), the First Fortune Playhouse (built in 1600), and the Bear Garden (used initially for baiting, and later reconstructed as the Hope Playhouse in 1613). Henslowe and Alleyn served jointly as the Masters of the Bulls, Bears, and Mastiff Dogs under James I. Then, following Henslowe's death in 1616, Alleyn carried on as Master of the Royal Game, adding the Second Fortune Playhouse to his set of theatrical investments, as well as a private playhouse called Porter's Hall (which seems not to have been used for theatrical performances outside of one conjectural performance). At his death Alleyn had achieved social prominence in a variety of capacities – as an actor, theatre owner, churchwarden, courtier, Lord of Dulwich Manor, and as a patron of the poor. Today he is remembered in the continuance of Dulwich College, which he founded in 1619 as a school for poor scholars and a home for pensioners.[2]

9 Edward Alleyn's ring

Alleyn's signet ring consists of a plain gold setting which frames a bezel (the top portion) of sardonyx intaglio (the engraved design) depicting the Alleyn coat of arms: a chevron (bent bar) between three cinquefoils (star design), two above the chevron and one below (Plate 9).[3] In style and design it is typical of heraldic signets produced in the late sixteenth and early seventeenth centuries in England, although the

[2] The standard, though unhappily outdated biography of Alleyn is by G. L. Hosking, *The Life and Times of Edward Alleyn* (London, 1952). Biographical sketches were written by W. S. Wright, 'Edward Alleyn, Actor and Benefactor', *Theatre Notebook*, 20 (1966), 155–60; George F. Warner, 'Edward Alleyn', *DNB*, vol. 1, pp. 327–30; and William Rendle, 'Edward Alleyn', *The Genealogist*, n.s. 2 (1885), 241–55. E. K. Chambers, *The Elizabethan Stage*, 4 vols. (Oxford, 1923), vol. 2, pp. 296–8, and G. E. Bentley, *The Jacobean and Caroline Stage*, 7 vols. (Oxford, 1941–68), vol. 2, pp. 346–9 offer reliable, short accounts of Alleyn's professional life. See also supplemental material in S. P. Cerasano, 'Edward Alleyn's Early Years: his Life and Family', *Notes and Queries*, 34 no. 2, (1987), 237–43. J. R. Piggott provides an overview of Alleyn and Dulwich College in *Dulwich College: A Brief History and Guide to the Buildings* (n.p., 1990), pp. 5–12. John H. Astington has taken up the issue of Alleyn's appearance in 'The "Unrecorded Portrait" of Edward Alleyn', *Shakespeare Quarterly*, 44 no. 1 (1993), 73–86. Alleyn's silver-gilt chalice, as well as his ring and his seal, are housed at Dulwich College.

[3] The Alleyn coat of arms, recorded by the College of Arms as MS 2c. 26, fol. 73v, would technically be described as an argent (silver) background on which are placed a chevron (bent bar) dividing three cinquefoils gules (red, five-pointed stars). In Alleyn's later life these arms were merged with 'gules, a lion of England, and a chief of France Ancient', the Henslowe arms. The latter information was given by Alleyn to the heralds during their Visitation of Surrey in 1623, three years before his death. It is recorded and illustrated in W. Henry Rylands, ed., *The Visitation of the County of Buckingham, 1634* (London, 1909), p. 2. The connection between Alleyn and his father's coat of arms is discussed in S. P.

precise date at which it was made is difficult to determine. Sardonyx – a reddish translucent stone streaked with white – was commonly used for heraldic signets because the stone is hard enough to allow fine etching and strong enough to hold up under reasonable pressure. Consequently, the intaglio, with its incised design, allowed the ring to be used conveniently in place of a larger seal. A signet was acceptable as a means of identifying its owner, and more practically, as a way of sealing documents. In many portraits of the period men typically have removed a glove to show off their signet rings; and art historians frequently make use of the signet design to identify a subject of an otherwise unidentified portrait. Similarly, signet seals were occasionally substituted for signatures altogether although, at other times, the signature and the seal appear together. Originally heraldic signets were restricted to members of the aristocracy; but by Alleyn's time they had become fashionable among wealthy merchants and other persons of rank. Thus, many references to signets appear in wills, as bequests; and because they were family treasures many Renaissance signets have been well preserved.[4]

Among the actors of Alleyn's era several notable players endorsed their wills with seals. Nicholas Tooley who performed with the King's Men (alongside William Shakespeare) for eighteen years, and who was living in Cuthbert Burbage's house at the time of his death, set his seal to his will in 1624. John Shank – another of the King's Men, noted for his roles as a clown – also set his seal to his will. Thomas Downton, an established player and a professional colleague of Alleyn's, ended his will with the phrase 'sealed with my ring and subscribed with my hand', leaving his son 'one ring of gold with a lion rampant and two great letters of his name'. William Browne, who performed with Queen Anne's and Prince Charles' companies, and was the stepson of a prominent actor, left his mother 'my house clock, my pocket watch, my gold seal ring, my best beaver hat, and all my wearing apparel'. William Shakespeare who, after several attempts, ultimately succeeded in obtaining a coat of arms, distinguished carefully between his signature and his seal. He signed his will: 'In witness whereof I have hereunto put my hand', the word 'seal' having been first written in before 'hand', and then carefully crossed out.[5]

In addition to the many documents which bear the impression of Alleyn's signet ring, the ring itself is prominently displayed in Alleyn's portrait which currently hangs in the board room at Dulwich College. In it, Alleyn has removed his glove to display the ring worn on the last finger of his right hand, the hand being held in a slightly unnatural position so that the ring could be shown clearly. In both the exposure and the placement of the ring Alleyn was following contemporary convention. As some well-known portraits suggest – those of Sir Nicholas Bacon (1597, Montacute House) or

Cerasano, 'Edward Alleyn's Early Years: his Life and Family', *Notes and Queries*, 34 no. 2 (1987), 237–43, especially pp. 237–8. Alleyn's arms were painted at various places in Dulwich College, and, in 1681, on two stones at Pye Alley in the northeast of London, marking the place where Alleyn was born. On 9 March 1654 a turner was paid to fit a bone handle to the College seal. (Cited in the weekly account books of Dulwich College, and quoted in Frances B. Bickley, *Catalogue of the Manuscripts and Muniments of Alleyn's College of God's Gift at Dulwich. Second Series* (London, 1903), pp. 14, 17, 34.)

4 For information concerning the creation, design, and use of signet rings during this period see Gerald Taylor and Diana Scarisbrick, *Finger Rings from Ancient Egypt to the Present Day* (London, 1978), especially pp. 23–9; C. Oman, *British Rings, 800–1914* (London, 1974); Yvonne Hackenbroch, *Renaissance Jewellery* (London, 1979); and Diana Scarisbrick, *Rings: Symbols of Wealth, Power, and Affection* (London, 1993).

5 The wills were all filed in the Prerogative Court of Canterbury. They are now housed at the Public Record Office (Chancery Lane), catalogued as: Nicholas Tooley (PROB 11/144, fols. 427v–428), John Shank (PROB 11/170/53r–54r), Thomas Downton (PROB 11/146, fols. 167v–168r), William Browne (PROB 11/166, fols. 317v–318r), and William Shakespeare (PROB 1/4).

William Cecil, Lord Burghley (*c.* 1585, Glasgow Art Gallery), to cite two well-known examples – men tended to wear signets on either their index finger or their little finger because it was most convenient to seal a document by simply bending the hand under toward the wrist when setting seal to wax, thus eliminating the need to remove the ring. Therefore, although the pencil drawing of Alleyn's portrait done in 1790 by Sylvester Harding (and conjectured to represent some repair work done on the portrait) shifts the ring to the third finger, it is much more likely that Alleyn would have worn the ring on the last (smallest) finger as it is represented in the portrait, especially since there is much evidence that he used the signet regularly to endorse documents. The earliest extant document in Alleyn's collection which bears the seal (as made by the ring) is dated 28 February 1610. But many documents housed at Dulwich College bear Alleyn's signet. Alleyn apparently used it regularly throughout his later life. Upon his death he left both his ring and his seal to the College, doubtless expecting subsequent masters of Dulwich to use them for the purposes of validating documents.[6]

Fortunately, the masters kept Alleyn's ring in mint condition, as was generally the case for Renaissance signet rings. Unlike mourning rings or remembrance rings, many of which were melted down, signets were generally well preserved, and very few show any sign of alteration. (Not only could the stone be damaged in the process of alteration, but alterations were rarely made for any reason. Apparently, those who inherited a ring simply wore it on whatever finger was comfortable.) Consequently, many examples of signet rings survive in pristine condition. Moreover, English

[6] The Alleyn portrait was inscribed in 1626, the year of his death, but the date presumably refers to Alleyn's bequest rather than the date that the portrait was painted. (See Peter Murray, *Dulwich Picture Gallery* (London, 1980).) The Harding drawing is housed at the Dulwich Picture Gallery; it was made in preparation for an engraving of the portrait. Murray notes that it shows differences in the gloves, cuffs, and position of the ring (p. 35). In fact, the engraving, if studied closely, shows only the most basic similarity to the portrait in its present state; and it might well be that it was not meant to duplicate the portrait in the condition in which Harding found it in 1790. In addition to the alterations noted by Murray the engraving shows a different background, including a column and tile floor, and there is drapery behind Alleyn's left shoulder. The head is tilted further to the left than it is in the portrait, creating a more unnatural pose. The subject's left arm is extended further from his body, apparently to allow for the introduction of fur trim which borders the cloak he is wearing. (The sleeves of his cloak also bear the sort of velvet bars characteristically adorning the sleeves of academic robes.) Moreover, Alleyn is dressed in breeches and hose, and the shoes have platforms with ties, none of which is suggested by the original. Despite the fact that the background from the portrait has darkened over the years there is no trace of these elements in the original, and some, it might be argued, indicate a later style of portraiture than the original. Therefore it is likely that Harding contrived his own sense of what the portrait looked like, reconceiving it in terms more appropriate to the portraiture of the later eighteenth century. With an updated floor and background, and wearing the robe more like that of the masters at Dulwich, Alleyn was made to look more contemporary. George Romney's portrait of James Allen – an eighteenth-century portrait (also housed at the Gallery) – shows the same robe as that which appears in the Harding engraving – a master's robe, not necessarily the robe of a Jacobean nobleman.

Interestingly, Sylvester Harding wasn't a professional artist or an engraver by trade. In the words of one commentator he was 'a man of many occupations – actor, miniaturist, portraitist, author, engraver – and none for long. Etching, of course, entered into his repertoire, but not to much extent or of great quality.' (See Maurice Arnold Grant, *A Dictionary of British Etchers* (London, 1952), p. 97.)

The earliest seal made from Alleyn's signet can be found on Muniment 35 (George F. Warner, *Catalogue of the Manuscripts and Muniments of Alleyn's College of God's Gift at Dulwich* (London, 1881), p. 237). Henslowe also had a signet ring, now presumably lost, that appears on other of the Henslowe–Alleyn papers. A good example is MS 2, no. 19, fol. 51r (Warner, *Catalogue*, p. 75), a commission by Henslowe and Alleyn licensing John Morgan and Richard Tyler 'To take up and provide, for his highness, bears, bulls, and dogs'. Here Alleyn's and Henslowe's seals appear, side by side, each below the owner's signature, a relatively common practice.

signet rings outnumber those from the Continent, in part because the great English collections were formed early on.[7] Although there is no record of the original purchase of Alleyn's ring, the fact that signets were made to order rendered them much more costly than the average ring. Some of those costs are suggested by one of Shakespeare's fellows, John Heminges, who bequeathed 10*s* to each living sharer in the King's men to make remembrance rings; and Shakespeare himself left '26*s* 8*d*' each to Heminges, Condell, and Richard Burbage.[8] Nevertheless, the accounts kept by Philip Henslowe during the period when he ran a pawnbroking business (in the plague years, 1593–4) indicate that heraldic signets were only valuable to those who had a right to use them. For four gold rings – one, a seal with a saracen's head – he lent 40*s* (£2). For a collection of items, including various articles of clothing, four gold hoop rings, and '1 seal ring with a griffen's head' (perhaps, but not necessarily, a heraldic signet) he lent only £5. One ring bearing a saracen's head and another ring with two 'stones' brought a slight 14*s* for both. As a result, Henslowe's pawn accounts suggest that signet rings brought no more substantial a price than ordinary rings when they were pawned; and the paucity of identifiable signets among the many rings that Henslowe records reconfirms that signets were most valuable to their owners, and that heraldic signets were normally passed down in families from father to son.[9]

If biographers and cultural historians would draw certain kinds of conclusions from Alleyn's signet ring, cultural anthropologists would use the evidence supplied by the ring to speculate on very different questions. Alleyn's well-preserved ring – with its unblemished, substantial bezel and its solid gold hoop – offers tangible evidence that can be used to estimate Alleyn's physical size, one of the most important factors that influenced his portrayal of the Tamburlaine role. For years, theatre historians have assumed that Edward Alleyn was a man of extraordinary height, a conclusion based on two distinctly different types of evidence: first, the dimensions of the Alleyn portrait, which emphasize Alleyn's stature and proportion (the breadth of his shoulders and large size of his hands, for instance); and second, the contemporary descriptions of Alleyn's acting style which imply that he crowded the dimensions of the Rose stage even as his portrait seems to crowd the canvas upon which it is painted.

The Alleyn portrait is dated 1626, the year of his death. At the time Alleyn was sixty years old, but the portrait clearly represents a man at an earlier stage of his life, one closer to middle age. It is the only known portrait of Alleyn, and thus there is nothing with which to compare it. The canvas measures 80¼ × 44⅞ inches (203.8 × 114 cm, or 6 feet 8¼ inches) in height. Except for 2–3 inches of blank space at the top and bottom Alleyn spans the entire canvas, the suggestion being that he stood roughly 6 feet 2–4 inches in height. Some early historians – not taking into account that Alleyn does not reach the entire length of the canvas – hypothesized that his height matched that of the portrait, that he literally stood 6 feet 7–8 inches.

In the portrait Alleyn is dressed in a long black gown. The background of the portrait is plain and drab, in part because the paint has darkened over time. In style and composition it has been said to resemble other portraits produced by the workshop of Marcus Gheeraerts II (d. 1635); however, the mixed quality of the painting would seem to contradict this. The portrait lacks consistency overall, the face being much better executed and more detailed than the rest of the painting. And while Alleyn's

---

[7] Taylor and Scarisbrick, *Finger Rings*, p. 29.

[8] Heminges' will is transcribed in Bentley, *The Jacobean and Caroline Stage*, vol. 2, pp. 643–5.

[9] R. A. Foakes and R. T. Rickert, eds., *Henslowe's Diary* (Cambridge, 1968), pp. 146, 148, 150–1, 153–4, 156, hereafter abbreviated *HD*. Shakespeare's arms are discussed by E. K. Chambers, *William Shakespeare*, 2 vols. (Oxford, 1930), vol. 2, pp. 18–32, especially p. 23. His arms were merged with those of his son-in-law (John Hall).

hands stand out because of their large size and the detailed signet on his small finger, the hands are not portrayed as well as the face. In addition, it might be argued that the Alleyn portrait shows a distinctly different sense of technique and composition than other portraits produced by Gheeraerts' workshop. Even in basic things the differences are glaring: there is no evidence of underpainting in the Alleyn portrait, for instance. Moreover, all the interest lies in the top half, which features Alleyn's face and hands starkly represented against the black background. The size of the portrait, coupled with its uninteresting lower half, has prompted some scholars to conclude that it could only have been painted to suggest Alleyn's unusual height, that there is no other reason for its composition, perhaps apart from simple ostentation, that would have motivated an artist to paint such a large portrait. Given the amount of paint required of the artist the portrait was clearly expensive to produce; but if the depiction of actual physical size was not at issue, then it seems a rather expensive venture for such an uninteresting picture.[10]

In assessing Alleyn's height theatre historians also cite contemporary descriptions of Alleyn's portrayal of Tamburlaine, a role that seems to demand an actor of majestic, imposing presence. Early on in the first part of the play Mycetes notes that Tamburlaine's force can only be countered by 'a great and thund'ring speech' (1.1.3). He is 'a terror to the world, / Measuring the limits of the empery / By east and west as Phoebus doth his course.' Menaphon characterizes him more specifically:

> Of stature tall, and straightly fashionèd,
> Like his desire, lift upwards and divine;
> So large of limbs, his joints so strongly knit,
> Such breadth of shoulders as might mainly bear
> Old Atlas' burden . . .
>
> His arms and fingers long and sinewy,
> Betokening valour and excess of strength:
> In every part proportioned like the man
> Should make the world subdued to
> Tamburlaine. (2.1.7–11; 27–30)[11]

And Theridamas likewise describes Tamburlaine's stature:

> For he is gross and like the massy earth
> That moves not upwards, nor by princely deeds
> Doth man to soar above the highest sort.
> (2.7.31–3)

Alleyn apparently achieved his desired effect through both his vocal strength and his physical presence so that, in his portrayal, Tamburlaine's assertiveness and success would have been partially a function of his imposing stature. Tamburlaine would have appeared to be taking over the play world of the Rose stage in military, spiritual, geographical, and physical terms. In criticizing Alleyn's acting style Ben Jonson complained that Alleyn's roles have 'nothing in them but the *scenicall* strutting and furious vociferation'. Thomas Dekker and Thomas Middleton both linked 'stalking' with Tamburlaine. Similarly, Everard Guilpin noted Alleyn's 'stalking and roaring'; and Hamlet's speech to the players alludes to an Alleyn who 'strutted and bellowed'.[12] In the Induction of Marston's

---

10 Murray, *Dulwich Picture Gallery*, offers a photograph of the Alleyn portrait (no. 443).

11 Citations are from *Tamburlaine the Great*, ed. J. S. Cunningham (Manchester, 1981).

12 Ben Jonson, 'Timber, or Discoveries', in C. H. Herford and Percy Simpson, eds., *Ben Jonson* (Oxford, 1925–52), vol. 8, 587. Thomas Dekker's reference to 'Death (like a Spanish Leager, or rather like stalking Tamburlaine)' appeared in *The Wonderfull Yeare* (1603), C4v; Thomas Middleton wrote in *The Black Booke* (1604), D1r that the 'Spindle-shanke Spyders which showed like great Leaders with little legges, went stalking over his head, as if they had been conning of *Tamburlayne*.' Everard Guilpin refers to Tamburlaine in *Skialetheia* (1598), B2v. Hamlet's well-known remark is at 3.2.34. Two essays which deal largely with Alleyn's acting style are W. A. Armstrong, 'Shakespeare and the Acting of Edward Alleyn', *Shakespeare Survey 7* (1954), 82–9, and A. J. Gurr, 'Who Strutted and Bellowed?', *Shakespeare Survey 16* (1963), 95–102. Richard Levin offers a comprehensive list of Tamburlaine references in 'The Contemporary Perception of Marlowe's Tamburlaine', *Medieval and Renaissance Drama in England*, 1 (1984), 51–70.

Antonio and Mellida (*c.* 1599) Feliche cites the force of Tamburlaine's voice: 'What rattling thunderclap breaks from his lips?' But among the many contemporary comments about, and allusions to, Alleyn's stature Joseph Hall characterized the excitement of Alleyn's tremendous power most vividly in *Virgidemiarum* (1597):

One higher pitch'd doth set his soaring thought
On crowned kings that Fortune hath low brought:
Or some upreared, high-aspiring swaine
As it might be the Turkish *Tamburlaine*.
Then weeneth he his base drink-drowned spright,
Rapt to the threefold loft of heavens hight,
When he conceives upon his fained stage
The stalking steps of his great personage,
Graced with huf-cap termes and thundring threats
That his poor hearers hayre quite upright sets.
Such soone, as some brave-minded hungry youth,
Sees fitly frame to his wide-strained mouth,
He vaunts his voyce upon an hyred stage,
With high-set steps, and princely cariage:
Now sooping in side robes of Royaltie,
That earst did skrub in Lowsie brokerie.
There if he can with termes Italianate,
Big-sounding sentences, and words of state,
Faire patch me up his pure Iambick verse,
He ravishes the gazing Scaffolders.

So influential was this portrayal that J. S. Cunningham thought that Shakespeare alluded to Alleyn when Ulysses describes Patroclus' imitation of:

A strutting player whose conceit
Lies in his hamstring, and doth think it rich
To hear the wooden dialogue and sound
'Twixt his stretch'd footing and the scaffoldage.[13]

For however tall Alleyn seemed, the historical Tamburlaine was renowned for his height as well as for his limping gait, the supposed legacy of a battle wound. Petrus Perondinus noted in 1553:

He had a tall and lofty stature, was bearded, and broad across
the shoulders and chest, and he was equally well-proportioned
and robust in all his limbs, with the exception of one foot,
where he was not so strong, and it was apparent that this
caused him to limp, with a mis-shapen gait. He had a fierce
countenance, and the deep-set eyes in the knitted brow
expressed the savagery of his warlike spirit, striking fear
and terror into onlookers. So very strong were his muscles,
that he could throw the strongest of the Scythians on the
wrestling-floor, and he could easily bend the string of a
huge Parthian bow with his brawny arms past his ear, and
pierce a brazen mortar with the point of a javelin.[14]

Other histories of the Turks also helped to fuel the Tamburlaine craze of the 1590s, making the mythic conqueror – called 'mighty' more than by any other epithet – larger than life. By the time Alleyn performed the role in Marlowe's plays the audience expected a conqueror of histrionic excess who, as Marlowe wrote, 'threatened the world with high astounding terms'. Tamburlaine inspired both fear and awe, and Marlowe's play was enormously popular in its time. The first recorded performance of *Part I* at the Rose Playhouse was on 28 August 1594. By 19 December 1594, *Part II* was also in production; and both parts played regularly in the repertory of the Lord Admiral's Men for over a year. As a play that featured

[13] Joseph Hall, *Virgidemiarum* (1597–8), in *The Collected Poems of Joseph Hall*, ed. A. Davenport (Liverpool, 1949), p. 14; Cunningham, *Tamburlaine the Great*, pp. 31–2.

[14] Petrus Perondinus, *Magni Tamerlanis Scythiarum Imperatoris Vita* (1553) is printed, with a translation, in Cunningham, *Tamburlaine the Great*, pp. 324–9.

carefully orchestrated rituals of entrance and exit, coronations, a town burning, a banquet, and the abuse of political hostages, the *Tamburlaine* plays exploited spectacle on a grand scale. Marlowe's plays were 'large texts' that excited audiences through ceremony and stately effect. Cosroe's taunting – 'Come, Tamburlaine, now whet thy winged sword / And lift thy lofty arm into the clouds' – seems most natural when addressed to an actor whose very stature would have helped to create some of the play's terror and revulsion.[15]

Because of its unusual size Alleyn's ring, in corroboration with literary and anecdotal evidence, helps to recreate a sense of the scale on which Alleyn and Tamburlaine worked. The diameter of Alleyn's ring measures 1.7 cm (or a size P in the equivalent of a modern, English jeweller's measurements). A study of extant rings from the late sixteenth and early seventeenth centuries demonstrates that this size is highly unusual. It is at least two sizes larger than the average ring size of the period, and three sizes larger than the average size of most extant signet rings. During the period the size N ring seems to have been the most common, with sizes M and O being relatively popular sizes as well. For signet rings, the average size is slightly smaller – size M being the most popular, with L and N also showing in significant numbers throughout the pool of extant evidence. Because so many signet rings were worn on the smallest finger, however, their average dimensions are predictably smaller than those of other rings.[16]

Using what are known to statisticians as regression predictions modern anthropologists can estimate Alleyn's height and weight. Of course such calculations only provide a rough approximation of anatomical dimensions. Some variables cannot be taken into account – for instance, any fluctuation in body mass that occurred after the ring was made, or the possibility that a person could well have been taller and thinner than the results of the equation would suggest. Yet despite these qualifications, it would seem that Alleyn was – at the shortest possibility – approximately 5 feet 9–10 inches tall, and he probably weighed approximately 130–150 lbs (at the upper end of the estimation). By today's standards this would not qualify Alleyn as a Herculean actor; but in consideration of the size of the average person of the 1590s – as we can judge it from tournament armour, or furniture, or architectural dimensions – Alleyn would probably have been significantly taller than most men of his time. Wearing a pair of boots would have added 1–2 inches to his height, bringing him up to a height of around 6 feet tall. Thus, the portrait of Alleyn at Dulwich might well have been slightly exaggerated if we expect it to reflect the physical reality of Alleyn's size. But in all likelihood it was not intended for that purpose. The size of the portrait was probably meant to suggest eminence and social stature rather than physical size. Furthermore, in consideration of the fact that, for the most part, only the nobility were painted full-length and in such magnitude the Alleyn portrait might be more reflective of Alleyn's upward mobility and his social aspirations than his actual size.[17]

15 *HD*, pp. 23–6 records the dates of the plays in repertory. Two articles of Tamburlaine's costume were recorded in Henslowe's inventory (13 March 1598): 'Tamburlynes cotte [coat] with a cop[p]er lace' and 'Tamburlanes bre[e]ches of crymson vellvet' (pp. 321–2).

16 Taylor and Scarisbrick, and Oman catalogue well over one thousand rings among them, over two hundred of which are from the late sixteenth and early seventeenth centuries. Nearly half of these are signet rings.

17 Data for correlation of ring size with living stature and weight were obtained from Dr Kenneth A. R. Kennedy of Cornell University and Dr Claire C. Gordon of the US Army Natick R, D, and E Center. The unpublished data that furnished the regression equation were originally prepared from the 1988 Anthropometric Survey of US Army Personnel of which Dr Gordon was the project director. I would also like to thank Dr Daniel Hendrick of the Department of Mathematics at Colgate University who worked out the final estimation of Alleyn's height and weight. There are no good published data concerning the issue of height during the Renaissance. Cultural anthropologists tend to estimate average height and weight based on extant material objects, such as the size of furniture, tournament armour, doorways, or remnants of clothing, as I suggest.

Most importantly for theatre historians, a sense of Alleyn's stature helps to recreate a sense of his stage presence in terms of the Rose Playhouse where the *Tamburlaine* plays were performed. Although perfectly reasonable for purposes of performance the dimensions of the First Rose Playhouse stage were more modest than theatre historians had imagined before the excavation of the playhouse site in 1989. On a stage just over 16 feet deep (from front to back) and 26 feet 10 inches at its front, Tamburlaine entering on his chariot drawn by captives would probably have looked as though he was a giant conqueror of mythic proportions. Although there is no specific evidence relating to how high up the stage was from the ground, spectators standing in the pit, looking upwards, would have viewed Alleyn from a perspective that would have added further to the sense of physical eminence that he projected. And any movement in which Alleyn spread his arms full-length to his sides would have underscored the impression that Tamburlaine was capable of lifting his arms into the clouds. Given these possibilities it is easier to visualize the extreme brutality and incredible pride that were so central to Alleyn's impersonation of Marlowe's egoist.[18]

Coincidentally, Alleyn's dimensions correlate roughly with those of the historical Tamburlaine. In 1941, the Russian anthropologist Mikhail Gerasimov described the exhumation of the Tamburlaine buried at Samarkand in 1405:

> Within the coffin lay a skeleton on its back with folded hands and outstretched legs. The skull lay on its left side, the face turned towards Mecca . . . His contemporaries described him as a red-bearded man of tall stature and extraordinary bodily strength.

The skeleton in the grave was that of a powerfully built man of 5 feet 8 inches with a fused right elbow and knee. The thigh bones of the left leg were characterized by their massiveness. Despite his lameness, and the natural physical compensation that the rest of the skeleton had undergone as a result, there was little sign of weakening. Tamburlaine was sixty-nine years old when he died, but:

> The massiveness and strength of the sound bones, their strongly developed relief, the breadth of the shoulders, [for a Mongol] all afford grounds for supposing that Timur was an exceedingly robust man. Despite his athletic muscles he must have been lean, which is natural enough if we remember that an unsettled life of warfare with its hardships, deprivations and contingencies is hardly likely to lead to obesity.[19]

Whether Marlowe had heard anything but rumours of Tamburlaine's stature would be impossible to prove. Contemporary sources, such as Perondinus' *Vita*, would have provided ample suggestion of Tamburlaine's legendary physical might and his unusual weight, as judged by his contemporaries; while Marlowe's interests in an extravagant theatrical style easily fell in line with Tamburlaine's conquests. Yet it was more than the extent of Tamburlaine's nomadic conquests that made him so famous. His campaigns were known for ostentation and massacre, and his leadership for naked ferocity. On stage at the Rose Playhouse Tamburlaine's heroic acting conquered Theridamas not only with rhetoric, but with imposing presence and, probably, unusual stature as well. The evidence supplied by Alleyn's ring reconfirms that, in part, Alleyn's physical size helped to create the portrait of the conquerer for which Tamburlaine was known in the 1590s.

---

18 Julian M. C. Bowsher and Simon Blatherwick record the stage dimensions from the data in their archaeological report. These results are most accessible to scholars in their article 'The Structure of the Rose', in *New Issues in the Reconstruction of Shakespeare's Theatre*, ed. Franklin J. Hildy (NY: Peter Lang, 1990), pp. 55–78, especially pp. 63–4. The Rose Playhouse was subsequently enlarged and the stage area moved back. The new stage area was slightly larger than that of the first playhouse. It had a depth of 18 feet 4 inches and was more of a rectangular shape than the first stage; but, like the first stage, the second stage had a slightly tapering front (Bowsher and Blatherwick, p. 70).

19 M. M. Gerasimov, *The Face Finder*, trans. Alan Houghton Broderick (London: Hutchinson, 1971), pp. 129, 132, 134–7.

SHAKESPEARE PERFORMANCES IN ENGLAND, 1992–1993

PETER HOLLAND

If there is one cry heard more often than any other when the state of the arts in England is being discussed, it is the accusation that the arts are treated far too much of the time as if nothing significant ever happens outside London. Sponsorship, Arts Council grants and, above all, press coverage are all subject to the grave charge of being London-centred. For a theatre production to be reviewed in the national press it seems it must travel to London before it can be noticed. Of course the claim is put too strongly; of course theatre reviewers are occasionally to be seen in the regions and some papers have regional reviewers of great brilliance. Yet there is truth in the argument nonetheless.

For Shakespearians in England the similar accusation might be 'Stratford-centrism'. Niky Rathbone's listings in *Survey* show the extraordinary quantity of Shakespeare activity in the professional theatre across the country. Yet few Shakespearians, even those most devoted to productions, see more than a tiny fragment of it.

But, even for the most Stratford-centred, it was striking how firmly the centre of attention to the Shakespeare theatre industry shifted to London at the close of 1992 and early in 1993. The RSC opened a Shakespeare production in London; an innovative touring production arrived at the Riverside; the Royal Court, the Royal National Theatre and the West End were all responsible for important productions. In a year in which there were fewer new Shakespeare productions in Stratford than we have become used to in recent years, only five in total, there is equal balance between Stratford and London in the ten productions I shall be reviewing. Yet I must regret that I can say nothing of Shakespeare in Manchester and Crewe, in Exeter and Nottingham. I have been well aware that I cannot report for *Survey* on many productions of, it is rumoured, great intelligence and brilliance.

LONDON

For the first time since the company's opening productions at the Barbican, the Royal Shakespeare Company premiered a new Shakespeare production at its London home. While the changes between Stratford and London have often meant that productions making the transfer have appeared at least nearly new, the decision to open Adrian Noble's *Hamlet* there marked a clear policy change and its overwhelming box-office success proved its worth to the company's coffers. The idea was also a consequence of the company's occasional difficulties in cajoling star-performers into a two-year commitment; Kenneth Branagh, Noble's Hamlet, is far too busy to stay with the RSC that long. Instead the production could run in London from December 1992 until it moved to open the 1993 Stratford season in the main house with a straight run of performances, playing opposite Sam Mendes' production of *Richard III* in the Swan theatre, and had closed

10 *Hamlet*, 3.2, RSC, Barbican Theatre, 1992: 'Give me some light': Claudius (John Shrapnel) stops the play

by late spring, never to be seen again. In a remarkably short time-span it could thus be seen for as many performances as most RSC Shakespeare work.

If the production's advance publicity was, inevitably, dominated by the presence of Branagh, the production itself was as much dominated by Noble's decision to use a fully conflated text of Q2 and F. Basing his decision less on any textual theory than on a delightfully innocent greed to do as much of a *Hamlet* as he possibly could (given that he was unlikely to direct the play for many years to come), Noble created his own conflation and allowed the enormous result full rein. The production ran at least four and a quarter hours (rather more the night I saw it), with a five-minute pause before the play-scene (3.2) after nearly two hours and only one full interval after the Fortinbras scene (4.4), forty-five minutes later.

As the vast expanse of the text unfolded, some scenes took on new weight and scale when played at fuller length than usually allowed. Claudius' duologue with Laertes (4.7.1–134), for instance, was striking in its extent and spaciousness; yet, in spite of the fine performances by John Shrapnel and Richard Bonneville, the scene seemed shorter on tension and conspiracy than in its normal truncated form. The gulling of Laertes and Claudius' fascination with Lamord had more time without justifying their larger presence in the shaping of the whole play.

Noble's production was, indeed, unequivocally shaped, with Bob Crowley's design as emphatic as possible. The colour changes in the three panels of the performance, from white through red to a grey drained of all life, and the enormous stage effects, like the vertiginous seating for the on-stage audience that filled the back wall throughout the central section of the performance, demanded the audience's attention as controlling motifs. As important, though, was the production's exploration of the depth of the stage. In front of the downstage edge, as it were in the orchestra pit, was a fairly rank and unweeded garden, with flowers and herbs rather obviously in place for Ophelia's mad horticulture; the crosses in among the plants keyed the presence of death and fertile ground for the grave-digging later. Not content with Shakespeare's opening, Noble added an entry for the ghost who emerged, hand first, through the soil of the graveyard like some corpse in a poor horror film, before stalking the whole depth of the stage and, as the broad cyclorama at the back lifted, exiting at the furthest upstage point, establishing for the production its full extent of depth.

The space at the rear beyond the cyclorama, a space marked as a world beyond, was the entry-route for the players and for Fortinbras and his army, in both cases apparently at the Elsinore railway station, where Hamlet appeared to be leaving Denmark for England by the boat-train. It was also the direction in which the funeral procession headed at the end where, as the cyclorama lifted again, the ghost could be seen with outstretched arms welcoming his most loving son. Such evident structuring, such over-emphatic underlining worked against the production's flow, enforcing a pattern of formal articulation rather than the energies of events that more readily shaped the performances.

Crowley's extravagances often made life difficult for the actors: the glaringly scarlet closet created on the abandoned stage of the players' performance had no correlation with Jane Lapotaire's nervy and vulnerable Gertrude who was supposed to be living in it – only the photograph of Claudius on the dressing-table suggested her touch. The bedroom had to be surrounded by the accoutrements of the court stage so that Claudius could turn a spotlight on Hamlet when interrogating him later, echoing Hamlet's turning the same theatre light on him during the chaos of his disruption of the performance. For the last section of the play, the stage was covered in grey parachute silk, under which, as Ophelia pulled it away, were large heaps of decaying wreaths and a piano, all offering a mass of obstacles for the actors to negotiate.

The piano shared the production's frequent obviousness of design. There is, of course, little point in putting a piano onstage unless someone is going to play it. It had earlier been seen in Ophelia's room in 1.3, a space whose decorated furniture hinted that it was still a nursery, with her doll's house lodged on top of her wardrobe. Joanne Pearce's Ophelia, first seen in bed wearing nightdress and bedsocks, washing perfunctorily at the wash-stand (a child's cat's-lick and a promise), before cuddling her brother on the bed, started playing the piano (not terribly well) when Laertes left. Polonius (David Bradley), a strictly authoritarian father as well as efficient bureaucrat, loomed large beside her as she played, leading her off at the end of the scene by the hand like a small child, as he pocketed the silver-framed photograph of Hamlet that had stood on her bedside table.

Pearce's Ophelia's closeness to her father was already strongly marked in this scene; so too was his concern for her, strikingly differentiated from his attitude to Laertes whose parting embrace he spurned while giving him a ring (which, in due course, Laertes would later give his distracted sister). In 2.1, set in Polonius' office, with a skyscraper tower of filing cabinets, Bradley in frock-coat combined magnificently the natural spy, the far-thinking politician and the now anxious father, putting a coat around Ophelia who had thrown a shawl over her nightdress and pulled on black boots, already giving firm indications in her reactions to her encounter with Hamlet of what will appear later. After the 'nunnery' scene, when Hamlet came close to raping her when she tried to kiss him, throwing her to the ground and finally spitting on her, Pearce's distraction was terrifyingly inevitable. When she tried to play the piano here to calm herself, Polonius firmly closed the piano-lid to stop her.

Her madness in 4.5, played both as extreme in its neurosis and detailed in its naturalism, was deeply distressing. Characteristically for this production, she had the time to explore the scene fully. Clutching the suitcase in which she had earlier kept Hamlet's 'remembrances' (3.1.95) on top of her wardrobe, she combined loss of lover and loss of father, with Polonius effectively superimposed on her existence by her wearing his clothes, blood-stained shirt and all, a remarkable and powerful invention. But when at the end of the scene she headed for the piano to accompany her mad songs and to play a fragmented version of the piece she had played in 1.3, the large prop seemed banal, a glib reference to her father.

It is this curious cross between satisfying depth and frustrating superficiality that characterized Branagh's Hamlet. First seen with his back to the audience, wearing a black coat with a prominent black armband, Hamlet had very carefully separated himself from the court, placed on the opposite side of the very wide stage and spreading through a part-drawn curtain, a group dominated by Claudius in a comfortable white suit with a glass in one hand and a fat cigar in the other, easy and confident. Claudius' summoning of Hamlet into the action (1.2.64)[1] brought a light up on him as he turned first away from the court before facing them, hands clasped tightly behind him like Prince Charles, stiff and unmoving as Gertrude tried to embrace him. The rigidity of grief, though, did not sit comfortably on Branagh whose easy warmth as an actor and natural preference for comedy was continually being reined in behind a mood of introspection. Branagh's earlier stage Hamlet (for his Renaissance Stage Company in 1988) was often accused of being too dashing and impetuous.[2] Now there was a clear superimposition of thoughtfulness, focused, above all, on the profundity of his love for his father. At his best, inevitably, in acerbically mocking Polonius (and teasingly donning a straitjacket to do it), Branagh's Hamlet seemed so intensely on the verge of swashbuckling action that it was increasingly difficult to see what was preventing him from stabbing Claudius at once and dashing offstage with Ophelia tucked under one arm. The melancholy was too self-evidently performed (by Branagh rather than Hamlet), a disguise laid over his normal style. Only in his delivery of 'How all occasions' (4.4) did the stillness grow out of the character and the soliloquy as the expression of thought convince. Only in the savagery of his treatment of Osric (Guy Henry as little camp as Ian Hughes' Reynaldo was extreme) did the aggression towards people become more than mannered. By comparison the brutality to Ophelia and to Gertrude, whom he came close to feigning to rape in the closet scene just as the ghost entered, was designed more as theatrical effect than credible facet of character. Hamlet simply does not sit comfortably with Branagh's considerable skills and he seemed miscast. Branagh also, I must report, acted much of the performance on autopilot, lazy in his responses, confident in the anticipation of the standing ovation he duly received; it is some time since I have seen an actor quite so contemptuous of the audience.

With Branagh so much the star, many other performances paled: Shrapnel's Claudius, for instance, was better at collapsing to the floor on the news of Laertes' invasion than at demonstrating the usurper and murderer, his indecision most clearly seen when, after his attempt at prayer (3.3), he found the sword that Hamlet has left behind. Bradley and Pearce apart, I was

---

1 Shrapnel's Claudius had cautiously eyed Hamlet earlier, leaving a pause after 'And now' before taking the easier option and turning to Laertes (1.2.42).

2 See the fascinating comparison of reviewers' comments on Branagh 1988 and 1992 in the *Independent* 23 December 1992, p. 15.

11 *Richard III*, 4.4, Northern Broadsides, 1992: King Richard (Barrie Rutter) asks Queen Elizabeth (Ishia Bennison) to help him woo her daughter

impressed only by Rob Edwards' Horatio, whose jumper and corduroy suit defined him as a man who did not belong at Claudius' urbane Elsinore and who therefore had to watch 'The Mousetrap' in borrowed tails too big in the waist and short in the leg for him, and by some of the smaller roles, like Richard Moore's top-hatted lugubrious Victorian undertaker, a very superior gravedigger.

Branagh and Noble, who had worked so successfully together in *Henry V* years before, now made an uneasy partnership, with the director trying both to showcase the star-actor and to deliver a production both huge and fresh. The result was heavyweight in the worst senses, its invention unfocused. In a production that seemed for the most part to perceive the play as family drama, the spectacle of set and star became an obstacle, not a benefit, the play's language, often well spoken, submerged beneath effect. Perhaps a cut text is better; at the least, Noble proved the blurred effect of conflation.

While Noble's *Hamlet* indulged in its sheer length, no one could accuse Barrie Rutter's production of *Richard III* of taking its time. Spoken at high speed, the text whistled by, concentrating attention on the thrill of the unfolding narrative, the vitality of the characters' relationships and the verve of the actors, much more than on the possible virtues of individual line-readings. Only rarely so fast as to be breathless, the lines had an easiness and immediacy, almost a contemporaneity, by the way they seemed to fit the actors' tongues so naturally.

Rutter's company, Northern Broadsides, had toured the production widely and triumphantly across the north of England before a season at the Riverside Studios in London. The actors, mostly from Yorkshire, were allowed, usually for the first time in their professional careers, to use their natural voices in a classical play. The company was mocked by some critics for doing Shakespeare in Yorkshire accents, most noticeably by John Peter in a swingeing attack on 'a piece of karaoke theatre in which Shakespeare provides the orchestra, and the actors have fun providing the voices', which he found condescending.[3] But the actors were not choosing accents but instead allowing their voices to relax from conventions of Received Pronunciation and official Shakespeare diction so that the text's fluency and excitement was not mediated by an imposed accent, the convention of classical theatre that all speech has the accent of London. If the result was that 'Naught to do with Mrs Shore?' (1.1.99) sounded more like 'Nowt to do wi' Mistress Shawah?' or 'Something we will determine' (3.1.190) was adapted into 'Summat we will do', it seemed a small price to pay for the infectious energy of the production.

Defiantly played as cheap theatre, with a shoulder-pad borrowed from Bradford Northern Rugby League club for Richard's hump and an old fur coat as the queen's robe passed from Elizabeth to Anne and then offered by Richard to Elizabeth again for her daughter, Rutter's production enjoyed its theatricality. The rival armies of Act 5, for instance, slowly donned boiler-suits and clogs during the build-up to Bosworth where the generals were wheeled around mounted on porters' trolleys and the armies stamped thunderous rhythms in their clogs. Richard died at the hands of the ghosts whose sticks and clogs enacted a folk-ritual of exorcism of the devil. His corpse was placed inside the wire enclosure that had been a permanent presence on audience right and on whose perimeter fence articles symbolizing Richard's victims had accumulated in the course of the performance. The drumming of the clogs slowed and quietened and eventually stopped as Richmond spoke of 'this fair land's peace' (5.8.39). The soldiers, copying Richmond, took off their clogs and dungarees, dumping the paraphernalia of war on the body of the cause of bloodshed, closing the enclosure fence on him and leaving on the opposite side of the stage towards a strong light streaming through open doors. I have never before found the end so complete, the sense of purification of the demonic so absolute, the calm of the new order so effective. If the result is simplifying, it is also fine theatre, powerful and thoughtful and, above all, clear in its communication of what Bosworth has accomplished.

The battle sequence was, by some way, the largest of the production's effects. More often, the energy of narrative came through with the rapidity of naturalism. The disputes of the rival factions took on overtones of a family squabble in a gritty northern realist drama of the 1950s, with Ishia Bennison's splendid Queen Elizabeth someone who the others clearly thought had got above herself in her gold dress and mink coat. In 1.3 Polly Hemingway's Margaret, a bag-lady who has wandered into the court, could be calmed by Dave Hill's authoritative but benignly soothing Buckingham, making sure there was no fuss, but alone with the other women in 4.4 she could kick Elizabeth to the ground, pull the hair of the Duchess of York, and leave the stage with clenched fist raised triumphantly aloft like a street-fighter who has beaten up rivals. But none of these moments

---

[3] *The Sunday Times*, 13 December 1992, p. 8/20.

diminished the text; the implications of the struggles of dynastic factions or the threat of Margaret's prophetic curses were no less powerful for the recognizability of the characters. Rutter's Richard was no less dangerous for appearing an engaging and impish comedian with a prancing walk (wearing one shoe and one clog) and one hand permanently thrust in his trouser pocket. The worried conversations of the citizens (2.3) came over all the more concerned since the fate of the nation was in hands insufficiently different from their own.

Rutter's production was more than happy to find comedy outside Richard himself in, for example, Clarence's diminutive murderers, a good six inches shorter than their victim, or the Duke of York in 2.4, an adult in school-cap playing games on the benches, a school-boy bored by adult conversation. But on the immense width of the Riverside stage, moves of anger were frighteningly large as Richard, furious at Hasting's 'If' (3.4.73), pursued him at high speed across the whole stage-width. The transitions of mood were startlingly fast as comedy or gentleness modulated into evil: Richard planted a sweet kiss on Anne's forehead before pushing her at Catesby to be taken off to murder. The audience could not help but admire Richard's brassneck, that northern word for arrogant nerve, even as his actions disgusted.

Rutter's production proclaimed its regionalism but it also trumpeted its sheer, unabashed pleasure in the play with a directness that more conventional work is embarrassed by. Where some productions seem almost to be apologizing for doing Shakespeare at all, Northern Broadsides shows why he was the English Renaissance's most popular dramatist and why he should continue to be the centre of vitality in our theatre culture. If that is 'condescending' it is a condescension more companies should copy.

Part of the problem that Northern Broadsides addresses is the placing of Shakespeare in English culture. Central to the work of the RSC or a classical company like the Royal National Theatre, Shakespeare is a figure on the periphery of the vision of the English Stage Company at the Royal Court. The last time the company had turned to Shakespeare had been in 1980 (*Hamlet* directed by Richard Eyre); now, as his valedictory production to mark the end of his reign as the theatre's artistic director, Max Stafford-Clark directed *King Lear* on the Court's tiny stage.

Eyre's *Hamlet* is best remembered as the production where the ghost's lines were spoken by Hamlet himself; Stafford-Clark's *King Lear* will probably be remembered as the production where the Fool (Andy Serkis) made his first entry in drag. It might also be remembered for the way its opening conversation between Kent (Philip Jackson) and Gloucester (Hugh Ross) was set in a urinal or for Oswald urinating over Kent (not in the stocks but buried up to his neck) or for the Fool, obstinately refusing to vanish after 3.6, graffiti-spraying on the back wall 'What a piece of', leaving open the question whether the quotation is to end 'rubbish' or 'work is man'. But such cheap effects, cocking a snook at tradition, while they may be part of the Royal Court's own traditional pose of liberal radicalism, suggest a production more glib than was the case.

More thoughtful, though equally predictable, was the production's attempt to provide a context of contemporaneity by staging the last scenes as echoes of Bosnia. Across the battlefield wandered refugees with their possessions loaded into a supermarket trolley[4] or clutching a ghetto-blaster or a bicycle, taking cover as they fled from the explosions that blasted chunks out of the brickwork of the set. At the end, as Kent prayed by the corpses of Lear and Cordelia, two gravediggers rapidly

[4] Some props seem peculiarly 'in' some years: a supermarket trolley could also be seen in Rutter's *Richard III* as the source of the 'rotten armour', mostly plastic, in 3.5.

12 *King Lear*, I.I, The Royal Court Theatre, 1993: 'Nothing': Cordelia (Cara Kelly) and Lear (Tom Wilkinson)

shovelled up mounds of earth, two soldiers in sunglasses and holding automatic weapons unrolled barbed wire and two women lit candles. But such images of civil war and torment, for all their power as theatrical imitations of all too familiar newsreel, were intrusions into the production's play-world, over-emphatic additions to make a point more superficially than the resonances created elsewhere. Stafford-Clark's *King Lear* had no need of such devices to prove the play's relevance.

Earlier, Stafford-Clark's view of the play's politics had emerged from the production's creation of a dominantly male, public-school homosocial world. Entering in riding coat and breeches, Tom Wilkinson's Lear, nowhere near 'fourscore', was an energetic colonel with beetling eye-brows, walrus moustache and a monocle, an efficient ruler busy signing the papers Gloucester handed him, smug in his authority and enjoying his elder daughters' glee at their shares of the kingdom and their performance of affection as Regan kissed and nuzzled Lear's hand, refusing to let it go. It seemed natural for Kent's exile to be marked by Lear's cutting off his uniform ribbons. At Goneril's house, Lear, in red hunting-coat, goosed the serving maid who was setting the dinner table and loved the officers' mess games as Oswald was kicked in the groin and his mouth stuffed with butter by Lear's two knights. The Fool, a camp queen in full Edwardian evening dress, kissed Kent full on the mouth and mocked Lear by bending him over, pretending to spank him with a whip and to bugger him to the cheers of the others. Goneril's fury was not only fully justified by these 'not-to-be-endurèd riots' (1.4.186) but by the exclusive masculinity of Lear's attitude to gender. This Lear, who knew, even as he ignored Cordelia's exit in 1.1, that he had made a terrible mistake, would have found it a questioning of his sense of his own masculinity to change his mind. His self-assurance in contradicting Kent in the stocks ('No, I say' 2.2.196) revealed the absolute confidence of a man who simply cannot bear to be wrong. Only the gay Fool, whose working-class accent broke through the sounds of camp whenever he was moved, could be perceived by Lear as caring for him. In 1.5, looking like a blowsy whore in padded underwear and ragged tights, the Fool's comfort was both a function of his drag performance and yet moving, as he powdered his nose and then showed Lear his own reflection in the mirror in the lid of his powder-compact.

Goneril and Regan had adopted differing ways of dealing with their father: Goneril (Lia Williams) adopting riding breeches as if to be Lear's son, Regan (Saskia Reeves) playing at being daddy's little girl, an act she repeated with her husband. But neither strategy would work; for women, other than the Fool's male imitation, could not possibly penetrate this Lear's shell. Madness was a retreat into a still more private world. Edgar's 'Look where he stands and glares' (Quarto, 13.19) was an accurate description of Lear's post-traumatic shock. In his encounter with Gloucester, Wilkinson's Lear was to be seen wandering to and fro behind the central doorway at the rear of the stage, muttering his lines to himself, allowing the audience to laugh at this ruin of a man but making his contact with Gloucester painful as the king tried to comfort him, patting Gloucester's bald head as 'a good block' (4.5.179). Death, too, became another form of privacy, as Lear's death rattle in his throat and drumming heels, an extraordinarily long drawn out agony, shocked and horrified the audience on and off stage, even as Kent lovingly cradled the dying man. It was inevitable that a man of such physical strength should be stretched inordinately long on the 'rack of this tough world' (5.3.290).

Beside the clarity of Lear's progress, the production's gimmicks were only distractions. It was difficult to concentrate on Lear's death as the corpse of the hanged Fool swung to and fro at the back of the stage, providing a cheap referent for Lear's line. But the production benefited more from such support as Peter-Hugo Daly's brutal Cornwall, heating a spoon on the flame of his lighter to remove Gloucester's eyes, and Iain Glen's Edgar, a corduroy-suited aesthete with a smoker's cough transformed brutally to a self-wounded, pitiably shaking Poor Tom, plucking out the sprigs of rosemary that had pierced his chest. More than the corduroy suit seemed to connect this Edgar to Rob Edwards' Horatio at the Barbican.

In the tiny space of the Royal Court, the immediacy of Edgar's individual pain spoke more eloquently of Bosnia than the activity of the company's supernumeraries. The threat beyond was better captured by the distant rumble of the tube-trains under the theatre than by offstage gunfire. The company's radicalism lay in its emphasis on the play's despairing humanity in a state in which central authority had collapsed, not in the gestures of heterodoxy in stage effect.

Richard Eyre's 1980 *Hamlet* at the Royal Court was strikingly fresh; his *Richard III* at the National Theatre, after his move to become its artistic director, strong and provocative. But his *Macbeth* there was awe-inspiring only in its awfulness. The production sharply divided the critics when it opened, some finding it 'whole-hearted and exciting' (Martin Dodsworth, *TLS*) while others found only a travesty. I saw it late in its run by which time Alan Howard, always notorious for becoming more self-indulgent in the course of a run, had made Macbeth into a hysterical neurotic while most of the cast were going about their business in

13 *Macbeth*, Royal National Theatre, 1993: Macbeth (Alan Howard)

the perfunctory manner of actors who would rather have been in any other show than this. I was grateful that the play was performed without an interval since the lure of leaving halfway would have been almost irresistible.

Any production of *Macbeth* that throws away the first scene is hinting at trouble to come. Here, the voices of the unseen witches could be heard over throbbing music while behind a curtain torches flashed. As the curtain dropped, Macbeth was seen in a ring of flames, the production's motif of the witches' power, suggesting a desire for sponsorship by British Gas. It was the last moment at which Howard's Macbeth was seen still. Thereafter, he twitched and shook to such an extent that a Duncan as pragmatic as Robin Bailey's would undoubtedly have locked him up. Howard's way with Shakespearian verse used to be quite mannered; by comparison with his Macbeth his past excesses had a glorious normality. The lines were screamed and chanted, twisted and fragmented, stretched and gabbled into a nonsense that harked back to satiric descriptions of the worst nineteenth-century barnstorming styles. Most often keening in a nasal whine, Macbeth could also be heard cackling maniacally on his exit after the murder of Duncan or panting nervously while Macduff went to wake Duncan, trying any verbal tic to animate the lines.

Anastasia Hille, as Lady Macbeth, could hardly be blamed for keeping her distance from this Macbeth, a man perfectly capable of making his wife go with him at the end of 3.2 by the simple expedient of picking her up and carrying her off over his shoulder. Hille simply lacked the technique for such a demanding role, offsetting the intriguing idea of casting a Lady Macbeth so much younger than her husband. Announcing that Macbeth 'shalt be / What thou art promised' (1.5.14–15), she stood with legs astride, punching the air like a football fan, a gesture more charming in its innocence than as a threatening premonition of her future actions. Going through regular costume changes, for instance from a sleeveless nightdress for 1.5 to a high-collared black velvet gown for 1.6 to a silver lurex number for 1.7, she had little chance to shine, at her best in an unsentimental sleepwalking scene.

Elsewhere the production mixed styles pointlessly. The witches started as social outcasts swigging from a hipflask as they clustered round a camp-fire at the edge of the dark woods seen at the back of the stage; they had entered the castle for their second encounter with Macbeth in 4.1, conjured up by Macbeth's nightmares. The apparitions were explicitly linked to other characters: Macduff holding the armed head, Lady Macbeth the bloody child, Malcolm as the crowned child. But the parade of kings was limply glimpsed and shadowed on curtains. The Lady Macduff scene was played with purest naturalism as her three children in their neat dressing-gowns breakfasted on porridge and boiled eggs while a nurse rocked the baby. The English scene was, intentionally I hope, a caricature with Malcolm adopting a priggish Oxford accent while sitting with Macduff in wicker chairs in an English garden as a servant served glasses of cool lemonade. By the end Macbeth seemed to have turned into Dracula, biting Young Siward in the neck, before fighting a duel with Macduff in which the actors were all too plainly counting their moves. Wounded, Macbeth helped Macduff's dagger to his neck. His head was stuck on the hilt of a flaming sword and then, as the stage emptied, the witches came forward, wrapped up their grisly trophy and retreated back into the woods.

When actors as good as Paul Moriarty (Ross) and James Laurenson (Macduff) do so little with their roles or when the trundling on of massive semi-circular battlements only serves to leave Banquo and Fleance stranded meaninglessly far from the audience, any possibility of vitality has clearly drained away. I find it difficult to believe that a good production could ever have deteriorated so far and must side with those who at the start saw only a farrago.

A Shakespeare production opening in the West End, rather than transferring there, is an even rarer event than one opening at the Barbican or the Royal Court. It must have taken courage for Thelma Holt to back the production of *Much Ado About Nothing* by a director as young, though as promising, as Matthew Warchus, even with an encouraging programme-note from Kenneth Branagh, whose film version opened in London during the run. The pre-publicity for the film must have helped and may, I suspect, have conditioned the choice of play. Certainly the production deserved to succeed and the prospect of commercial Shakespeare in London, if hardly likely to be a regular event, undoubtedly varies the diet.

I would, however, be hard put to it to indicate in what ways Warchus's production differed from an RSC one. Some undercasting of the smaller roles went with a certain obviousness of playing but worse has often been seen in Stratford. Janet McTeer (Beatrice) and Mark Rylance (Benedick) have both played major roles for the RSC. Perhaps Warchus's production took more care to underline the plot, with Borachio at the end of 2.2 left alone onstage as he silently imagined, with the help of projected photographs, his encounter with Margaret; but such clarification of narrative is positively desirable, even if this was not necessarily the best way to do it.

By comparison with the banal populism of Branagh's film version, Warchus's work was usually thoughtful and often deeply perceptive. Far from being overly centred on the central performances, this *Much Ado* was full of fine detailing of other roles: Margaret sitting in mourning outside Hero's monument in 5.2, trying to be witty but crushed by her part in the events, Don Pedro (Jack Ellis) in the last scene deeply shamed by Don John's capture and the public humiliation at his share in the success of his brother's plot, or Kevin Doyle's fine Don John, immured indoors in a dark interior with a massive window through which he can watch Claudio embracing Hero in 2.2, a trapped and caged man, bitterly and comprehensibly angry and resentful at being trapped by his defeat in battle.

There was good and, to me, new comic business as well: Don Pedro deliberately using a watering-can to water the concealed Benedick in 2.3, Dogberry (Gerard Kelly) interrogating his prisoners in a lawyer's gown like some would-be Irish Marshall Hall, or Benedick in the opening scene, bested by Beatrice in the dialogue, suddenly sinking down clutching his heavily bandaged head (hence her accusation of 'a jade's trick' 1.1.138), before flinging the bandage aside to reveal no trace of a wound, when left alone with Claudio at 1.1.154. Beside such invention, the playing of the dance in 2.1 in Wild West costume and cod John Wayne accents or the opening of the monument in 5.3 to show a red sepulchre with the wedding dress on a stand as if in some bizarre boutique were oddly banal mistakes.

Neil Warmington's design, sometimes rather bland, was dominated by cupids, three of whom, armed with bows, hovered over the gulling of Beatrice and Benedick. But these benign cupids were offset by the image of a painted cupid with the eyes torn off, an emblem of love blinded that was only healed when the missing strip of painting was found watching the tomb inside the monument, a canopied space previously used as the wedding-chapel in 3.5. The set for the gulling had a net of roses descending from a cupid's hand, a net of love for Benedick's concealment. The cupids' bows allowed for targets onstage, behind which Beatrice hid, becoming, quite literally, a moving target for the merciless and surprisingly brutal attack on her 'carping' by Hero.

Hero's last line in the scene, 'Some Cupid kills with arrows, some with traps' (3.1.106), became troubling, not least to Hero and Ursula, a questioning of their own responsibility in this action. They were right to be troubled for a significant part of the motivating force of the plot against Beatrice and Benedick was the hurt that Beatrice's rejection of Don Pedro's totally sincere proposal of marriage caused him. Made to appear a complete fool by her formal rejection, 'No, my lord' (2.1.306), his anger fuelled the plot as an act of revenge.

McTeer's Beatrice, tall and, from the start, at ease with herself, bare-legged and wearing sensible brogues, strode the stage in complete control, giving Hero a glass of Dutch courage before the wooing or coming to call Benedick to dinner (2.3.233) munching a banana. The gulling unsettled her magnificently. After her soliloquy at the end of 3.1, spoken slowly and mournfully to the accompaniment of a melancholy viol, the scene ran straight on, as Benedick entered newly shaved of his drooping moustache, trying to sing 'Sigh no more' in a cracked voice. The two sat awkwardly on benches, not knowing how to start the conversation, how to begin to express what they felt, until, at the entry of Don Pedro, Claudio and Leonato, Beatrice ran off and Benedick stuffed the paper with the words of the song in his mouth. His complaints of the toothache (3.2.20 and 64) were justifed by the large lump in his mouth caused by the paper. By the end, her willing acceptance of his kiss ('Peace, I will stop your mouth' 5.3.97) echoed and transformed her earlier advice to Hero ('Speak, cousin. Or, if you cannot, stop his mouth with a kiss' 2.1.291–2), advice which, when Hero followed it, had caused Beatrice a loud groan.

McTeer's Beatrice was perfectly balanced by Rylance's Benedick. Rylance looked particularly short alongside McTeer who could swing him around in the dance in 2.1 whenever Benedick tried to escape. Always fresh in his conception of a role, Rylance equipped Benedick with a Belfast brogue, enabling him to combine both the gift of the gab and an offhand delivery, almost, but never quite, throwing lines away by muttering them half to himself. Almost coarse early on, the 'bugle' he does not want to hang 'in an invisible baldric' (1.1.226) unequivocally phallic, Benedick was left a complete wreck by his treatment at the hands of the conspirators. 'Love me! Why, it must be requited' (2.3.212–13) became 'Love me! Why? It must be requited' and the audience, looking at this bedraggled crushed figure, could find no answer to the question other than laughter. Increasingly gentle as the performance developed, this Benedick was nervous and engagingly awkward in his wooing in 4.1 and his gentle concern in 5.2, putting his arm caringly round Beatrice as he asked 'And how do you?' (5.2.82), was sincerely moving. Throughout Rylance increasingly showed the private, vulnerable man behind the public show and the audience loved what it saw. Often understated, always provocative, this was as fine a Benedick as I have seen. In generating and accommodating central performances as fine as these, Matthew Warchus showed that the Queen's Theatre in Shaftesbury Avenue is a convenient staging-post on the route to Stratford.

STRATFORD

Though the Stratford season may have been foreshortened by the runs of *Hamlet* and *Richard III*, it was certainly not short on anything else. It was, quite simply, one of the greatest Stratford seasons I can remember, production after production of a quality of imagination and achievement of the highest order, both in the company's Shakespeare work in the Royal Shakespeare Theatre and The Other Place and, even more emphatically, in the non-Shakespearian work in the Swan and The Other Place.[5] Not all were individually great productions but cumulatively it was a magnificent vindication of the approaches that, falteringly in the last two seasons, Adrian Noble had established.

David Thacker, for instance, whose work in the previous season had been so disappointing, was firmly back to form. I must admit to

[5] This included outstanding productions, in the Swan, of Eliot's *Murder in the Cathedral*, Wycherley's *The Country Wife*, Goldoni's *The Venetian Twins* and, at The Other Place, of Ibsen's *Ghosts*.

having approached his production of *Julius Caesar* in The Other Place (prior to its tour) with depressing expectations. There were two particular grounds for impending gloom: the first was the sad history of the play in recent Stratford productions; the second a general dislike of promenade productions.

The settled perspectives of the audience to the action in a conventional seated theatre deserve, of course, to be disrupted sometimes but I always find in promenade shows that, sooner or later, I end up in the wrong place to see a particular scene. In this, *Julius Caesar* was no exception. I cannot be sure that I made the right sense of the quarrel scene since I was staring at Brutus' back rather than seeing his face, and my concentration on the battle wavered while I nursed the bruises caused by a soldier planting a size eleven army boot squarely on my foot as he charged off stage through the smoke. On the press night, when I saw it, there was the added distraction of watching the critics. The sight of Michael Billington taking notes was almost as intriguing as whatever Casca was doing standing next to him. Such problems may be accidental rather than substantive but they certainly affected my experience of the performance.

Nonetheless promenade is one possible answer to the perennial problem of the crowd (the major disaster of recent main-house productions). The brilliant staging of the Forum scene, with the promenading audience and actors mingled among them in the crowd staring up at Brutus or Antony on their towers as the light gently accentuated the crowd's rapt faces, showed why the choice of style made sense, helped by the hard-working concentration of the crowd-actors, binding the audience together into a group, if not a mob. Of course it was possible for members of the audience to resist the experience, to hold themselves separate from this integration into the action and to observe uncomfortably the actors performing next to them. Since only half of the audience was promenading while the audience seated in the gallery could observe both action and 'on-stage' audience, the opportunity for individuals to feel awkward was certainly present. But resistance to the infectious effect was difficult in the face, quite literally, of the actors' intense concentration. In the scenes of privacy, the almost voyeuristic intrusion into Brutus' lonely attempt to weigh his commitment to the conspiracy (2.1.10–34) or the attempts by Brutus and Portia to define the nature of their marriage (2.1.232–308), say, pose a quite different and no less substantial problem, but here too the quality of performance was very nearly enough to win me over.

I have more serious hesitations about the production's contemporaneity. Playing Caesar as Yeltsin, Calphurnia as Raisa Gorbachev, and giving the battle scenes overtones of civil war in Bosnia have peculiar consequences, here as in the Royal Court's *King Lear*, for if *Julius Caesar* celebrates, as we are celebrating, the overthrow of dictatorships like those of Eastern Europe, it is also a play far more uneasy about the manipulability of the mass of the people than I would like to be about the fall of Ceaucescu or the events of Tiananmen Square. That republican conspiracy can lead to further empires disdains the people's yearning for freedom. It was one of those cases where the use of the analogy would not hold, where the production rode roughshod over the possibilities of difference, rather than the generalized repetition across history that the analogy provoked. Still, the sight of David Sumner's splendid Caesar playing to the television cameras with the assurance of Yeltsin or Clinton on walkabout, beaming but surrounded by bodyguards, was too good to miss.

The analogy also controlled the production's visual language. Fran Thompson's set, a red-carpeted circle with blue surround with four massive portals or platforms at the corners of The Other Place, carried in its colours and in its banners with their central stars strong overtones of Soviet style. But it also left resonances of an arena, a football stadium or a circus ring within which the drama was played out. The drama of Thacker's production was not one of the politics of ideology but of the humanity and hence corrupted nature of commitment, a commitment generated by individual psychology rather than political analysis. In the cautious indirections of Brutus' language ('What you would work me to I have some aim' 1.2.163) could be heard, in this context, the dangers of being overheard, the risks in speaking plainly. But while Jeffery Kissoon's Brutus articulated his actions in terms of a political theory, Rob Edwards' Cassius, the finest I have ever seen, was driven by a personal loathing for Caesar of frightening intensity.

This Cassius foregrounded his sneering contempt for the gap between the public image of Caesar (marked by his face staring from the walls in the mass of posters) and the private limitations (echoed by Caesar's superstitious analysis of dreams and his ghastly hiding behind his wife's fears as a mask for his own). In his wild behaviour in the storm (1.3), high and a bit drunk in his rain-soaked shirt, he was able to focus this personal hatred, ripping one of the posters as he talked to Casca. In the quarrel with Brutus, Cassius allowed us to see his real concern, a simply desperate need to be loved by Brutus: 'Have you not love enough to bear with me / When that rash humour which my mother gave me / Makes me forgetful?' (4.2.175–7) – and Edwards' rasping, mocking enunciation of 'mother' suggested the unloved child in need of the love and reassurance that an adult man alone could give him. Not in any way homosexual, Edwards' Cassius could only find meaning in the homosocial world, the male camaraderie of conspiracy.

Julius Caesar became a play centrally about this male bonding in a fiercely patriarchal society, to the extent that Brutus' willingness to listen to Portia in 2.1 appeared almost abnormal, at least in this world where women could be so easily marginalized as Calphurnia rushed out of the room choking back tears when Caesar had decided to 'go forth' or when, in a rather glib image, a woman pushed a dead soldier in a pram across the battlefield of Philippi. When Portia explored what her marriage to Brutus meant to both of them (Francesca Ryan superb here and in her nervous anxiety with Lucius later, in 2.4) she spoke of a modern partnership of which the play has no other exemplar and even the news of her death became only grist to the public image of Brutus before his officers in 4.2. Cassius, hugging Brutus as the conspirators left the orchard at 3 a.m., became some sort of rival to this marriage, though the gesture was also to be echoed in that embrace in which Brutus would stab Caesar.

Caesar, oscillating between his suit and full army uniform, heavily bemedalled, for ceremonial occasions, met his death in the full panoply of public event, standing at a lectern with a microphone to address the senate, turning 'Are we all ready?' (3.1.31) into a tutting aside at the conspirators' nervous whisperings whose words he could not hear.

But Caesar's very visible self-confidence in public modulated into the private self-confidence of Barry Lynch's Antony. There is always something terribly dangerous about Barry Lynch's smile. Having played the whole forum scene remarkably low-key, especially after his private speech to the corpse ('O pardon me, thou bleeding piece of earth') was delivered as the most colossal and violent verse paragraph of rage, Lynch appeared almost unable to control the energies he had unleashed. Wearing Caesar's bloodied and ripped jacket, hanging loosely on him like a giant's robe upon this dwarfish thief, he seemed wrapped up rather in himself. Only when Octavius' officer arrived as Antony was hanging on one of the set's ladders (3.2.254) did the play of that smile over his face show his real relish of what he had achieved, intensified in the first scene after the interval as he rocked his chair back, so easy with himself as the triumvirs pricked the names and a woman shredded dangerous documents. Lynch's oleaginous charm suggested a remarkable Iago sometime in the future.

14 *Julius Caesar*, 3.1, RSC at The Other Place, 1993: '*Et tu, Brute*': Brutus (Jeffery Kissoon) and Caesar (David Sumner)

The battle scenes were a logical culmination of the production's concerns; the sheer brutality, the casual slaughters, the deaths put on by cunning and forced cause were dominated by that moment when one of the guards killing prisoners removed his balaclava and turned out to be Caesar's ghost who smiled mockingly at Brutus. Philippi was, we know, a most hideous bloodbath, its casualty list of terrifying size for a battle of the period. It was also civil war; the indistinguishability of the two sides in their battle fatigues added immeasurably to the moral as well as visual murkiness of the fighting; there were not even the racial divisions of the type that differentiate the sides in Bosnia. There could be here no full close, only the exhaustion of self-destruction. The deaths of Brutus and Cassius seemed almost incidental, certainly unheroic, and the last speeches of Antony and Octavius provided no summing-up. *Julius Caesar* was a firm justification of Thacker's appointment as the RSC's Director in Residence.

Thacker's production of *The Merchant of Venice* was also outstanding proof that he had exorcised the demon of the main house. Indeed having wondered last year whether the main house was now an insoluble problem for directors I now feel more than a little foolish, for the first three directors to work there this season showed that it need have no terrors, only an exceptional power and potential.

I have always preferred to believe that *The Merchant of Venice* is not anti-semitic but that directors have usually lacked the perceptive ability to show how it is not. Thacker's production was the most coherent and convincing demonstration that the play need not be. Bryan Cheyette's review in *TLS* summed up the production as arguing that 'If even an assimilated and cultured Jew can become a bloodthirsty skullcapped and gaberdined racial killer, then how can we possibly trust any of them?' But Cheyette seemed to have missed Thacker's careful use of Tubal to place and define the audience's attitude to Shylock.[6] Thacker increased Tubal's presence in the play. He was onstage in 1.3 when Bassanio and Antonio come to borrow the money from Shylock. David Calder's Shylock really did not have the 3,000 ducats available (1.3.51–4) and Tubal's whispered offer solved the problem: 'Tubal, a wealthy Hebrew of my tribe, / Will furnish me' (55–6). Skullcapped from the start, offering advice about Shylock's biblical analogy to Jacob like a resident rabbinical scholar, Nick Simons' Tubal marked in the course of the play his increasing distance from Shylock's maniacal pursuit of Antonio. When Shylock announced 'I will have the heart of him if he forfeit' (3.1. 117–18) he put his hand firmly on an open book, a prayerbook I presume, on his desk and Tubal registered horror at this abuse of religion. In Shylock's confrontation with Salerio and Solanio (the two halves of 3.1 were reversed), Tubal made clear his total rejection of Shylock's course of action, a response underlined by the placing of the interval here. It was an unspoken plea from Tubal that drew from Shylock the acerbic 'Tell not me of mercy' (3.3.1) as Antonio was going to jail. At the trial scene, while Antonio was backed by his friends, Shylock was conspicuously alone, the seats behind him empty.

Calder's approach to Shylock was extremely clear and logical. He began as a man desperate for assimilation – no skullcap for him – his voice cultured and anglicized except when he mocked the stereotype jew his visitors expected to find ('Fair sir, you spat on me on Wednesday last' 1.3.124). His statement 'I would be friends with you, and have your love' (1.3.136) was totally sincere and he really could not understand their gentile contempt. At this stage Shylock's desire for integration made him not so much a jew, more jew-ish; Antonio's comment 'gentle Jew' (1.3.176) drew from Shylock compliant laughter, followed by a grimace at the audience asking for complicity in his mockery of these odd things gentiles found funny. Such a view of the character had, of course, to underplay Shylock's aside of hatred (1.3.39–50) as much a possible and the speech left its jarring resonance across the scene.

But, seen at home in 2.5, listening to Schubert on his compact-disc player and hugging a photograph of Leah, this cultured man did not deserve his treatment. It made of Jessica's betrayal (a rather disappointing performance from Kate Duchêne) both something difficult to make sense of and something far more culpable, a commitment to the triviality of the yuppie culture, all champagne and portable telephones, of the production's view of Venice as modern stock-exchange. Everything that followed in Calder's performance was a direct response to the traumatic shock of the loss of Jessica, as he searched desperately through the crowd of animal-masqued carnival revellers, shouting her name in a sequence added to the end of 2.6.

The revenge on Antonio was simply the consequence of Antonio's availability as victim. Wishing Jessica 'hearsed at my foot and the ducats in her coffin' (3.1. 83–4), Shylock tore open his shirt to reveal the star-of-david underneath (as Antonio's open shirt in the trial scene revealed a crucifix). By the trial scene, Shylock

6 Compare John Barton's comment on a workshop exploration of 3.1: 'It's what [Tubal] thinks of Shylock that perhaps tells an audience how the Jewish community look at Shylock. It seems to me that this scene often goes wrong because Tubal is played as a snivelling, sympathetic side-kick to Shylock. What both of you did as Tubal was to be dispassionate, detached and in the end disapproving. And that's terribly important to maintain the right balance of sympathy in the play.' (*Playing Shakespeare* (1984) pp. 178–9.)

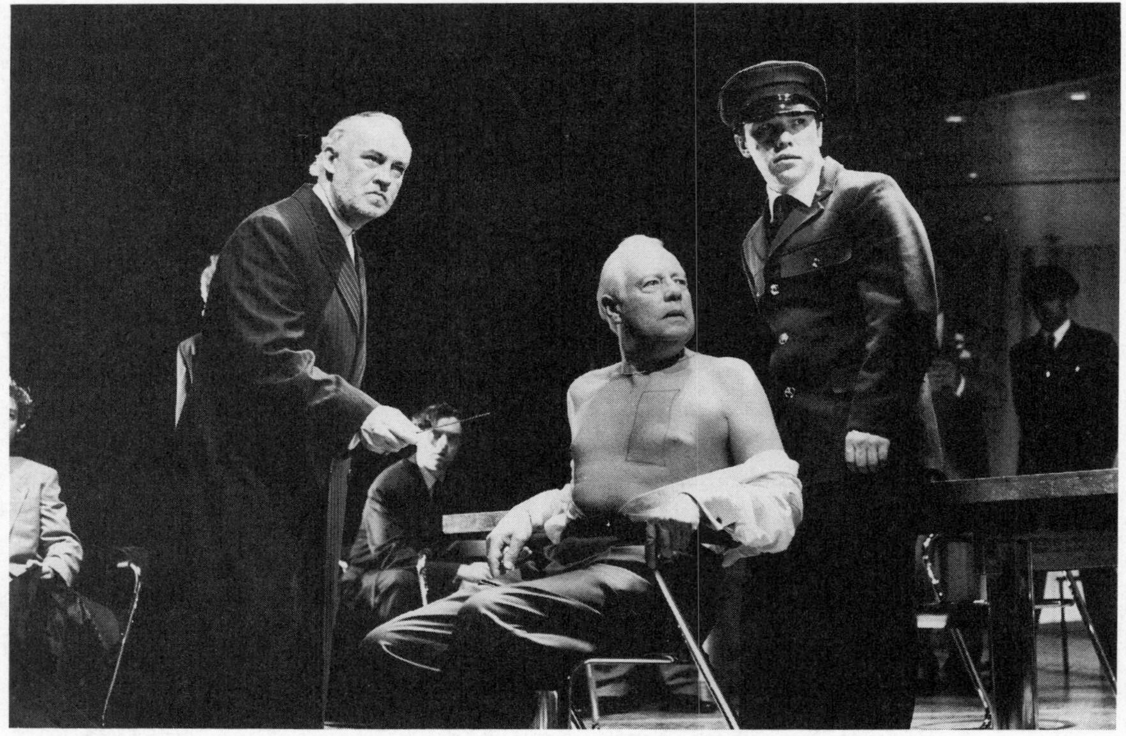

15 *The Merchant of Venice*, 4.1, RSC, 1993: 'Tarry a little': Shylock (David Calder) and Antonio (Clifford Rose)

had turned himself into the image of a religious jew, with skullcap and gaberdine and with the star-of-david now worn outside his collarless shirt. His use of the symbols of religion was now demonstrably an abuse of religion and race, becoming a jew only because it focused his traumatized existence. It was Shylock himself who now appeared the anti-semite.

Calder was matched by Clifford Rose's Antonio, tight-lipped and precise, a man whose hidden sexual habits were probably very nasty indeed. Shaking uncontrollably with terror in the trial scene – the first Antonio I have seen to need guards to hold him down – as Shylock marked out the pound's-worth on his chest with a marker pen, he ended up, legs buckling, draped over Bassanio, which was where, I presume, he wanted to be. He had tried embracing Shylock and been rejected (3.3.4); he had tried shaking hands with the Duke and been rather pointedly ignored. Only Bassanio could console him now. Owen Teale's cheerily good-natured Bassanio missed the caddishness of the man, first cousin to Claudio in *Much Ado About Nothing*, though there was something endearingly clumsy about his suggestion to 'Wrest once the law to your authority' (4.1.212), rating horror from everyone else at its corruption of law, and something ingratiating about his appearance at Belmont, unruly hair now slicked down like the Prince of Morocco's.

Thacker's vision of Venice was of a generalized racism: when a black yuppie spoke feelingly to Solanio and Salerio, in the bar where they had gone with a couple of secretaries, of Antonio – 'A kinder gentleman treads not the earth' (2.8.35) was transferred to him –

he was very pointedly ignored. It was a pity then that he had not allowed the resonance of the same emotion in Belmont, for Portia was neatly sanitized by the cutting of her vicious final comment on Morocco (a sympathetic performance by Ray Fearon, pitiable in his anguish at failing), 'Let all of his complexion choose me so' (2.7.79), a line which deliberately echoes his first line in the play, 'Mislike me not for my complexion' (2.1.1).

Penny Downie, caught in a sterile Belmont backed with a translucent screen, blossomed unexpectedly when Bassanio chose correctly. Suddenly, there were flowers and a brilliant costume, replacing her earlier black dress. But the arrival of Salerio with the news of Antonio's arrest had suddenly and startlingly allowed sight of the Venetian high-tech world through the now transparent screen. The process was reversed when for Act 5 tree projections filled the back wall of the stage and Venice seemed invaded by the spirit of Belmont, a take-over bid entirely in keeping with the monetarist world of the production. But Thacker's attentions were hardly directed at the Belmont scenes and that side of the play seemed dull by comparison with the events in Venice.

One of the great strengths of this year's Stratford season was the casting in depth. Of *The Merchant of Venice* cast I must mention Mark Lockyer's Graziano, wearing a mesmerizingly awful tie, his shallowness in the first scenes growing brilliantly to a near-hysteria of impotent rage in the trial scene when he was left spitting at Shylock, and Chris Luscombe's amazing proof that Lancelot Gobbo, long thought the least funny of Shakespeare's clowns, can be deliriously funny, especially when out for an early-morning jog with his walkman in 5.1.

Only once did the production falter, when, at the end of the trial scene, Shylock, crawling to his feet with his back to the audience, trying to control himself in the gathering darkness, suddenly rounded on the audience and glowered threateningly. I realized it was offered as a parallel to the focus on the prim and smug authority of Antonio spotlit at the very end of the play but the look was just too enigmatic.

There were many enigmas in Adrian Noble's production of *King Lear*, facets of Anthony Ward's design and passages of the play that never came fully into focus. But, after the disappointments of his *Hamlet*, it was immensely satisfying to find Noble so unquestionably back to form. Using a conflated text, cut by about 400 lines, the production was as vast and cosmic as the play demands. Again and again it demonstrated its achievement, creating a vision of the play as powerful and as moving as one could wish for.

Productions of *King Lear*, however good, are foredoomed unless the Lear himself is good enough. Robert Stephens possessed the role with an authority as absolute as Lear's own rule. When a teenager, I remember complaining of Artur Schnabel's records of Beethoven piano sonatas, with all the arrogance of youth, about the fluffs and doubles in Schnabel's playing. 'Ah but', a far wiser mentor told me, 'never mind about the few wrong notes. Just listen to all the right ones.' It was appropriate advice for Stephens' Lear. There were many lines fluffed and rewritten – on some nights many more than on others. Sometimes the new lines were nonsensical; sometimes the metre went haywire as a result. Certainly there were nights when, for Shakespeare scholars, the fluffs loomed large and troubling. But then Shakespeare scholars are by their very nature a pedantic breed. And one would have had to be, like the onstage audience Lear addresses at the end of the play, 'men of stones' not to be wrenchingly moved by Stephens' Lear. If with John Wood's Lear, the last in the main house, one could not help but observe the technique that was producing the effects, admiring the actor's skills that created the emotional charge of the performance, with Stephens it seemed plain wrong to hold oneself removed, observing how he did it. If this Lear did not make one weep, no perform-

16 *King Lear*, 3.4, RSC, 1993: Kent (David Calder) and Fool (Ian Hughes) watch Edgar (Simon Russell Beale) and Lear (Robert Stephens)

ance ever will. Capable of terrifying violence, as his threatening Goneril with his riding-whip in 1.3 made frighteningly clear, and capable of equally terrifying love, as Cordelia was stood on a chair like a prized pupil for her answer in the first scene, Stephens' Lear became increasingly trapped in a world of his own making. Kent (the authoritative David Calder) could not help, nor, even, could contact with the Fool, played by Ian Hughes so much less eccentrically than most other recent Fools – no need for drag here – and being so much more tender and moving as a result, making his final exit in 3.6 in the wrong direction, away from Kent and Lear, in a state of suicidal despair, carrying a knife which Lear had dropped.

No one could really touch this Lear, wrapped up in the private terror of the descent to madness. Even the scene with the blind Gloucester was frighteningly lonely with Edgar, immobile through most of the scene, able to do no more than touch his father's shoulder consolingly as Gloucester wept uncontrollably. The line down for Stephens' Lear from the easy, genial assumption of authority at the start was controlled, its steps plainly marked. The trauma of the loss of control was as much physical as mental as the anguish appeared almost like a sequence of strokes or a succession of heart attacks – as in a sense they are. This transformation of the mental into the physical was crushing, leaving the audience as helpless as observers as the other characters onstage.

Above all, it was a descent of which Lear himself was painfully aware: Stephens made of 'O Fool, I shall go mad' (2.2.459) nothing more or less than a statement of fact, all the more chilling for his consciousness of the inevitability of the process. Nothing could penetrate this self-inflicted collapse.

Of course to call Lear's agony self-inflicted is to give a hostage to fortune. But Noble's treatment of the evil elsewhere in the play placed it in a context far removed from Lear himself. The grand guignol, almost melodramatic excesses of Simon Dormandy's psychopathic Cornwall, for instance, searching Edmund's wound with intrigued fascination in 2.1, or the mannered playing of Goneril and Regan (both roles undercast and underdirected), making them more than ever like Cinderella's ugly sisters, did not deny the horror of their actions but put them into a different play-world, one which could not really affect the solipsistic universe of Lear. Only as they stared after Lear towards the impending storm, trying to convince themselves that they had had no choice and had done the right thing (3.1.461–5), was there a hint of a child's affection.

Something similar happened in the Gloucester action. David Bradley, like Stephens, started quietly, almost underpowered as he coasted through his scene with Edmund (1.2). Only at his blinding did this Gloucester unleash his power. No Gloucester I have ever seen has so awfully demonstrated the blinding as sheer physical pain, for usually the discovery of Edmund's evil and the wronging of Edgar is allowed to take precedence over the enveloping agony of the act. Bradley, by contrast, caught in the coldest possible white spotlight, let the awful horror of torture have its fullest unbearable extent, so that the care for Edgar ('Kind gods, forgive me that, and prosper him!' 3.7.90) existed in spite of and through that overwhelming experience of the extremity of physical suffering. Taking the interval after the blinding (as Hytner did and Peter Brook before him), Noble left Bradley's Gloucester staring sightlessly at an immense moon suspended over the stage as the biggest of all the big effects of Anthony Ward's design came into its own: the globe cracked and sand poured from it as, as Lear predicted, 'all germens spill at once' (3.2.8). The impact of this extravagant device was so perfectly in keeping with the play's cosmic vision that it would have been impossibly curmudgeonly to resist its theatrical truth.

Great productions of huge plays like *King Lear* understand the rhythm of the text. Noble allowed the play to unfold over its full extent, building slowly towards the emotional extremes of pain and grief that would be needed in the last stages of the action. The result was the only major flaw in the production, the underplaying of the opening. Lear's stylish regency court, a world of apparent rationality which would disintegrate to the limits of unreason, turned tensely at the king's approach but the production did not reveal a cause either for that nervous anxiety or for Lear's actions. Stephens' Lear certainly believed himself to have been 'So kind a father' (1.5.33). He was, as Michael Billington commented, 'a man spoilt by a lifetime of adulation' (*Guardian)*, beaming at every one, until, just before his exit (1.1.265), he paused, marking both the power and regret at what he had done, signalling a man who had never had to undo anything and certainly incapable of starting to do so now. Later, too, he settled to 'pray' (3.4.27), framing the word to hint at its unaccustomed significance. There was almost too much geniality in 1.1 with its polite court laughter and even applause at Cordelia's 'Nothing', little sense that the future of the nation was at stake.

Noble's production was played out over a map of England which papered the stage floor and on which the Fool, gagged and with odd stockings like some bizarre footman, painted the red lines of the division of the kingdom, as the court – and Cornwall in particular – craned to see how the shares would be established. Gradually the paper map ripped and shredded from the moment of Edgar's entry as Poor Tom in 3.6 until it was finally removed in the civil war of the last battle. But the production did not seek to explore the politics of the play's view of nation. Only the careful nature of the apportionment of the three shares, with Cordelia's third a wedge that prevents the lands given to Goneril and Regan from touching at any point along their borders, suggested a politics of rule here. Instead the line from individual through family led without interruption to the pitiless universe beneath which these characters crawled.

So many characters had to make this journey until the survivors could line up facing the sandheap and the globe as the production's final image. John Normington's Albany moved from earlier ineffectuality to belated authority, a man trying to make sense of the war he is engaged in ('For this business, / It touches us as France invades our land' Q 22.26–7). Simon Russell Beale's Edgar moved from the endearingly naive bookish scholar, reading in the midst of the court hubbub at the start, to the muddied, wounded figure whose body contorted to the poses of the *Icones* of Andreas Vesalius and who sang his fragments of tune with an unworldly beauty. This Edgar was so traumatized by the blinding of his father that he repeatedly sought to revenge it, blinding Oswald with his staff as he killed him and trying to gouge Edmund's eyes with his thumbs at the end of their savage duel, making clear what drove his vision of connectedness: 'The dark and vicious place where thee he got / Cost him his eyes' (5.3.163–4). Even Owen Teale's Edmund, a cheery swashbuckler who could engage the audience's complicit laughter with a little shrug of the shoulders as he tricked his brother, could lose almost all his charm.

But such performances paled beside Stephens. I must mark three crowning moments. In the scene with Gloucester (4.5) he alone could find the connection between the fragmented shards of his language, revealing the supreme logic of madness, unafraid of the audience's laughter, our temporary comfort while we experienced a painful link between sight and feeling, as in Edgar's lines, which, oddly, were cut: 'it is, / And my heart breaks at it' (4.5.137–8). Indeed, Stephens throughout encouraged laughs, for instance as he unthinkingly directed 'Follow me not' (2.2.234) at Kent still stuck in the stocks. In the reunion with Cordelia, this shattered King rising from his hospital bed, wearing woolly socks and braces, embraced Cordelia with such force that all the violence of his love came flooding back, though the power was offset by a distracting vision of eighteenth-century musicians playing overly sentimental music on the sand-heap at the rear of the stage. At the end, his grief was mixed with equally fierce anger, turning Cordelia's body over roughly, even, in some performances, kicking her corpse, until, at 'Look there, look there', he pulled Cordelia's corpse by the hand, crawling across the stage, and focused his eyes with all that remained of his strength – and how could anything remain by this stage? – on a vacancy on the edge of the stage that he had filled but which the audience could only find unbearably empty.

Noble's productions, whatever their problems, demonstrate a consistent command and mastery of the Main House stage. For Sam Mendes, whatever his success in the Swan and The Other Place, a debut production in the Main House must still have been a daunting task. Mendes' production of *The Tempest* was as confident a debut there as I have seen, far better than anyone else's in recent years. But after the brilliance of his *Troilus and Cressida* in the Swan or his *Richard III* in The Other Place I unreasonably expected something magnificent whereas it was only very good.

The problem lay most particularly in his

choice of Prospero. The critics were hard on Alec McCowen's Prospero. It certainly was an underweighted, small-scale performance, underplaying the grandeur of the part's emotion and turning him into a grumpy Victorian father, neither magus nor duke. Always a fine comedian, he was happiest with the light touches, blowing the dust off his ducal crown as he took it out of its red velvet crown-box as he began his narrative ('Twelve year since' 1.2.53) or eyeing the rather affronted Ferdinand and Miranda whom he has been warning of unchastity with a richly knowing 'Well' (4.1.56). Paul Taylor was not unreasonable in suggesting that this 'donnish, avuncular, mildly eccentric figure' was 'a conjuror who'd go down well at a children's party but not a man who would have to struggle desperately to conquer vengeful desires' (*The Independent*). It was easy to see that this man was a fine tutor for his daughter, comfortably self-mocking as he called himself her 'schoolmaster' (1.2.173), but McCowen was not helped by Mendes' predilection for putting him up a ladder at the back of the stage, a point from which I would defy any actor, even Robert Stephens, to dominate that stage, and especially an actor like McCowen whose best work and best effects have always been in smaller theatres. In the Swan McCowen would have been magnificent; on the main stage the performance lacked the authority this theatre, as much as the part, demands.

McCowen was also not helped by the production's concentration on Ariel. Noble's previous production of *King Lear* is better remembered for its Fool (Sher) than its Lear (Gambon). Mendes' *Tempest* runs a comparable risk, especially given Simon Russell Beale's brilliance as Ariel in doing what was asked of him.

The production opened with Ariel emerging from a wicker theatrical skip onstage and swinging a suspended lamp to set the storm in motion, defining from the beginning the theatricality of the production and its domination by Ariel as stage-hand. It is, though, I believe, quite simply a mistake to have Ariel visibly controlling the storm (and Prospero, too, was visible through the scrim) for there are few stage effects in Shakespeare quite as thrilling as the realization that the hyper-realism of the opening scene, so quickly and economically accomplished, is really only a trick, not of the company of actors but of the play's magician. Mendes made so much come out or go into the theatrical basket of tricks or a folding screen painted with a cloudscape that he sometimes refused to allow the play its own theatrical effects. The dividing line between theatre and existence that makes of Prospero's connection between the great globe itself and his pageant something hovering between metaphor and reality became a line too immediately and permanently blurred, once the interpenetration of art and life was as complete as here.

But what Mendes had recognized is Ariel's curious fluidity in the play, the only character not bound to particular groups of other characters, unlike even Prospero himself. This superior house-servant controlled and stage-managed all the play's spectacles, down to the spirits' planting of flowers on the stage floor for the first lords' scene (2.1). It was appropriate that the spirits of this island were not 'of monstrous shape' as Gonzalo suggests (3.3.31) but rather servants displaced from the first-class restaurant of a passing ocean liner. Ariel as the harpy, in blood-stained mess-jacket and clawed talons from which red streamers spewed, looked like a waiter who had eaten one of the diners.

I really cannot better Paul Taylor's description of Ariel's more normal appearance: 'His far from sylph-like form crammed into a blue silk Mao suit, he pads about barefoot making ninety-degree turns and looking like a *Stepford Wives* equivalent of Wishee Washee.' This robotic effect, while paying tribute to Beale's stillness and control, rather drastically delimited his range of expression, turning his separation from the human world into a fact, rather than an unbridgeable gulf. There could here be no sense of loss or yearning in Ariel's lack of affections, 'Mine would, sir, were I human' (5.1.20), only the efficient tones of service in that deferential 'sir'. As he transformed Prospero's pattern-book of pop-up toy theatre instantly into a full-size Pollock's for the masque and peopled it with spirit automata, Ariel was the play's shape-changer. As perfect servant himself of course he did not betray any emotion, even when reminded of his past pains. Prospero's affectionate treatment of him, stroking his cheek or calling him nicknames, met with no response, though the style had to ignore his earnest enquiry of Prospero 'Do you love me, master? No?' (4.1.48). Freed at the end, Ariel met the benign gaze of Prospero by spitting full in his erstwhile master's face, a superb invention, pinpointing the patronizing nature of our assumption that the perfect servant enjoys serving and that Prospero's treatment of him is not in its own way as brutal and humiliating a servitude as Sycorax's. His final exit, through a previously invisible door in the stage's back wall, from the stage's blue room into a world of dazzlingly white light, was poignant and enigmatic: what after all is there behind the back wall of the stage?

Ariel's style of service was parodied by Stephano (whose costume echoed the island spirits), here played by Mark Lockyer as a cross between Bluto in Popeye and Barry Humphries' Australian cultural attaché, Sir Les Patterson. Stephano inevitably turned Caliban into a version of himself; his servant was as like himself as a servant as he could manage, just as David Bradley's Trinculo, a jittery northern ventriloquist with Little Tich boots, was accompanied by his own mirror likeness in his dummy. If the dummy inhibited Bradley, locking his hands in supporting the prop, it also gave Ariel's ventriloquism ('Thou liest' 3.2.45) a physical focus as the dummy moved uncontrollably in Trinculo's hands. Characteristically the clowns' exit to 'Freedom, high-day! High-day, freedom!' (2.2.185) was back into the wicker skip under Ariel's control, not into freedom at all but the entrapment of the actor in the role.

The Stephano and Trinculo scenes were helped immeasurably by David Troughton's marvellous Caliban, bald and with long hooked fingernails only on his left hand (all the better to dig pignuts with), able to move from the huge rage of hatred to child-like cowering as Sarah Woodward's energetic and gutsy Miranda, no fair English rose she, flew at him at 'Abhorrèd slave' (1.2.354). His announcement 'This island's mine', spoken while hiding in the basket, sounded like a child's grumble from behind the bedroom door. This Caliban – or was it only a spirit version of him? – turned up as one of the reapers in the masque, breaking out of his role to roar threateningly at Prospero and thereby cueing the abrupt ending of the masque. It was no surprise that this Caliban should so touchingly describe the island's noises. What was unfairly harsh was Mendes' cutting of the text at the end so that, rather than being able to hope for pardon in return for a bit of housework ('As you look / To have my pardon, trim it handsomely' 5.1.296–7), he was locked into the theatrical skip, still roaring in pain. This was a particularly brutal cut, though I was sorry that another bit of trimming deprived the audience of the chance of seeing Simon Russell Beale as a 'nymph o'th'sea' (1.2.304). The coldness surrounding Ariel disconcertingly threw audience sympathies back towards Caliban.

With court scenes that never quite caught fire, Mendes' *Tempest* seemed, for all its ingenuity and strong lines of interpretation, still hampered by the very size of the stage. Anthony Ward's set, enveloping the actors in a single massive space, part cell, part shore, often left characters unhelpfully lost in space. Only in the fine celebration of theatricality in the masque did the change of scale from the Swan appear fully accomplished. Throughout there was always much to admire but admiration seems too objective a response, as cold as this Ariel.

17 *The Tempest*, 2.2 RSC, 1993: 'Freedom, high-day! High-day, freedom!': Trinculo (David Bradley), Stephano (Mark Lockyer) and Caliban (David Troughton) in the costume skip as Ariel (Simon Russell Beale) enters to pull it away

It would be good to report that the strengths of the season continued to the final Shakespeare production but they did not. Ian Judge's vision of *Love's Labour's Lost* began promisingly by choosing to set the play in an Edwardian Oxbridge. The loss of a court setting, hardly a significant feature of recent productions in any case, was more than offset by the immediately recognizable world of 'academe' in which young men, in single-sex colleges, had to balance their commitment 'to live and study here three years' (1.1.35) against such temptations as 'to see a woman in that term' (37). Nathaniel became a college chaplain, Holofernes a 'Professor of Latin' (according to the programme), Moth (Christopher Luscombe) a well-scrubbed student chorister and Costard a local delivery boy – though it was not clear where Daniel Massey's dull Don Armado fitted into this community. The dons discussed the hunt in 4.2 while watching a town-vs-gown cricket match, Costard making his entrance (4.2.81) as a batsman just bowled. In 5.1, they arrived somewhat the worse for wear after dining at High Table, Holofernes (John Normington) clutching his napkin like a miniature Pavarotti and rising to peaks of drunken fury at the barbarities of Don Armado's assaults on 'orthography'.

With the stage floor littered with piles of books, looking suspiciously like those in Prospero's cell in Mendes' *Tempest*, and, when the walls of the college drew away, a prospect of Oxford's dreaming spires revealed in the distance, the pastoral ambiguities of the play could

18 *Love's Labour's Lost*, 3.1, RSC, 1993: Moth (Christopher Luscombe) and Don Armado (Daniel Massey) play Oxbridge word-games while Costard (Mark Lewis Jones) watches

be precisely focused on groves of academe. The arrival of the Princess and her entourage – by train, cleverly suggested by a plume of smoke darting across the top of a wall – was not only a matter of gender but also of style, their superb succession of costumes by Deirdre Clancy looking like a series of Edwardian fashion plates, contrasting sharply with the students' blazers. In response, the men metamorphosed into white ties and tails, though they were also to be seen in dressing gowns and pyjamas in 4.3 as they wandered the college courts at night with their love poems and, memorably, as four Rasputins with sunglasses for their Muscovite disguise.

All this was so promising and so well supported by fine verse speaking and by Jeremy Northam's breathlessly enthusiastic Biron, Owen Teale's nervous King of Navarre, on the verge of fainting at the prospect of mockery (5.2.390), Guy Henry's very long Longaville and Robert Portal's Dumaine (whose risqué jokes embarrassed the others at 4.3.278–9). Even the unevenness of the women could have been borne, especially with Paul Greenwood's stylish Boyet, thankfully free of the camp that usually dominates the role.

But such ample resources of comedy must in *Love's Labour's Lost* be balanced by an understanding of love and this the production signally failed to provide. Every expression of love was heavily underscored by Nigel Hess's overscored music swelling beneath; the young men's poems became songs and Don Armado's farewell to valour (1.2.172–6) an excess of musical ardour. The saccharine sentimentalism of musical pastiche smothered any possibility of accurate depiction of emotion under its clichés. The fault did not only lie with the music; Judge's versions of love were all of a piece with such faked romantic feeling. Jenny Quayle's Princess, for instance, fluttering her eyelashes and gazing with big round eyes, offered an engaging parody of naiveté but her self-mockery was left stranded when her invitation to the King at the end, 'Come challenge me' (5.2.798), was made with such an unselfconscious, richly sensuous promise of mutual sexual desire. Even the pain of the Worthies mattered far less than it should, especially against the operatic excesses of the heroes' performances, though the blocking of the scene was effective, young men clubbing together on one side of the stage while the women stiffly showed their annoyance with their lovers' behaviour on the other.

Judge's transpositions at the end epitomized the problems. Don Armado's line 'The words of Mercury are harsh after the songs of Apollo' (5.2.914–15) followed Mercadé's last line (714). The ladies too left the darkening stage, the King's offer to 'bring you on your way' (860) spoken only to the Princess's departing back. In a glibly melancholic gloom and to the sound of distant gunfire, Biron's ironic comment on the time-limits of plays was addressed to the audience. We had been watching, it appeared, the long hot summer of 1914 and few of these men would survive in the trenches the required year and a day. This is both unnecessary and cheap for the play contains no warnings of war and the slaughter of the trenches is too weighty a sudden imposition for the last moments of a production of *Love's Labour's Lost*.

Nonetheless, Biron's lines provoked applause as the audience assumed the play was over. Only after the first bows did Armado offer the song. The exquisite balance of Spring and Winter was lost – no change here to a wintry world of ending – as the two sides were identical, Nathaniel in a cuckoo costume set against Holofernes' owl complete with mortar-board. A final company chorus to ram home the fun of a good family show was followed by Don Armado pointing the way to the exits: 'You that way, we this way'. Such treatment denied the play's discriminating perception of the knife-edge of loss, replacing it with theatrical banalities. In a season where so little was banal, the disappointment provoked by this *Love's Labour's Lost* was all the keener. This production seemed to be aiming rather too obviously for a West End transfer.

PROFESSIONAL SHAKESPEARE PRODUCTIONS IN THE BRITISH ISLES, JANUARY–DECEMBER 1992

compiled by

NIKY RATHBONE

Most of the productions listed are by professional companies, but some amateur productions and adaptations are included. Information is taken from reviews and programmes held in the Birmingham Shakespeare Library. Details have been verified wherever possible, but the nature of the material prevents corroboration in every case.

ALL'S WELL THAT ENDS WELL

The RSC at the Swan Theatre, Stratford: June 1992–
Director: Sir Peter Hall
Designer: John Gunter
Music: Guy Woolfenden
Helena: Sophie Thompson
The Countess: Barbara Jefford
Bertram: Toby Stephens

ANTONY AND CLEOPATRA

The RSC at the Royal Shakespeare Theatre, Stratford: October 1992–
Director: John Caird
Designer: Sue Blane
Music: Ilona Sekacz
Antony: Richard Johnson
Cleopatra: Claire Higgins

AS YOU LIKE IT

Cheek by Jowl: Tour continues. See *Shakespeare Survey 46*.

Joe Dixon won the Ian Charleson Award for his portrayal of Rosalind.

The RSC at the Royal Shakespeare Theatre, Stratford: April 1992–
Director: David Thacker
Designer: Johan Engels
Music: Gary Yershon
Rosalind: Samantha Bond

Greenwich Theatre, London: April–June 1992
Director: James Robert Carson
Designer: Kathy Strachan
Rosalind: Jemma Redgrave

New Shakespeare Company, Regent's Park: June 1992–
Director: Maria Aitken
Designer: Bruno Santini
Rosalind: Cathryn Harrison
Jaques/The Film Director: Betty Bourne
Conceived as a film with the chief roles played by 'professionals' the other roles by 'enthusiastic amateurs' with 'close-ups' and 'repeats'. The Director/Jaques was played by the drag artist Betty Bourne. Some reviewers felt the conceit upstaged the play.

Ludlow Festival: June–July 1992
Director: Alan Cohen
Designer: Claire Lyth
Rosalind: Victoria Wicks
Jaques: Ken Drury

Wales Actors' Company: Tour of Welsh castles and open-air sites: July 1992–

Director: Ruth Garnault
Rosalind: Manon Edwards

Touchstone Theatre, The Gulbenkian Studio Theatre, Newcastle: September 1992
Director: Damian Brant
Rosalind: Annie Aldington
Set in the 1920s.

Film version

Sands Films: UK première: Chichester Film Festival: July 1992
Director: Christine Edzard
With James Fox, Griff Rhys Jones, Cyril Cusack, Miriam Margolyes
Set in an urban wasteland.

THE COMEDY OF ERRORS

The Original Shakespeare Company at the Mermaid Theatre, London: Two performances only in January 1992
A reconstruction of Elizabethan conditions of staging.

New Victoria Theatre, Newcastle-under-Lyme: September 1992–
Director: Chris Martin
Designer: Lis Evans

The RSC/Royal Insurance tour: October 1992–
Also touring to Brussels, Madrid, Hong Kong and Perth, Australia
See *Shakespeare Survey 46*.

Redgrave Theatre, Farnham: October 1992
Director: Graham Watkins
Designer: Janey Gardiner
Victorian seaside setting.

CORIOLANUS

Renaissance Theatre Company at Chichester Festival Theatre: May–June 1992
Director: Tim Supple
Designer: Bunny Christie
Music: Andrew Poppy
Coriolanus: Kenneth Branagh
Aufidius: Iain Glen
Volumnia: Dame Judi Dench
A traditional production, using a large cast of local amateurs to augment the important crowd scenes.

HAMLET

The Roaring Girl's Hamlet: The Warehouse Theatre, Croydon and tour: January 1992–
Director: Sue Parrish
Designer: Anny Evason
Music: Claire van Kampen
Hamlet: Ruth Mitchell
Moll Cutpurse/Claudius: Alexandra Mathie
Additional material by Claire Luckham
An all-female cast playing the full Folio text. The play was set in London in 1605 and presented by Moll Cutpurse.

Second Age, The Riverbank Theatre, Dublin: February 1992–
Director: Alan Stanford
Designer: Robert Ballagh
Hamlet: Frank McCusker
Played in the round. The production focused on domestic relationships, and was intentionally set in an indeterminate period.

The Lyric Theatre, Belfast: February–March 1992
Director: Charles Nowosielski
Designer: Kerry Dunn
Hamlet: Andrew Price

Classic Theatre Productions, Shakespeare's Globe Theatre, London: April 1992
Producer/Director: Raymond Bootle

Cleveland Theatre Productions, The Nuffield Theatre Studio: May 1992
Hamlet: Nabil Shaban
Set in a modern-day security bunker. Nabil Shaban is a disabled actor.

The Medieval Players, Civic Theatre, Scunthorpe and tour of the UK, Denmark and Germany: May 1992–

Director: Ben Benison
Designer: Emma Ryott
Hamlet: Patrick Knox
A production of the First Quarto version. In the autumn this production played in repertoire with *Fratricide Punished*.

Compass Theatre (Sheffield) tour, with *King Lear*: June 1992–
Director: Neil Sissons
Hamlet: Paul Rider

The Riverside Studios, London, Nottingham Playhouse and tour: September 1992–
Producer: Thelma Holt
Director: Robert Sturua
Designer: Giorgi Meskhishvili
Music: Ghia Kancheli
Hamlet: Alan Rickman
Gertrude: Geraldine McEwan

Naked Theatre at the Garter Lane Theatre, Waterford: and the Everyman Palace Theatre, Cork: November 1992
Hamlet: Declan Conlon
A new company of seven actors in a production which emphasized the comic aspects of the play.

Theatre Clwyd, Mold and tour: November 1991–2
See *Shakespeare Survey 46*

Natural Edge Theatre Company at the Theatre Museum, Covent Garden: December 1992, January 1993

The RSC at the Barbican, London: December 1992–
Director: Adrian Noble
Designer: Bob Crowley
Music: Guy Woolfenden
Hamlet: Kenneth Branagh
Gertrude: Jane Lapotaire
Transfer to Stratford March 1993.

Adaptations

Hamlet, the Tragedy of a Fat Man
The Shaw Theatre, London: June 1992
Director: Professor Iovhannes Pilikian, author of the book *Hamlet, Tragedy of a Fat Man*
Hamlet: Steve Varnom
Advertised as the eighteen-stone Hamlet, and presented as part of the World Classical Theatre season. The text was severely cut. A production with this title was listed in *Shakespeare Survey 42*; it is not clear whether this is the text played in that production.

Ophelia by Jeff Wanshel
The Rialto Theatre, Derry, Eire: November 1992
Ophelia: Camille L. Jeter
Hamlet: Troy Kotsur
Directors: Will Rhys and Robbie Barnet
Designer: David Hays
Performed for the National Theatre of the Deaf; the part of Ophelia was played entirely in sign language. Although the play was based on *Hamlet*, it also contained elements of *Romeo and Juliet*.

HENRY IV Parts I and II

The RSC at the Barbican, London
See *Shakespeare Survey 46*

HENRY VI Part III and RICHARD III

The Wars of the Roses
Stafford Shakespeare Company at Stafford Castle: July–August 1992
Director: Geoffrey Davies
Designer: David Neal
Music: Rick Wakeman
Henry VI: Rob Clilverd
Queen Margaret: Annie Corbier
Gloucester/Richard III: Tom Watt

JULIUS CAESAR

The New Victoria Theatre, Newcastle-under-Lyme: March 1992–
Director: Martin Harvey

Designer: Lis Evans
Brutus: Roger Llewellyn
Antony: Oliver Beamish

Adaptations

Caesar!
Deal Theatre Project: Summer 1992
Professional actors conducted a series of workshops leading to a complete performance of *Julius Caesar*.

Roman Voices
Opening Acts Theatre Company, tour of Scottish schools: Autumn 1992

KING LEAR

The Royal National Theatre, tour with *Richard III*. See *Shakespeare Survey 46*.

Tabard Theatre, Uxbridge: April–May 1992
Director: Kate Bone
Music: John Martin and Warren Saire
Lear: Duncan Bonner
A very cut production with an exceptionally young Lear, apparently in his mid thirties.

The Rose Theatre Company, tour, with *That Way Madness Lies*: April 1992–
That Way Madness Lies was a half day workshop on the journey of transformation experienced in *King Lear*. The company is an independent touring co-operative company. The production made use of masks, singing, percussion and colour contrasts.

Compass Theatre (Sheffield) and The Crucible Theatre, Sheffield tour with *Hamlet*: June 1992–
Director: Neil Sissons
Lear: Nick Chadwin
Set in an indeterminate period on a bare stage hung with huge 'thunder sheets'. Well reviewed.

Kaboodle Productions, Forest Arts Centre, New Milton and tour: September 1992–
Directors: Lee Beagley and Josette Bushell-Mingo
Designer: Amanda Bracebridge
Music: Andy Frizell
Lear: Lee Beagley
A study in uncompromising force and militarism, with Japanese and Balkan elements to the costumes and set. Well reviewed.

Second Age at the Tivoli Theatre, Dublin: November 1992
Director/Designer: Alan Stanford
Lear: Timothy West

LOVE'S LABOUR'S LOST

Manchester Royal Exchange: September–October 1992
Director: James Macdonald
Designer: Kandis Cook
Berowne: Linus Roache
Rosaline: Suzan Sylvester
The King of Navarre: Stephen Tompkinson
Don Armado: Bernard Bresslaw
A feminist reading; the men were portrayed as people of limited capability, intoxicated by lust, and the women would not be wooed.

MACBETH

The ESC, national and international tour, opened at Warwick Arts Centre, February 1992
Director: Michael Bogdanov
Designer: Claire Lyth
Macbeth: Michael Pennington
Lady Macbeth: Jenny Quayle
The production toured first with *Twelfth Night*, then toured abroad. It returned to the UK to tour with *The Tempest*; Tony Haygarth took over as Macbeth and Lynn Farleigh as Lady Macbeth. The ESC also toured Africa with an adapted version for a company of six, aimed at non-English-speaking audiences, and using mime and ritualistic dance. Directors: Michael Bogdanov, Teddy Kiendl.

The Schiller Theatre, Berlin at the Mermaid Theatre, London: January–February 1992
See *Shakespeare Survey 46* for details of the production previously seen in Dublin.

Button Hole Theatre Company at the New End Theatre, Hampstead: February–March 1992
Director: Christopher Geelan
Designer: Sarah Millington
Macbeth: Ian Reddington
Lady Macbeth: Sally Montemore
A modern-dress production.

Stafford Shakespeare Company, The Gatehouse Theatre, Stafford: March 1992–
Director: Geoffrey Davies
Macbeth: Andrew Barrow
Lady Macbeth: Elli Mackenzie
Richard Todd took a cameo role as the Porter.

D.P. Productions, the Princess Theatre, Torquay and tour: April 1992–
Director: Ian Dickens
Designer: Richard Baker
Music: Matt Marks
Macbeth: Paul Darrow
Lady Macbeth: Pamela Salem/Mary Conlon
Set during the Jacobite rebellion. Well reviewed.

Rain Dog at Glasgow Arts Centre and Glasgow Citizens' Theatre: April 1992–
Director: Robert Carlyle
Macbeth: Alexander Morton
Lady Macbeth: Caroline Paterson
An all-Scottish cast performing in Scots accents. The action was cut to two hours.
Rain Dog is a new Scottish company.

Cutting Edge Theatre Company, tour: June 1992
Macbeth: Mark Hopkins
Lady Macbeth: Carol Reynolds
The company was started by Mark Hopkins in 1992, and produced the play with workshops as a schools production.

Talawa at the Cochrane Theatre, London: September 1992
Director: Stephen Rayne
Designer: Gerald Lidstone
Set in contemporary Africa.

Point Blank Theatre Company, tour: Autumn 1992
Director: Sion Taylor
Macbeth: John Killoran
Lady Macbeth: Janice Morell
A cast of six touring nationally. Many minor characters were omitted.

The Watermill Theatre, Newbury: September–October 1992
Director: Euan Smith
Macbeth: Douglas Henshall
Lady Macbeth: Caroline Loncq
The production also toured to Tokyo and Argentina.

Astra Theatre Company at the Duke of Cambridge, London: October 1992
Director: Caroline Gardiner
Designer: Sarah Nelson
Macbeth: Ged McKenna
Lady Macbeth: Anna Macmin
A restrained production set in nineteenth-century Russia.

Screaming Blue Murder Theatre Company, Leeds Civic Theatre, October 1992
Director: Jo McCarey
Played as a black comedy set in eleventh-century Scotland.

Harrogate Theatre: October–November 1992
Director: Andrew Manley
Designer: Julie Henry
Macbeth: Peter Forbes
Lady Macbeth: Catherine Prendergast
Set in a post-nuclear holocaust world. The weird sisters carried geiger counters, and the rest of the cast resembled New Age travellers.

The Everyman Theatre, Cheltenham: October–November 1992
Director: Martin Houghton
Designer: Nettie Edwards
Macbeth: Julian Bleach
Lady Macbeth: Dilys Watling
The witches re-appeared in other roles, to indicate their pernicious influence. Sexual lust was also an important theme. The production

was linked to an actors' residential weekend, and to a production of *Lady Macbeth* by Jean Binnie at the Richardson Studio Theatre, also directed by Martin Houghton, with Tina Jones as Lady Macbeth.

Access Theatre Company, Tara Arts Centre, Wandsworth, London: November–December 1992
A new theatre company, dedicated to producing neglected plays and classics.

MEASURE FOR MEASURE

The RSC at the Young Vic, London: March–April 1992
See *Shakespeare Survey 46* for details

Contact Theatre, Manchester: April 1992
Director: Brigid Larmour
Designer: Simon Banham
Isabella: Katherine Rogers
Angelo: Simeon Andrews
The Duke: Paul Brightwell
A rather slow production set in an indeterminate period, which received mixed reviews.

London Bubble, touring London parks with their tent: June 1992
Directors: Jonathan Petherbridge and Adrian Jackson
Costumes: Hannah Mayall
Isabella: Sandra Yaw
Angelo: Barry Killerby
The Duke: Bev Willis
A production which concentrated on the theme of male-dominated society.

Chester Gateway Theatre: November 1992
Director: Ian Forrest
Designer: Juliet Watkinson
Angelo: Mark Spalding
A modern-dress production.

Adaptation

Measure for Measure, adapted by Dominic Power and Andrew Hilton
Show of Strength Theatre Company at the Hen and Chicken, Bristol: November–December 1992
Director: Andrew Hilton
Angelo: Tim Crouch

THE MERCHANT OF VENICE

The Sherman Theatre, Cardiff: February 1992–
Director: Jamie Garvin
Designer: Jane Linz Roberts
Shylock: Kenneth Gardnier
Portia: Rakie Ayola
Antonio/Old Gobbo: Owen Garmon
Shylock was played by a black actor in a production which focused on racial issues and was set in a non-specific period.

Theatre Set Up, tour: June 1992–
Director: Wendy McPhee
A cast of seven in a traditional production touring open-air sites.

The Library Theatre, Manchester: October–November 1992
Director: Chris Honer
Designer: Michel Taylor
Shylock: Peter Whitman
Portia: Kate Paul
Antonio: David Kelsey

The Northcott Theatre, Exeter: November 1992
Director: John Durnin
Designers: Kit and Meg Surrey
Shylock: Patrick Romer
Portia: Susan Twist
Antonio: John Glenforan
A production which emphasized the themes of trade and commerce.

THE MERRY WIVES OF WINDSOR

The RSC at the Royal Shakespeare Theatre, Stratford: August 1992–
Director: David Thacker
Designer: William Dudley

Music: Guy Woolfenden
Falstaff: Benjamin Whitrow

A MIDSUMMER NIGHT'S DREAM

The New Shakespeare Company, Regent's Park Open Air Theatre: June 1992–
Director: Ian Talbot
Oberon: Ken Bones
Titania: Jane Maud
Bottom: Dinsdale Landen
The fairies were played as insects in a production which focused on the lovers.

The Queen Mary Players at the Shakespeare Globe Museum Theatre: June 1992
Director: John Ramsden
Set in the 1920s.

Tymescythe Theatre Company, in the garden of the Rose-in-Vale Hotel, Mithian, Cornwall: July 1992
Director: Cedric Messina

The Royal National Theatre, the Olivier Theatre, London: July 1992–
Director: Robert Lepage
Designer: Michael Levine
Music: Adrian Lee and Peter Salem
Titania: Sally Dexter
Oberon: Jeffery Kissoon
Bottom: Timothy Spall
Puck: Angela Laurier
The production used the contrast between the white actress playing Titania and the black actor playing Oberon to advantage. Played on a mud-covered stage.

Dream-Makers, open-air production at Cannizaro Park, Wimbledon: August 1992
Director: Leo Dolan

Illyria Theatre Group, Penshurst Place, Tonbridge: September–October 1992
A professional group of five, who also toured schools with a children's version.

Sheffield Crucible: October 1992
Director: Michael Rudman
Designer: Kendra Ullyart
A Victorian setting. The 'dream' was seen through the imagination of Theseus.

Salisbury Playhouse: October 1992
Director: Deborah Paige
Designer: Isabella Bywater
A modern-dress production with the lovers in scruffy sweaters and holed socks and Puck as a mischievous schoolgirl. The fairies were played as menacing spirits.

Adaptations

The Royal National Theatre, workshop production, touring Cambridgeshire schools: February 1992–
Director: Bridget Panet
Five actors using a slightly modernized text in a one-hour production which cut the mechanicals and focused on Oberon, Titania and the lovers.

MUCH ADO ABOUT NOTHING

The Oxford Stage Company, Sheffield Lyceum; national and international tour: July 1992–
Director: Alex Darie
Designer: Maria Miu
Music: Karl James
Beatrice: Marie Francis
Benedick: James Simmons
A multi-ethnic, multi-cultural production which used ethnic music and costumes to create a sense of tribal conflict. The action of the play is a brief lull in the fighting; at the end of this production Don John is returning with an army.

The Liverpool Everyman: October–November 1992
Director: John Doyle
Designer: Neil Warmington
Benedick: Guy Scantlebury
Beatrice: Jacqueline Dankworth
A cast of eight, doubling male and female roles.

Actions and Words Theatre Company, Bridge Lane Theatre, London: October–November 1992
Director: David Beaton
Beatrice: Melanie Wynyard
Benedick: Andrew Potts
Set in the 1920s.

New Triad Theatre Company, Theatre Gwynedd, Wales; and tour: November 1992–
Director: John Strehlow
Beatrice: Debbie Radcliffe
Benedick: John Hug
Set in the ninteenth century.

OTHELLO

The Everyman Theatre, Liverpool: February 1992
Director: John Doyle
Designer: India Smith
Music: Matthew Wood
Othello: Ray Fearon
Desdemona: Gillian Kearney
Iago: Tony Turner
Emilia: Joanne Stoner
Set in the 1911–12 Italian–Turkish war.

The Court Theatre Company, The Courtyard Theatre Club, London: 1992–
Director: June Abbott
Othello: Gary Lawrence
Performed by a group of young professional actors.

The Byre Theatre, St Andrews: September 1992–
Director: Maggie Kinloch
Othello: Danny Sapani
Desdemona: Deirdre Davis
Iago: Cliff Burnett
Set in the Second World War, in London and Cyprus, with Desdemona played as a debutante.

Adaptations

Iago, adapted and directed by Phil Willmott. Steam Factory at the Man in the Moon Theatre Club, London: March 1992

Othello, adapted by Ronald Selwyn Phillips
Deconstruction Theatre Company, Barons Court Theatre, Kensington, London: January–February 1992–
Director: Adam Roberts
Designer: Clodagh McGuinness
Othello: Christopher Toba
Iago: Yomi Michaels
Desdemona: Nina Sosanya
Set on an island off the African coast, with a white Othello and the rest of the cast black.

RICHARD III

The Royal National Theatre; international tour followed by a further UK season
See *Shakespeare Survey 46*

Northern Broadsides at the Marina Boatshed, Hull; northern tour and the Riverside Studios, London: June 1992–
Director: Barrie Rutter
Richard: Barrie Rutter
Buckingham: Brian Glover
Queen Margaret: Polly Hemingway
A new company, formed to stage performances of classic plays using northern accents. Non-theatrical venues, such as the Boatshed, were chosen for the northern tour. Set: Bare wooden benches around the acting space, with a steel cage at one end of the acting area.

The RSC at The Other Place, Stratford and tour: August 1992–
Director: Sam Mendes
Designer: Tim Hatley
Music: Paddy Cunneen
Richard: Simon Russell Beale
Queen Elizabeth/Prince Edward: Kate Duchêne
The RSC/Royal Insurance schools tour, 1992, returning to the Swan Theatre, Stratford in 1993. The production also toured to Japan and the Netherlands.

For Stafford Shakespeare Company see *Henry VI*

ROMEO AND JULIET

Bristol Old Vic: January 1992–
Director: Andrew Hay
Designer: Mick Bearwish
Romeo: Clarence Smith
Juliet: Geraldine Somerville
The 1760s stage conditions of this theatre, one of the few remaining Georgian theatre interiors, were re-created to make this production a closet drama. Several male roles were played by women.

Manchester Royal Exchange and tour: February 1992–
Director: Gregory Hersov
Designer: David Short
Music: Mark Vibrans
Romeo: Michael Sheen
Juliet: Kate Byers
A modern-dress production.

Zip Theatre, Wolverhampton and tour: April 1992–
A modern-dress mixed-race production with the Montagues played by Afro-Caribbean actors.

The RSC at the Barbican, London: June 1992–
See *Shakespeare Survey 46*.
The set was radically re-worked for the London transfer.

Adaptations

Romeo and Juliet. A modern adaptation by Ronald Selwyn Phillips, set on an island off Africa. The Capulets were depicted as indigenous Africans, the Montagues as white outsiders.
Deconstruction Theatre Company at the Barons Court Theatre, London: June–August 1992
Designer: David Evans Rees
Designer: Alban Oliver
Romeo: Christopher Toba
Juliet: Heather Imani

Heer & Romeo Devised by Jatinder Verma. Schools tour, with workshops, Tara Arts, and the Theatre Royal, Stratford East: September 1992–
Director: Philippe Cherbonnier
Designer: Magdalen Rubalcava
Performed by Tassia Messimeris and David Tse.
An exploration of the connections between *Romeo and Juliet* and Varis Shah's eighteenth-century Indian epic poem *Heer and Ranjha*.

THE TAMING OF THE SHREW

The RSC at the Royal Shakespeare Theatre, Stratford: March 1992–
Director: Bill Alexander
Designer: Tim Goodchild
Music: Jonathan Goldstein
Katherine: Amanda Harris
Petruchio: Anton Lesser

The Duke's Playhouse, Lancaster, open-air production in Williamson Park: June–July 1992
Director: Jon Pope
Katherine: Lucy Tregear
Petruchio: Chris Wright
Set during World War II. Kate in uniform, Petruchio as a GI. Christopher Sly became a tipsy ARP warden, beguiled by a troup of ENSA performers.

Heartbreak productions, tour of open-air sites: July 1992–
Director: Lewis Hancock
The First Folio text.
The actors worked only from their own parts and three-line cues.

Edinburgh Lyceum: October–November 1992
Director: Ian Wooldridge
Katherine: Kathryn Howden
Petruchio: Kenny Bryans

THE TEMPEST

Orchard Theatre Company, the Plough Arts Centre, Torrington, and tour of south-west England: February 1992–

Director: Stephen Powell
Designer: Meg Surrey
Music: Tom Nordon
Prospero: John Surman
Caliban: Bill Buffery
Miranda/Ariel: Andrea Gascoigne
Very simple props were used, with extraordinary special effects and music derived from Arabic and African folk-song. Well received.

Path Theatre Company, the Cochrane Theatre, London: August 1992–
A production using able-bodied, physically disabled and mentally handicapped actors.

Bristol Old Vic: October 1992–
Director: Andrew Hay
Designer: Mick Bearwish
Prospero: Ewan Hooper

The ESC, the Grand Theatre, Swansea, and tour with *Macbeth*: September 1992–
Director: Michael Bogdanov
Prospero: John Woodvine
The set was dominated by enormous metal pipes which represented the engine-room of the shipwrecked ship, and subsequently appeared to represent a nuclear power station.

The Ninagawa Company at the Barbican, London: December 1992
The company was invited to London as part of the LIFT theatre season. See *Shakespeare Survey 43* for details of their previous appearance at the Edinburgh Festival.

TWELFTH NIGHT

The ESC, UK and world tour with *Macbeth*: See *Shakespeare Survey 46*.

Forest Forge, tour of Hampshire: Spring 1992
Performed by a cast of six.

Wizzard Productions, The Duke's Head Theatre, Richmond and tour of fringe venues: February 1992–
Director: David Gillies
Designer: Naomi Wilkinson
Viola: Jan Dunn

Factotum Theatre Company, tour: August 1992
Director: Alastair Palmer
Designer: Jill Muirhead
Viola: Lisa Fornara
A traditional production.

Past Imperfect Theatre Company, the Drill Hall Arts Centre, London: October 1992
Director: Philip Osmet
Designers: Charlotte Malik and Kevin McKeon
Viola: Susan Cole
Sebastian was played as a bouncy bisexual.

Liverpool Playhouse: October 1992–
Director: Gillian Diamond
Designer: David Roger
Viola: Serena Gordon
Malvolio: Roy Marsden
A traditional production set in the Elizabethan period.

Berserk Theatre Company, the Arches, Glasgow: December 1992
Set in 1920s Berlin and performed with Dietrich songs.

THE TWO GENTLEMEN OF VERONA

The RSC at the Barbican, London: October 1992–
See *Shakespeare Survey 46*.

THE WINTER'S TALE

Theatre de Complicite, tour: January 1992–
Director: Annabel Arden
Designer: Ariane Gastambide
Mamilius/Paulina/Time/Old Shepherd: Kathryn Hunter
An imaginatively staged production with a very effective change from Bohemia to Sicily, achieved by the cast disassembling and reassembling themselves as they circled round the stage. Kathryn Hunter was particularly praised

for her performance. First performed at the Sydney Festival, Australia.

The RSC at the Royal Shakespeare Theatre, Stratford: July 1992–
Director: Adrian Noble
Designer: Anthony Ward
Music: Shaun Davey
Leontes: John Nettles
Hermione: Samantha Bond

ATTRIBUTED PLAYS

Arden of Faversham
Arden's House garden, Faversham: September 1992
Producer: Alan Pope

THE SONNETS AND POEMS

L.O.V.E. An adaptation of the sonnets set to 1970s disco music.
Volano Theatre, Swansea, tour: Autumn 1992

Love

Unity Theatre, London, tour: November1992

VENUS AND ADONIS

The Citizens' Theatre, Glasgow: November 1992
Directors: Matthew Radford and Malcolm Sutherland
Venus: Siobhan Stanley
Adonis: Matthew Radford
Text adapted by Matthew Radford.

MISCELLANEOUS

Enemy to the People: Shakespeare and revolution, a compilation from Shakespeare's Roman plays devised by Michael Bogdanov and Michael Pennington.
The ESC, international tour: February 1992–
Director: Tim Carroll

The Animated Shakespeare
Cartoon versions of the plays, abridged by Leon Garfield, Island World Video
First titles in the series:
Hamlet, *Macbeth*, *A Midsummer Night's Dream*, *Romeo and Juliet*, *The Tempest*, *Twelfth Night*.
Each video is about thirty minutes long, using original text with narration. Techniques involved in the animation include painting on glass, puppets and cel animation.

THE YEAR'S CONTRIBUTIONS TO SHAKESPEARE STUDIES

1. CRITICAL STUDIES

reviewed by David Lindley

GENERAL STUDIES AND COLLECTIONS

At the very moment of finishing this review the British Prime Minister, John Major, has denounced 'airy-fairy theory' as part of a more general demonizing of the inheritance of the sixties which has marked the last year or so of political discourse in Britain. It is tempting to see Brian Vickers's counterblast to current literary theory, *Appropriating Shakespeare* (New Haven and London: Yale University Press, 1993) as animated by very much the same hostility. It has been greeted already with considerable enthusiasm by those who feel alienated from, threatened by or contemptuous of the directions in which critical practices have been moving for the last thirty years or so. Like John Major, Vickers sees the sixties as the cause of our going astray. Unlike the politician, however, Vickers mounts his attack not out of a vague nostalgia and determined anti-intellectualism, but through a detailed and systematic scholarly critique of the appropriation (or misappropriation) of the work of Saussure which he argues underlies French literary theory. In subsequent chapters Vickers attacks each modern 'heresy' in turn. Deconstructionists don't understand how language works; psychoanalysts are doomed to failure because their founding father is a fraud; new historicists just don't do their history well enough; feminists (like everyone else) misread the texts because of their determination to find their own political/ideological theories represented therein; Christians and (some) Marxists – oddly bracketed together – are guilty of treating texts as allegories. There are many shrewd hits in the course of the book and some occasional touches of pure *vituperatio* that enliven what is sometimes a rather stodgy (and very long) text. But, though one might sympathize with Vickers's complaints against the self-righteousness and self-aggrandisement frequently indulged in by certain proponents of this or that master story, I cannot but feel that in so determinedly attempting to crush the excesses of some current critical exegesis, Vickers fails to take on board the fact that the intellectual landscape has been inevitably and irrevocably changed. Old certainties needed to be explored and questioned, and they cannot, as Vickers seems to imply, be reinstated as though the last thirty years had never been. In particular, Vickers does not offer any model for the negotiation between the past text and the present reader which would answer the very real problems in this most fundamental of critical activities that more recent writing has brought to the surface. Indeed, Vickers himself makes some surprisingly authoritarian pronouncements about what Shakespeare and his contemporaries might or might not have believed. Is it really true – could it indeed ever have been true – that Shakespeare's 'presentations of social unrest . . . derive from historical sources, and are never keyed to contemporary events' for example? So too, though he accuses his adversaries of selective reading of the Shakespearian texts, his own selection from their work is frequently partial and tendentious. This is certainly an important book; it is one of the best-primed cannons yet fired against current theoretical approaches to Shakespeare. But its central failure, to my mind, is its lack of self-awareness of its own implication in the current cultural scene.

The tone of the other major reconsideration of currently fashionable theory could not be more different. R. A. Foakes is prepared to accept that recent approaches have generated 'methods of opening the plays out rather than seeking to pin them down', and ready to recognize the cultural construction of his own writing. His aim is not to bring back an imagined golden age of empirical criticism, but to find a way to remedy what he sees as the lack of attention to the aesthetic shape of the plays which has limited more recent approaches. *Hamlet versus Lear* (Cambridge: Cambridge University Press, 1993) begins with chapters chronicling the reception of the two tragedies from the nineteenth century onwards, making obvious but necessary points about the relationship of critical positions to their contemporary political and cultural attitudes; we then move to a discussion of the relationship of F and Q texts of both plays – and Foakes suggests (rightly in my view) that rather too much has been made of the destabilizing tendency of these revisions. Finally readings are produced of each of the plays in which claims are made for the possibility of 'recuperating a sense of the whole play and of artistic design not in an immutable "formal perfection", but as generated, like meaning, out of a collaboration between viewers or readers and Shakespeare's texts'. The detail of these readings seems to me stronger than the larger case made for them as exemplars – the contrast between *Hamlet* as a play obsessed with memory and deeply Christianized with *Lear* as a play that has no past nor religious frame of reference is forcefully made, for example. Even if the book as a whole does not quite hang together, in its attempt to do justice to recent theory while pointing to what it excludes this is a pleasant contrast to Vickers's aggressive extremism.

Nonetheless, a good deal of the most interesting work I have encountered this year draws its inspiration from recent theoretical developments. Two books emanating from a Cultural Materialist perspective make an instructive contrast one with the other, and illustrate the strengths and weaknesses of the approach. With *Will Power* (London: Harvester, 1993) Richard Wilson establishes himself as one of the most committed and passionate exponents of a criticism that places Shakespeare's work within 'the local situation it occupies within discourses of material power'. Unlike the history of most New Historicists, with its privileging of the free-floating anecdote, Wilson's work is marked by its scholarly, comprehensive and particular establishment of contexts. A number of the essays in this book (on *Coriolanus*, *As You Like It*, *Julius Caesar* and the comedies) have been considered in earlier reviews, but to them is added a new, long, and complex chapter which takes Shakespeare's own Will as its starting point. Wilson demonstrates that Shakespeare's testamentary exclusions were typical of the way in which the rights of the individual testator to determine the destiny of his property were being instated in place of older customary controls of inheritance during the early seventeenth century, and sees them as a sign of larger cultural shifts. This then becomes the springboard for the understanding of patriarchal and paternal control in the comedies, and, crucially, for an extended and suggestive reading of *King Lear* as 'mapped precisely in time and place, on the edge of customary culture, at a point when the liberty won by Tudor testators impacts on the partibility descending from time immemorial'. Finally, Shakespeare's Will is interpreted 'as a paradigm of Shakespearian poetry, which works to impress the identity of the single writer onto a nexus of genres . . . that had formerly been common heritage'. For all the forcibleness and abundant scholarship of these essays, there are times when Wilson's strategies seem dangerously reductive. Beginning his chapter on the late plays with the medical practice of Shakespeare's son-in-law Dr Hall, for example, he argues that 'the discursive function of the romances is revealed to be the Harveian project of separating childbirth from those wayward sisters already demonised in tragedy'. I just do not believe that these plays can be thus rigidly delimited. *Will Power* is a book that will provoke extreme reactions – but it is one that cannot be ignored.

Derek Cohen's *Shakespeare's Culture of Violence* (London: Macmillan; New York: St Martin's Press, 1993), though it shares Wilson's politics, could not be more different in the manner of its execution. Cohen relentlessly pursues the single question of whether 'the plays are exposing or simply complying with patriarchal structures', taking as axiomatic the proposition that the foundation of those structures is a violence that they define and legitimate, attempting to demarcate justifiable and criminal violence. Cohen traverses the second tetralogy of history plays, three tragedies involving the murder of women, and *Macbeth*, charting the ways in which violence functions in each of them. At times his paradigm is revealing – particularly perhaps in his discussion of Othello's desperate attempt to legitimate the killing of Desdemona, but at others it seems both circuitous and simplified – as, for example, in the suggestion that Cordelia dies 'to validate a structure of nature and kinship that patriarchy has consolidated as its own'. Compared with Wilson's careful attempt to define terms, Cohen's use of 'patriarchy' is frequently no more than gestural, his observations on social class unnuanced and untroubled by historians' debates on this highly contentious issue. There is little reference outside the texts to a material history which might substantiate its central proposition.

Victor Kiernan's *Shakespeare, Poet and Citizen* (London and New York: Verso, 1993) is also written from a Marxist perspective, and one might expect a historian to provide some of the precision of detail missing in Cohen's book. Kiernan concentrates on ways in which Shakespeare registers the shifts from feudalism to a new individualism in the plays of the 1590s, but though he offers a number of suggestive ideas, especially about Shakespeare's attachment to virtues defined through valorous conduct, and his effort as 'a social critic . . . to sketch a pattern of truly "aristocratic" behaviour' Kiernan's readings are very bland. There is, indeed, a lack of any satisfactory theoretical model for the ways in which literature and history may be conjointly read.

By contrast with these books' assumptions about the values implicit in Shakespearian texts Katherine Maynard suggests that his work espouses a politics based on 'shared responsibilities, communal interests put before self-interest; a social system that rewards merit and hard work; social relationships based in equity and reciprocity'. These values, she contends, in 'Shakespeare's Georgic Nationalism' (*History of European Ideas*, 16, 1993, pp. 981–9), are ambivalently represented in the histories, but emerge triumphant in the last plays. It all depends where you start from, I suppose.

Psychoanalytic criticism makes no claim to be speaking in terms that Shakespeare's culture would have recognized, its resolute anachronism being one reason for Vickers's particular hostility. *The Undiscover'd Country* (London: Free Association Books, 1993), edited by B. J. Sokol, opens with a measured defence – one curiously enough enlisting such approaches to a turn against 'current trends' in Shakespeare criticism – and in the varied essays that follow the sympathetic reader will find interesting material. The strongest essays seem to me to be Lyn Stephens' '"A Wilderness of Monkeys": A Psychodynamic Study of *The Merchant of*

Venice', which explores the 'surprising savagery and ruthlessness' of the play with some telling comments on Antonio's manipulative inadequacy, and on the ways in which Portia and Shylock respond to the various constraints laid upon them, and B. J. Sokol's own contribution on *The Tempest*, justly observing that much recent criticism begins 'by assuming that the only human relations having real significance are relations of power', and arguing instead for the inner struggle of Prospero as the play's motor.

Source studies are, to some at least of the newer critics, impossible territory, implying as they do authorial control of the text, and from the critic a control upon the limits of interpretation defined by specific, detailed and demonstrable relationships. But, paradoxically enough, the notion of intertextual dialogue can act as a valuable stimulant even for critics who wish to retain contact with Shakespeare the individual author. Two books, neither of them unaware of recent debate though both 'traditional' in their underlying assumptions, demonstrate how familiar ground can be freshly ploughed.

Leah Scragg's *Shakespeare's Mouldy Tales: Recurrent Plot Motifs in Shakespearian Drama* (London and New York: Longman, 1992) examines the playwright's treatment of six motifs – sibling confusion, gender exchange, scolding, substitute coupling, exile, and putative death – in order to demonstrate the dexterousness of Shakespeare's artful transformations of his sources and insistent reworkings of his own dramatic structures. It is a book in a series specifically designed for the student and general reader – and the introduction on imitation, together with frequent summaries of the plots of plays are clearly there to help this audience. In closely detailed consideration and comparison of plays Scragg shows herself a sensitive and discriminating reader. It is a book to be recommended to students – and more experienced scholars will find, for example, her treatment of the reworkings of the motif of banishment from the early histories through to the romances, as well as her discrimination between the uses of the bed-trick in *All's Well* and *Measure for Measure*, enlightening.

'My aim in this book', says Brian Gibbons, of his *Shakespeare and Multiplicity* (Cambridge: Cambridge University Press, 1993), 'is to take some examples which focus on Shakespeare's art of translating – or better, transfiguring – material into the three-dimensional language of theatre.' It is a purpose amply vindicated in the work that follows. Studies of *Cymbeline* and the matter of Britain, *Measure for Measure* and its relationship to Whetstone's *Promos and Cassandra*, *Antony and Cleopatra* and Marlowe, are all richly argued, informed by a strong sense of the plays in the theatre, and of the ways in which they can be remade in a contemporary context. The essay on *As You Like It* argues convincingly for the pervasive influence of Sidney's *Arcadia* on Shakespeare's imagination, an influence that has, it seems to me, been consistently underrated in the past; but perhaps the most powerful of all the chapters in this continuously stimulating book is that entitled 'Shakespeare's "Road of excess": *Titus Andronicus, The Taming of the Shrew, King Lear*'. The links between their 'dramatisations of cultural systems under pressure' are persuasively presented, and the relationships of the two tragedies to Marlowe's *Tamburlaine* are profitably explored. This is a consistently readable book, free from jargon, but not therefore from subtlety. It demonstrates, perhaps even more convincingly than Foakes's book, that one does not have to become a disciple of a theoretical school in order to have benefited from some of the procedures that the last thirty years or so have made possible.

A rather more self-consciously theoretical perspective on Shakespeare's borrowing is offered by Linda Woodbridge, in her crowded but stimulating article 'Patchwork: Piecing the Early Modern Mind in England's First Century of Print Culture' (*English Literary Renaissance*, 23, 1993, 5–45). She builds an analogy between patchwork, quilting, cannibalism and the literary methods of Shakespeare and his contemporaries to suggest ways in which early modern culture was linked to, absorbed and redirected 'old tales, redolent of that vanishing world – rural, feudal, chivalric, parochial, magical, oral'.

Attacks on Bradleian notions of character predate current theoretical squabbles, but character-study is still often seen as one of the major symptoms of a regrettable allegiance to 'liberal humanism'. It is perhaps a sign that the hegemony of theory is waning that new attempts are being made to find ways of talking about character that do not simply lapse into novelistic, nineteenth-century descriptive modes. Two books this year attempt the task, neither, it must be said, with complete success.

Imtiaz Habib is interested in the discontinuities of Shakespearian characterization, which he suggests may be related to anamorphic painting. If this might seem to imply a Greenblattian approach, Habib's *Shakespeare's Pluralistic Concepts of Character: A Study in Dramatic Anamorphism* (Selinsgrove: Susquehanna University Press; London and Toronto: Associated University Presses, 1993) is in fact much less ambitious. He attempts to categorize and distinguish different ways in which Shakespeare manipulates multiple perspectives 'in an attempt to probe dramaturgically the ambiguity and relativism of changing human perception and experience'. Underneath it all, however, is a conviction that the plays are a continuous attempt to find 'the core of human personality that remains identifiably whole and unchanging in the flux of experience and that can be described and understood through art'. Christy Desmet's *Reading Shakespeare's Characters* (Amherst: University of Massachusetts Press, 1992) is altogether more ambitious. At its centre is an exploration of the role played by rhetoric in fashioning and representing character. She draws on rhetoricians from Plato to Paul de Man, taking in Coleridge and other eighteenth- and nineteenth-century critics in the course of the study. The book begins strongly, with a discussion of Ophelia's rhetorical description of Hamlet which points out the way in which 'observer and observed fashion themselves by reading one another through a repertoire of shared rhetorical forms', and ends with a good chapter on the problematic representation of 'female rhetoricians', Venus, Isabella and Helena. In between, a discussion of three late eighteenth-century studies of Falstaff is stimulating, but chapters examining the function of particular rhetorical forms – epideictic in *Cymbeline*, hyperbole in *Othello*, *King John* and *The Winter's Tale*, and the proverbial in *King Lear*, for all their moments of revealing insight, seem to me much less clearly focused. This is a book which will repay consideration, but one that seems ultimately not yet fully thought through.

Desmet's comments on eighteenth-century shifts of critical perspective can usefully be complemented by Jean I. Marsden's 'The Individual Reader and the Canonized Text: Shakespeare Criticism After Johnson' (*Eighteenth Century Life*, 17, 1993, 62–80) which charts the way in which responses to Johnson's edition mark out a shift from consideration of the 'overall effect of the play and its observation of poetic justice' to a more atomized concentration on moments of feeling, individual speeches and characters considered in isolation from the plot.

There are valuable reflections on the idea of character, too, in Douglas Lanier's '"Stigmatical in Making": The Material Character of *The Comedy of Errors*' (*English Literary Renaissance*, 23, 1993, 81–112). A thorough investigation of the play, of the conditions of its performance, including the special features of its rendition as part of the Gray's Inn revels, leads to a recognition that 'Shakespeare demonstrates that character is in effect an ongoing inference we make from outward marks, a hypothesis that demands constant interpretive support.' The essay not only takes the play more seriously than has perhaps been customary, it also offers insights that go well beyond the particular focus on one play.

Of the books on character M. M. Mahood's *Bit Parts in Shakespeare's Plays* (Cambridge: Cambridge University Press, 1992) is perhaps the most appealing. It is grounded in the practicalities of performance (with frequent reference to actual stagings of the plays), as it investigates the varieties of functions served by the Messengers, Gentlemen, Ladies-in-waiting and others, named but briefly present, who populate the plays. After setting out some of the various functions that such characters might serve – as scene-shifters, providers of bridge-passages, 'feeds' and foils for major characters and the like – Mahood considers six representative plays in more detail. The writing is consistently a pleasure to read – as for example when she observes that 'it is hard to believe in corruption boiling and bubbling in Vienna, as the Duke later describes it, when all that rises to the surface is Froth'. The book is packed with possibilities for the theatre director – as for example the conjecture that a Servant's failure to recognize Isabella when he introduces her to Angelo might indicate that she has actually taken her vows and appears dressed as a nun. The whole study is founded on the conviction that the 'imaginative fulfilment of even the most inexperienced actor and the most humdrum audience may underlie the vibrant contradiction felt in so many of Shakespeare's minimal characters between their perceived social insignificance and their felt individual significance'. Not at all a book for the theorist (many of the larger interpretations of the plays are very traditional) it is yet full of particular moments of perception.

COMEDIES

One of the features of Shakespeare criticism in recent years has been the ever-increasing attention devoted to the comedies. But they are still the plays that students find most difficult, and least appealing. Two books offer approaches to the earlier comedies that undergraduates will find useful. Camilla Slights, in her *Shakespeare's Comic Commonwealth* (Toronto, Buffalo and London: Toronto University Press, 1993) distances herself equally from C. L. Barber and Northrop Frye, from the model of subversion and containment as from that of psychological maturation, proposing instead that all the earlier comedies are concerned with the ways in which 'society adjusts to meet challenge and change, and individuals adjust – consciously or unconsciously, willingly or unwillingly – in order to take their places within society'. Hierarchical paradigms, she argues, are not overturned, though their inconsistencies might be exposed. Many of the individual chapters have insightful comments to make. Slights's discussion of *Love's Labour's Lost* as a 'treatment of the impact of humanist education on an hierarchical society', of the language games of *Much Ado About Nothing*, and of patterns of gift-giving and reciprocity in *Twelfth Night*, for example, are all useful. It is a blessedly clearly written book, even if its horizons are somewhat limited. Gunnar Sorelius' survey of the comedies up to *A Midsummer Night's Dream*, *Shakespeare's Early Comedies: Myth, Metamorphosis, Mannerism* (Uppsala, 1993) argues that these early plays explore the way the individual self is constructed 'through love in a world of Ovidian metamorphic instability and chance'. It is a straightforward line, and some of the parallels he draws with classical texts and with contemporary mannerist art are suggestive. There is, however, a certain leadenness about the style – and the grudging response to Bottom, who 'remains throughout the same selfish and unobservant character' is typical of a kind of earnest simplification that runs through many of the analyses.

There have been a number of discussions of the sources of the comedies, and it may be helpful to notice them together. In an article spread over two issues of *The Review of English Studies* (43, 1992, 467–87 and 44, 1993, 1–15) entitled 'Aristotelian Wealth and the Sea of Love: Shakespeare's Synthesis of Greek Philosophy and Roman Poetry in *The Merchant of*

Venice', Isabella Wheater suggests that the play echoes 'a particular combination of ethical vocabulary' that Shakespeare found in Aristotle's *Nichomachean Ethics*; indeed she argues that he absorbed the logical structure of the classical text 'in its entirety, with all Aristotle's central concerns and large articulations underpinning the play's plot, characterization and language'. Particularly useful is her discussion of the idea of wealth, both material and symbolic, and her deployment of Aristotle's differentiation of categories of friendship. The argument extends further, to take in significant refashioning of *Il Pecorone*, and to suggest other mythical stories and classical texts that impinge upon the play. Not all the parallels are equally persuasive, and the effect is rather to smooth out the theatrical troublesomeness of the play, but this is an article that will have to be taken into account in any subsequent discussion. Another source for the play is offered in Joan Ozark Holmer's 'Miles Mosse, *The Arraignment and Conviction of Vsurie* (1595): A New Source for *The Merchant of Venice*' (*Shakespeare Studies*, 21, 1993, 11–44). Whether Shakespeare knew this particular text or not, the parallels between their discussions of usury are suggestive. Robert S. Miola, in 'New Comedy in *All's Well That Ends Well*' (*Renaissance Quarterly*, 46, 1993, 23–42) convincingly demonstrates that the play is fashioned from motifs deriving both directly from the classics, and from Shakespeare's own earlier reworkings of Latin New Comedy. Especially helpful is his identification of Parolles and Bertram as a 'splitting' of the figure of the *miles gloriosus*.

The variety of emphases in other critical works makes it perhaps more useful to consider them play-by-play, rather than attempting the kind of categorization into critical schools that Vickers sees as an awful sign of theory's domination. I begin with a scatter of single articles.

J. L. Calderwood's 'Coming Out in Shakespeare's *Two Gentlemen of Verona*', (*ELH* 60, 1993, 857–68) is a typically inventive piece. He discusses the play as a narrative of Shakespeare's 'coming out' as dramatist, as a story of leaving home, and one which ultimately locates the place of desire in the cross-dressed Julia, who becomes 'a reassuring means of reconciling auto/homoerotic mutuality with the heterosexuality which patriarchy and the generic conclusion of comedy require'. On the way we have amusing readings of Lance's little narrative, and a number of unsupportable puns: 'The grass/grace homonym conjoins the pubic with the divine', he says – but I just don't believe it.

A number of writers in recent years have severely modified older assumptions about the function of 'symbolic' music in the plays. In an important article, 'Hands, Feet and Bottoms: Decentering the Cosmic Dance in *A Midsummer Night's Dream*' (*Shakespeare Quarterly*, 44, 1993, 325–42) Skiles Howard does the same for dance. Distinctions are made between popular and courtly dance – and suggestions offered for the ways in which each figured both class and gender hierarchy. I am not convinced that these distinctions were as absolute or as stable in the period as they are made to seem. The music for dances moved between the popular and the courtly; and the contention that dance always figured the woman as subservient needs qualification. What of Elizabeth's own prowess as a dancer for example, or the complicated relationships of power figured in the dances of female masquers in the early seventeenth century? But there is plenty here to suggest further avenues for thought and research.

The Merry Wives of Windsor's difference from other comedies is frequently remarked. It is explored as a humours comedy which, unlike the romantic plays, 'resists sexual adventure by exposing it as unhealthy fantasy' by Grace Tiffany in 'Falstaff's False Staff: "Jonsonian" Asexuality in *Merry Wives of Windsor*' (*Comparative Drama*, 26, 1992, 254–70).

The wrestling match in *As You Like It* is the

focus of Cynthia Marshall's attention ('Wrestling as Play and Game in *As You Like It*', *SEL*, 33, 1993, 265–88). She usefully contextualizes the contest and suggests ways in which, as both sport and earnest, it is an apt prelude for the later action of the play, acting as 'mimetic violence, as game, as spectacle, and, eventually as metaphor'. The conclusion, that wrestling 'demonstrates how social codes are continually being made, broken and remade' showing in 'its spectacle of violence, the ongoing process we call culture' has a certain humourless predictability about it.

It is, however, *Twelfth Night* which has attracted by far the most attention. Generations of students and playgoers have had problems with the scene of Malvolio's tormenting. Chris R. Hassell, Jr in 'Malvolio's Dark Concupiscence' (*Cahiers Elisabéthains*, 43, 1993, 1–22) suggests Luther's discussion of the deluded self-righteousness of those whose belief is in salvation by merit rather than grace as background for understanding a Malvolio who 'ends as he begins, rich of self-love, darkly ignorant, heathenish and concupiscent in righteousness, and imprisoned in all these figurative ways by Goodman Devil'. It is an ingenious exegesis, even if it cannot quite explain away the problem. The gender politics of the play most fascinate theorists – and, it must be said, most interest the average undergraduate these days. Three articles dealing with this topic might well be taken to illustrate both the benefits and dangers of the approach. Lisa Jardine in 'Twins and Travesties: *Twelfth Night*', in Susan Zimmerman, ed. *Erotic Politics* (London: Routledge, 1993, pp. 27–38), argues that young boys and women, existing in a relationship of dependence and obedience, were both potentially vulnerable and sexually available when outside the confines of the home. In the case of *Twelfth Night*, she argues, 'the erotic potential of service is appropriately contained within the admissible boundaries of the patriarchal household'. Her contention that 'eroticism . . . is not gender-specific, is not grounded in the sex of the possibly "submissive" partner, but is an expectation of that very submissiveness' is a valuable widening of the scope of much of the recent commentary on cross-dressing in the theatre – even though I think it still slips too easily from one kind of love to another. Because erotic and sexual boundaries were differently perceived in the sixteenth century it does not, I think, follow that there were no boundaries at all. In contrast to this tightly argued essay comes Dympna Callaghan's '"And all is semblative a woman's part": body politics and *Twelfth Night*' (*Textual Practice*, 7, 1993, 428–523). She devotes a good deal of time to Malvolio's reading of Maria's letter, particularly to the C's, U's and T's which, in her view, 'put Olivia's private parts on display for everyone's amusement'. Somehow this letter both 'feminizes, ridicules and castrates' Malvolio, as well as leading to the amazing suggestion: 'that Malvolio comically presents himself as having familiarity with Olivia's private parts, can also be read as a claim to have engaged in mutual masturbation'. No amount of citation of accounts of the fondling of females at the theatre or in court cases can justify this nonsense. In an altogether more modest, but suggestive essay Martha Ronk focuses on Viola's two emblematic speeches – the 'willow cabin' and Patience speeches – to suggest something of the problematic doubleness in her character and dramatic function as 'a central character who is richly and complexly gendered, who is both dramatic and allegorical, both imprisoned and free, both silent and a voice echoing to the hills'. ('Viola's (Lack of) Patience', *Centennial Review*, 37, 1993, 384–99). On a related but distinct theme Karin S. Coddon adds another piece to the growing pile of criticism dealing with social, rather than gender, instability with her '"Slander in an Allow'd Fool": *Twelfth Night*'s Crisis of the Aristocracy' (*SEL*, 33, 1993, 309–25).

'The medical metaphor in *All's Well* bears the largest burden in articulating the alteration of socio-political reality', argues Julie Robin

Solomon in 'Mortality as Matter of Mind: Towards a Politics of Problems in *All's Well That Ends Well*' (*English Literary Renaissance*, 23, 1993, 134–69). She develops at length the contrast between Galenic medicine's belief in knowledge's limits and Paracelsian ambition, as a figure for the play's 'series of oppositions between knowledge and mortality, private wish and public reality, and culture and nature'. The prioritization of medicine as the topic which 'allows Shakespeare to dismantle sure distinctions about where nature ends and culture begins' seems, in the end, rather overstated, but there are many stimulating ideas in this account. That more space does not necessarily lead to clearer argument is demonstrated in a book-length study of the play, *Shakespeare's Courtly Mirror: Reflexivity and Prudence in 'All's Well That End's Well'* (Newark: University of Delaware Press; London and Toronto: Associated University Presses, 1993), by David Haley. He deals with medicine and alchemy, but suggests also the play's relationships with biblical story (especially that of Ahab) and what he sees as Boccaccio's agnostic secularism. Uncontentiously he argues that the play as a whole is concentrated on analysis of the court and courtly behaviour. More surprisingly, perhaps, Bertram is viewed positively as a figure in pursuit of an heroic self-determination, and Helena divested of the quasi-allegorical function she is frequently given. Crucial to his analysis of these characters, and his view of the play's design as a whole, are concepts of 'reflexivity' and 'heroic prudence', concepts which, despite Haley's definitions and frequent iterations, I find slippery in the extreme. Some of his readings seem to me distinctly odd, wilfully running against the grain of the text, and the whole is elusive.

Two contrasting articles on *Measure for Measure* both have sexuality as their theme. Mario Digangi, in 'Pleasure and Danger: Measuring Female Sexuality in *Measure for Measure*', (*ELH*, 60, 1993, 589–610), takes issue with feminist critics who have found this play unreadable. The pleasure a feminist reader (and possibly a Renaissance woman) can take, she suggests, comes from 'reading oppositionally'. In a surprising move, Mistress Elbow, the only legitimate wife in the play, though she never appears, is invoked as an agent for destabilizing the familiar patriarchal trinity of virgin/wife/whore, rendering suspect even the middle term. The play's anxiety about female sexuality, therefore, itself 'opens the way for a feminist reading of female pleasure and the dangers it poses to male rule'. I'm still not sure how one moves from the first to the second element in this proposition – but as a male reader I suppose that's only what might be expected? I found rather more of benefit in a soundly researched essay by Victoria Hayne, 'Performing Social Practice: The Example of *Measure for Measure*' (*Shakespeare Quarterly*, 44, 1993, 1–29), which sets the play in the context of the debate about the regulation of sexual appetite that brought Puritans into conflict with the Ecclesiastical Courts during the early seventeenth century. The article is valuable for its documentation of this contest, and the contention that the comedic form of the play is itself an act of mediation between extreme views is plausible.

Shortly before his death in 1987 the Bulgarian scholar, Marco Mincoff, published his study of the romances, *Things Supernatural and Causeless: Shakespearian Romance*, a book originally written during the 1970s. It is now reissued, by the University of Delaware Press (Newark, 1992), with some unspecified 'revision'. In striking contrast to both older and newer critics who have given these plays a special place in the canon, Mincoff attacks those who would see them as marked by an especial profundity. To him romance is self-evidently an inferior genre; he asserts that the ideas contained in the last plays are unsurprising, and comments unfavourably on the thinness of their characterization. Yet he still wishes to claim for the romances a capacity to lay hold on a sense of wonder. *The Tempest* is 'a miracle of perfect blending', *The Winter's Tale* (perhaps the play for which he finds most to say) invests its commonplace ideas with 'emotional and imaginative power'. I find this contradictory attitude confused rather than enabling.

Peggy Muñoz Simonds, in sharp contrast, takes *Cymbeline* very seriously indeed. Her *Myth, Emblem, and Music in Shakespeare's Cymbeline* (Newark: University of Delaware Press; London and Toronto: Associated University Presses, 1992) harks back to an earlier critical era in its explication of the play as a Neo-Platonic, Orphic celebration through a minute reading of all its elements against the iconographic tradition represented in the emblem books. In this enormously scholarly, but fragmented work there are many revelations – the discussion of Imogen's bedchamber and of the image of the ivy and elm, for example, are especially illuminating. It must be agreed that systems of correspondences were part of the habitual mental furniture of the Renaissance; overall, however, the process by which a link is made between some detail in the play and a pictorial emblem, which then becomes the basis of an elaboration of the significance of that detail, expands signification but freezes dramatic potential. I learnt a good deal from the book, but ultimately do not feel closer to the experience of the play itself, which seems altogether more complicated and less secure than Simonds makes it.

Two rather bland essays consider the genre of *The Winter's Tale*. Verna A. Foster suggests that the audience is prepared for Hermione's resurrection by the way tragic possibility is continuously deflected in the earlier part of the play (*Cahiers Elisabéthains*, 43, 1993, 43–56), while Robert Henke suggests that the mixed genre of this play 'exemplifies the "unwritten poetics" of tragicomic dramaturgy as most thoroughly articulated by Guarini' (*Comparative Drama*, 27, 1993, 197-217). Neither of these essays breaks much new ground, but a more surprising context for the play is proffered by Donna B. Hamilton, in '*The Winter's Tale* and the Language of Union, 1604–1610' (*Shakespeare Studies*, 21, 1993, 228–52). Hermione, she suggests, deploys a rhetoric that echoes James's pleas for his project of Union, and she contends that the difficulties and dangers of the scheme are figured in the relationships of Bohemia and Sicilia. It is an ingenious, but to me unpersuasive argument.

Caliban is discussed in three essays. Victor Bourgy presents him as 'the invisible reference point, from which radiate concentric ripples of meaning' (*Cahiers Elisabéthains*, 43, 1993, 35–42). More suggestive is a brief note in the same journal (57–60) by Martin W. Walsh, linking Caliban's song of freedom to hiring customs, where 'heavy wine-drinking and the rural labourer's illusion of freedom' prevailed. The 'colonial' reading receives a new twist in Mark Taylor's engaging piece, 'Prospero's Books and Stephano's Bottle: Colonial Experience in *The Tempest*' (*Clio*, 22, 1993, 101–13). He draws attention to the way Caliban's urging of his co-conspirators to seize Prospero's books counterpoints Stephano's calling upon him to 'kiss the book' which is his bottle, and argues that Caliban makes the same interpretative mistake with both, in failing to perceive the metonymy that each enacts. He points to Hariot's description of an analogous confusion amongst the Amerindians about the properties of the Bible to argue that a book 'is not mainly a physical object but rather a convenient way of representing that which can reside in such an object and also in a human head, but only the head of a man taught the reading lessons that were never offered Caliban'. Pierre Iselin considers the liminal, double nature of music in *The Tempest* in his '*The Tempest* et ses Musiques: Mythe et Dramaturgie' (*Etudes Anglaises*, 46, 1993, 385–97), its implication both in mythic symbolic narratives and in the practicalities of theatrical manipulation.

HISTORIES

Henry V receives more attention than any other of the histories this year. It is a play which often divides critics along predictable political lines, provoking polarized responses. Antony Brennan's *New Critical Introduction* in the Harvester/Twayne series (1993) attempts a more balanced view. Central to his argument is the history of the play in performance – where he notes the scale of cuts that have enabled performers to simplify the text's effect. Crucial, too, is his reading of the Chorus as presenting a view of events which the play itself wants us to recognize as but partial. His *Henry V* is a play which sets out 'the paradox of political leadership which Shakespeare explored throughout his career' (116), enabling us to see the conscious manipulation of self-image by its hero and to register the cost and the fragility of his triumph but yet not tipping into mere satire. I could have wished for rather more contextualization in terms of the late-Elizabethan political situation, but it is a solidly executed reading, and the frequent reference to recent productions, including widely circulated film versions, is likely to be stimulating to students. Henry's strategies of self-presentation are considered also by Kathryn Kunkel, in 'The Crown That Ate Prince Hal' (*Papers of the Shakespeare and Renaissance Association of West Virginia*, 52–61), succinctly analysing the ways in which Henry as King continuously and consistently denies his own agency in events and is, in her view, totally unable to reconcile private and public roles. A subtler and more challenging view of Henry's earlier career also emphasizing his instability as a character but linking it to 'an unease about theatrical mimesis written into the plays' is offered by Matthew H. Wikander in 'The Protean Prince Hal' in *Comparative Drama*, 27, 1993, 295–311. He concludes that 'the *Henry IV* plays are ambivalent about theatre insofar as they are ambivalent about kingship, and they are ambivalent about kingship insofar as kingship is theatrical'. The argument is not novel, but the association of the critics' problems with Prince Hal with anti-theatrical prejudice gives an interesting slant to a familiar topic.

How far Shakespeare's sympathies lie with the common soldiers is a central question for a number of these critics. How to view Jack Cade's rebellion in the earlier *Henry VI, 2* poses similar problems. Paola Pugliatti settles for the compromise verdict that it could be read simultaneously in different ways by attempting to look at the way the play as a whole dramatizes and inflects its sources. She suggests that the play consistently emphasizes the corruption of the noble class, and therefore gives some credence to the view that Cade's rebellion is produced by them, even whilst abhorring the egalitarian tendency of the rebels themselves ('"More than history can pattern": The Jack Cade rebellion in Shakespeare's *Henry VI, 2*', *Journal of Medieval and Renaissance Studies*, 22, 1992, 451–78).

Two of the least-discussed history plays are represented in successive issues of *Theatre History Studies*. B. A. Kachur discusses a spectacular staging of *King John* in 1899, in 'Shakespeare Politicized: Beerbohm Tree's *King John* and the Boer War' (12, 1992, 25–44) and suggests that the nature of the performance was conditioned by the Boer War, which had long been anticipated and began shortly after the first performance. A chiming with patriotic fervour accounts for the choice of the play, and for the shaping of the text that Tree gave it – and the failure of the War to deliver the anticipated quick victories led Tree to shift to escapist plays, and never to restage this one. Tree's performances were noted for their historical 'accuracy'. Hugh M. Richmond suggests that such historical pedantry of presentation has marked the performance history of *Henry VIII*, but sees this as a proper response to the play's own preoccupation with 'truth', signalled by its alternative title, *All is True*. In his view the BBC television Shakespeare, with its 'authentic' settings, gets the play right – and he suggests, in opposition to 'current literary theory', that 'criticism of the play has proved convincing in direct proportion to its acceptance of a realistic mode of performance for it'. ('Shakespeare's Last Experiment in Verismo: A Performance Approach to *All is True*', 13, 1993, 47–62) The argument, it seems to me, begs as many questions as it answers.

TRAGEDIES

Only one general book on the tragedies has come my way this year. Zulfikar Ghose's *Shakespeare's Mortal Knowledge* (London: Macmillan, 1993) seems to be written in innocence of all criticism of the plays (except Eliot on *Hamlet*), in ignorance of the problematic nature of the texts themselves, and without very much to offer except a personal, not to say idiosyncratic commentary (eight pages out of thirty-two on *King Lear* are devoted to the proposition that Cordelia speaks as she does because she wants to be disinherited in order to ensure that she marries France).

Juhani Rudanko offers an approach to three tragedies, *Othello*, *Coriolanus*, and *Timon of Athens*, based on linguistics, and promising an escape from 'contingent historicism', since linguistic research aims at the discovery of 'universals' that 'support the idea that man is an essence'. *Pragmatic Approaches to Shakespeare* (Lanham, New York and London: University Press of America, 1993) subjects each of the three plays to particular analyses, discussing, for example, some of the linguistic strategies of 'topic control' that Iago deploys in his persuasion of Othello, or the ways in which 'case grammar' might be applied to soliloquies, producing 'indices of agentivity' for Othello and Iago. The simple question one must ask of a study such as this is whether the considerable labour of categorization of linguistic utterance enables clarified perception of what is going on in the plays. Rudanko observes in his concluding remarks that 'linguistic approaches are not very fashionable'. Though I am not expert enough to judge his contribution to linguistic theory, I fear that few literary students will be prepared to take on board the technicalities of such linguistic description when the rewards seem to be confirmation of the fairly obvious, rather than startling new insights.

Hamlet, according to Foakes, has slipped from its position as 'Shakespeare's greatest play'. It has to be said that this year it has not produced a particularly good selection of commentary on it. *Hamlet Studies* collects James R. Andreas's reflections on the language of Hamlet and Claudius as respectively the 'vulgar' and 'polite', the dialogic and monologic of Bakhtin; Larry S. Champion's discussion of proverbs in the play; a disarmingly modest piece by Neil L. York speculating on why American Revolutionaries found *Hamlet* a congenial text for co-option and parody; William E. Sheidley's introduction to, and translation of, Louis Henry's 1816 ballet version, which leaves Hamlet in possession of the Danish crown at the end, and A. Banerjee's not very persuasive suggestion that Jimmy Porter in Osborne's play is 'a modern Hamlet'. I was not much persuaded, either, by James O. Taylor's 'The Influence of Rapier Fencing in *Hamlet*' (*Forum for Modern Language Studies*, 29, 1993, 203–15), which argues that the rhetorical figure of 'penetrative words' is analogical to the play's preoccupation with fencing. Film and television versions of the ending are described in a rather unfocused piece by H. R. Coursen in the *Selected Papers of the Shakespeare and Renaissance Association of West Virginia* (16, 1993, 1–14), drawing attention especially to the question of whether or not Fortinbras' arrival is cut. Rather more is on offer in David Thatcher's sceptical account of Horatio's final summary of the action in 'Horatio's "Let me speak": Narrative Summary and Summary Narrative in *Hamlet*' (*English Studies*, 74, 1993, 246–57). But much the best essay I have encountered is Luke Wilson's '*Hamlet*, Hales v. Petit and the Hysteresis of Action' (*ELH*, 60, 1993, 17–56). He has some fascinating things to say about the issues of intentionality and the fictive and retrospective process of story-making involved both in legal discourse and in the play, and he embeds his discussion in a complex consideration of agency and intention in current historicist criticism.

A much more interesting clutch of articles is devoted to *Troilus and Cressida*. James P. Bednarz returns to the suggestion that it was the play in which Shakespeare administered his 'purge' to Ben Jonson in *Shakespeare Studies*, 21, 175–213 ('Shakespeare's Purge of Jonson: The Literary Context of *Troilus and Cressida*'). Peter Hyland's 'Legitimacy in Interpretation: The Bastard Voice in *Troilus and Cressida*' (*Mosaic*, 26, 1993, 1–13) suggests that Thersites' claim to be a bearer of 'truth' has been systematically underplayed by critics, and argues that belated insistence on his bastardy marks Thersites out as '"the illegitimate voice", the spokesman for a whole constituency of those who have been marginalized'. Feminist criticism has long been interested in the figure of Cressida and her oppression. With the current controversy about date-rape hovering in the background, Grace Tiffany argues in somewhat paradoxical fashion that 'sympathetic' evaluations of Cressida which emphasize her imprisonment by male values are unhelpful; instead, she claims, the feminist critic should recognize the degree to which Cressida consents in her self-erasure. 'Rather than positing that female decisions are determined by a patriarchal universe', she concludes, 'we may study the ways that universe is ratified by female consent.' ('Not Saying No: Female Self-Erasure in *Troilus and Cressida*', *Texas Studies in Literature and Language*, 35, 1993, 44–56). Gary Spear focuses, by contrast, upon the representation of masculinity, or at least of effeminate males, in the play. As he rightly suggests, 'effeminacy' is a very elusive term within the language of Renaissance England, and he goes some way to elucidating its function in this particular play. Especially useful is his noting of the way 'effeminacy' can signal an 'excess of masculinity'. (It is perhaps a pity he did not consider the play's musical scene, which concentrates ambivalence of effeminacy and desire interestingly.) This essay raises ideas that could profitably be extended.

Two articles concern themselves, rather predictably, with the issue of Othello's blackness. James R. Aubrey makes a useful, if not entirely original, survey of contextual material on Elizabethan attitudes in 'Race and the Spectacle of the Monstrous in *Othello*' (*Clio*, 22, 1993, 239–50), and offers the possibility that the frequent association of blackness with 'monstrous birth' can be taken as a metaphor for Iago's 'impregnation' of Othello's mind. A much more highly theorized, though perhaps not more helpful, approach to this question is Arthur L. Little Jr's '"An essence that's not seen": The Primal Scene of Racism in *Othello*' (*Shakespeare Quarterly*, 44, 1993, 304–24). It is a clotted and anxious essay in its attempts to stake out a difference for his approach from other critics who have tackled the same subject. For him, it is the 'scene of sexual intercourse' between Othello and Desdemona which 'functions, for the on- and off-stage audience alike, as the sexual site and sight of the play's racial anxieties', and the play, in his view 'probes Othello's blackness', its metaphoric origins as well as literal presence.

Geoffrey Aggeler contextualizes notions of pity in *King Lear*, setting the Stoic expulsion of pity as a virtue against Calvin's acceptance of it to argue that Edgar's progress can be charted as a movement from 'bad pity' to 'good' (*Neophilologus*, 77, 1993, 321–32). It is the pity that both Gloucester and Lear discover for those they have neglected that has focused a good deal of recent critical debate about the extent of Shakespeare's radicalism. Judy Kronenfeld, in '"So distribution should undo excess, and each man have enough": Shakespeare's *King Lear* – Anabaptist Egalitarianism, Anglican Charity, Both, Neither' (*ELH*, 59, 1992, 755–84) surveys some of these critical responses, and in a carefully documented essay analyses Gloucester's key terms 'distribution' and 'excess' to argue that the radicalism of his sentiments can be, and has been, overstated. Demonstrating the omnipresence of just such terms in a wide range of contemporary discussions of charity she takes issue, too, with attempts to see Gloucester as in some way ventriloquizing a popular perspective, arguing instead that rich and poor alike habitually distinguished charity from egalitarianism. This is an excellent essay, attending closely to the semantic and cultural fields of the play's words. It seems to me to be 'historicism' ('old' or 'new') that is really attempting to do what historical scholarship should.

As Derek Cohen notes, Lear is often compared with Timon of Athens, but in his 'The Politics of Wealth: *Timon of Athens*' (*Neophilologus*, 57, 1993, 149–60) he argues that the later(?) play is 'less transformative in its impulses'. Though 'the poor are the dirty little secret of both worlds' they are more passionately acknowledged by Lear, for Timon 'sees poverty as a grotesque deformation of his desert'. For Cohen this releases the revolutionary possibility of the play since there is no attempt to suggest that the system could be ameliorated, but recognizes that it may only be excoriated in Timon's outbursts.

Much more has been written on *Macbeth*, though not a great deal that seems to me particularly productive. Anthony Paul's *The Torture of the Mind: 'Macbeth', Tragedy and Chiasmus* (Amsterdam: Thesis Publishers, 1992) is a book which seems unsure of where it is going. The shades of the doctoral thesis from which it grew hang round its rather pedantic explication of the presence of the rhetorical figure of chiasmus in the play, a figure which Paul sees as central not only to its language but to the dramatic patterning of the deaths that punctuate the play. This discussion seems only tangentially connected to the latter part of the book, which treats largely of the play's central figures, and particularly of Macbeth's journey 'into a forbidden and dangerous place'. Paul has no time at all for any attempt to read the play in terms of its contemporary political context, and this gives a disembodied feel to his exegesis. It is a disappointing book.

Freud had problems with Lady Macbeth; Anny Crunelle Vanrigh suggests that this is because the play is not concerned with the oedipal scene, but the pre-oedipal 'where the son, in order to secure permanent symbiosis with the mother kills the figure planning to force him into unwelcome growth'. ('*Macbeth*: Oedipus Transposed', *Cahiers Elisabéthains*, 43, 1993, 21–34). The argument is a less persuasive version of that advanced by Adelman. In a wide-ranging essay Stanley Cavell offers a tentative mapping of intimations about the play, its relationship to history, its speech and silences and its presentation of the marriage of the Macbeths. He writes in an insistently self-questioning style which leaves at least this reader very uncertain as to where he is being led. Suggestive though some of the ideas are, the article would have benefited from tighter and clearer focus (*Raritan* 12.2, 1992, 1–15 and 12.3 1993, 1–15). James L. O'Rourke offers a much more decided reading, in which '*Macbeth* engages the central problem of a Christian metaphysic, the conflict between divine omniscience and human free will, and emerges with the gloomiest of verdicts, as neither Divine Providence nor human volition can account for the action of the play.' ('The Subversive Metaphysics of *Macbeth*', *Shakespeare Studies*, 21, 213–27).

Two essays of very different kinds consider the protagonists of *Antony and Cleopatra*. In a complex argument, bringing together contemporary psychoanalysis and Burton's analysis of melancholia, Cynthia Marshall suggests that Antony's fragmented identity 'opens an interior space between governing self-image and performance in the world' – a space 'inhabited by melancholy'. The extension of her argument is that the yearning for stable, interior identity not only characterizes Antony, but defines the nature of the audience's response to the play and to its characters, so that '*Antony and Cleopatra* shows love and melancholy to be the mutually constituting terms of a subject's identifications.' It is an ambitious essay, and makes a fruitful contribution to this year's crop of books and articles reconsidering the notion of 'character', even if in execution it is rather less than clear (*Shakespeare Quarterly*, 44, 1993, 385–408). Cleopatra is the subject of Laura Severt King's 'Blessed when they were riggish: Shakespeare's Cleopatra and Christianity's Penitent Prostitutes' (*Journal of Medieval and Renaissance Studies*, 22, 1992, 429–49). The bulk of the article establishes the tradition, but in the last few pages she suggests that Cleopatra distinguishes herself from it, and endorses the separation of whore and saint that had become common in Shakespeare's period, and is the Roman view within the play.

REPRINTED ESSAYS

John F. Andrews collects a variety of responses to *Romeo and Juliet*, from Traversi in 1956 to Hodgdon in 1989, in the Garland series. It is a more balanced survey than many in this series, with essays grouped under the headings of 'Language and Structure', 'Performance' and the play 'as a Product of Elizabethan Culture' (New York and London: Garland, 1993). Two *New Casebooks* have appeared, on the History plays, edited by Graham Holderness, and *King Lear*, edited by Kiernan Ryan. Their tenor can perhaps be deduced from the dust-jackets, which claim that the first 'aims to problematise rather than merely reflect traditional methods and assumptions', and the second offers 'dissent from the traditional critical assumptions which have obstructed the reappraisal of this drama for our time'. Both are serviceable collections for students, and both are clearly introduced by their editors – but one does wonder whether newness is necessarily so transparently progressive, and whether the abandonment of the old form of the series, which gave a wide chronological span of criticism, is not an uncomfortable mark of a certain kind of professional arrogance. Students can be encouraged to historicize their reading of older criticism without its being so relentlessly disparaged. And that, really, is where this survey began, for the near contempt which both these collections appear to demonstrate for earlier criticism is precisely what fuels the bitterness of Vickers's riposte. The overplus of antipathy in both, it seems to me, inhibits really fruitful debate.

2. SHAKESPEARE'S LIFE, TIMES, AND STAGE
reviewed by MARTIN WIGGINS

I

There were only two books in the 'Theatre' section of the *Times Literary Supplement* listings page in the issue for the week ending 15 February 1990. One was called *Theatre Semiotics*. The other was *Broadway Anecdotes*.[1] It is a memorable juxtaposition which neatly defines the epistemological range of the subject, albeit in terms of its extremes: knowledge can be either unapproachably abstract or insignificantly concrete, with the attendant dangers of, on the one hand, producing entries for Pseuds Corner (of which more later), and, on the other, achieving mediocrity as mere anecdote is loosed upon the world. The best work in the field usually cultivates the art of landing gracefully between two stools, and there are many ways of doing so with distinction.

A perennial interest, at the theoretical end of the scale, is the interpretation of what actually happens at performances, not in the sense of recording hard fact but of developing a more precise understanding of the process of theatre in general. Several critics this year have converged, from the very different angles of texts, productions, and theory, on the issue of how and where authority is located in performance. At two extremes of the debate we find Ralph

[1] *Times Literary Supplement* (1990), p. 155.

Berry and Balz Engler. For Berry, who has published a book of short and miscellaneous stage-centred essays, *Shakespeare in Performance* (Basingstoke and London, 1993), the play shapes the playgoers, an exercise he calls 'The taming of the audience' (p. vii) and examines in relation to *King Lear* and *Richard II*. Engler, however, uses reception theory to underline the audience's importance in shaping both performance and text.[2] Other critics, giving more attention to the separate claims of the author (or the text), see a more complex set of negotiations and appropriations as the various empowered parties seek to arrogate authority to themselves. The key moments, shows Robert Smallwood, are the opening ones: empirical evidence from a range of modern productions shows how a pre-text, a 'little directorial dumb show', allows the director to create 'a free space for himself before the authorial text comes along to restrict that freedom and to cramp his style' (p. 73).[3]

In the earlier theatre, this hinterland between real life and play was occupied by the prologue, which could serve a similar function, proposes Robert Weimann in a complicated but suggestive article. He offers a distinction between prologues which confer authority upon the performers, subordinating 'our poet', and those which claim it for the poet and treat the actors merely as a medium of conveyance: university-educated playwrights tend to produce the latter type, he suggests, while professional hacks like Shakespeare opt for the former.[4] This is a potentially valuable taxonomy, though Weimann does not always apply it where he might: for instance, he identifies Marlowe's prologue to *Tamburlaine the Great* as a seminal example of the playwright-orientated type, pointing the way forward to the authorial authority which became increasingly the norm as the period wore on; but he does not mention the sequel's equally suggestive reversion to the 'our poet' rhetoric which the earlier play so strikingly disavowed.[5]

Ralph Berry's book ranges freely over many theatrical topics – casting is an especially frequent concern – but his ultimate goal is textual interpretation: he seeks to assimilate performance criticism to the traditional concerns of literary criticism, commenting in the Preface,

> Theatre history, as I view it, is less a fascinating study in itself than a means of knowing the plays. Through the record of performance, one sees what the plays *are*. (p. vii)

It is not a conclusion borne out by the work of Marvin Rosenberg, who approaches performance with a similar agenda. His inordinately vast *The Masks of 'Hamlet'* (Newark, 1992) has emerged from the University of Delaware Press in the company of reissues of his earlier works on three other major tragedies.[6] The new book runs to nearly a thousand pages and draws on as many sources, though inevitably the documentation of particular bits of stage business is less thorough than theatre historians might like, or need.[7] As in the earlier books on *King Lear* and *Macbeth*, all these different performance options are carefully listed and presented sequentially in a structure analogous to that of the play itself: as if through the compound eyes of a fly, we see, synoptically,

---

2 Balz Engler, 'Uber den Applaus bei Shakespeare', *Deutsche Shakespeare-Gesellschaft Jahrbuch 1993*, ed. Werner Habicht and Günther Klotz (Bochum, 1993), pp. 85–98.

3 Robert Smallwood, '"Beginners, Please"; or, First Start your Play', ibid., pp. 72–84.

4 Robert Weimann, 'Authority and Representation in the Pre-Shakespearean Prologue', in Elmar Lehmann and Bernd Lenz (eds.), *Telling Stories: Studies in Honour of Ulrich Broich on the Occasion of his 60th Birthday* (Amsterdam and Philadelphia, 1992), pp. 34–46.

5 *The Second Part of Tamburlaine*, Prol. 3.

6 *The Masks of 'Othello'* (Berkeley and Los Angeles, 1961); *The Masks of 'King Lear'* (Berkeley, Los Angeles, and London, 1972); *The Masks of 'Macbeth'* (Berkeley, Los Angeles, and London, 1978).

7 It is especially unfortunate that Rosenberg often suppresses the names of performers: for some reason Ophelias suffer from this most of all, becoming the syntactic property of the director or the actor playing Hamlet.

multiple discrete versions of the same moment. Locally illuminating though it often is, this procedure does not, in Berry's terms, show us 'what the play *is*'; it merely presents a bewildering dazzle of alternatives, a *Hamlet* that has never existed, except perhaps in the crazier flights of some post-structuralist imagination.

What suffers from Berry's purely literary approach to theatre history are the non-verbal elements of any performance, and, as Graham Parry points out in an account of the Jacobean masque, much of the impact of any production derives from such elements, from music and dance to swordplay – the subject of a lucid and practical study by Charles Edelman, *Brawl Ridiculous: Swordfighting in Shakespeare's Plays* (Manchester and New York, 1992) – and what Dennis Kennedy calls 'scenography'.[8] By this he means all aspects of theatrical design, from costumes and sets to the permanent architecture of the stage itself, and even the visibility or otherwise of other members of the audience, all of which are considered in his book, *Looking at Shakespeare: A Visual History of Twentieth-Century Performance* (Cambridge, 1993).

The opening chapter offers a careful exposition of the nature and limitations of visual evidence, which should be required reading for every theatre historian, particularly in view of recent work by John H. Astington which calls into question the evidential value of several familiar images that we had thought were reliable representations of the seventeenth-century stage.[9] Kennedy gives a thorough account of the main scenographic movements of the century, and is especially notable for his close consideration of the to and fro of Anglo-Continental design influence, from Craig to Reinhardt to Barker, and so on. Occasionally it seems that his thinking is unduly dominated by a simple dichotomy defined by the presence or absence of a proscenium arch, with the result that, for example, the Swan Theatre in Stratford is virtually ignored, its scenographic implications taken to be a mere extension of those of the very different space across the road, The Other Place. With so much packed into the book, however, including many very necessary illustrations, it is hard to quibble about particular omissions, even when one of them is an important and much loved theatre.

The wider movements of intellectual and ideological history provide Paul Whitfield White with his supra-anecdotal context in his study of a neglected because pre-Shakespearian period of the English stage, *Theatre and Reformation* (Cambridge, 1993). No scholar of Tudor drama will be surprised by his contention that, in the middle of the sixteenth century, the theatre played an important part in the dissemination of Protestant ideas, but if the book has an unremarkable central thesis, it is nonetheless a valuable contribution to the subject in its attention to the practical realities which governed the theatre business at the time: the surviving plays acquire a firmer professional context from White's painstaking consideration of performance spaces, touring itineraries, and the theatre's patrons from educationalists to noblemen.

However, a corollary of this emphasis on Reformation theatre's uses in official culture, both establishment and oppositional, is that the book risks underestimating another of its aspects. From Luther to the Ranters, radical Protestant discourse could also be unrespectable: vandalism and bad manners are valorized, authority-figures are mocked and buffeted, and turds fly about, bringing doctrinal controversy to the playground level of 'That's you, that is.' Drama was no exception to this subversive, 'punk' tendency: the London theatre of early 1559 was so scurrilous that the government had to institute formal censorship procedures in

[8] Graham Parry, 'The Politics of the Jacobean Masque', in J. R. Mulryne and Margaret Shewring (eds.), *Theatre and Government under the Early Stuarts* (Cambridge, 1993), pp. 113–14.

[9] John H. Astington, 'The Origins of the *Roxana* and *Messallina* Illustrations', *Shakespeare Survey 43* (1991), pp. 149–69, and '*The Wits* Illustration, 1662', *Theatre Notebook*, 47 (1993), 122–40.

order to mollify outraged Catholic ambassadors, so it is unsurprising that the plays now exist only as traces rather than texts. White does not ignore this material altogether, but he is not notably assiduous in assessing its significance: this study attends more to the morally and politically creditable theatre of the sixteenth century, and attends to it well; but the concern remains that his partial picture is all too close to the one which the Reformation authorities wanted seen.

Two good books at the concrete if not the anecdotal end of the spectrum are, in a sense, biographies, though unconventional ones in that neither describes a subject that was ever biologically alive: one deals with a fictional character, the other a theatre. Self-consciously addressing himself to 'ordinary readers' (p. 9), John Gross writes *Shylock: Four Hundred Years in the Life of a Legend* (London, 1992) with a literacy and readability that puts many academic Shakespearians to shame. What he sacrifices is sustained and detailed analysis. In discussing productions he is content, for example, to trust to reviews: there is no evidence that he has consulted prompt-books or other theatrical archive material. Short cuts are often taken, giving the book a bitty, portrait-gallery quality, a limitation which becomes most acute when, after discussing the play itself and its theatrical life, Gross turns to Shylock's broader place in cultural history. This breadth often means a failure of focus: there is a tendency to spill over into the larger pool of Jewish literary representations in general, with the search for Shylock conducted by fishing for salmon in both. Undoubtedly there is a need for a full study of Shylock's influence on Jewish stereotyping in later literature and culture; John Gross provides a good survey of the material, but not the study itself.

Shylock's development, unlike that of a human life, is a gyre: it consists of the periodic repetition of the same actions, differently construed. Perhaps this is why it is difficult for non-specialists to understand the loss occasioned by ignorance of stage history so keenly as they might with 'lives' which take a more linear progress through time: we may lack the finer points of interpretation in an eighteenth-century performance, but at least we have the play itself.[10] In contrast, we cannot even guess at the sort of entertainment staged at London's Victoria Theatre during its time as a Temperance Music Hall: even the most basic records have not survived. In his generously illustrated account of one of London's oldest surviving playhouses, *The Old Vic Theatre: A History* (Cambridge, 1993), George Rowell does his best to fill in the major gaps in our knowledge of the theatre's nineteenth-century life, but there is still much that can probably never be rescued from the scrip of oblivion.

Writing with clarity and a more than occasional crackle of dry wit, Rowell follows the Old Vic from its origins in 1818 as Joseph Glossop's Coburg Theatre, taking in its temperance years under Emma Cons and its emergence as a major Shakespearian venue under her redoubtable niece, Lilian Baylis. Anecdote and gossip enliven his account: we hear, for example, of Ben Greet trapping Miss Baylis in her office in order to extort an apology to an ill-used stage manager, or of the Board's mistrust of the theatrical young Turk it had appointed as director, Tyrone Guthrie. Without reducing the book to a trivial collection of *Waterloo Road Anecdotes*, details like these add the dimension of human actuality to the potentially dry facts of history.

The final chapter or so, in which Rowell brings the history up to the present day, has less

[10] Of course it is especially important to know whether or not a play was actually performed in a given period, which is why Hugh M. Richmond's discovery of a couple of adaptations of *The Two Noble Kinsmen*, dating from 1795 and 1864, is a more than usually valuable contribution to an otherwise blank stage history between Davenant and the Old Vic: 'The Persistent *Kinsmen* of Shakespeare and Fletcher', *Notes and Queries*, 238 (1993), 232–4.

of this sort of juice. For obvious reasons of confidentiality, he quotes less freely from the minutes of more recent Board meetings, and the Governors, who became such important players in the time of crisis after the National Theatre company left the Old Vic in 1976, remain anonymous, though successive Presidents and Chairmen are named in an appendix. Like a parachutist dropping below radar level, every chronological survey tends to lose objectivity and perspective as it reaches recent times. Rowell and Gross both become more political towards the end of their respective books, Gross latently so as, in a single chapter, he skims over Shylock's complex history since the Second World War and gives a sceptical account of recent trends in academic literary criticism, Rowell more overtly in his unsurprising identification of government under-funding of the arts as a factor in the Old Vic's present uncertain position.

If scholars can never write a satisfactory history of recent theatre, though, what they can do is concentrate on the immediacy of performance criticism, a case in point being Miriam Gilbert's excellent analysis of *Love's Labour's Lost*s she has seen (and some she presumably has not), which has appeared in the 'Shakespeare in Performance' series.[11] Thorough, careful, sensitive work like this is valuable not only in enriching our understanding of the play and its theatrical life, but in laying down for the future the sort of detailed evidence that current scholars from Paul Whitfield White to George Rowell have had to do without.[12]

II

Guesswork is the primal eldest curse of English Renaissance drama studies. In the absence of detailed production records from the period – even *Maiden Lane Anecdotes* would be welcome – scholars will always have to piece out our ignorance with their minds, and if Roslyn Lander Knutson is, perforce, no exception in *The Repertory of Shakespeare's Company, 1594–1613* (Fayetteville, 1991), at least her speculations are informed by a broad knowledge and a generally plausible sense of the role of commercial imperatives and theatrical fashion in the operations of the Chamberlain's and King's Men. The book analyses the company's repertory from its formation in 1594 to the burning of the Globe in 1613 (a neat cut-off point which entails the signal inconvenience of stopping just short of *The Duchess of Malfi* and *The Two Noble Kinsmen*), suggesting and, where possible, demonstrating empirically what we should already have known (but often didn't) through the application of common sense. For example, when read with an eye to theatre management rather than finance, Henslowe's records show that the Admiral's Men managed their time providently, creating rehearsal opportunities at the start of a season (which Knutson takes to be the autumn) by allowing the daily repertory to rely initially on continuations of plays with which they were already familiar; though we cannot prove that other companies did the same, she reasonably contends that it would have been sensible for them to do so.

In other respects her analysis of Henslowe's Diary is more questionable. In particular, she seeks to use his gallery receipts as a means of calculating the size of the audiences in that part of the theatre, apparently forgetting that the design of the playhouse itself is an unknown factor in the equation: if the Rose and Fortune punters progressed through the yard to reach the gallery, paying penny by penny as they went (as has been inferred from Platter's account of the Globe), then the gallery takings indicate larger numbers than if entry to the different parts of the auditorium was *via* three

11 Miriam Gilbert, *Love's Labour's Lost* (Manchester, 1993).

12 For the same reason, the most valuable part of Samuel Crowl's book, *Shakespeare Observed: Studies in Performance on Stage and Screen* (Athens, Ohio, 1992), is his interesting rehearsal diary for the 1980 RSC *Romeo and Juliet*.

separate entrances outside the theatre (as has been inferred from the actual remains of the Globe).

Assumptions about the genre, dating, and revival of the plays themselves are also contentious, though helpfully set out in a checklist of the company's known plays. There are some misjudgements: it is strange to find *The Fair Maid of Bristol*, a play concluded in patent imitation of *Measure for Measure*, assigned to the previous repertory year.[13] There are also some simple errors: Knutson is evidently unaware, for instance, of Webster's share in the text (as well as the induction) of the QC version of *The Malcontent* (p. 105). However, it is on the reconstruction of a pattern of revivals that the book's argument turns, and this too is insecurely founded.

Knutson infers that a play has recently been revived from the appearance of allusions or a new edition of the text. Plausible though this hypothesis is in many individual cases, it can scarcely be applicable as a general principle: there was indeed a connection between the market for plays in the theatre and on the bookstall, but without a wider study of fashions in book publication we cannot take it that reprinting is invariably evidence of revival. Moreover, the analysis of allusions is not always sufficiently informed by a sense of the wider context. For example, *Gesta Grayorum*'s mention of Plautus in relation to *The Comedy of Errors* is taken to indicate that the play's popularity lay in its Plautine associations (pp. 62–3), without considering the representativeness or otherwise of a Gray's Inn audience. Other allusions are interpreted with an extraordinary literal-mindedness: the characters in the induction of *The Malcontent* are not actually Burbage, Condell, and Lowin, for example, so 'Condell's' reference to the appropriation of *Jeronimo* by the Blackfriars company cannot be taken, as Knutson takes it (p. 92), as unambiguous evidence that the King's Men were angry with their eyas rivals; and it seems remarkably humourless to read Manningham's joke about the sexual exploits of Burbage and Shakespeare as evidence that the latter played the part of William the Conqueror in a revival of *Fair Em* (p. 62).

It is natural that scholars like Knutson should rarely feel content with imponderables, but regrettable that they do not always recognize the limitations of their cases. In his Oxford edition of *Macbeth*, Nicholas Brooke showed laudable caution in his consideration of the play's position in the canon: '*Macbeth* was probably written . . . close . . . to *Antony and Cleopatra*, but whether before or after I do not know.'[14] Such caution is less apparent in a note by David Farley-Hills, who is keen to convince us of *Antony and Cleopatra*'s priority.[15] One of the principles on which he bases his claim is his own suggestion in an earlier book that Shakespeare frequently alludes to his immediately preceding play;[16] accordingly, he posits, Macbeth's reference to Mark Antony (3.1.58) is an instance of the same kind of retro-thinking on Shakespeare's part. The problem is that no such proposal can have a general application. Many creative artists – Dickens, for instance – anticipate themselves as often as they refer back,[17]

---

13 Richard Proudfoot, 'Shakespeare and the New Dramatists of the King's Men, 1606–1613', *Later Shakespeare*, Stratford-upon-Avon Studies, 8 (London, 1966), p. 238. Knutson (p. 115) presumably follows the assumption of E. K. Chambers that the play's court performance 'must have been during the Christmas of 1603–4' (*The Elizabethan Stage*, IV.12), but unless we are to assume substantial imitative revision as well as possible memorial reconstruction, the earliest plausible date of composition can hardly be earlier than the reopening of the theatres in April 1604.

14 *Macbeth*, ed. Nicholas Brooke (Oxford, 1990), p. 64.

15 David Farley-Hills, 'The Position of *Antony and Cleopatra* in the Canon', *Notes and Queries*, 238 (1993), 193–7.

16 David Farley-Hills, *Shakespeare and the Rival Playwrights, 1600–1606* (London and New York, 1990), pp. 41, 78–9.

17 For example, Dickens refers to Utilitarian education in *Bleak House* (1852–3), written just before *Hard Times* (1854), and to the French Revolution in *Little Dorrit* (1855–7), anticipating *A Tale of Two Cities* (1859).

and this seems also to be true of Shakespeare, unless of course David Farley-Hills proposes to use the same method to date *Henry V* after *Julius Caesar*, or *Twelfth Night* after *Troilus and Cressida*.[18]

The other main argument Farley-Hills has to offer is that, in the traditional order of the canon, Shakespeare seems 'unaccountably barren of new plays' (p. 196) during the winter of 1605–6. But it is only only an over-confident acceptance of out-of-date hypotheses about the composition of other plays that gives the illusion of a vacancy: if *King Lear* dates from late 1605, not 1604–5 as Farley-Hills believes, if *Timon of Athens* belongs before *Coriolanus* rather than *Lear*, and if *All's Well That Ends Well* is a Jacobean play of 1604–5, one of the Oxford editors' most plausible reassignments about which Farley-Hills has nothing at all to say, then the breach is filled and there is no need to close it up with *Antony and Cleopatra*. Of course, it is always valuable to be reminded that it is convenience rather than evidence that sometimes determines our sense of the plays' sequence, but the work of David Farley-Hills has not moved us beyond Nicholas Brooke's uncertainty.

Ultimately it is the discovery, provision, and analysis of documentary evidence which whittles away the indeterminate regions of our subject. For example, statistical function-word analysis has decisively ejected *Edmond Ironside* from the Shakespeare apocrypha, and if, sadly, *Cardenio* has not turned up (despite the extravagant claims recently made by Charles Hamilton), there have nonetheless been many welcome additions to the available material.[19] Masayuki Yamagishi's *The Henslowe Papers Supplement: The Theatre Papers* (Kyoto, 1992), for instance, aims to supply texts of all the theatrical documents in the Dulwich collection which were omitted from the selections by Greg and Foakes and Rickert.[20] There are one or two otiose inclusions (article 18 appears in all three editions, for example) and, regrettably, four omissions of what Yamagishi calls 'inadequate and corrupted documents' (p. v). Articles 142–4 are badly mutilated, it is true, but palaeographers have coped with such difficulties before, and although article 20 is in all likelihood a forgery, this need not diminish its interest in some respects; other, equally spurious documents are included in the collection. It is frustrating that Yamagishi's efforts leave us still several documents short of the full set of transcripts.

S. P. Cerasano has investigated Henslowe's association with Simon Forman, enabling her tentatively to link the Diary's collection of spells with his first visit to the conjurer in 1596. Other valuable finds in Forman's papers include another record of his theatregoing, eleven years earlier than the better-known 'Book of Plaies', giving a detailed account of a lost Admiral's play of 1600, *Cox of Collumpton*; and the fact that Henslowe was forty-two at the time of his second visit to the astrologer in February 1597. The latter discovery has more significance than may at first be apparent: it now emerges that, in comparison with other Elizabethan impresarios like Langley, Woodliffe, or James Burbage, Henslowe was a relatively young man when the Rose opened in 1587. Indeed, Cerasano goes on to suggest that the theatre of the 1590s was a young man's world: the most successful figures, Alleyn, Shakespeare, and the Burbage brothers, had all been born in the 1560s.[21]

---

[18] See *Henry V*, 5.0.26–8; *Twelfth Night*, 3.1.50–5: both passages, and indeed *Macbeth*'s reference to Antony, seem to show Shakespeare 'thinking around' a topic, which happened to become the subject of one of his next plays. Perhaps there is a basis here for speculation about other ideas which he abandoned.

[19] M. W. A. Smith, '*Edmund Ironside*', *Notes and Queries*, 238 (1993), 202–5; 'Will's will is clue to identity of long-lost tragedy of necrophilia', *The Independent*, 13 July 1993, p. 1.

[20] W. W. Greg (ed.), *Henslowe Papers, being Documents Supplementary to Henslowe's Diary* (London, 1907); R. A. Foakes and R. T. Rickert (eds.), *Henslowe's Diary* (Cambridge, 1961).

[21] S. P. Cerasano, 'Philip Henslowe, Simon Forman, and the Theatrical Community of the 1590s', *Shakespeare Quarterly*, 44 (1993), 145–58.

E. A. J. Honigmann and Susan Brock deal with maturer concerns in their diligently researched *Playhouse Wills, 1558–1642* (Manchester, 1993). It is a volume which makes an unexpected but not unwelcome inclusion in the Revels Plays Companion Library series: a substantial and valuable gathering of documentary evidence like this might seem more at home as a Malone Society *Collection*. The book benefits most conspicuously from its placement in being able to furnish a more extensive introduction than would have been possible elsewhere: the editors' account supplies not only a clear explanation of the legal context of the wills, but also an analysis of some of the ways in which they provide information, directly and indirectly, about 'the social, financial, religious and sentimental lives' (p. 26) of members of the Elizabethan and early Stuart theatrical community. Even so, the apparatus could usefully have been more extensive still, for the annotation is relatively sparse, and the indexing inadequate: a volume of this sort needs not only an index of proper names but also of bequests, without which it is impossible to determine (for example) how many theatre people left books, or Bibles, or bedding (second-best or otherwise).[22] It is a shame that the exemplary archive-work of Brock and Honigmann in digging out so much previously unpublished material could not have been better served in this respect; but ultimately it is those unpublished wills which make the volume nonetheless one of exceptional value to scholars and biographers.[23]

The inevitability of guesswork seems not to trouble Felix Pryor: it is, in fact, the principal medium of his scholarship in *The Mirror and the Globe* (London, 1992), an investigation of possible literary relations between Shakespeare and Marston. Those relations, he suggests, were characterized by an antagonism which led Shakespeare to write the 'rugged Pyrrhus' speech in *Hamlet* as a parody not of Marlowe's but Marston's style as heard in *Antonio and Mellida*. It seems an inefficient parody that would avoid some of the more distinctive features of Marston's writing – notably slubbery snottery – and an inefficient interpretation that demands our reading an otherwise unsupported irony into Hamlet's expressed appreciation for the passage.[24] The most serious problems with the theory, however, appear in the contortions and contradictions of Pryor's argument about the identity and circumstances of the 'tragedians of the city' (2.2.329) who bring the Pyrrhus play and others to Elsinore.

Most critics have interpreted Hamlet's reference to 'an eyrie of children' (2.2.339) as an indirect allusion to the Children of the Chapel. Pryor, however, devotes much literal-minded ingenuity to identifying the eyases as Marston's company, the Paul's Boys: otherwise, he points out, Hamlet-Burbage, joint owner of the Blackfriars Playhouse, would have been publicly attacking his own tenants; that the war of the theatres saw several other skirmishes between Globe and Blackfriars is conveniently overlooked.[25] Pryor cannot have it both ways, but that doesn't stop him trying: not only have the players been driven to touring by the emergence of a children's company identifiable

---

[22] Shakespeare's will offers little help to Park Honan, who has made a determined but inconclusive effort to trace the disposition of the dramatist's Bible; an eighteenth-century inscription suggests that it came into the Hart family *via* Shakespeare's sister, Joan: 'Shakespeare's Bible and the Harts', *Notes and Queries*, 238 (1993), 231–2.

[23] Outside theatre history, two other sets of useful documents, one primary and one secondary, have become more accessible, thanks to Joan Larsen Klein, who has edited *Daughters, Wives, and Widows: Writings by Men about Women and Marriage in England, 1500–1640* (Urbana and Chicago, 1992), and John Haffenden, who has collected William Empson's work on 'Donne and the New Philosophy' to become the first volume of his *Essays on Renaissance Literature* (Cambridge, 1993).

[24] Pryor doesn't consider the more plausible possibility that the gloomy Dane, who spends a long time telling professional actors their job, might just be a bad critic.

[25] Indeed, if one interprets the 'war' as a publicity stunt, then these two companies' being the main combatants might actually be *because* of Burbage's financial interest in both playhouses.

with the Paul's Boys, they are also themselves identified *as* the Paul's Boys on a Continental tour, which at least makes sense of their having a 'Marston' play in their repertory; the evidence for their being an adult company is dismissed, J. M. Robertson fashion, as a survival from an earlier draft of *Hamlet*. Ultimately he throws out even his own preceding case when he posits that Shakespeare, unlike Jonson, is less concerned in the passage with personalities than with a style of acting and an attitude to theatre: if, as he says, 'It is not Marston that matters, but Marston's play and the actors that take part in it' (p. 173), then why bother with specific reference to Marston, which could only give offence?[26] This is not a book notable for its consistency of argument.

Pryor needs *Hamlet* to hit back at Paul's rather than Blackfriars because he believes Paul's hit back: having given Shakespeare a small-minded riposte to *Antonio and Mellida*, he reads *Antonio's Revenge* as an equally petty remonstrance; this also makes it imperative for him to pull back the date of Shakespeare's play, implausibly, to 1599 or early 1600. Simple priority is the key factor in his model of artistic influence, which has the rhythm and sequentiality of a tennis match.[27] But in commercial competition, the common-sense principle that one play or the other must have come first does not always operate: *Antonio's Revenge* could indeed have been written from Marston's viewing of *Hamlet*, or *Hamlet* from Shakespeare's viewing of *Antonio's Revenge*; but, equally, either play could also have been written in response to the knowledge of a similar, forthcoming play in the other company's repertory. There is no need to infer a bitter personal interplay between the two dramatists (even if it may have existed) to account for phenomena that are explicable as professional rivalry alone.

This is not an altogether barren book: it contains a few illuminating suggestions. Shakespeare's decision to represent the Ghost in armour, for example, is interestingly associated with the vogue for armed prologues and epilogues, started by Marston in *Antonio and Mellida* and continued in, among others, *Troilus and Cressida*. The possibility of an imaginative association between the two Shakespeare plays leads on to speculation that the excisions in the Folio version of *Hamlet* were made by Shakespeare with the intention of exploring the ideas more fully in *Troilus*. These notions are undeveloped, but not foolish. It is a pity that, in general, the book is notable chiefly not for them but the obsessive tenacity with which Felix Pryor pursues conclusions which are not only unprovable but also unlikely.

III

Poor Middleton! It seems that conscientious writers of student handbooks on his work, such as Martin White's in the Macmillan English Dramatists series, will forever play safe by relegating the recently identified parts of his canon to an uncertain and largely unread hinterland. *The Revenger's Tragedy* alone weighs too heavily to be ignored or skimped, but the upshot of its inclusion is that *The Atheist's Tragedy* gets to accompany it, and the book has to be entitled *Middleton and Tourneur* (Basingstoke, 1992). This is not to say that Tourneur's play is unworthy of attention, and, though shackled primarily through historical accident, the two most conservative and most moralistic writers of Jacobean tragedy would

[26] But then Pryor sees Marston everywhere. For instance, he suggests that, not content with guying him as Crispinus in *The Poetaster*, Jonson introduced Marston as the figure of Envy in the prologue to the same play. Presumably this was after a sex-change operation: Envy is female in Jonson's Ovidian iconography.

[27] Shakespeare v. Marston concluded, he believes, with the older dramatist temporarily absorbing the younger to write his own play in Marston's cynical vein, *Troilus and Cressida*. Pryor thus joins those critics whose narrow view of Shakespeare cannot account for his plays unpleasant other than as anomalous works which must be explained away as products of some outside influence.

not have made strange bedfellows, had White been inclined to discuss them together.[28] Moreover, he provides a competent account of the texts he chooses to discuss; the volume is especially pleasing in giving serious if brief critical attention to Middleton's early non-dramatic writings and emphasizing their thematic relevance to his later work.

The book's drawback is that, however much White tries to develop this sense of the imaginative and intellectual continuity of the canon, he is always hampered by a cautious reverence for its traditional limits: in particular, that characteristically Middletonian newcomer, the 'second' *Maiden's Tragedy* gets unduly compendious coverage in proportion to its interest and merits, not because White himself questions the attribution but because others have, and space is at a premium. At root there is a failure to distinguish degrees, or kinds, of uncertainty, apparent in the appended list of Middleton's writings: an asterisk confers the black spot of doubt on a title, producing a category in which works that are now more or less generally accepted as Middleton's, like *The Revenger's Tragedy* and *The Maiden's Tragedy*, rub serifs with generally rejected attributions like *Blurt, Master Constable* and *The Spanish Gipsy*, and even with *A Match at Midnight*, given in part to Middleton by F. G. Fleay in one of his wilder flights of fancy.[29] It seems that, like the Struldbruggs in *Gulliver's Travels*, silly theories, once born, will be with us forever; in other words, White retains (and so perpetuates) old and discredited ideas, while presenting the best efforts of modern scholarship in the same light. In a series like Macmillan English Dramatists, so self-consciously re-presenting the plays for today's readers, so self-assertively up-to-date, such conservatism is the more inappropriate.

Middleton does better by T. H. Howard-Hill, who has edited *A Game at Chess* for The Revels Plays (Manchester, 1993). His text chooses between the various manuscript sources with informed eclecticism, and thirty-two documents pertaining to the play are usefully collected as an appendix. Many features of the edition will help uninitiated readers with a difficult play. The *dramatis personae*, always a key tool for the first-time student, is inventively laid out in two columns corresponding to the black and white houses, with the Fat Bishop aptly positioned between the two. Some of the notes are especially valuable in teasing out the dialogue's implications about such matters as the precise sectarian allegiances of certain pawns: Howard-Hill thus makes available the play's subtler differentiations which the omnipresent black and white of the chess motif might otherwise obscure.

On the other hand, the notes sometimes give more help than is necessary. Even though nobody is ever likely to be introduced to English Renaissance drama through *A Game at Chess*, one can accept that there may be some inexperienced users of the edition who need telling that a Machiavel is an 'unscrupulous schemer' (3.1.121), or even that perdition is 'damnation' (2.2.175) and epicures are 'gluttons' (5.3.28). However, no English-speaking reader should require glosses for *facetious* ('jocular', 4.2.20) or *waste* ('squander', 2.2.167); the unanticipated irony of the latter is comment enough.

There are also a few errors of fact and judgement, which are the more regrettable in the scholarly context of an edition. For a critic to misattribute a Jacobean play or misname a Warwickshire village is a regrettable but minor matter (even if a pedantic reviewer decides to

[28] In practice, Tourneur ends up shoved into the last few pages: White resists integrating the two in order to express structurally his cautious sense of *The Revenger's Tragedy*'s interstitial (and, one might add, impossible) position between the canons; as the bulkier and more important body of work, Middleton comes first, leaving the chapter on *The Atheist's Tragedy* at best a loosely attached coda.

[29] F. G. Fleay, *A Chronicle History of the London Stage* (London, 1886), p. 203. For an expression of reasonable doubt, see Stephen Blase Young (ed.), *A Match at Midnight* (New York and London, 1980), pp. 22–37.

mention it anyway).[30] In editions, however, the cancer cells of error are at their most malignant, because they have most opportunity to travel: editions are, after all, a point of access, for readers to a text, and for texts to the future. What a shame, then, that Howard-Hill retails, in his introductory comments on the typicality of the fifty-five-day delay between licensing and staging (p. 17), the naive notion that a play's first recorded performance – often at court – was also its première: that might well be true of *A Game at Chess*, but is hardly likely in the case of, say, *The Changeling*, a play which, he claims, took nearly twenty months to reach the stage after it was licensed early in May 1622. A shame, too, that he has plumped for the wrong assassin in his note on 'the killing of a heretical prince with a poisoned knife' (4.2.111–12): the play's New Mermaid editor, J. W. Harper, offered as alternative possible referents the killers of Henri III and Henri IV, Jacques Clément and François Ravaillac; Howard-Hill picks Ravaillac, presumably on grounds of recency, but the detail of the poisoned knife points unambiguously to Clément.[31] (In the context – a discussion of the *taxae poenitentiae* – it is also possible that the reference is less specific, and merely draws on well-known aspects of Clément's case.) It is too late to protect Revels readers from these minor blemishes on an important new edition, but let us hope that the play's future editors will not be misled.

George Buchanan's neo-Latin tragedy *Baptistes* and its anonymous seventeenth-century translation, *Tyrannical Government Anatomized* are less likely than *A Game at Chess* to demand fresh editions in the near future, so it is fortunate that their present editor, Steven Berkowitz, has done his textual work exhaustively.[32] A lengthy introduction covers the play from every editorial angle conceivable, including a strenuous refutation of the translation's attribution to Milton. What it does not seek to do is offer a critical account of the play: its considerable interest to historians and critics is left as a matter for brief suggestion in the Preface. This includes the curious notion that *Baptistes*, which was dedicated to the boy-king James VI when it was published in 1577, 'suggests a Scottish heritage for James I's remarkable tolerance of dissentient drama' (p. x). The cases of *Sejanus' Fall*, *Eastward Ho*, *The Isle of Gulls*, and the *Biron* plays might give cause to doubt that James *was* remarkably tolerant; and to read dissentience so untentatively in other plays of the period is, with a few exceptions, to confuse demonstrable fact with fashionable academic speculation. However, this small misjudgement need not diminish the edition's value in providing texts of the two versions of an out-of-the-way and politically interesting play.

The political school of criticism has been concerned, as ever, with various kinds of alterity – sexual, geographical, psychological. In the case of Duncan Salkeld's important study of insanity, *Madness and Drama in the Age of Shakespeare* (Manchester and New York, 1993), the initial object is to establish that his topic is indeed 'other' than discourse: in traditional criticism, he points out, 'madness has been regarded not in opposition to reason but as a kind of superior rationality, an insanity close to genius, in which truths which normally remain hidden are grasped' (p. 18). For him, however,

> Madness is a sign of the 'bonds crack'd' and produced out of reason's failure and self-contradiction. Its concept has only a negative value, marking a loss or lack of sanity, syntax and power. (p. 154)

---

30 Douglas Bruster gives the two parts of *The Honest Whore* to Heywood (*Drama and the Market in the Age of Shakespeare*, p. 32 and index), though they are correctly assigned elsewhere; John Gross turns Snitterfield, home of Shakespeare's grandfather, into 'Snittersfield' (*Shylock*, p. 46), one of the book's many trifling inaccuracies.

31 See, e.g., Marlowe, *The Massacre at Paris*, 24.73–6. Comentators associated both assassins with Jesuit attempts to control royal 'heresy', but Ravaillac's knife was not poisoned.

32 Steven Berkowitz (ed.), *A Critical Edition of George Buchanan's 'Baptistes' and of Its Anonymous Seventeenth-Century Translation 'Tyrannicall-Government Anatomized'* (New York and London, 1992).

Once disentangled from his *devoir* of theory (which sometimes seems there more to validate his ideas than enable them), Salkeld's case is persuasive and humane, attending more to the human suffering encoded in stage madness than to its supposedly ennobling or educative consequences. At the same time, drawing on Foucault, he takes insanity as a phenomenon which, though beyond ideology, is nonetheless legible as a critique of it: its presence – for Salkeld, ubiquity – in English Renaissance drama is a disturbing reminder of the limitations – for Salkeld, failures – of rational discourse.

The underlying point here is the familiar one that the recognition and recovery of repressed alternatives is a means to effect social change. The issue is, perhaps, felt with more urgency in North America, for reasons especially apparent in the latest hefty New Historicist serving of post-colonial guilt-feelings, *New World Encounters* (Berkeley, Los Angeles, and Oxford, 1993). These essays on early cultural relations between Europe and the Americas are written around what the volume's editor, Stephen Greenblatt, calls 'the vision of the vanquished' (p. viii): this manifests itself in everything from the essays' interest in the marginal to the publishers' tricksy disorientation devices like putting the running-titles at the bottom of the page rather than the top. For Shakespearians, uncomfortably but unavoidably more concerned with victors than vanquished, the most relevant piece is Jeffrey Knapp's clever if overlong and repetitive account of the economic and cultural anxieties underlying Elizabethan criticisms of tobacco – an import from the aboriginal North Americans which sapped English vigour and so gave an ironic victory to the colonized vendors.

There is a political paradox here which can apply as much to the radical school of criticism itself as to the objects of its attention: every act of empowerment risks undermining itself. All too often, literary studies which focus on formerly oppressed groups use the argument to work out a deep-seated anger at that oppression, with the result that the analysis tends to alienate the uncommitted through its unattractive zealotry and aggression, however much they may sympathize with the broad political principles that underlie it; the self-assertion of such books tends ultimately to confirm the ghetto status of 'special interest lobby' against which they struggle. Bruce R. Smith's *Homosexual Desire in Renaissance England: A Cultural Poetics* (Chicago and London, 1991), a book which 'began, not as a manifesto, but as a dialog' (p. xi), is more constructive. Avowedly a contribution to modern gay politics as well as to literary and cultural history, it nonetheless stands or falls by the same criteria as any other academic study of any other subject.

In the event, it stands. Smith is admirably thorough in scotching the notion that Renaissance England was an uncomplicatedly homophobic culture, which sits ill with the overt homoeroticism of some of the period's works of art, such as Shakespeare's Sonnets. In a stimulating essay in *Shakespeare Survey*, Margreta de Grazia has suggested that the backdating of later cultural prejudices has led critics to read the Sonnets as potentially scandalous in their homosexual content, as they were to Steevens and Malone, when for contemporaries it was the risk of miscegenation with a dark lady that was monstrous.[33] Smith provides a sophisticated and plausible basis for her case in arguing that the reliance by previous commentators, particularly Alan Bray, on legal instruments and moralistic literature led them to present only a partial and biased version of Renaissance cultural attitudes:

> Moral treatises and verse satires may seem to speak directly and unambiguously about sexual experience, but they speak about it from the outside. Poems, plays, and fiction speak from the inside: they give us imaginative access to sexuality that may be oblique but all the more true for that. (p. 25)

Accordingly, the main body of the book is

33 Margreta de Grazia, 'The Scandal of Shakespeare's Sonnets', *Shakespeare Survey 46* (1994), pp. 35–49.

elegantly structured around a series of six concentric 'myths' which lead from the external homosociality of soldierly comradeship to the private homosexuality of the Sonnets. Each 'myth' is discernible in mainstream texts of the period, and each, he argues, is associated with a particular social institution, and 'enacts in symbolic terms what the relevant social institution fosters in actual behavior' (p. 22): thus the fictions of cultural representation connect meaningfully with the realities of socio-sexual practice, and Smith is duly able to provide a comprehensive alternative to Bray's bleak picture of an age of intolerance.[34] In this respect, *Homosexual Desire in Renaissance England* adds significantly to our knowledge of human experience in Shakespeare's time; in the ordinary persuasiveness of its distinguished analysis, moreover, it does far more than any amount of political assertiveness to move gay culture and gay issues into the intellectual mainstream, and to create, as Smith himself puts it, 'a more liberally imagined world for one of the many modes of human sexual desire' (p. 270).

I am sorry that I cannot be equally enthusiastic about *Erotic Politics: Desire on the Renaissance Stage* (London, 1992), to which Smith is also a contributor. Sexuality is an important topic in all its manifestations, and the volume contains some notable contributions. In particular, Kathleen McLuskie's identification of a titillating element in Renaissance texts which ostensibly condemn or satirize sexual irregularity – a phenomenon still evident in modern tabloid journalism – should further complicate the 'Alan Bray school' of analysis of early modern moralism; and Valerie Traub's essay interestingly uses plays by Shakespeare, Heywood, and Shirley to suggest that the period's conception of female sexuality was undifferentiated, without distinction between the lesbian and the heterosexual. Seen as a collection, however, the book has inadequacies which are attributable to a refusal to engage in the sort of liberal dialogue from which Smith's book originated.

The question-fixated Routledge copywriters hit the right note of presumptuous self-satisfaction in heading the back cover blurb, 'Why was the English Renaissance Theatre a Site of Erotic Pleasure?' Deletion of the first word would produce an equally pertinent question, but the collection's editor, Susan Zimmerman, offers no introductory survey of the recent literature suggesting an erotic dimension to the Elizabethan and early Stuart theatre: the essays may be founded upon that hypothesis, but it is taken to be self-evident fact rather than contestable theory. This is a common procedure in the book. The main body of Zimmerman's own essay, for instance, begins with the sentence, 'Julia Kristeva reminded us that monotheistic, patrilinear societies require the radical separation and incompatibility of the sexes, the demonization of women, and the centralizing of eroticism in the reproductive function' (p. 40). Actually, Kristeva cannot 'remind' us of anything of the sort, because, interesting though this is as an idea, it is not empirical fact, and never will be unless historians and anthropologists can find enough independent monotheistic and patrilinear societies to verify it. There is a concern here to avoid question and challenge – in a sense, a desire to stifle dissent – which also informs the obfuscations of Zimmerman's prose style. All texts may be opaque, as Stephen Greenblatt insists in his introduction to *New World Encounters*, but reading through Zimmerman's dense fog of unnecessary jargon, unexplained shorthand, and overabundant adjectives, one cannot help but add that some are more opaque than others.[35]

---

[34] Alan Bray, *Homosexuality in Renaissance England* (London, 1982). Bray's later position, which is closer to Smith's in its acknowledgement of a proximity and possible slippage between male friendship and homosexuality, only became available as the latter's book was going to press, and is accordingly acknowledged only in a note (pp. 284–5): Bray, 'Homosexuality and the Signs of Male Friendship in Elizabethan England', *History Workshop Journal*, 29 (1990), 1–19.

[35] Greenblatt, *New World Encounters*, p. xvi.

Sentences like this, from her decidedly unintroductory introduction, seem designed more to insulate her ideas than express them: 'any teleology, whether that of the Marxist dialectic or the Christian metaphysics, is seen to reify those transhistorical or transcendental notions that serve the interests of hegemonic structures in their exercise of power' (p. 1). Nobody should write like that: it is not only a mark of contempt for one's readership, but also, in courting inaccessibility, fundamentally anti-educational. Susan Zimmerman is certainly right in saying that our understanding of Renaissance sexuality has a long way to go after *Erotic Politics*.

Kathleen McLuskie ends her essay with a pertinent status report on cultural materialism: 'In our excitement at the discovery that Shakespearean drama was implicated in the real social relations of early modern England, we have perhaps neglected the formal and material circumstances of its operation' (p. 122). Douglas Bruster's attempt to establish a 'poetics of the market' (p. 11) in his book, *Drama and the Market in the Age of Shakespeare* (Cambridge, 1992) goes some way towards filling the gap. Relating the institutionalizing of the theatres to the general growth in capitalist activity in Elizabethan and Jacobean England, Bruster challenges Steven Mullaney's reading, in *The Place of the Stage* (Chicago, 1988), of their marginality: they were, he posits, as engaged as the city itself in the operation of market forces. This is more than a chapter in the history of theatrical finance: the influence of the market can also be traced in the output of the playhouses, from the texts' openness to a variety of possible ideological readings – a case of the drama trying to be all things to all (ticket-buying) men, in order to provide the heterogeneous playgoers with 'what they would' – to a preoccupation with what Bruster calls a 'materialist vision' (p. 38).

No doubt participating in the development of a new stage realism around 1600, analysed by Jonathan Haynes in his short book, *The Social Relations of Jonson's Theater* (Cambridge, 1992), the plays of the time were concerned, Bruster shows, with the way material things affect life as much as do ideals: for example, the vogue for 'humours' characters, obsessively focused on objects like Malvolio's yellow stockings and psychologically determined by the very fluids of their bodies, is taken as a symptom of this interest. Where the book's efficient analysis can perhaps be faulted is in its bias towards comedy. Bruster reinforces class stereotypes in suggesting that the lower social rank of comedy's characters makes them more rooted in material life than what he sees, narrowly, as 'the idealized and idealizing figures of formal tragedy' (p. 34). However, his discussion of linen in *Othello* brings out the extent to which tragedies can and do use objects and commodities as *foci* for less concrete relations between people; indeed, Inga-Stina Ewbank made the point about *Women Beware Women* as long ago as 1969.[36] The relative absence of tragedy from the discussion is, then, the book's major limitation: for example, its account of wittolry's use by Middleton as a narrative metaphor for capitalism should have included discussion of *The Maiden's Tragedy* and, again, *Women Beware Women* alongside the obvious comic instance of the device, *A Chaste Maid in Cheapside*. Perhaps a further study of the material concerns of Jacobean tragedy is in order now that Douglas Bruster has opened the way so stimulatingly.

Another of the consequences of the new attention to the commercial, market-driven nature of English Renaissance drama is that it will no longer be possible to draw the simple, sharp distinction between the artistic and the popular which has made the output of playhouses like the Fortune and the Red Bull as 'unfashionable' today with critics, audiences, and theatre companies as it was in the seventeenth century. These plays 'are supposed to

[36] Inga-Stina Ewbank, 'Realism and Morality in *Women Beware Women*', *Essays and Studies*, 22 (1969), 62–4.

have catered to public taste in a commercial and therefore inartistic way' (p. 190), comments Julia Gasper in her contribution to J. R. Mulryne and Margaret Shewring's eclectic and uneven collection of conference proceedings, *Theatre and Government under the Early Stuarts* (Cambridge, 1993); it is the word 'therefore' which is now untenable. Accordingly, the book gives some attention to the work of Dekker and Heywood alongside the more expected discussions of the court masque, the city pageant, the political plays of Middleton and Massinger, and the Master of the Revels – the last, by Richard Dutton, already superseded by his more extensive study, *Mastering the Revels* (Basingstoke, 1991).[37]

Alexander Leggatt's book, *Jacobean Public Theatre* (London, 1992), has a similar agenda, though here the mainstream of Jacobean drama is not quite so rigorously marginalized as in the Mulryne and Shewring volume: Shakespeare and Webster were there accorded only brief, scattered references, whereas Leggatt includes an interesting analysis of possible reasons for the commercial failure of the Red Bull production of *The White Devil*, and ends up by applying to *King Lear* his findings about the theatrical manifestation of early modern popular culture. To modern critical eyes, one of the most alien of the characteristics he identifies is a tendency to produce diptychal works which incorporate different and even contradictory points of view. In plays, suggests Leggatt, we should accept similar inconsistencies – so rife in the drama of Heywood in particular – as an index of their 'popular' status.

The problem is that such negative capability is implicitly patronizing: it betrays a failure to engage fully with the texts. A closer analysis would reveal that in each case of contradiction, there is a hierarchy of values in operation. For instance, two aspects of *Thomas, Lord Cromwell* which Leggatt identifies in close succession are its xenophobia, evident in its account of latin lustfulness and teutonic riot, and its high regard for acts of charity towards the poor. The prime exponent of the latter is Fryskiball, who is (Leggatt does not point out) a Florentine merchant living in London, his name an English attempt at 'Frescobaldi'. He is just the sort of person who excited popular displays of xenophobia (think of *Sir Thomas More* and the Lombards), but the play treats him favourably because of his charity. It is not simply that the different prejudices contradict one another, but that one has overruled the other.[38]

The point about engagement is important because another emphasized feature of popular culture is the generalization of particular experience into universal principles: the balance of general and particular is bound to be skewed in an account which refuses to pay attention to detail, and so to particularity. Readers of these plays, suggests Leggatt, should consider 'what would strike an audience immediately, in the heat of performance' (p. 2). What is not said is how far this depends, in any production, on what the performers intend should strike the audience. This means that we cannot ignore, as Leggatt suggests we should, 'effects that reveal themselves only on close and repeated study, effects that turn the scripts into opportunities for a reader' (p. 2). All actors are of necessity readers: they have to study their parts, closely

[37] One aspect of the argument of *Mastering the Revels* has been challenged in an article by N. W. Bawcutt, who has analysed a number of items relating to Sir John Astley's brief tenure as the Master, and finds it a less political appointment than Dutton had suggested: N. W. Bawcutt, 'Evidence and Conjecture in Literary Scholarship: The Case of Sir John Astley Reconsidered', *English Literary Renaissance*, 22 (1992), 333–46.

[38] A. J. Hoenselaars offers a more complex analysis of the relationship between the play's national stereotyping and its sympathetic portrayal of Fryskiball in his meaty monograph, *Images of Englishmen and Foreigners in the Drama of Shakespeare and His Contemporaries: A Study of Stage Characters and National Identity in English Renaissance Drama, 1558–1642* (Rutherford, Madison, and Teaneck, 1992), pp. 103–7. The book's coverage is wide and with its excellent, user-friendly index it will no doubt become the standard reference work on the subject.

and repeatedly, and in the process they will discover subtle nuances which they can bring out on stage. The idea that such nuances should be disregarded in a performance-orientated approach derives, ironically, from the antitheatrical myth of under-rehearsed, undirected Jacobean players struggling through plays which they know only from their own parts.

In practice, this means that attention to face value sometimes blinds Leggatt to the latent complexity of the popular plays he discusses. For instance, *When You See Me, You Know Me* is treated as an 'arbitrary' series of 'self-contained' and unconnected episodes (p. 107), underestimating the extent to which the various sequences cohere in showing the King operating on each of the various levels of royal responsibility (familial, public, and diplomatic); instead of narrative development, the play achieves thematic unity in representing episodically the various dimensions of its topic of regal authority. Misreadings are also on occasion the result of allowing a sense of theatre to predominate over other fields of interpretation. For example, Clem's remark, in *The Fair Maid of the West*, that he would not kill Bess Bridges even if he caught her 'pissing against a wall' becomes for Leggatt an example of theatrical self-consciousness as the male actor's gender is momentarily exposed (pp. 138–9). But this is a reading which privileges biology over culture: the material differences in male and female genito-urinary systems are taken to be more relevant to the passage than the fact that to stab someone as they were relieving themselves was well known at the time as an especially easy and cowardly way to kill.[39] Here, ironically, Leggatt finds more sophistication and less simple contradiction than is actually there.

Leggatt's advocacy of a reading method unlike the approach taken by conventional literary criticism also leads him to suppress the names of playwrights, thereby bringing us, he says, 'a little closer to the initial effect of these plays on audiences who would have associated them . . . less with an author than we do' (p. 4). This, too, is contestable: no doubt Jacobean audiences could forget some playwrights all of the time, and all playwrights some of the time, but Shakespeare at least seems to have had a reputation during his lifetime: the appearance of his name on Quarto title pages from 1598 onwards is an index of a commercial value that surely originated in the theatre, not the bookshop.[40] Leggatt is certainly right in stressing the importance of the theatre itself in Jacobean audiences' choice of play, which is one reason why the misunderstanding Red Bull auditory was so disappointed in *The White Devil*. What is more contentious is his implication that, if they went to see a Globe play like *King Lear* or *Macbeth*, they did not also in some sense go to see a Shakespeare play.

It must be said that Jacobean public theatre has not on the whole had good service from literary critics, and to a degree the tradition continues in *Theatre and Government under the Early Stuarts*: writing at least from empirical analysis rather than preconception, Kathleen McLuskie concludes her essay by remarking that the plays 'have only sporadic emotional and intellectual power and their politics do not easily transfer to the modern age' (p. 234). But if their artistry is in some ways different from what we are used to in literature, it does not follow that our established canons of criticism cannot illuminate them if applied with due care and sensitivity. Alexander Leggatt's book offers a strong and readable account of a neglected area of Jacobean drama, along with some useful alternative ways of reading what seem initially to be unpromising plays. My reservations about it derive from the fact that, in many cases, these ways of reading are predicated on latent assumptions which are unlikely to alter that general neglect.

---

[39] See *Arden of Faversham*, 2.97–8.

[40] Though it is true that *Venus and Adonis* was already a proven seller, having been through four editions in as many years.

IV

'A Lusty Account of the Gamesome Romps and Comic Caperings of Will Shakespeare, the Playwright, wherein you may find: Bawdy Houses. Gaming Dens. Bear Pits. Gallows birds, Cutpurses, and Royal Rogues. Love-mad Poets and Penniless Players. Foolish Politicians and Politic Fools. Mountebanks and Magical Things. Lusting Lords and Luscious Ladies. Aged Husbands and Merry Wives.' The cover blurb of John Mortimer's book of his television serial, *Will Shakespeare: The Untold Story* (New York, 1978), may not be among this or any year's contributions to our knowledge of Shakespeare's life, but it is a revealing response to the problem that faces any Shakespearian biography, whether celluloid or literary. The highly coloured list of contents contains a great many things that will make people buy the book, but very few of them have anything to do with Shakespeare; and, though extreme, this is also symptomatic. Underlying all Shakespeare's lives there is the great embarrassment that 'Shakespeare' the canon is much more interesting than Shakespeare the historical personage, at least insofar as the latter is recoverable today. Caught between wild speculation and dry documentation, biographers usually end up having to write mainly about something other than William Shakespeare.

With this limitation in mind, Peter Thomson's handsome illustrated account of *Shakespeare's Professional Career* (Cambridge, 1992) takes a welcome diversion from the beaten track: instead of dealing with Shakespeare's life and works, it is, Thomson announces, a book about his job. As such, it is valuable in retailing to a wider readership the gist and import of the discussions which have moved academic Shakespeare studies away from the Romantic obsession with the personal life of the artist. This is achieved most effectively in the book's consideration of the recently fashionable area of aristocratic patronage, in which the Stanleys are used as a case study.[41] The focus is on what might be called the indirect influence of the patron, on journeyman playwrights hired to write for the acting company bearing his livery: they may have received only a collateral benefit from his patronage, but his pleasure was nonetheless one of the imperatives they served. Thomson suggests, for example, that some scenes in English history plays, such as the Falstaff interlude in *Henry VI, Part 1*, were written to flatter patrons and their friends by representing the heroic deeds of their ancestors. One may balk at this concentration on a very small section of the theatre's possible audience, remembering A. P. Rossiter's remark (apropos of Sidney's definition of tragedy) about 'a row of stalls full of kings being shown what happens to tyrants', but the point is well taken that dramatists had to work to criteria which included compliment as well as commerce.[42] The interaction of the two systems and the accommodations that had to be made is an area that would reward further attention.

In practice, Thomson has to take a broadly biographical structure – his book is an account of a career as much as it is of a profession – and he gives cautious support to E. A. J. Honigmann's theory about the 'lost years': 'It can no longer be seriously doubted' (p. 65), he asserts, that those years were spent with players, and Lord Strange's Men, favoured by Honigmann, are likely enough candidates. With this in mind, it is a pity that Shakespeare's work as a professional actor, which was as much a part of his career as writing plays, tends to be relegated to the sidelines. Caution is understandable in

[41] Two useful studies of theatrical patronage in particular have appeared in the same issue of *Shakespeare Quarterly*, 44 (1993): Andrew Gurr, 'Three Reluctant Patrons and Early Shakespeare', 159–74; and Sally-Beth MacLean, 'The Politics of Patronage: Dramatic Records in Robert Dudley's Household Books', 175–82.

[42] A. P. Rossiter, *Angel with Horns* (London, 1961), pp. 258–9.

view of the lack of hard evidence, though even what there is can be passed over: Thomson scrupulously discounts the traditions that Shakespeare played old Adam and King Hamlet's ghost, preferring to believe that he gave up acting for scriptwriting, and came out of retirement in 1603 to appear in *Sejanus' Fall*; but the basis for this supposition is not stated, and there is no mention of the cast list for *Every Man in His Humour*, which indicates that Shakespeare was still acting at least as late as 1598.

Any account of Shakespeare's career which downgrades his work as a performer, and treats him as not only primarily but essentially a writer, risks lifting him out of the context of practical theatre altogether. Thomson's does not: for instance, he suggests that Shakespeare's skills in dramatic characterization developed from his intimate knowledge of the talents and habitual performance styles of the particular individuals for whom he wrote. What the book fails to convey, however, is the possible relevance of his own acting career to the less evanescent areas of his creativity: obviously the fact of having acted, having projected himself into other identities, must also have been an influence on his character-writing. Moreover, it follows from Thomson's arguments that, if Shakespeare did continue acting in some capacity, some of his roles must have been written for himself – another area which might be worth investigation, taking a lead from Molière studies.[43]

Ultimately *Shakespeare's Professional Career* is not itself a book of scholarship, so much as a popular work which assimilates a good deal of scholarship. It is understandable that it should also have assimilated a few out-of-date notions, such as the nature and function of theatrical 'plots' (p. 89), and the role of stenography in the production of bad quartos (p. 90); even the 'manifest allusiveness' (p. 114) of *Love's Labour's Lost* now seems less manifest than Thomson suggests. There are occasions when a little more scepticism might have been in order, such as in the confident and uncritical identification of Henslowe's *harey the vj* as one of Shakespeare's *Henry VI* plays, or of a 1603 engraving of Tamburlaine (reproduced on page 65) as a portrait of Edward Alleyn in the role.[44] One could also quarrel with the description of Kempe's jigs as 'soft pornography' (p. 103) – whatever that overused term may mean in this context – and with the account of playhouse manuscripts and their origins (p. 85). The latter makes the assumption that the scribal fair copy was chopped up into the actors' parts, after having been used as the basis for a further transcript, made without reference to the original holograph; this transcript, he believes, then became the prompt-book. It suits his argument to maximize the potential error content of the prompt-book, but he offers no evidence, palaeographical or otherwise, to link either it or the parts with particular stages in the chain of transmission. (Indeed one may doubt whether

[43] Gaston Hall, 'Molière's Roles Written for Himself', unpublished paper read at St Edmund Hall, Oxford, in 1989. See also his *Molière's 'Le Bourgeois Gentilhomme': Context and Stagecraft* (Durham, 1990). Of course, it is awkward that, even with the eccentric computer-aided guesswork being undertaken by Donald W. Foster – on which, see his over-confident article 'Reconstructuring Shakespeare I: The Roles that Shakespeare Performed', *The Shakespeare Newsletter*, 41 (1991), 16–17 – we are unlikely ever to achieve absolute certainty about Shakespeare's own roles. As John Gross says, 'Novelists are allowed to indulge in . . . speculation, critics and biographers do so at their peril – which does not mean that the idea may not have something in it' (*Shylock*, p. 323). But since we have good reason to believe that some parts were created by Shakespeare in more than the literary sense, even if we cannot find out the details by normal scholarly method, this sort of imaginative parlour game cannot be entirely worthless, so long as it is played with an honest recognition of its limitations. In this spirit, my own front runner is the character of Time in *The Winter's Tale*.

[44] The engraving's origins – as an illustration to Richard Knolles's *General History of the Turks* rather than a piece of theatrical portraiture – are not mentioned. The case for identifying the portrait as Alleyn has now been thoroughly demolished by John H. Astington, 'The "Unrecorded Portrait" of Edward Alleyn', *Shakespeare Quarterly*, 44 (1993), 73–86.

the theatre had a consistent practice at all: if for practical purposes a transcript is taken to be an identical copy, then surely either document could serve either purpose.) But these are minor reservations, and the book can nonetheless be warmly recommended to undergraduates, now that it has appeared in a paperback edition which is, unlike the original hardback, within their price range.

Part of the biographer's dilemma is the demarcation of territory. Contrary to the myth of 'Shakespeare's-life-on-a-postage-stamp', there is a substantial body of documentary material which might offer biographical evidence. Most of it was published in 1623 as *Mr William Shakespeare's Comedies, Histories, and Tragedies*. Of course, it is always dangerous to infer external biography from the plays – let *The Mirror and the Globe* stand as an awful warning – and since C. J. Sisson's British Academy Lecture they have also been a no-go area as a direct, Dowdenesque record of the dramatist's emotional and spiritual life. However, they can still be read, with due care and subtlety, as evidence of his reading and his intellectual interests and development. This is the point at which criticism traditionally takes over from biography, but it is a criticism which is driven by an essentially biographical curiosity: as Jonathan Bate says in the Preface to his excellent study of *Shakespeare and Ovid* (Oxford, 1993), 'If you admire a writer, it is natural to wonder which writers that writer admired.' (p. vii)

Bate's central assumption is a community of aesthetic experience between Shakespeare and his modern students and enthusiasts: his artistic emergence is envisaged as a paradigm of our own, except that, coming from a time when there was no Shakespeare for schoolchildren to study, resent, and occasionally fall in love with, Shakespeare himself had Ovid instead. In this respect, the book is a natural development from Bate's earlier work, with its underlying project to identify and analyse Shakespeare's place in a literary tradition which influenced new writing, particularly that of the Romantic poets. Now Shakespeare himself is constructed in the same terms, as the inheritor of Ovid. Bate's metaphor for this process of influence places literature as a supremely civilized practice: there is none of the military brutality implicit in the fashionable but nauseating critical rhetoric of 'strategy' and 'interrogation'; for Bate, literature is better compared with conversation, between author and author, and between author and critic.

Metaphor is, of course, a two-edged critical tool. This particular metaphor is appropriate to Bate's case in that, as he points out, Renaissance habits of thought tended to privilege a text's exemplarity rather than its singularity, so that, for an Elizabethan audience, Shakespeare's plays were *foci* for a vast network of associations with previous literature. In this respect, the text participates with its antecedents rather than fights with them. On the other hand, such influence is not the whole of Shakespeare's interest and appeal: otherwise we could not explain Shakespeare's survival in the (for the most part) classically uneducated late twentieth century, in contrast with, say, the late Augustan poets who also demand to be read for their exemplarity, and are consequently almost unreadable today without specialized taste and training. Perhaps Bate's overriding emphasis on the text's interactiveness leads him to underestimate the extent to which good writers also steal from one another: many of his examples of Shakespeare's allusions to and affinities with Ovid could also be interpreted as unconscious appropriations.

These are not, though, reservations which invalidate Bate's concern to remake some of the connections for modern readers. From *Titus Andronicus* – whose Rome is for him a sort of humanist academy of atrocity, whose graduates have learned from their schoolbooks how to be worse people – to the collaborations with Fletcher, and from the narrative poems to the Sonnets, he brilliantly demonstrates the fructifying presence of Ovid, overtly in the early and late work but also as a subtler 'underpresence' (p. 215) in the mature tragedies. In doing so, he reads the plays with such learning and subtlety that to attempt summary is to risk debasing the material. It is a fine book which rewards close attention.

Bate's lightness of touch is sorely missed in Wolfgang Riehle's overwritten study of *Shakespeare, Plautus, and the Humanist Tradition* (Woodbridge, 1990), in which he suggests that the influence of Plautus in Elizabethan culture has been underestimated, because previous scholars have been misled by the contemporary Continental taste for Terence. He explores the popularity of the classical New Comedy tradition – unbroken in the Middle Ages, he posits – in Renaissance humanism and throughout Shakespeare's career, but naturally his main focus is on *The Comedy of Errors*. Its links with Plautus are exhaustively examined: characterization, lexis, prosody, structure, all owe something to Shakespeare's Roman source in Riehle's analysis. The Appendix also attempts to demonstrate Shakespeare's debt to Warner's translation of the *Menaechmi*, but the argument depends on a highly tentative analysis of Warner's practice as a translator, and on that account fails to convince.

Three other books have also dealt, directly and indirectly, with Shakespeare's broader context in literary history. Virginia Cox's study of *The Renaissance Dialogue* (Cambridge, 1992) considers the flourishing of this critically neglected form in *cinquecento* Italy, but will also make valuable background reading for students of English literary dialogue from Thomas More to the pamphlet plays of the 1640s. More immediately applicable to Shakespeare is Richard Andrews's careful consideration of the generic traditions of Italian comedy in *Scripts and Scenarios: The Performance of Comedy in Renaissance Italy* (Cambridge, 1993), with frequent and illuminating reference to English dramatists' subsequent use of similar material. Meanwhile, Henry Ansgar Kelly surveys *Ideas and Forms of Tragedy from Aristotle to the Middle Ages* (Cambridge, 1993), and finds that medieval writers on the genre treat it as one practised by dead poets: Chaucer's tragic works are exceptional, he argues, and mark a revival of interest in tragedy, which was continued by Lydgate and Henryson, and ultimately the Jacobeans.

A more local study of Shakespeare's reading is provided by F. W. Brownlow in *Shakespeare, Harsnett, and the Devils of Denham* (Newark, 1993), published in revised form thirty years after it was submitted as a Shakespeare Institute Ph.D. thesis. The book combines a lightly annotated old-spelling edition of Samuel Harsnett's *Declaration of Egregious Popish Impostures* with a lengthy monograph, which includes a biography of Harsnett as well as a study of the book's occasion and reception. The key question about the *Declaration* is why, in 1602, Harsnett should have devoted so much attention to the Denham exorcisms of sixteen years earlier. For Brownlow, the book is current affairs in disguise: he relates it to the ecclesiastical politics of the turn of the century, and in particular to a pamphlet war between the church authorities and the discredited exorcist John Darrell. Rather like some disgruntled author haunting the correspondence columns of the *Times Literary Supplement*, Darrell proved to be a persistent answerer of published criticisms, and this, Brownlow argues, was the reason for Harsnett's using the Denham exorcisms as a stalking-horse: since the book did not overtly apply to him, Darrell could not respond to it without implicitly admitting a correspondence between the Denham affair and his own activities, and so acknowledging the charge of credulity over the sort of imposture that Harsnett sets out to expose. That Darrell fell silent after the publication of the *Declaration* gives credence to Brownlow's necessarily tentative theory.

Harsnett's book may initially have caught Shakespeare's attention because it contained information about fellow Stratfordians. Brownlow feels that it continued to exercise and trouble him as a crypto-Catholic. *King Lear* thus becomes a conscious reply to Harsnett, a contribution to the ecclesiastical debate which presents, in Edgar, the phenomena from which Harsnett tries to disengage his readers. Brownlow evidently wants the play to be sympathetic to the Catholic position on the Denham exorcisms, and in this respect his reading serves the latent but noticeable Catholic bias with which he writes.[45] However, it entails treating *Lear* as fundamentally a work of the same order as, say, most of Dryden's longer poems: a contribution to an existing intellectual debate rather than an originary work of fiction. This sits ill with Brownlow's recognition of the depth of the *Declaration*'s imaginative impact on Shakespeare:

> In writing *King Lear* Shakespeare did not, as we say, 'use' the *Declaration*; Harsnett's book is not in the ordinary sense a source at all. Rather the play is the result of an encounter with another text: a kind of dialogue has taken place between the cleric and the poet . . . (p. 118)

As Brownlow presents it, however, it is a dialogue characterized more by subcutaneous absorption than overt rejoinder: usefully, he adds to Kenneth Muir's list of parallels between the two texts, and stresses particularly the extent to which Shakespeare acquired rare vocabulary from Harsnett.[46]

It is as a case study of Shakespeare's response to his reading, and not as a disquisition on the politico-religious purpose of *King Lear*, that F. W. Brownlow's book is most valuable. Lives may be more commercial than close, scholarly source studies like this, but it is the latter which can show us more directly Shakespeare's mind at work. Perhaps, then, Shakespearian biography too should seek its future not in the pre-Fielding 'merrie England' of *Will Shakespeare: The Untold Story*, nor in the less fictitious theatre business of *Shakespeare's Professional Career*, but beyond the disadvantageous boundary that separates the poet's material from his intellectual life.

V

In the 1856 edition of the *Encyclopaedia Britannica*, Lord Macaulay sniped at what he considered the most 'slovenly' and 'worthless' imaginable edition of Shakespeare, that of Samuel Johnson ninety-one years earlier:

> That his knowledge of our literature was extensive is indisputable. But, unfortunately, he had altogether neglected that very part of our literature with which it is especially desirable that an editor of Shakespeare should be conversant . . . Johnson might easily, in a few months, have made himself well acquainted with every old play that was extant. But it never seems to have occurred to him that this was a necessary preparation for the work which he had undertaken.[47]

This stricture has none of the positivist sense of superiority with which the Victorians often looked down on their ancestors: Johnson is, rather, being attacked for a simple lack of editorial common sense. Modern scholars who have read their Margreta de Grazia will properly reply that this 'common sense' is actually a contingent procedure that was only established, by Malone, six years after Johnson's death: that, by 1856, he could be expected to have used that procedure shows how far Malone's innovations had come to be regarded as self-evident.

The trouble with long perspectives, whether

---

45 For example, to describe Edward Arden as having been 'executed as a Catholic on charges of treason' (p. 109), as distinct from a Catholic executed as a traitor, is to resurrect the anti-government line taken by the Jesuits in the 1580s (i.e. that executed recusants had been persecuted for Catholicism rather than prosecuted for criminality), and answered by Burghley in *The Execution of Justice in England* (1583).

46 If this should prove to be a general habit of Shakespeare's, it could have important editorial applications: many of *Hamlet*'s most inscrutable cruces, for instance, centre on rare words which Shakespeare may have picked up from his reading.

47 Thomas Babington Macaulay, *Selected Writings*, ed. John Clive and Thomas Pinney (Chicago and London, 1972), p. 148.

from 1856 or 1991, when *Shakespeare Verbatim* was published, is that they tend to simplify: 'God said, "Let Malone be", and all was light.' From the vantage of the 1790s, as Jonathan Bate shows in his contribution to an important collection of essays edited by Nigel Smith, *Literature and Censorship*, Malone's approach seemed less secure: like all revolutions, it had to be enforced by marginalizing or suppressing alternative positions. In this case, the opposition took the very different forms of Joseph Ritson's *Cursory Criticisms* (1792) and the Ireland forgeries of three years later. Bate shows how both embodied positions inimical to the Burkean political imperatives which inform Malone's editorial preoccupation with authority and authenticity: he was especially outraged that the 'Shakespeare' of the forgeries should call the crown a 'gyldedde bawble' (p. 71). Accordingly Bate interprets the closing down of the Ireland circus as a kind of anti-Jacobin censorship which contributed, as Nigel Smith puts it in his Preface to the volume, to 'the manufacturing of a Tory Shakespeare' (p. vii). It turns out that, for all Malone's importance in defining scholarly method, his Shakespeare is uncomfortably close to E. M. W. Tillyard's monarchical propagandist, while the more recent, plausibly sceptical views of the 'Elizabethan golden age' have an unlikely and embarrassing ancestor in William-Henry Ireland.[48]

An unwitting contributor to the ongoing redress of the eighteenth-century revolution in Shakespeare studies is Arthur Sherbo. The most recent product of his continuing quest to confer recognition on the bit-players of the time is *Shakespeare's Midwives: Some Neglected Shakespeareans* (Newark, 1992), in which he restores to visibility seven minor commentators from Tyrwhitt to the younger Boswell. These are people who have for the most part dwindled into a footnote or, in the case of Francis Douce, a shelfmark: in what Sherbo calls, after Samuel Johnson, the 'Age of the Single Scholiast' (p. 16), the twentieth century, they have escaped notice because they are not themselves editors (though Boswell's name is associated with the Third Variorum); this is inappropriate and unfair, he contends, since, in the 'closed society' (p. 14) that was eighteenth-century literary culture, the project of Shakespearian editing was far more a collaboration than a solo effort. The main object of the book seems to be merely to uphold the honour of the eighteenth century, in showing how far its scholars were responsible for insights which are usually attributed to commentators of the nineteenth; but in exposing a little more of the origins of Shakespearian knowledge, the book also makes a little less sustainable the sublime complacency of a Macaulay.

The other wing of this scholarly movement, the recovery of the alternative Shakespeares of the past, is among the concerns of Michael Dobson's distinguished book, *The Making of the National Poet: Shakespeare, Adaptation and Authorship, 1660–1769* (Oxford, 1992), which tells how Shakespeare became 'immortal', though sadly not how he became 'the Bard', another of the culturally loaded eighteenth-century epithets which have survived into modern usage (including, incidentally, Dobson's text). This is a process which, Dobson argues, was abetted by the making of temporary, disposable versions of the plays: Alternative Shakespeares begat Establishment Shakespeare.

The traditional account of Shakespeare's longevity, put foward by both Jonson and Johnson, held that his work survived because of its inherent greatness. Dobson shows, however, that literary and theatrical survival is actually a by-product of appropriation: Shakespeare became timeless by being made period-bound. The adaptations of the later seventeenth century, for example, keyed the plays in to the political anxieties of the Restoration: apolitical

[48] Jonathan Bate, 'Faking It: Shakespeare and the 1790s', in Nigel Smith (ed.), *Literature and Censorship, Essays and Studies*, 46 (1993), 63–80.

because old, they regularly served, as they did more recently in communist Eastern Europe, as a means of masking the theatre's engagement with sensitive topical matters. It is in these terms that Dobson offers a vindication of Nahum Tate: the rewritten *Lear*, with its longer bastard's role and its happy ending, becomes a propagandist parable about the Duke of Monmouth, rather than the act of cultural vandalism it is often taken to be. The continuing popularity of this version, still in the repertory in the nineteenth century, may be attributed to the appeal of its 'apolitical domestic pathos' (p. 83), though Dobson offers no answer to the question this begs about other similar adaptations – such as Otway's *Caius Marius*, also a prime example of domestic pathos – which did not share the Tate *Lear*'s endurance.

From the late Restoration onwards, Dobson argues, the making of the National Poet was also the domestication of the plays. Adapters increasingly sought to avoid a political Shakespeare, and so steered their versions towards the concerns of the common man rather than of state. Meanwhile, the developing sense of propriety at the end of the seventeenth century – forever associated with the name of Jeremy Collier – issued in a 'cultural decontamination project' (p. 125) in the first decade of the eighteenth, with the result that adaptation was necessary not only to suit new tastes but also to protect the reputation of Shakespeare; it was for this reason, Dobson suggests, that Shakespeare's name was omitted from *The Cobbler of Preston*. With the development of a new sense of the significance of authorship, the matter was increasingly seen in personal terms: William Shakespeare is abstracted from his plays, often to appear as a ghostly prologue conferring his authority on a revival or some other cultural project; eventually he is embodied, first in statuary and then, reincarnated, in the person of David Garrick. This created a quandary: on the one hand, with the birth of the author came a new regard for authenticity which found its ultimate exponents in editors like Capell and Malone, but on the other, the content of the plays – in particular, their low comedy and lower-class characters – was taken to reflect badly on their imaginatively reconstructed author.[49] Adaptation was at once a necessary and a furtive practice.

The book demonstrates, then, how Shakespeare was made 'respectable' – fit to be commemorated as a statue in Westminster Abbey, fit to be the focus of a fashionable ladies' club – by being made un-Shakespearian. In the long term, the result was to move the plays from the public arena of the theatre into the home, a development completed by the Bowdlers and the Lambs with *The Family Shakespeare* and *Tales from Shakespeare* respectively. The paradox – which will come as no surprise to readers of *Literature and Censorship* – is that this movement into private space was coterminous with the emergence of British imperialism, which made the middle-class version of Shakespeare one of the national exports of the later eighteenth century: as so often with bourgeois acts of censorship (which the Augustan 'decontamination project' essentially was), the agenda of the home demands the subjugation of the unruly outside world, and, once tamed, Shakespeare could go on to be a prime cultural instrument in furthering the process internationally. It is, Dobson shows, not entirely a coincidence that the period's notable admirers of 'the Bard' should have included Maurice Morgann of the Colonial Office.

The study of Shakespeare's reception – and in particular his reception in North America – will be significantly abetted by the publication of Richard Studing's *Shakespeare in American*

49 The French had their own version of the process, except that they subordinated Shakespeare to the neo-classical strictures of Voltaire rather than to middle-class notions of morality; the subject is extensively studied by John Golder in his book, *Shakespeare for the Age of Reason: The Earliest Stage Adaptations of Jean-François Ducis, 1769–1792* (Oxford, 1992).

Painting: A Catalogue from the Late Eighteenth Century to the Present (Rutherford, Madison, and Teaneck, 1993) and William L. Pressly's sumptuous *Catalogue of Paintings in the Folger Shakespeare Library* (New Haven and London, 1993). The latter makes available, seventy years on, the 'systematic survey' (p. 5) of Henry Clay Folger's art collection, which Folger himself began to think necessary in 1922: each of the 202 paintings is reproduced, described, and discussed, under one of five generic headings. The lion's share are 'Literary Illustrations', and Pressley's introduction to the section treats them as a neglected medium of interpretation, drawing interesting associations with the movements of written criticism. His introduction to 'Portraits of Shakespeare' is less satisfactory, in that his account of Shakespeare's life contains some obvious and basic inaccuracies: legend and speculation alike are retailed as fact, from Aubrey's tale of John Shakespeare the butcher to Baldwin's about Shakespeare's membership of Leicester's men (p. 263). It is unfortunate that some art historians may be misled by these claims, though presumably the volume was never intended to be a definitive source of information on Shakespeare's life. For definitive information on the Folger's paintings, however, it could hardly be bettered.

Richard Studing's catalogue is a vaster enterprise, and is understandably more of a record of work in progress; in fact, many of the paintings listed are at present unlocated. With two centuries of art history to cover, the introduction can only offer a whistlestop tour of the major figures, while the main body of the catalogue provides a generous but less than comprehensive selection of illustrations, some of them in colour. There are some casualties here: the impressionist work of Albert Pinkham Ryder is not at its best in black-and-white, for instance, and the entertaining kitsch of Ayres Houghtelling's teeming pictures suffers badly from undersized reproduction, a perennial problem in illustrated academic publications.[50] Less unavoidable is the absence of running-titles relating to the entries, which should be a standard time-saving feature of reference books. If this is an important failure of user-friendliness, however, it is also an isolated one, and the catalogue is especially laudable for the provision of a detailed subject index, organized character by character as well as play by play, which enables the reader to see at a glance the most popular areas of the canon among America's Shakespearian painters.

Interviewed on British television about the making of Kenneth Branagh's *Much Ado About Nothing*, Emma Thompson commented on the conscious internationalism of the film's casting: 'There's a dangerous and rather unattractive myth that the British do Shakespeare the best, which is not true and shouldn't be allowed to be true.'[51] A similar approach seems incipient in academic Shakespeare studies. Imperial Britain may have retailed to the world its cleaned-up version of 'the Bard', but the result has been manifold appropriations and transformations to suit various cultural circumstances. These other Shakespeares are sometimes studied in the countries of their origin, in books like *Shakespeare en España: Crítica, traducciones y representaciones* (Alicante and Saragossa, 1993), a collection of essays edited by José Manuel González, though, written as they are in Spanish, they are unlikely to be much read outside Spain and Latin America. Now, however, Anglo-American critics too are growing readier to pay attention to elsewhere's Shakespeares, partly because the work of scholars like Michael Dobson and Margreta de Grazia has exposed the contingency of their own tradition, and perhaps also in response to a sharper awareness, promoted by the New Historicists, of colonialism as an intellectual as well as a political issue.

---

50 Another example of this inadequacy is *Shakespeare's Professional Career*: some of the illustrations' captions draw attention to details that are all but invisible to the naked eye.

51 *Chasing the Light*, Special Treats Productions for BBC television, transmitted on 9 October 1993.

Two recently announced projects show that there is still much mileage in the subject. One is a new series from the University of Delaware Press, 'International Studies in Shakespeare and his Contemporaries', which aims to reprint the best contributions to scholarship by modern writers outside England and America, and which has kicked off with *Shakespeare and His Contemporaries: Eastern and Central European Studies* (Newark, 1993), edited by Jerzy Limon and Jay L. Halio. The other is next year's volume of *Shakespeare Survey*.

3. EDITIONS AND TEXTUAL STUDIES

reviewed by H. R. WOUDHUYSEN

> Well then; the promis'd hour is come at last;
> The present Age of Wit obscures the past:

It may seem a little extravagant to use Dryden's lines on Congreve to introduce a fully annotated text of *King Lear* based on the Folio alone, but after so much talk and work, it is a moment of some interest.[1] One question worth asking about recent textual work on Shakespeare is whether the past ten or so years have witnessed an editorial revolution or, less dramatically, a publishing one. Of course, some important matters have been valuably addressed, from the difficulties posed by modernization to the relationship between literary and theatrical texts. But the steady flow of impressive volumes from Cambridge and Oxford may make the reader occasionally pause to wonder how different in practice these editions are from those of a decade or more ago.

Jay L. Halio's edition of what has been called 'the bibliographer's Everest', *King Lear*,[2] is large and generous, with a lengthy critical and historical introduction and over eighty pages devoted to textual matters, including detailed comparisons of Q/F parallel passages and fully edited versions of Q-only passages. Halio takes a modest view of the editor's role; he is clear sighted and level headed, accurate and in control of his material. The result is an edition of the play which consolidates much recent *Lear* scholarship and brings aspects of its textual and theatrical history into sharp focus. It allows the reader to reconstruct most of the story – or at least one version of it – and gain access to the materials behind the play's two texts.

Halio starts with *Lear*'s composition which he argues had begun by spring or summer of 1605 (p. 1). Shakespeare had read the old play of *King Leir* and had been studying Sidney's *Arcadia*; his interest in fools and the nature of folly was complemented by a concern with exorcism and purgation stimulated by Harsnett's *A Declaration of Egregious Popish Impostures*. The contemporary genius of Montaigne was fused with the deeper reaches of the Cinderella story, morality plays, and the Book of Job. *Lear* was probably acted in 1605 although its first certain performance was at court on 26 December 1606 (p. 34). Nicholas Okes somehow got hold of Shakespeare's heavily revised manuscript foul papers of the play and printed them over the Christmas of 1607–8. It was the first play the new master printer Okes had attempted to print, and the combination of difficult copy and his inexperience caused considerable problems as the book passed through the press: the many corrections undertaken during this process were not always made accurately (p. 62). Two compositors set the book not by formes but seriatim. The first Quarto was reprinted in the second Quarto published in 1619.

---

1 *The Tragedy of King Lear*, ed. Jay L. Halio (Cambridge, 1992), in the New Cambridge Shakespeare Series.

2 Norman Sanders, 'Shakespeare's Text' in *Shakespeare: A Bibliographical Guide*, new edn, ed. Stanley Wells (Oxford, 1990), p. 29.

Before then, at some point, the play was revised and it is this later version which was printed from cast-off copy in the First Folio of 1623. Most of the play was set by the apprentice known as E, the rest by the more experienced B. The copy for F was probably partly derived from an annotated copy of Q2. Alternatively, the compositors may have used manuscripts and transcripts deriving from Q and from the playhouse: the issue is uncertain and Halio canvasses the differing views of Gary Taylor and Trevor Howard-Hill, and draws on Peter Blayney's unpublished research. He concludes that 'both a manuscript and an exemplar of Q2 influenced the setting of the Folio' (p. 67). The manuscript preserved theatrical changes and was therefore taken from, or identical with, the prompt-book: 'In general, then, substantive readings and alterations derive from the manuscript; accidentals and orthography from Q2' (p. 68). Although he admits that 'differences between Q and F' may be 'mixed and cumulative, and that autonomy can be claimed for neither in isolation' (p. 69), Halio essentially subscribes to the view that Shakespeare revised the play by annotating a copy of Q1. This was collated against the old prompt-book and a 'new prompt-book (or a transcript of it) became the copy for F, which was printed in consultation with Q2, copies of which were available in Jaggard's printing-house'.

The difficult task facing an editor of a single-text edition of the play revolves around distinguishing what is genuine authorial revision from changes which may have been caused by a scribe or compositor, and from revisions made in the playhouse with the author's agreement or against his wishes. Halio discusses the many variations between the two texts under the headings of 'Omissions and Cuts', 'Amplifications and Additions', and 'Rewriting, Substitution, and Recasting'. He then turns to 'The Timing of Interventions' tracing possible changes through the processes of making a fair copy of Shakespeare's foul papers, of rehearsals, and of the preparation of copy for F. He usefully emphasizes that these changes were not made all at once, but may have evolved over several years. After his detailed analyses of some fifty-five Q-only passages – almost all illustrated with reproductions from both Q and F – Halio states that 'The weight of the evidence clearly indicates that F represents a revised text of *King Lear*, with Q reflecting a version of the original' (p. 288). The reviser, he believes, is to be identified with Shakespeare who on stylistic grounds can be judged to have been responsible for the additions, but may equally have had a hand in the theatrical cuts. Even when it comes to the omission of the 'mock trial' in 3.6 in F, Halio admits that Shakespeare may have had reasons for the cut, 'But authors – even Shakespeare –', he continues 'are not always the best judges of their own work, and theatre directors (who are notorious for making alterations of their own, regardless of whose play it is) seldom cut the mock trial in 3.6' (p. 270).

Halio's lucid and fair-minded presentation of a great deal of complicated material is highly impressive. And yet, it is possible to feel that the promised hour has not quite come, that the present editorial age has not really eclipsed the last. Some readers may still feel that difficulties remain about what has emerged almost as a canonical view of *King Lear* and of its texts. Halio is aware that the current consensus may be as flawed in its own way as the earlier theories about the play – the theories which led to conflated editions. John Henry Newman wrote that 'Ten thousand difficulties do not make one doubt': but will Halio's scrupulous dealing with the fifteen hundred or so difficult Q/F variants dispel the doubt which may still lurk in some minds? It is possible to trace a pattern of revision to the roles of the Fool, Albany and Goneril and to study the changes made to the parts played by France and by the French King in F, but doubts over such essential elements as the mock trial in 3.6, the servants' dialogue at the end of 3.7, the dialogue between Kent and the Gentleman after 4.2, and even the reassignment of the play's last speech in F from Albany to Edgar, tend to linger.

These local difficulties bring some broader questions to mind. Does it necessarily follow that F is a later version of Q? Might not Q and F essentially derive from the same document containing all or most of the readings in the two texts? Why are the revisions both so delicate and so savage? It seems unlikely that these revisions were made because the play was too long. As Halio points out, while F is some two hundred lines shorter than Q, the cuts – occurring mainly after 3.5 – scarcely have a significant effect on the play's overall length. They 'alter the ethos of several characters', but 'are sometimes offset by additions or amplifications' (p. 71). And does their almost exclusive concern with plot and character reflect our own critical interests – traditional ones admittedly – rather too neatly?

Three further areas may be of particular interest to those thinking about the play and its different versions. First, it would still be valuable to know how and under what circumstances Okes got hold of the manuscript from which he printed the play. Halio admits (p. 62 n. 5) that the question remains open, but it is one which poses a fundamental challenge to our understanding of Shakespeare's relations with both the theatre and the stationers, to say nothing of our attempts to make sense of his views of his own art. Secondly, Halio is disappointingly reticent about the date at and circumstances under which he believes Shakespeare revised the play. In the stemma on p. 70 the revision is dated '1611–12?', and earlier (p. 69 n. 5) he cites Gary Taylor's essay on 'Date and authorship' in *The Division of the Kingdoms* in addition to a forthcoming study by Donald Foster. As he admits, Halio's date for the revision is 'quite late': the Oxford *Textual Companion* places Folio *Lear* in 1610.[3] Finally, there is the problem of censorship. Halio accepts that F was subject to the 1606 Act against profanity (see the note to 1.2.115 where Q's 'Fut' has been cut), and that some passages in Q may have been offensive to James I and his court (see p. 294), but has little to say about the role censorship may have had in determining some of the play's most distinctive features (but cp. p. 296 on the French). When he comes to discuss 4.5.157–62, 'Plate sin with gold ...', Halio refuses to accept Chambers' argument that 'the lines were cut from Q because of censorship' since 'censorship would hardly affect foul papers' (p. 286). Censorship might not be able to prevent Shakespeare's writing politically or socially unacceptable material; however, it might well cause a printer – especially one who had licensed his copy – to think twice about printing it.

It was not Halio's task to answer all of these questions, but to produce an edition of the play which would reflect the current editorial view that F is a later and, to put it crudely, 'better' version of the play. Within these limits what sort of an edition has he produced? The text and the collations are on the whole very accurate and the most jarring error is the reproduction as the first illustration of the title-page of *King Leir*, when the Introduction (p. 1) clearly refers to the first quarto of *King Lear*.[4] Halio sticks to F readings as often as he can; even so he substantively emends F from Q on some sixty or so occasions. Most of F's rejected readings appear

---

[3] Stanley Wells and Gary Taylor, *William Shakespeare: A Textual Companion* (Oxford, 1987), p. 131.

[4] The following errors affect the text: 1.4.61 *for* 'I have not seen him these two days' *read* 'I have not seen him this two days'; 2.4.11 *for* 'What's he that has so much thy place mistook'; *read* 'What he that hath so much thy place mistook'; 4.3.0 F calls for 'Gentlemen' rather than a 'Gentleman' in the scene; 4.5.193 *for* 'an you get it' *read* 'and you get it' – elsewhere, unlike Oxford, Cambridge prints 'and' where it means 'if'.

The main errors in the textual commentary, excluding ones concerning spelling or punctuation, are: 1.1.205 *for* 'To auvert' *read* 'To auert'; 1.4.238 *for* 'thourt disuentur'd' *read* 'thourt disuetur'd'; 3.4.116 *for* 'tode pole' in uncorrected Q *read* 'tode pold'; 3.7.2 F (TLN 2061) does not read 'hin' but like Q 'him'. Among the Q-only passages, line 1 in number xxiii on p. 306 should read 'and yet it is danger' rather than 'and yet 'tis danger'.

to be the result of simple compositorial inaccuracy, but Halio identifies some characteristic errors as resulting from dittography (1.1.69, 4.6.32, 5.3.77), crowding (1.1.174, 281, 5.3.231), simple omission (1.1.208, 2.1.70, 3.4.120, 4.4.41, 4.6.25, 5.1.13, 5.3.224), compositorial sophistication (4.1.14), faulty plurals (5.3.78, 82), modernization (4.5.18, 114, 145, where F has 'yond' for Q's 'yon'), and straightforward misreading of manuscript copy (2.4.28, 3.4.50, 3.6.27(?), 4.2.44). Halio's list of emendations – helpfully marked in the textual commentary by asterisks – is well worth studying. He adopts or follows Oxford on a few occasions such as at 1.1.150, 'ne'er feared to lose it', 4.1.10, 'My father, parti-eyed', describing Q2's and F's 'poorely led' as making 'sufficient, if feeble, sense', 4.3.3, 'fumitor', and 5.3.119, 'honour'. Halio's own emendations are largely confined to changes to stage-directions and to punctuation. Having already edited the play once in 1973, at 1.1.182 he retains the speech-heading which he then gave to Cordelia, but rejects his similar assignment at 1.1.156. One significant and not altogether happy change Halio makes is to follow F's usual practice and to print the form 'Edmond': Q has 'Edmund'. *The Oxford Dictionary of Christian Names* describes 'Edmond' as a French form often used for Edmund in the Middle Ages, but still used by some families later.[5] To modern eyes, 'Edmond' looks, and from some lips will no doubt sound, rather odd.

The Introduction itself is on the whole sensible and to the point. Its account of *Lear* 'on stage and screen' is thorough, especially in stressing the long-standing rule of Tate's adaptation, and at times diverting – as when Halio recounts the legend that the audience 'tittered to see the diminutive actor', Kean, 'struggling under the weight of Mrs W. West's Cordelia' (p. 41), or when he describes Kemble 'wearing a white wig and mustachios, a jewelled and feathered hat, false shoulders, and a lace collar and white stockings' in the part (p. 43). In the end, Halio sees the play as presenting its audience with something almost unbearably real (pp. 33–4). He locates one of the play's most characteristic moments in his acute comment on Gloucester's fall (p. 22), drawing a parallel between 'The trick Edgar plays on his father's imagination' and 'the trick Shakespeare plays on ours'. F, he argues, makes the play more 'anti-romantic', heightening its 'nihilistic energies' (pp. 12, 28) but, at the same time, he can state that Q has a harsher ending (p. 34). Despite its 'outrageous and preposterous extremities', the *Lear* world 'is not without redeeming elements that may rescue us from despair' (p. 28).

Above all, Halio is a close reader of the play's plot. Noting that in Edgar's first three appearances before 3.4 he says nothing of Lear's situation, Halio wonders 'Is it possible that Edgar has no knowledge and only now learns of it?' (p. 20). Again and again in the commentary he draws attention to the play's plotting and its concern with narrative (see, for example, 2.1.29–30, 3.7.15, 4.4.4, 4.5.222–3, 274, 5.1.54–5). The problem is that close observation sometimes turns into a questionable editorial coerciveness. So that 3.4.32–3 ('O I have ta'en / Too little care of this') prompts the comment 'By assuming responsibility for the wretched state of his subjects, Lear takes a major step forward in understanding himself.' Sometimes these observations are Halio's own, on other occasions he cites previous commentators: Gloucester's 'away he [Edmund] shall again' (1.1.27–8) provokes Halio into quoting Kenneth Muir '"Perhaps these words seal Gloucester's doom"'; Edmund's 'conversion' at 5.3.190–2 is described, drawing on John Reibetanz's *The Lear World*, as showing that he '"becomes humanised" in the course of *King Lear*, discovering the limitations and passions that being human involves . . .'. He draws particularly heavily on Marvin Rosenberg's

[5] E. G. Withycombe, *The Oxford Dictionary of Christian Names*, 2nd edn (Oxford, 1959), p. 89.

The Masks of 'King Lear' and the result is not always very happy. The most unfortunate or contentious example of this practice is Halio's comment on 4.6.39 when Cordelia says Lear 'wakes': 'These words signal the moment of greatest emotional tension in the play.' But other comments also readily provoke dissent, such as Albany's 'Great thing of us forgot!' (5.3.210), which shows he 'reveals an inability from here on to take effective and timely action, which justifies his relinquishment of the throne at the end'. And although Halio is clearly moved by Lear's 'Cordelia, Cordelia, stay a little' (5.3.245) he revives the old and unfortunate editorial practice of passing critical judgement when he comments 'The eloquence and poignancy of this simple utterance are unsurpassed.' However justified this remark may be locally, few readers would wish to see editors indulging generally in this sort of commentary.

Of course the commentary is by no means always conducted at this level and it is full of valuable material, born out of close observation. But it is surprising to see such a technically proficient editor, who has produced an edition of a kind which has been so long awaited, directing his readers' responses so forcefully. Halio's edition makes an important contribution to *Lear* studies and deserves prolonged and close use: it is bound to provoke debate and discussion about many aspects of the play. He has faced its textual problems head on and given a comprehensive and detailed account of them: it deserves to command attention and stimulate critical response.

Towards the end of his Introduction Halio writes 'Were a fully annotated and collated parallel-text edition feasible, the reader could study all of the changes between Q and F in detail' (p. 81). René Weis's edition of the play for the Longman Annotated Texts series (of which the present writer is a General Editor), provides just such a parallel text.[6] Both texts have been modernized with Q printed on the left-hand page and F on the right. The layout does not attempt a typographically exact match between the two – such as Michael Warren sought to achieve in his photo-facsimile of the play – but opening for opening the two texts are made to match each other. In 4.3 the right-hand side of the page is left blank except for the commentary. This is printed at the bottom of both pages and is cued initially to Q, but F variations are constantly pointed out and discussed; F-only readings are signalled within the commentary and duly have their own annotation. There is no textual commentary and the reader has to take some textual details on trust, but Weis fully discusses what he sees as the significant Q/F variants. Although the commentary pays particular attention to these variants, it is also meant to be sufficiently full to explicate the play for the more or less uninitiated reader. Where Weis comments on differences between Q and F, as he frequently does, he is not afraid to say which reading he feels is 'better' or more dramatically effective: for some key scenes and characters in the play, his feelings clearly favour the version that Q represents. Halio's edition appeared too late for him to be able to make use of it (p. vii).

Weis's introduction is dense: he writes forcefully, conveying a great deal of information in a limited space. He introduces the initial textual problem and usefully summarizes the main Q/F differences scene by scene (these are again summarized in the headnote to each scene) and character by character. It is F's assigning of the play's final lines to Edgar rather than to Albany which supplies Weis with the point of departure for his exploration of the two texts of the play. This reassignment leads him on to question whether F's reduction of Albany's part 'appears on some imaginative balance sheet as credited to Edgar' (p. 9). Weis argues that F does cut Albany's part heavily, but not in such a

[6] *King Lear: A Parallel Text Edition*, ed. René Weis (London and New York, 1993), in the Longman Annotated Texts Series.

way as to disqualify him from speaking the last lines. Instead, by looking at Gloucester's and Lear's deaths, and the promise of Kent's demise in Q which is played down in F, he suggests that *The Tragedy*'s ending is to an extent redeemed 'from near-total darkness' (p. 13). He then turns to the Fool's part in F and makes much of the possibility that his role in that text was censored, but he also notes the changes which affect him in 2.4 and 3.2, but especially in 3.6. There Lear's 'Then let them anatomize Regan' shows the bad join which remains in F after the trial scene – present in Q – had been cut. Where Halio (3.6.33–4) sees 'An acceptable non sequitur, given the context of mad speeches', Weis detects 'botched surgery' (p. 23). This could have been the result of censorship, which also played a significant part, he argues, in relation to the war in the play. Nevertheless, the presence of this line in F, he believes, shows that it too must be connected in some way to Shakespeare's foul papers. In a brief passage on 'The two-text "Lear" and theatrical performance' (p. 34), he notes that in his 1990 production of the play, which was based mainly on F, Nicholas Hytner still included the trial scene in 3.6 from Q.

Despite, or perhaps because of, his complex analysis of the two texts' differences and discontinuities, Weis's position is an essentially sceptical one: he addresses many of the issues raised by Halio, but approaches them with a strong measure of doubt. His main aim was to steer a course between 'the Scylla of conflation' and 'the Charybdis of full-scale revision, because the evidence as I have set it out does not clearly support either position' (p. 33). That evidence leads him to put forward a theory of more or less continuous copy: Shakespeare's foul papers, used in the setting of Q, also generated the prompt-book on which F drew (pp. 5, 32–3). Weis seems implicitly to favour an early date for Shakespeare's further work on the play and to contest Taylor's dating of the revisions to 1610–11 (p. 13 n. 8). In the end, he admits that Q and F 'differ in several important ways', and (or perhaps, but) 'that these do not necessarily form part of a systematic revision' (p. 34).

The publication of both Halio's and Weis's editions at about the same time allows readers to reconsider the play which must form a test case for those interested in the question of Shakespeare and revision. If it is accepted that Shakespeare revised *King Lear*, the imaginative and critical implications of the differences between Q and F, despite the treatment they received over a decade ago in *The Division of the Kingdoms*, still deserve investigation. Halio's acceptance of the party line about the play leads him to provide a sound and more than serviceable edition of F; Weis's passionate scepticism has led him to a parallel-text edition supported by a full consideration of the merits of both Q and F. Without a doubt in this case there has been a revolution in the way editors look at the texts of the play and in which publishers are prepared to issue them. A new, conflated, eclectic text of *Lear* may, at the moment, look an unlikely prospect. However, furnished with both parallel texts and buttressed by editions which print unique Q/F passages as appendices, it might be dangerous to deny that *Lear* for most readers and theatre-goers, and even for a few scholars, is not still, imaginatively at least, a single-text play.

In addition to Halio's *Lear*, the other New Cambridge volume to appear recently is the third part of Michael Hattaway's *King Henry VI*.[7] Although there are some familiar features to this edition, it is worth pausing for a moment to remark on Hattaway's considerable achievement in producing an account of the trilogy which is coherent and thought provoking. He has not just made the plays accessible to a new audience, but has done an enormous amount to bring their dramatic power and political concerns to the fore. Even where it is

[7] *The Third Part of King Henry VI*, ed. Michael Hattaway (Cambridge, 1993), in the New Cambridge Shakespeare Series.

contentious, Hattaway's view of the trilogy is always stimulating, and his defence of its integrity is refreshing, although it will not be accepted by all readers and editors.

For him *3 Henry VI* portrays 'the final degradation of chivalry', the destruction of 'what is left of the commonweal', a 'ritualised anarchy' in which England is reduced to being 'a wilderness of tigers': the play is an 'epic of cruelty' (pp. ix, 1, 15, 19). His concern throughout is with what the plays have to say about the politics of the mid-fifteenth century and their treatment of the political aspects of individuals' lives (pp. 4, 9). He notes that they 'are not vehicles for star performers' and suggests – a little disingenuously – that they fell out of favour from the seventeenth century because 'Perhaps they were too radical and anti-establishment' (p. 8). What they have are 'bold dramatic patterns, strong theatrical rhythms, the cumulative effects of deeply etched stage images' (p. 9). After the Marxicizing account of *2 Henry VI*, especially of Cade's rebellion, Hattaway turns for the third part to anthropological contexts, particularly to Julian Pitt-Rivers' *The Fate of Shechem*. Hattaway is largely concerned with the role of the individual in a turbulent world and the part that honour plays in primitive or at least feudal societies: he notes, for example, that both the words 'crown' and 'father' occur more often in *3 Henry VI* than in any other play in the canon (p. 14) – but then it might be argued that they would. His most potent idea is that Shakespeare 'was offering a suggestion that an examination of the relationship between *feudal* ideals and opportunistic political behaviour might tell us more about an age than, say Spenser's romanticising evocation of *chivalric* ideals'. 'Principle' he argues, 'gives way to politics, and chivalry . . . serves only to sustain a fiction of feudalism' (pp. 17–18). Depending on how an audience looks at it, this is all very promising or deeply depressing: Shakespeare's history 'serves as an art of demonstration' rather than one of 'interpretation' – the only powers determining what happens are earthly ones (p. 27). Even then, there are no heroes (p. 30) and the play's secularized view of politics and history allows it to ask hard questions about 'the relationship between political action and moral value' and about loyalty, authority, and justice (p. 36).

Hattaway has not substantially revised his view of the trilogy's 'Date and occasion' and the textual note for *3 Henry VI* can also be largely carried over from that before *2 Henry VI*. He has one interesting new comment, that previous editors over-punctuated, achieving 'rhythmic monotony', whereas 'there is more enjambment in early Shakespeare than might be supposed from some modern editions' (p. 63). Since F was set from Shakespeare's manuscript or 'foul papers', but with some reference to an early print, and since the octavo first edition derives from a memorial reconstruction of London performances (pp. 202–3), Hattaway sees that his task is to base his text on F, but to use O for details of staging in performances in which Shakespeare may have had a hand. F was set by compositors A and B using a partially marked-up authorial manuscript (pp. 205–7); where they had difficulty with this copy they consulted Q3. Cuts in O may have been caused by censorship, but equally they may simply be the result of abridging the play (p. 207). O's memorial status is reflected in its echoes of other plays which may have belonged to Strange's or to Pembroke's Men. These recollections are listed in Appendix 2, along with passages from O which do not appear in F or which vary considerably from it.

Hattaway draws more heavily on O in *3 Henry VI* than he did on Q in *2 Henry VI*. He prints several whole lines from O (1.1.174–5, 2.1.113, 2.6.8, 4.7.59, 5.1.80–2, 5.6.80, 90–1), which he believes improve F's sense and dramatic texture.[8] As with the earlier play, F's compo-

[8] A line may also be missing at 1.4.16, where Hattaway adopts Collier's emendation 'Ned cried' for F's 'And cried'.

sitors are found to be guilty here and elsewhere of eye-skip on an alarming scale. At least six of the omitted lines may have been missed because of eye-skip, but other words and phrases need to be emended, he believes, usually from O, for the same reason or because of dittography (see, for example, 1.1.91, 106, 2.1.131, 2.5.36–7, 2.6.80, 3.1.40, 3.2.110, 3.3.11, 4.8.12, 5.1.38). Hattaway resorts to O's readings in a few places (1.1.261, 2.2.30, 3.1.55, 3.3.124, 5.1.102) and is tempted by them in others (2.1.127, 144, 5.1.42). Few of these are crucial, although there is a real difference between Henry's love at 3.3.124 being described as an 'eternal plant' as in O and its being an 'external' or visible one in F. O's theatrical origins lead Hattaway to include a drummer at the beginning of the second act. More significantly he has the father-killing son and the son-killing father in 2.5 enter separately, rather than forming some sort of tableau by coming on together. Clarence is made to whisper with Gloucester, then take his red rose out of his hat, and throw it at Warwick in 5.1. On the other hand, he detects actors' gags in O's versions of 3.2.11 and 25.

Although he has a slight tendency to keep his options open, this is a sensible approach to some of the play's problems and it should not be assumed that Hattaway has given himself an easy ride with its text. He notes the suppression of Edward Brooke's name (which O got slightly wrong) in F at 1.2.40, but suggests it was 'censored out – or tactlessly inserted by a reporter'. Similarly, O's 'aspiring *Catalin*' instead of F's 'murtherous *Macheuill*' at 3.2.193 probably derives from the reporter's inaccurate memory, 'although it could be an (authorial?) correction of the anachronistic' reference. '(Authorial?)' correction and revision are invoked elsewhere (1.1.14, 2.3.7–13 for Salisbury's presence in the scene and 2.6.42–4 for foul-paper revision during rehearsal which then, slightly surprisingly, found its way into O). There are several well-considered textual notes (see, for example, 1.4.16, 2.5.119, 3.1.24–5 and 5.2.44). Hattaway prints two new substantive emendations of his own. At 3.2.170 he has Gloucester say 'Until this head my misshaped trunk doth bear', explaining that F 'obviously makes little sense' and characteristically adds 'but whether from authorial inadvertance or compositorial error we cannot tell': most editors find no difficulty with F's 'Vntill my mis-shap'd Trunke, that beares this Head'. In a line in a passage which is contaminated in O, 4.2.2, he seeks to restore the metre by reading 'men' for O/F 'people', which works well; he prints other emendations at lines 12 and 15 in the same scene.

A leading textual decision was to reject the Oxford editors' retitling of the play, and to point out correctly (p. 21 n. 3) that *Richard Duke of York* 'has critical as well as textual implications': he believes the less-familiar title was actually used, but 'only when the play was being toured' (p. 201 n. 2). On a smaller scale he rejects Oxford's scene breaks after 4.3.27, attributing the line break in F's 'very uncrowded column' to 'defective casting off', and after 4.8.32 where he interprets F's '*Exeunt*' as referring just to the Lords, leaving Henry and Exeter on stage together. Hattaway's annotation is always helpful and to the point. He struggles manfully with the historical characters and events behind Shakespeare's play, but leaves his own critical view of the trilogy to his introduction: where Halio relies heavily on recent critics in his commentary, Hattaway frequently cites Johnson with a great deal more point and success. While Hattaway's overall interpretation of the plays may well cause scepticism and dissent in some readers, his ideas are strongly held ones arising from a close familiarity with the trilogy and its background. His is an important critical and editorial achievement – furthermore, his text and collations in this part, bar a few minor slips, are accurate.[9]

[9] The following errors affect the text: 1.1.153 *for* 'Think not that King Henry' *read* 'Think not that Henry'; 1.1.261 *for* 'thou wilt with stay me' *read* 'wilt thou stay

After twelve volumes from Cambridge in the last four years, Oxford is still a little way behind; but four recent editions of plays mean that the series is approaching its half-way mark. The books remain handsome, reasonably pleasing to the eye, even if some of the illustrations are sometimes so small and murky that it is hard to make out what is going on in them. The four plays – *All's Well That Ends Well*, *The Merchant of Venice*, *Much Ado About Nothing* and *As You Like It* –[10] are all comedies with relatively straightforward texts, which are on the whole handled accurately. The plays' different levels of annotation vary widely, with New Arden editors gaping in amazement or spinning in their graves, to see long runs of pages where the text fills two-thirds or three-quarters of the page and the commentary the meagre remainder. There must one day be a prize for the Oxford or Cambridge editor who manages to print a page of text without any annotation. With generally impeccable texts and sufficient annotation, for most readers the appeal of the Oxford series must rest heavily on their introductions, which – like most of the Cambridge ones – are of a fairly high standard. These four plays, at least, invite lively and contentious discussion.

Susan Snyder's introduction to *All's Well* is certainly lively.[11] She begins by taking the play's story from Boccaccio to Shakespeare, stressing the playwright's critical juxtaposition of wish-fulfilment and fairy-tale elements and the 'unromantic social realities of Early Modern Europe' (p. 5). One of the means he uses to achieve this effect in which 'the tale of the clever wench' is deconstructed (p. 6), is the play's explicit concern with sexuality. The bed-trick is just one aspect of this, 'the sexualizing of Helen and Bertram' another (p. 11). The play asks questions about the crossing of social barriers (p. 13) and about notions of honour and the nature of war (pp. 14–15). Snyder locates *All's Well* among the problem plays, exploring links between Hamlet and Bertram (p. 19), but concentrating on the difficulties which have been associated with Helen. The play sets her up for the admiration of critics 'but they cannot truly admire her' (p. 30), because of the contradictions of her 'stance' as 'aggressive and submissive lover', 'miracle-worker and down-to-earth arranger of the sexual rendezvous' (p. 39). One way of negotiating these extremes is to reconsider the play's genre, and Snyder brings out its links mainly with morality plays. But she extends its generic associations to embrace the Sonnets, pointing out that the play 'centres on "a provincial gaining entrée to court circles by virtue of a rare skill", passionately attached to a handsome, shallow self-centred young nobleman who does not respond in kind': indeed, she goes so far as to suggest that the play may touch on some of Shakespeare's own social resentments (pp. 44–5). The explicit nature of Helen's desires which some critics find disturbing can be attributed to the dramatist's creation of what she describes as 'a revolutionary heroine who appropriates male prerogatives of desire and sexual initiative' (p. 48). In the end the play's knottiness, Snyder argues, may reflect Shakespeare's 'own unresolved love experience': the whole may 'thematize the inadequacy of comedy as a genre' (p. 52).

There is much meat to chew on in Snyder's introduction: although she concentrates her attention almost exclusively on Helen, she uses her complex role to open the play up. However, she does rather surprisingly close down one potentially interesting avenue of approach. Snyder is opposed to identifying *All's Well* with *Love's Labour's Won* and is content to date

---

with me'; 4.3.19 *for* ''Tis to be doubted if he would waken him' *read* ''Tis to be doubted he would waken him.' One error in the textual commentary is at 1.1.124 where *for* 'Are we not both *Plantagenets*' *read* 'Are we not both both *Plantagenets*.'

[10] Full details of the Oxford Shakespeare editions are given in the notes below: *All's Well* in n. 11; *Merchant* in n. 16; *Much Ado* in n. 19 and *As You Like It* n. 22.

[11] *All's Well That Ends Well*, ed. Susan Snyder (Oxford, 1993) in the Oxford Shakespeare Series.

the extant play to 1604–5. Indeed she explicitly dissociates *All's Well* from *Love's Labour's Lost* (p. 22), even to the extent of claiming that *All's Well* is the only of Shakespeare's plays to have a title 'that makes a statement' (p. 49). Yet there are evident links between the two plays, from their joint concern with the nature of endings, to their settings in nearby parts of southern France, to what looks like a deliberate progression in Shakespeare's naming which goes from 'Mote' or 'Moth' to 'Paroles', from the word to spoken words. This is not to claim that *All's Well* can be safely identified with *Love's Labour's Won*, but that it might be illuminating to consider it in relation to *Love's Labour's Lost*. There is a further work which Snyder does not mention which can be associated with both extant comedies. One of the leading stories in Sidney's *New Arcadia* concerns Helen (or Helena), Queen of Corinth, and her dogged and devoted pursuit in love of the ambiguous character Amphialus. One distinctive piece of information that the reader is given about Sidney's Helen is that she is skilled in medicine and the implication of her last significant appearance in Book 3 is that she will be able to restore Amphialus to health after his suicide attempt. It may be worth pondering on the fact that while Shakespeare kept most of the names from the story which he found in Painter's version of Boccaccio, he changed Giletta's to Helen.

The received view is that the Folio text of *All's Well* shows a play still evolving. Snyder's textual introduction is much indebted to Bowers's 1979 and 1980 accounts of the play's text, and she follows the Oxford line in arguing that F was set from revised foul papers which appear also to have been lightly annotated 'in anticipation of a revival or of the Folio printing itself' (p. 54). Traces of Shakespeare's revising hand can be found throughout the play, not least in Diana's evolution out of Violenta and in Helen's first being thought of as Helena (pp. 56–7).[12] Snyder also devotes a great deal of space to the characters usually known as the French lords G and E, but who also appear simply as lords, Frenchmen and French G and E, and Captains G and E. She believes that Shakespeare regularized their designations for reasons of 'dramatic economy' (p. 61). In this reading of the evidence it is scarcely surprising that confronted with foul papers, authorial revisions and playhouse annotation in one manuscript, compositor B helped by compositors D and C in the first formes found the task of setting the play for the Folio difficult. The manuscript, Snyder concludes, 'had been considerably worked over after the first writing' (p. 65), resulting in what has been called the worst-printed play in the Folio.[13]

Nevertheless, even if an editor can guess at or strongly suspect the cause of corruption in a text, this does not necessarily mean that emendation is made any the easier. Snyder sticks to F where she can, defending its readings, for example, in the difficult exchange between Lafeu, the Countess and Bertram in 1.1.55–60, in Paroles' odd calculations in 1.1.149, or the Clown's 'You're shallow, madam, in great friends . . .' at 1.3.42 and so on.[14] On the other hand, despite the difficulty of the copy, she detects few of the sorts of errors which Hattaway, for example, identifies as characteristic of foul papers. Compositor D is found guilty of omission at 1.3.114 (see also 2.5.52); there is a suspicion of dittography at 3.7.47, and Shakespeare himself appears to be the source of the error at 5.3.313. Two important editorial changes which Snyder makes concern Helen. The first is to call her by that name rather than Helena. The second is that she accepts Gary

[12] See also the commentary at 1.3.127.2, 2.3.270, 272, 4.3.74.1 and 5.3.157.

[13] Cp. *Textual Companion*, p. 493.

[14] See also 1.1.40–1, 167, 1.3.202, 'cap'cious and intenible', 223, 'manifest experience', 2.3.263–4, 'commission . . . heraldry', 270, 'sweet heart', 2.5.91, 4.2.38, 'men make rope's in such a scarre' ('Since none of the proposed emendations is convincing, I leave it unaltered'), 4.5.5–7, 5.3.50, 'Scorned a fair colour' and 5.3.72, 'O nature, cesse!'.

Taylor's radical proposal that when Helen comes on in 2.1, she is in disguise which avoids problems with Lafeu later on (see 2.3.46). Her first of two substantive emendations is attractive: she prints 'To give some labourer's room' at 1.2.67 on the grounds that where F has 'Labourers' only one is properly called for. A later one is rather more awkward, for at 4.5.40 she replaces F's 'a has an English maine' not with Rowe's usual 'name' but with 'mien', postulating 'mein' or 'meine' in the manuscript. The trouble is, as she admits, that although the minim error is possible, Shakespeare does not use 'mien' elsewhere. Snyder's text and collations are almost completely accurate, her commentary full and helpful.[15] She draws some suggestive parallels between *All's Well* and other works – thus the group of mourners at the play's opening is reminiscent of *Hamlet*, Helen's retreat 'from the unanticipated acceptance of a suit not seriously intended' at 2.3.78 is like Beatrice's position in *Much Ado*, and Helen's sonnet at the beginning of 3.4 identifies her with the erotic and sacred concerns of the genre. The concentration on Helen in Snyder's introduction is motivated by a desire to address 'the schizophrenia of critical reaction' to the play (p. 49). If Snyder is, finally, not quite successful in this, it is of course because part of the play's power lies in its unwillingness to be tied down: Snyder knows this, but has all the same managed to produce a valuable and thoughtful edition.

If Helen dominates *All's Well*, there can be little doubt that, despite the relative smallness of his part, Shylock supplies a convenient focus for critical attention in *The Merchant of Venice*. Not content with the task of editing *King Lear* for Cambridge, Jay L. Halio must have felt time was hanging heavily on his hands and decided to produce *The Merchant* for Oxford a year later.[16] The virtues he brought to work on the tragedy are all present in his edition of the comedy, as unfortunately are some of his weaknesses. While editing and annotating a Folio-only text of *Lear* must have been a comparatively new experience, Halio is able to draw on previous editions of *The Merchant*, especially M. M. Mahood's for Cambridge. What he did not have access to, until his edition was being printed, was John Gross's *Shylock: Four Hundred Years in the Life of a Legend*, which complements and supplements quite a lot of what he puts into his introduction. This is a careful and conscientious piece of work, but in it Halio focuses almost entirely on Shylock, the question of anti-Semitism, and the role of bonds and of trials of all kinds in the play's construction. Halio does not go as far as the Oxford editors did in printing 'or Otherwise called The Jew of Venice' as the play's subtitle, but he clearly assumes that Shylock is, so to speak, at the heart of the play. Of course this is true, up to a point, but in attending to Shylock Halio does not let the play's concern with love and lovers, disguise and music get much of a look in. He is unreceptive to the idea that homosexuality plays an identifiable part among Antonio and his friends (pp. 31–2).

What Halio has to say about Shylock is in fact rather good. Tracing the history of Semitism in England to Shakespeare's time, he is able to point out that Shylock is 'the first stage Jew in English drama who is multi-dimensional and thus made to appear human' (p. 9) and that it 'is impossible to maintain a simple, single response' to his behaviour (p. 12). Halio is particularly adept at bringing out the complicating effect that Shylock's desire for revenge has on the reader or on the audience. He draws attention to the 'motives that are as repulsive as

[15] One error in the text of the play occurs at 3.6.85–6 *for* 'Is this not a strange fellow' *read* 'Is not this a strange fellow'. In the collation at 2.1.60 F's variant should be 'see' not 'fee', which was Theobald's emendation; there is a similar long s/f error at 5.3.216 where F reads 'insuite comming' not 'infuite comming'. In addition to the alterations to lineation recorded in Appendix D, the following are worth noting: 3.5.80–1 are one line in F (TLN 1705) and 5.3.270 is set as prose in F (TLN 2998).

[16] *The Merchant of Venice*, ed. Jay L. Halio (Oxford, 1993), in the Oxford Shakespeare Series.

they are comprehensible' in his speech 'How like a fawning publican he looks' (1.3.38–49), which is often cut from productions sympathetic to Shylock (pp. 39–40). He also signals what he takes to be 'the real point' of Shylock's 'Hath not a Jew eyes?' outburst – that it is a plea for and justification of revenge: in the speech 'Shakespeare identifies Shylock with the rest of humanity, but a humanity depraved by revenge' (p. 46 and see 3.1.62 and 114). After the trial, Shylock's final monosyllabic words in the play show that his 'diabolical lust for revenge' has been purged and that 'no longer a serious menace or a comic butt' he can be seen as simply human (p. 54). Halio's history of *The Merchant of Venice* in performance moves between those two extreme portrayals of Shylock with great skill: his account is genuinely illuminating.

It is at the local level that Halio's commentary appears rather over-determining, as it does in his edition of *Lear*. When Shylock replies to Antonio's question 'Or is your gold and silver ewes and rams?' by saying 'I cannot tell; I make it breed as fast', Halio comments on 'breed' (1.3.93) 'Shylock uses the term metaphorically, with sardonic humour that evidently annoys Antonio': this may be so but Antonio could respond with 'The Devil can cite Scripture for his purpose' in other ways than just with annoyance. And when Shylock goes on to mention the 'Three thousand ducats . . . ', Halio states (1.3.100–1) that he is 'Deliberately musing aloud', which again coerces the reader into one interpretation of what is going on. The line 'I never felt it till now' (3.1.81–2) provides Halio with another directorial moment when he maintains that 'The emphasis should be on "I", as David Suchet spoke it in the 1981 RSC production' – but whether he spoke it in this way in every performance is a moot point.[17] It is of course a fine line to walk between telling the reader how the play ought to be performed or describing what is going on in the characters' minds and having a clear view of or a good idea about what is happening. Much of Halio's commentary is very attentive and well thought out, although occasionally he reveals some strange prejudices, as when he states that the County Palatine's 'dour disposition suggests a middle European' (1.2.43). To take just two examples, he is good on Shylock's speech rhythms and the way 'his clipped phrases emphasize his slightly unidiomatic speech' (1.3.138) and valiant in defence of Jessica's last line ('I am never merry when I hear sweet music', 5.1.69) which he says 'means that music puts her into a contemplative or reflective attitude, and Lorenzo's reply explains why'.

The play's theatrical success may have led to its being registered within a year or so of its first performance: Halio dates its writing to 1596–7 and makes the valuable point that some of its prose, for example, Shylock's 'Hath not a Jew eyes', anticipates Falstaff's (p. 29). The quarto of 1600 was probably set not from 'the prompt-book but some manuscript, very likely a fair copy, possibly in Shakespeare's own hand' (p. 86). The main problem the two compositors faced seems to have been recurrent type shortages (pp. 88–90). A second quarto from Jaggard's shop was printed in 1619, but although it shows some signs of pedantic editorial activity, no manuscript was consulted (pp. 90–1 and see 2.2.20). When the play was prepared for the First Folio a copy of Q1 was collated against a playhouse prompt-book, which appears to have been censored but also to have had a few readings revised (p. 92). Halio takes his text from Q but records a good number of Q2 and F variants. Apart from a few slips the text he prints is correct.[18] He rarely has

[17] See also 2.2.170 and 4.1.370–3.

[18] At 3.4.32 *for* 'there will we abide' *read* 'there we will abide'. Lorenzo's 'Leave hollering, man' at 5.1.43 may have rather an American ring. In the collation at 4.1.206 F agrees with Q and does not read 'course'. Halio is not always quite accurate in recording Q/F readings, for example, at 1.1.98 F reads 'dam' as well as Q1–2 and at 1.3.102 Q/F read 'beholding' as well as Q2. There is no need to note that 4.1.1 is set as two lines in Q/F, where they are set in their usual form. The collation needs taking back on p. 122 and n. 4 on p. 75 belongs correctly on p. 77. In the useful and interesting table of speech prefixes for Shylock, on p. 230 F's O1a should refer to Q1a.

cause to depart from Q, which he defends even to the point of allowing Morocco to have Hercules 'beaten by his rage' in his dice-play against Lichas, because the suitor 'tends to confuse things' (2.1.32–8). Textual difficulties arise because of the nature of the manuscript copy (1.1.27, 113, 'It is' for 'Yet is', and 3.1.72.1) and because of compositorial simplification (2.6.14 'younger' for 'younker'). Shakespeare himself may have changed his mind while in the course of composition. Signs of this include Antonio's entrance at the end of 2.6, the switch of Lancelot's surname from 'Job' in its Italian form to 'Gobbo' (p. 90), and perhaps Lancelot's announcement of his master's return to Belmont (5.1.49). The awkward question of the 'three Sallies' might also be related to this (p. 87).

Yet generally the compositors of Q did an excellent job and Halio is restrained in his emendations. One important exception to this is his acting on Mahood's proposal that 'the lovely garnish of a boy' (2.6.45) is correctly 'the lowly garnish of a boy': Q's 'louely' is 'an old but possible spelling of *lowly*, or a compositor's misreading of "lowly"', he argues and then characteristically asserts that his reading 'better fits the context' than the traditional one. Not everyone will agree with him, and 'lovely boy' has resonances within the play which make it an attractive reading. Halio also believes that the first syllable of Shylock's name was probably pronounced with a short *i* in Shakespeare's time (p. 23 and 3.5.14–15), but he does not or cannot make the form visible in his text. He does, however, in the modern way, turn the familiar 'Gratiano' into 'Graziano' as the 'correct' form of the name, which Shakespeare would have wanted.

Halio must have pondered the strangeness of editing plays from foul papers, not least the difficulties Okes's compositors faced in setting the text of *Lear* and the strenuous efforts they made to correct it as it passed through the press. With *The Merchant of Venice* he could reassure himself that the copy for Q was a transcript, perhaps even by Shakespeare, of his foul papers. Had he been editing *Much Ado About Nothing* he might have been overcome by a feeling of déjà-vu. For *Much Ado* like *Lear* was set seriatim from foul-papers and yet the resulting quarto is of a very different nature. One compositor worked on the comedy, but two were responsible for the tragedy. Can the radical differences in the quality of the resulting quartos be attributed to the compositors, to Simmes's far greater experience than Okes in printing playtexts, or to the nature of the underlying copy, or to a combination of all three elements? It is striking to look at Simmes's quarto and then to look at Okes's, and to observe how much editorial emendation the one needs compared to the other just to get it to make sense. Simmes's compositor was evidently much more experienced in this sort of work than Okes's yet, if anything, had a tendency according to the play's latest editor, Sheldon P. Zitner, to 'make minor omissions, substitutions, interpolations, and transpositions' (p. 80).[19] Apart from the usual confusions and indecisions about characters' names and some exits and entrances, Shakespeare's foul papers seem to have been in a fairly good state. Even though it was set from Q, collated against a lightly annotated promptbook, F could hardly 'improve' on Q's text (p. 87). F's omission at 3.2.33–5 might have been caused by fear of offence during a revival in 1612–13 for the marriage of Princess Elizabeth to the Elector Palatine and at 4.2.17–20 by the 1606 Act against profanity.

The result is that while keeping an open mind about F, for example its 'Heavenly, heavenly' in the funeral song at 5.3.21 for Q's 'Heavily, heavily', Zitner rarely has to depart from Q. He does so when considering Beatrice's 'base (though bitter)' disposition as Benedick describes it in Q (2.1.208); adopting Alan E. Craven's emendation he reads 'base and bitter' on the grounds that although Q can be

[19] *Much Ado About Nothing*, ed. Sheldon P. Zitner (Oxford, 1993), in the Oxford Shakespeare Series.

explained it is 'still cryptic'. He adopts another of Craven's conjectures at 2.3.214, sorting out Q's 'one an opinion of an others' by reading 'one opinion of the other's'. Several of Zitner's own emendations are founded on Oxford ones. For example, in the first line of the second verse of Balthasar's song in 2.3, 'Sing no more ditties . . .', despite having to rhyme with 'so', he emends Q's 'moe' to 'more'; later in the same scene he accepts Stanley Wells's conjecture that Q's 'loue' for 'loved' in Beatrice's reported speech (2.3.148) is a misprint and in 5.1.38 he has 'pish' as an indifferent variant of 'push'. At 2.3.252 he believes that the amount of pleasure Beatrice takes in Benedick's message is made sharper if it is 'just so much as you may take upon a knife's point and not choke a daw withal' rather than enough to choke the bird: the emendation, which originates in the Collier Folio, rather depends on the view editors take of jackdaws.[20]

At one point in his introduction Zitner refers to 'the modern critical view that *Much Ado*' is 'clever, but essentially cold and empty' (p. 68). Zitner does his best to combat this judgement and in his introduction as well as in his commentary is keen to open up possibilities in interpreting the play, rather than to close them down. Thus he writes of 'knots to be cut by directors, not untied by editors' (p. 18) and of the possibility of reading the play as 'a sunny comedy with avoidable implications', he says that 'The text allows this, but also more. As Robert Frost said, the poem is entitled to everything in it' (p. 74). He assigns 'all the Watch speeches to A WATCHMAN, leaving the individuation to the actors', varying their number and character 'as each production warrants' (p. 83). Zitner's introduction as a whole is solid and well done, emphasizing the play's mixture of 'romantic plot . . . overlaid with harsh realism' (p. 3). The realism contributes to the play's 'secular temper' and allows its characters, which Zitner discusses one-by-one, to be placed socially with some accuracy (see, for example, p. 49). Although his approach concentrates on *Much Ado's* 'increasing definition of character', Zitner is a little reluctant to give much away about what he thinks of the play. He acknowledges that to some Messina is 'a cold and artificial place' (p. 36), but is liable to take the quite unexceptionable line that it 'is a play about gender differences' (p. 72). There may be a hint of criticism implied in his description of the play as representing 'courtship among Messina's gilded youth', but on the whole Zitner keeps his cards close to his chest – perhaps some of the play's chilly cleverness is bound to make an editor cautious. Certainly, some might think the view that 'the play's most intense moment' comes when Beatrice and Benedick are left alone at the end of 4.1. (p. 56) is an unexpected one.

Nevertheless, Zitner pays close attention to the play's plot and asks some pertinent questions about it (see, for example, p. 43, 1.2.8, 2.1.1, 2.2.46, 3.2.123, 4.1.269 and 5.1.174). He is eager to maintain that the Watch's and (the still pleasantly anglicized) Borachio's apparent nonsense makes sense of some kind and to trace any

[20] One error in the text occurs at 5.1.303, *for* 'and lock hanging by it' *read* 'and a lock hanging by it'. In his desire to show that what the watch says sober and Borachio drunk makes sense of some kind, Zitner rather radically but silently modernizes Dogberry's 'aspitious' in Q/F 3.5.44 to make him tell Leonato that they 'have indeed comprehended two auspicious persons'. There are a few errors in the collation: Don Pedro is called 'Don Peter' in the first as well as the ninth line of the play and an ellipsis has dropped out between 'being' and 'brother' in Q's variant reading at 1.1.151. Zitner records the added indentation at 5.3.24–7 but not at 3.1.107–16. Like Halio he has had trouble with the setting of the collation which needs taking back or over on pp. 163, 197 and 199. Other signs of haste in the book's production include page numbers running backwards in an article cited in a footnote on p. 15 and an unfilled cross reference on p. 204. More confusingly, in the Textual Introduction (p. 80) the inverted 'g' in Q's 'Song' should refer to 2.3.63 not 5.3.12. There are some slips in the recording of the play's lineation: 4.1.155–8 are set as prose in Q; 5.1.52–3 ('Marry . . . thou.') are set as one line in Q/F; and at 5.1.106–7 the second of the three lines ends on 'you' in Q not 'No'.

debts to Kyd that he can find. Although some of his commentary is in parts a little on the brief side, he is good on the play's handling of fashion and can be expansive: discussing Leonato's accusation of Claudio's 'nice fence' (5.1.75), Zitner points out that Shakespeare may have been influenced by Vincentio Saviolo's *His Practise in Two Books* of 1595 and that Shakespeare may have met him since the Italian was in partnership with Burbage when he leased 'the fencing school at which Saviolo taught for use as part of Blackfriars Theatre'. At times there is something pleasantly traditional and reassuring about Zitner's editing: Francis Willoughby's *Ornithology*, 1678, is cited to prove that 'a partridge wing' (2.1.149) is 'almost meatless but delicious', and 'Doublets', it is maintained (2.3.18), 'were so varied in design and so elaborately ornamented that one might well have to stay awake to design one that was distinctive.'[21]

Alan Brissenden's edition of *As You Like It* also goes far to show that a modern edition can be excellent and follow familiar lines at the same time.[22] His commentary is full of interest and displays a lively curiosity. He pays particular attention to the play's bawdy language, to first and early citations from the *OED* and to how directors and actors have cut, reshaped, and performed the play. Again and again his detailed observations on the play are engaging and provocative. Parallels and contrasts in its plot and in its tone receive careful attention, but his observations are never coercive: the commentary is used to open up the play. When he gets to Rosalind's 'I will weary you then no longer with idle talking' (5.2.49–50), he is descriptive rather than prescriptive: 'The rhythms become more stately, an air of mystery and high seriousness is generated, and there is a growing sense of ritual . . .' He quotes extensively from Lodge and to good purpose. Without constructing over-elaborate arguments he points out the play's recurrent themes concerning Robin Hood, the golden age, time and so on. He is equally good on less familiar subjects, such as wrestling (1.1.119, 150, 1.2.196.1), the weight of Adam's five hundred crowns ('"more than a bag of sugar"', he writes quoting an expert from the Ashmolean Museum, '"but you wouldn't need both hands"' (2.3.39)), palm-trees (3.2.169–70), and hunting scenes (4.2). Brissenden is a reliable guide to the play's extraordinary verbal and dramatic richness. At a more local level, he denies that 'a great reckoning in a little room' (3.3.11–12), especially in its comic context, need allude to Marlowe, but notes of course the later direct reference to the 'Dead shepherd' (3.5.82). Touchstone's 'This is the very false gallop of verses. Why do you infect yourself with them?' (3.2.109–10) is traced back to Nashe's *Strange News*. Shakespeare's own presence in the play might extend to the tradition that he played Adam (2.7.166.1, 167) and to William's 'fair name' (5.1.22) which was also the playwright's.

More controversially, Brissenden wants to relocate the play from Ardenne or the Ardennes in north-east France to the south-west where Lodge sets his romance, between Bordeaux and Lyons (p. 39). Consequently, he is able to print Arden with a clear conscience and, while he accepts that the play is strictly speaking entirely set in France, he can argue that Shakespeare wanted to suggest Arden in Warwickshire to his audience (pp. 40–1 and 1.1.109). This dual focus – that the play is set in France and in England, although of course it takes place in 'a fabulous forest' for which there is no map – is one of Brissenden's chief concerns in

[21] A quite different sort of commentary on the play, very largely of a purely linguistic kind, is supplied by Holger Klein in his edition of the same play (Salzburg Studies in English Literature: Elizabethan and Renaissance Studies, 113 (1992)). The commentary, which shows extensive use of the *OED* and the concordance, is longer than the text of the play and is printed after it. This is an edition which those working on the play may well wish to consult over particular difficulties.

[22] *As You Like It*, ed. Alan Brissenden (Oxford, 1993), in the Oxford Shakespeare Series.

his Introduction. 'Doubleness', he writes, 'informs many aspects of the play itself' (p. 23) and he pursues the theme through the two sets of quarrelling brothers, Orlando and Oliver and the two Dukes, the contrasting pair of Touchstone and Jaques, the play's concern with punning, Rosalind's dual sexual roles, the two Olivers and the two Jaqueses. This is all very well done without any straining after mere cleverness and Brissenden weaves into his argument strong accounts of Rosalind and of the education which Orlando receives in the forest. Arden is a place of talk and of metamorphosis. Brissenden stresses the second of these, insisting that 'Hymen presides over the grand transformation of single men and women into husbands and wives' (p. 20); consequently, he must be taken seriously as an independent god, not merely considered as a character dressed up for the part, and that the episode represents an early theophany (p. 19).

The play's pastoral element stimulates discussions of talk, time, and music, raising again the question of satire. Brissenden argues that since the satirist Jaques' name puns on 'jakes' it would have struck Shakespeare's contemporaries – rightly and wrongly – as an allusion to Sir John Harington's *The Metamorphosis of Ajax*, 1596. The combined effect of the Bishops' 1599 ban on satirical and obscene works, a ban which could be applied to Jaques' name and to his role, of Harington's position as the Queen's godson and of his links with the Earl of Essex led to the play's being stayed in 1600 and perhaps to its never having been performed during Shakespeare's lifetime (pp. 2–4, 50). He does not, incidentally, refer to Ajax in *Troilus and Cressida*, written within two or three years of the Bishops' ban. This is a very ingenious theory, although not an entirely new one or at least a new one based on old materials, but it does pose some problems. Brissenden is agnostic as to whether Shakespeare meant Jaques to allude to Harington. If he did not mean to, he must have been very shortsighted given that he was writing the play more or less at the same time as the Bishops' ban. If he did mean to allude to Harington then that has some interesting implications for his dramatic career which deserve to be more fully explored. Although Shakespeare's hero shares the same name as Ariosto's and although Harington translated *Orlando Furioso*, the parallel passages which Brissenden cites from Harington's works do not suggest a specific debt to the satirist. Shakespeare, he says, 'satirizes the satiric mode rather than any individual' (p. 31).

Satire and obscenity play an important part in Brissenden's account of the play in performance. He is keen to point out that Jaques's seven ages of man speech is a deeply cynical one which is then challenged by Orlando's generous and humane entrance carrying the ancient Adam (pp. 30, 32 and 2.7.166.1). But he is mainly concerned with the way in which Rosalind's robust humour and characterization have been variously toned down, brought out, or generally altered in production. There are, he argues, essentially three different modern versions of the role (the longest Shakespeare wrote for a woman), 'the hoyden, the wit, and the modern intellectual' (p. 72). Brissenden gives a generous account of how the part has been played and what opportunities the text gives for bringing out her various aspects, concluding that 'It is her capacity to contain and give expression to such diversity in love that makes her the greatest of Shakespeare's comic heroines' (p. 84). His account of the play is constantly alert and entertaining: if the reader is tempted to ask for more – on talk (some reference to Erasmian copiousness, perhaps) or on pastoral (Sukanta Chaudhuri's excellent book on the subject might have been useful) – it is only because what is already there is so good.

Brissenden brings real enthusiasm to the critical side of his edition: as well as full notes on the subject, he devotes a separate appendix to the sexual overtones of the word 'wit' in Shakespeare's works. Sometimes he is a little careless about details, so that in the introduction the author of *The Golden Bough* appears in the unlikely guise of Gordon Frazer (p. 68) and the *Arcadia* published in 1590 is said to have appeared six years after Sidney's death, which occurred in 1586 (p. 43). Similarly there is a disappointing number of minor errors in Brissenden's text and he is very cavalier in recording changes to his lineation of verse and prose.[23] In spite of these slips his textual policy is sound: he sticks to F as far as he can, while remaining non-committal about the exact nature of the copy from which the three compositors worked. Compositor D's preference for the spelling 'Rosaline' is linked to his work on *Love's Labour's Lost* (1.2.274), while B is convicted of setting prose as verse (2.6) to make space and avoid beginning the next scene at the bottom of the page and of doing the same at 3.4.1–13.[24]

Even where many editors emend F, Brissenden defends its readings.[25] His few emendations are either traditional (2.7.53–7: 'Not to seem senseless of the bob'; 5.2.93 'obedience' for F's repetition of 'observance'; 5.2.109 'I satisfy' where F fails to repeat with 'satisfi'd'; 5.4.21 'your' for F's unmetrical 'you your' and 5.4.109 'her' for 'his' demanded by confusion over Rosalind's sex), or more recent, such as at 3.5.129 where he adopts Oxford's 'Have I more cause to hate him' for F's unmetrical 'Have more cause to hate him'. The only emendation of his own which he puts forward is to accept Knowles's conjecture that F's 'Euen daughter' at 5.4.143 should read 'Even-daughter', meaning '"even as if you were my daughter"'. Although *As You Like It* does not quite afford the editor the holiday that nearly seventy years ago at the beginning of their Cambridge edition Quiller-Couch and Dover Wilson said it did,[26] Brissenden has lived up to Helen Gardner's remark which he quotes at the beginning of his introduction – that it is 'the last play in the world to be solemn over' (p. 1). His edition generates a feeling of excitement about the play and is very pleasing.

After a fairly intense study of these editions of six plays the question of the value and direction of bibliography after the age of Bowers still remains. Of course, work on *King Lear* has produced editions of a kind no publisher would have been eager to undertake until recently. On the other hand, scholars who really embrace a revising Shakespeare may find it difficult to convince publishers to issue other two-text plays in parallel or single-text forms. Furthermore, apart from *King Lear* the five other plays appear in fairly conventional dress. The stage directions and the problems of modernization have been reviewed; the degree to which the collations record the emendations and conjectures of later editors has been severely limited; the problems of lineation have been reconsidered and (in theory at least) a great deal more care is meant to be taken over recording editorial changes to the lining of verse and of prose; the introductions and sometimes the commentaries to the plays pay a great deal of attention to their histories in performance. All of these may be considered developments for the better. Yet looking at the texts of the plays themselves, it is hard not to feel that editorial caution is in the ascendant. Editors

---

23 The following errors occur in the text: 1.1.57 *for* 'this other hand pulled out thy tongue' *read* 'this other had pulled out thy tongue'; at 4.3.183.1 the SD '*Exeunt*' has been omitted; 5.4.129 *for* 'Or have a women to your lord' *read* 'Or have a woman to your lord'. Brissenden does not record editorial emendations of F at 3.3.18 'it may be said', for 'may be said' and at 5.2.18 that Oliver's '*Exit*' has been supplied.

24 Brissenden's explanation for this second relining by B confusingly implies that these are the last lines of the play.

25 In defending F Brissenden writes that: at 1.3.95 F 'sounds natural and affectionate', at 1.3.136 'F's meaning . . . is acceptable, and more theatrical', at 2.1.5–11 'F's reading is perfectly acceptable', at 2.3.59 'the repetition adds to the high moral tone of the scene as a whole', at 2.7.72–3 'F's text is intelligible', at 3.5.11 'F's punctuation makes good sense' and at 5.4.192 'F's reading is more theatrically effective'.

26 *As You Like It*, ed. Arthur Quiller-Couch and John Dover Wilson (Cambridge, 1926), in The New Shakespeare Series, p. vii.

may occasionally surrender to a moment's daring and print 'Edmond' or 'Graziano' or stick their heels in and insist on *The Third Part of Henry VI* or 'Arden', but on the whole there is something comforting in the very familiarity of these most recent editions. It is a moot point as to who deserves the thanks for this – the editors, the general editors, or the publishers.

BOOKS RECEIVED

This list includes all books received between September 1992 and September 1993 which are not reviewed in this volume of *Shakespeare Survey*. The appearance of a book in this list does not preclude its review in a subsequent volume.

Berchtold, Jacques. *Des Rat et des Ratières: Anamorphoses d'un champ métaphorique de saint Augustin à Jean Racine*. Geneva: Libraire Droz, 1992.

Chaudhuri, Sukanta, ed. *An Anthology of Elizabethan Poetry*. Delhi: Oxford University Press, 1992.

Epstein, Norrie. *The Friendly Shakespeare: A Thoroughly Painless Guide to the Best of the Bard*. New York: Viking, 1993.

Fleissner, Robert F. *Shakespeare and the Matter of the Crux: Textual, Topical, Onomastic, Authorial, and Other Puzzlements*. Lewiston, Queenstown, Lampeter: Edwin Mellen Press, 1991.

Hilton, Julian, ed. *New Directions in Theatre*. Basingstoke: Macmillan, 1993.

Marlowe, Christopher. *Doctor Faustus: A- and B- Texts (1604, 1616)*. Ed. by David Bevington and Eric Rasmussen. The Revels Plays. Manchester: Manchester University Press, 1993.

Mills, Howard. *Working with Shakespeare*. Hemel Hempstead: Harvester Wheatsheaf, 1993.

Norris, Christopher, and Nigel Mapp. *William Empson: The Critical Achievement*. Cambridge: Cambridge University Press, 1993.

Plautus, Titus Maccius. *Menaechmi*. Ed. by A. S. Gratwick. Cambridge: Cambridge University Press, 1993.

Shakespeare, William. *Measure for Measure*. Ed. by Jane Coles and Rex Gibson, Cambridge School Shakespeare. Cambridge: Cambridge University Press, 1993.

Shakespeare, William. *The Tragicall Historie of Hamlet Prince of Denmarke*. Ed. by Graham Holderness and Bryan Loughrey, Shakespeare Originals: First Editions. Lanham, Maryland: Barnes and Noble, 1992.

Shakespeare, William. *The Taming of A Shrew*. Ed. by Graham Holderness and Bryan Loughrey, Shakespeare Originals: First Editions. Lanham, Maryland: Barnes and Noble, 1992.

Shakespeare, William. *Much Ado About Nothing*. Ed. by Holger Klein, Salzburg Studies in English Literature. New York: Edwin Mellen Press, 1992.

Smidt, Kristian. *Unconformities in Shakespeare's Later Comedies*. Basingstoke: Macmillan, 1993.

Tanselle, G. Thomas. *The Life and Work of Fredson Bowers*. Charlottesville: The Bibliographical Society of the University of Virginia, 1993.

Tave, Stuart M. *Lovers, Clowns, and Fairies: An Essay on Comedies*. Chicago: University of Chicago Press, 1993.

Taylor, Gary, and John Jowett. *Shakespeare Reshaped, 1606–1623*. Oxford: Clarendon Press, 1993.

INDEX

Listing within the alphabetical sequence of titles of books and plays indicates that the books, or editions of the plays, are considered in the review articles.

INDEX

INDEX

INDEX

INDEX

INDEX

INDEX